Richard Hargrave, William P. Hargrave

Sacred Poems of Rev. Richard Hargrave

with a biography of himself and biographical sketches of some of his coadjutors

Richard Hargrave, William P. Hargrave

Sacred Poems of Rev. Richard Hargrave
with a biography of himself and biographical sketches of some of his coadjutors

ISBN/EAN: 9783337845865

Printed in Europe, USA, Canada, Australia, Japan

Cover: Foto ©Lupo / pixelio.de

More available books at **www.hansebooks.com**

Sacred Poems

OF

Rev. Richard Hargrave, D.D.

WITH

A BIOGRAPHY OF HIMSELF,

AND

BIOGRAPHICAL SKETCHES OF SOME OF HIS COADJUTORS.

EDITED BY HIS ELDEST SON,

REV WM. P HARGRAVE, A. M.,

OF THE NORTHWEST INDIANA CONFERENCE.

DEDICATION.

To the Memory of my Beloved Father,

The tender husband,
The loving father,
The faithful pastor,
And the great preacher;
With memory phenomenal,
Imagination Miltonic,
With reason Baconian,
With courage Pauline,
With enthusiasm wonderful;
In faith and hope boundless,
In charity Christ-like,
In labors abundant,
In sufferings patient,
In perils often,
In heat, cold, and storm;
With the voice of the clarion,
With the eye of an eagle,
The nostril of the war-horse,
The chest of a lion,
And the whole man Titanic!
And all that he was,
From youth to old age,
Consecrated to God,
And given to men.

W. P. H.

PREFACE.

AT the Northwest Indiana Conference of the Methodist Episcopal Church, for the year 1879, and on the fifth day of the session, the Rev. A. A. Gee, D. D., and several others, presented the following resolution, which was adopted:

"WHEREAS, Our venerated and departed brother, Rev. Richard Hargrave, has left his unpublished manuscripts with his son, Hon. W. P. Hargrave, for such use as he may deem best; therefore,

"*Resolved*, That we approve that action, and should Judge Hargrave deem it advisable to publish a posthumous volume, we pledge our influence to its circulation among our people, as a *souvenir* of our translated brother."

Situated as the writer has been, mainly owing to the exacting duties of the pastorate, it has not been practicable for him to comply with this request, and to prepare these writings for publication until now. But it is hoped that the work will be no less acceptable now than if published at an earlier date.

The writings of Richard Hargrave are, it is thought, of permanent interest and value; and his biography and that of his coadjutors in the ministry, must delight those who enter into the spirit of heroism by which they were actuated, as they have entered into the incalculable benefits of their life-work.

A word with reference to the *poems* of Richard Hargrave. After reading his autobiographical sketch, showing the meagerness of his early advantages, the reader will not expect the finished, classical verses of a Tennyson or a Longfellow; but, in the language of Dr. Ridpath: "There was something almost Miltonic in the majestic imagery and heavy tones of this pioneer harp of the Western wilderness. Nor can it be doubted that even with the changed spirit of poetry and the variable standard of criticism, which are set up from time to time, the poetry of this venerable apostle of our primitive commonwealth has in it the quality of life and the true spirit of the bard."

The reader will find in these poems the communings of a devout soul with God, a deep study of *The Word*, and an embodiment of its most striking scenes, as well as its profoundest teachings, in appropriate and touching verses.

The few miscellaneous poems published are, in the main, of a *subjective* character; and, while they are in sympathy with universal humanity, give an inside view of the heart and life of the writer. Also a number of hymns are published, now for the first time, which can not fail to inspire in the reader a devotional spirit.

It occurred to us that, in connection with these poems, there ought to be published a biography of Richard Hargrave, one of the most eminent names of Western Methodism—an idol of the people, especially in Indiana; who, as the testimony of Bishop Simpson and many others will show, was, in many regards, unequaled by any of his contemporaries; who, by reason of certain special endowments, became great on certain lines of work.

This biography is a new departure; it may be called a *symposium*. It opens with an autobiographical sketch (not found until after his death), covering the first three years of his ministry. This contains the story of his wonderful conversion—the " old, old story," upon which, as related by himself, thousands have hung with delight; his call to the ministry, and certain doctrinal difficulties with which he met, and over which he triumphed. This is followed by a picturesque account of the experience of an itinerant in that early day; together with brief sketches of some of the eminent men of that period. A number of these sketches can not be duplicated.

As Hargrave's ministry covers all the history of Methodism in Indiana, from the early date of 1825 to his death in 1879, and as "his plume was seen in the thickest of the fight" at all times, he is necessarily one of the most interesting personalities of Western Methodism. His name was a *household* word among Indiana Methodists. On his death-bed he told the writer that his stated ministry had extended into ninety out of the ninety-two counties in Indiana. There is no other record at all approaching this. He was fifty-eight years a minister, and for thirty-five years in the saddle.

Following this autobiographical sketch are carefully and ably written sketches of him by such men as Rev. William Graham, D. D., Rev. C. H. Benson, D. D., Rev. John L. Smith, D. D., Rev. A. A. Gee,

D. D., Rev. C. A. Brooke, D. D., John Clark Ridpath, LL. D., and a number of others; also "Recollections of my Father," by the writer. The reader who passes over any of these sketches will have reason for regret.

Attention is also asked to the biographical sketches of the brethren themselves, contained in this volume—beginning with "The Old Guard," and including the men of the present generation. With but few exceptions they were companions in the labors, joys, and sufferings of the itinerancy for many years. Many of them have long since gone to their reward; some are lingering till they shall hear the welcome release; and others still vigorously endure the heat and burden of the day.

A few names do not appear among the sketches, which we had hoped to obtain. Among these we may mention Dr. A. A. Gee; the veteran, Rev. J. M. Stallard, Dr. J. W. T. McMullen, and Dr. Samuel Godfrey. These are eminent preachers.

Many other names would have graced our pages—men known and honored in the Conference—had space permitted.

By an oversight in the make-up of the book, the sketches of two or three of the brethren are included under the title, "Letters Concerning Richard Hargrave." The table of contents points out these sketches.

That the book may prove a welcome addition to the literature of the Church, bringing light and joy to every reader, is the hope and prayer of

THE AUTHOR.

CINCINNATI, OHIO, August, 1890.

CONTENTS.

	PAGE.
AUTOBIOGRAPHICAL NOTES,	13

BIOGRAPHICAL SKETCHES.
  By William Graham, D. D., ... 65
  " Rev. Joseph Tarkington, ... 80
  " H. C. Benson, D. D., ... 82
  " John L. Smith, D. D., ... 90
  " Rev. G. H. McLaughlin, ... 94
  " C. A. Brooke, D. D., ... 97
  " Rev. G. W. Stafford, ...104
  " J. W. Greene, D. D., ...107
  " Rev. Allen Lewis, ... 108
  " Letter from same, ...110
  " Rev. W. J. Spaulding, Ph. D., ...111
  " W. R. Goodwin, D. D., ...112
  " W. H. Hickman, D. D., ...114
  " Rev. Noah Lathrop, A. M., ...116
  " Rev. Nelson Greene, ...120
  " A. A. Gee, D. D., ...124
  " Rev. Francis Cox, ...134
  " Rev. Wm. A. Smith, A. M., ...139
  " Rev. Ezra R. Lathrop, A. M., ... 141
  " John Clark Ridpath, LL. D., ...143
  " Rev. H. N. Ogden, A. M., ... 147
  Bishop Simpson's Introduction to Hargrave's Sermons, 140

LETTERS CONCERNING RICHARD HARGRAVE.
  From Rev. W. W. Jones, ... 154
  " S. Beck, D. D., ...157
  " Rev. B. H. Bradbury, ... 158
  " Rev. J. Hull, ...159
  " Rev. J. B. DeMotte, ...161
  " Dan Yount, Esq., ... 164
  " Philander Wiley, D. D., ...166
  " Rev. J. J. Claypool, ... 168

CONTENTS.

	PAGE
Letter from Rev. R. Hargrave to his daughter,	171
Memoir of Mrs. Lathrop,	173
Letter from Rev. O. C. Haskell,	174
" " Rev. L. L. Smith,	177
" " Rev. L. C. Buckles (Personal Sketch),	178
" " Rev. H. L. Kindig, " "	179
" " Rev. E. R. Johnson, " "	181

RECOLLECTIONS OF MY FATHER, REV. RICHARD HARGRAVE.
   By Rev. William P. Hargrave, A. M., ... 182

THE OLD GUARD.
  Rev. John Strange, ... 210
  Rev. Edwin Ray, ... 225
  Rev. James Armstrong, ... 236
  Rev. Nehemiah B. Griffith, ... 237
  Rev. William Beauchamp, ... 238
  Rev. William Cravens, ... 240
  Rev. George Locke, ... 243
  Rev. James Havens, ... 248
  Rev. Allen Wiley, ... 249
  Rev. C. W. Ruter, ... 250
  Rev. Augustus Eddy, ... 251
  Aaron Wood, D. D., ... 253
  Rev. Daniel DeMotte, ... 258
  Rev. Wade Posey, ... 265

MORE RECENT COADJUTORS.
  William Graham, A. M., D. D., ... 270
  Henry Clark Benson, D. D., ... 288
  Rev. Greenly H. McLaughlin, ... 291
  Sketch of Mrs. Elizabeth McLaughlin, ... 296
  George M. Boyd, D. D., ... 299
  John L. Smith, D. D., ... 302
  Charles A. Brooke, D. D., ... 305
  S. T. Gillett, D. D., ... 315
  James Wilson Greene, D. D., ... 318
  Rev. Geo. W. Stafford, ... 326
  William R. Goodwin, D. D., ... 327
  John Clark Ridpath, LL. D., ... 329
  Rev. Allen Lewis, ... 333
  Rev. Samuel Beck, ... 337
  Rev. Henry M. Middleton, A. M., ... 339

	PAGE.
Rev. D. M. Wood,	342
Rev. T. F. Drake,	343
Rev. Noah Lathrop, A. M.,	344
Rev. Albion Fellows, A. M.,	347
Stephen N. Fellows, D. D.,	350

SACRED POEMS.

OLD TESTAMENT SCENES.

Creation by The Word,	357
Redemption by The Word,	360
Abel's Faith,	362
The Call of Abraham,	363
God's Covenant with Abraham,	365
Destruction of Sodom,	367
The Trial of Abraham's Faith,	372
Jacob's Dream,	378
Jacob Wrestles with the Angel,	379
Joseph's Coat,	383
Lost Joseph,	386
Judah's Plea for Benjamin,	389
Moses,	393
The Flight of Israel out of Egypt,	395
Moses Called to Die,	401
Joshua and the Captain of God's Host,	404
David,	408
Elijah Meets Ahab,	411
Elijah Flees Before Jezebel,	415
Isaiah's Vision,	419
The Babylonish Captivity,	422

NEW TESTAMENT SCENES.

The Birth of Christ,	427
Simeon and Anna,	431
John the Baptist,	432
Temptation of Christ,	434
Bethesda's Pool,	437
Christ Calms the Sea,	438
Christ Raiseth the Widow's Son,	440
Christ Restoreth the Nobleman's Son,	442

	PAGE.
Blind Bartimeus,	445
Christ's Entry into Jerusalem,	446
Christ Weepeth Over Jerusalem,	448
Transfiguration of Christ,	449
The Resurrection of Christ,	451
Christ's Ascension,	454
Millennial Triumph,	457

HYMNS.

Trusting in God,	461
A Prayer for Protection,	462
Zion's Glory,	463
Access to God through Christ,	464
Consecration to God,	465
The Majesty of God,	466
Seeking Perfect Love,	467
The Christian Race,	468
Fight the Good Fight of Faith,	469
Rest of Faith,	470
Prospect of Death,	471
Longing for Heaven,	471
God's Worship,	472
God's Ways,	473
The Day of God,	474
The Eight Beatitudes,	475
Adieu to Life,	476

MISCELLANEOUS POEMS.

Reminiscences,	478
Early Friends,	479
Life's Early Memories,	480
Mirza's Vision Versified,	483

AUTOBIOGRAPHICAL NOTES

OF THE LATE

REV RICHARD HARGRAVE.

OF MY PARENTS AND GRANDPARENTS.

MY parents were natives of Sussex County, Virginia. My father, William Hargrave, was the oldest son of Thomas Hargrave.* He (Thomas) was a Quaker by education, but was converted before the Revolutionary War, and had joined the Methodists. Having conscientious scruples as to bearing arms, he served as a cook during the war; but returned home sick of a fever, and in a few days expired in the triumphs of the Christian's hope. He was a man of ardent piety, and on some occasions would shout the high praises of God in his devotions, for which his old Quaker friends called him "Crazy Tom."

A better solution of the matter we have in the following account, given by himself: "Before my soul enjoyed the great *second blessing*, I weathered the storms of life, like a house with some shingles off, and some panes of window-glass broken, and the door ajar; but since that great blessing, the shingles are all on, the glass in the windows, and the door is shut.

---

* I have heard my father say that his great-grandfather emigrated from England and settled in Virginia among the early colonists.—W. P. H.

It is a storm, but it is all outward; it does not break in upon my peace." This same state of holiness my grandmother sought after her husband's death, and it cheered her lonely widowhood, and often made her shout in family devotions.

When my grandfather died, my father was ten years old. He said that for six years his father's prayers followed him like a voice, wooing him from the pleasures of sin. On a calm summer evening he went to the grave of his father, and sealed his vows to serve God and be a Christian. Soon after that he found peace in believing.

My father's grandmother Lane was a *Churchwoman*, who, for her good works, was called the *Dorcas* of the old Jamestown parish, where she long resided. There she heard George Shadford preach a sermon on the *new birth*. She at first grew angry at the preacher, and looked for an officer to take him from the pulpit; but before the sermon was ended she felt the truth, like a two-edged sword, pierce her heart, and she cried out for mercy, and soon felt the healing of Gilead's balm. She invited the man of God to her house, and soon my father's mother found peace with God. Thus the unfeigned faith that was in my father "dwelt first in his grandmother Lois, and his mother Eunice."

How much this heaven-descended boon shed its unction upon *my* young heart I know not, but my father said at my birth that in answer to pleading prayer, he had obtained the witness that I would be his "preaching boy." When a little more than seventeen years of age I received license to preach. At that time my father, in tears, referred to his ever-abiding impression as to my call to the ministry, and said that in my most wayward days he had never faltered as to his belief in my preaching the gospel. He also said that his father, while Bishop Asbury was preaching on one occasion, obtained a like evidence as to *his* call to the gospel ministry. These presentiments were not so subject to severe criticism in those days as in these days of less faith and more philosophy.

EARLY HISTORY IN VIRGINIA.

My mother's father, William Ellis, was a Churchman. She gave the last time that her parents danced. It was at the wedding of her oldest brother. Parson Blackgrove led off the *reel;* but it was the last that they ever shuffled. Soon afterwards my grandfather was converted. He, being a prominent man in the community, soon reared the first meeting-house in those parts. This house is noticed, in the old bound Minutes, as the place of holding the early Conferences, thus: " Met at Ellis's, Va.; adjourned to Baltimore."*

My mother gave substantially the following account of Parson Blackgrove's conversion. Colonel

---

* See Strickland's " Life of Asbury," pp. 126, 129, as to the meeting of this Conference, April 17, 1782: "As the Conference was approaching, he [Asbury] directed his course toward the place of its meeting, which was *Ellis's*, in Sussex County; from which place, according to a resolution of the previous Conference, it was to be adjourned to Baltimore." There is a foot-note, in pencil, in my father's copy of the book, as follows: " Ellis was my grandfather. (Signed,) R. Hargrave."—W. P. H.

Lewis invited the parson to dine with him. This, however, was only to get him to talk with his lady on the subject of her religious melancholy, as he called it. So, after dinner, he politely introduced the matter, and left the parson and Mrs. Lewis to converse upon the subject of experimental religion. The conversation was as follows:

Mrs. Lewis—" Parson, let me ask you two or three questions."

Parson Blackgrove—" Say on, Madam."

Mrs. L.—" Well, Parson, were you ever born again ?"

Parson B.—" No, Madam, except it was in my baptism."

Mrs. L.—" Did you not feel moved by the Holy Ghost to take upon you the office of an elder in the Church of God when the bishop asked you that question at your ordination?"

Parson B.—" No, Madam."

Mrs. L.—" How, then, can you call yourself either a Christian or a gospel minister?"

This last question was a nail in a sure place; and the parson desired her to proceed with a recital of her Christian experience, which she gladly did. He became deeply convinced of sin, and forsook his polite balls, and fox-chases, and grog, and became so sober that many feared he was going beside himself. After a short time, however, the parson reascended the pulpit, and told his religious experience, and ever after preached experimental religion with great zeal.

He, with Parson Jarrett, used to attend the conferences in the chapel above referred to. My mother used to assist in waiting on the members of the Conference, the most of whom—thirty in number—made their home at my grandfather's house. She said that Parson Jarrett was a very large man, of genteel and dignified bearing. His presence was hailed with interest by the Conference, and he gave his advice freely, and his opinions were highly prized by Mr. Asbury and all concerned. After the Methodists took ordination under Dr. Coke, the parson met with them no more. He used to say to Mr. Asbury: "You have left your mother; I must give you up."

When Parson Blackgrove saw his end approaching, he requested that James Morris, a Methodist local preacher, should preach his funeral sermon, adding: "Though he is not a learned man, he is one of the best gospel preachers I have ever heard."

My grandfather Ellis grew restless in his mind upon the subject of slavery. He once suffered an attack of fever, and his *deed of emancipation* was not made out. This, however, he attended to promptly, and intrusted the recording of the deed to his oldest son, who evaded it, saying: "The preachers have been influencing my father,[*] and he is now too low to be a judge of such matters." Soon the family were called around his sick-bed to hear, as it was thought, the parting words of the holy

---

[*] He may have guessed pretty shrewdly, judging from the following record: "At the session of the General Conference of 1780, slavery was denounced, and 'traveling preachers' owning slaves were required to emancipate them. At *Ellis's preaching-house* [Conference held there 1783] it was now required that 'local preachers' should follow this example, whenever the civil laws would allow them." (Stevens's Hist. Am. Methodism, p. 168.)—W P H.

man. He was famishing under the old cruel treatment of giving calomel, which prohibited the use of cold water unconditionally. His cry was, "Water! water!" My uncle burst into tears, and said: "I will not see my father die begging for water!" So saying, he ran to the well and brought a quart of cold water. By this time my grandfather was speechless. Some water was put into his mouth, and he revived, and soon made signs, and they continued giving the water till he drained the cup. He could then speak, and said that he was burning to death with the fever and medicine. He got well "like a charm," and God added fifteen years to his useful life. He lived to see his emancipation papers recorded, by which he freed forty slaves. He often said that he thought he would then have died, but for the suppression of his emancipation papers. He came to his end by mortification of his right arm, which had been bruised by accident. My mother said he was the happiest dying man she ever saw. The morning of his departure, my mother asked him him how he had rested the night previous. He said: "Daughter, on the bosom of Jesus. He bore my sufferings for me." He shouted to his last breath the praises of his God.

Thus my mother was taught piety and humanity, and was a confirmed emancipationist.

My father gave the following as the reason for his convictions of the evils of slavery: There lived in their neighborhood a farmer, who owned a slave who was a good blacksmith. He was a good master, and gave the slave the Saturdays of every week to work for himself. By this means the slave had all the necessaries, and some of the luxuries, of life. His wife lived only a few rods from him, and ate at his own table. They had some four or five children that were well clothed and fed, and all were happy. On this family the rigors of slavery had not as yet come. But in time his wife's master failed, and his wife and children were sold to the Georgia Negro-traders. This was to the blacksmith slave an awful occurrence. He begged the traders to buy him; but his master asked fifteen hundred dollars for him, and would not take one dollar less. This the traders would not give. As a last act of grace, he was permitted to go with them as far as Petersburg in handcuffs, and in a few days was to return. He came at the appointed time, but with blood-shot, sunken eyes, "wild with enormous woe." He lay down on his bed to die. His sighs and lamentations so affected the young heart of my father that he vowed never to take one day's service from a slave after he was competent, in law, to free him. This purpose he kept till he was one and twenty, and then he recorded his "emancipation papers." The poor slave soon died, evidently of grief. Alas for humanity, when such things are still continually recurring! But vituperations against the system of slavery seem useless.*

My father, William Hargrave, married Sallie Ellis in the year 1785. Six children were born to them in old Virginia. In 1803 they removed to Caswell County, North Carolina. On December 5th, of that

---

*This reads as if written a long time since, as indeed it was. We can hardly realize that such outrages were ever perpetrated upon American soil.—W. P. H.

year, I was born in that land "sore punned at by witlings and scorned by the fool." It has, however, its sacred associations, and with all its "failings, I love it still." Its climate is pleasant. It is very healthful in those parts, and generous friendship abounds in social life.

EARLY LIFE.

Perhaps the first entry upon the tablet of my memory is the circumstance of my falling head-foremost into a "gum" spring. My head rested on the bottom. My sister rescued me from an untimely death. She wept with tender emotion, and parents and friends gave way to demonstrations of great joy when I was taken home.

When I was a school-boy I was attacked with congestion of the brain. This was from thrusting my head, when warm, into cold spring-water. The pangs which I endured on the day of my attack were keen and indescribable. The school-teacher was compelled to send me home. After a severe illness of some days I was suddenly relieved, and could then appreciate the goodness of God in my restoration; and for days I loved to dwell on pious verses of hymns, and I thought of angels and heaven, and felt that I wanted to go to the good world. In a childish way I wished to see the pretty things which I had heard were there. For weeks I had no relish for sinful mirth, but loved solitude and serious meditation. I felt so subdued and melted in heart, and such love for everybody, that I am of opinion that my heart was then changed, though but eight years old. After awhile I sinned this good frame away.

I take the liberty here to insert a curious event that occurred in my sixth year. My mind became strangely occupied with the thought of having a soul, and the philosophy of the idea seemed to stagger and oppress me, till it employed my soliloquies when alone. I say *philosophy,* for I desired to understand the connection between the soul and body, and to know whether the soul *went all through the body,* in my childish thought. One day my mother sent me to an aunt's to borrow some shuttles, and when I was passing near a ravine I heard my father's voice, when he spoke to his plow-horse, echo in the distance. I give the detail of the mental reverie I then had:

> The green, mossy spring by the sycamore-tree
> Is relic momentous and sacred to me;
> 'T was there that I sated my thirst when a child,
> In charge of a loved one most gentle and mild.
>
> Its cool, gushing waters meandered the hill,
> My birthplace in nature, whose memory still
> Brings fond recollections of days that are gone,
> And friendships, and pleasures, and scenes that are flown.
>
> The woodland below it, where warbled the thrush,
> 'Midst wild, darkling bowers where fountains did gush;
> The paths where I rambled the morn of my life,
> Not versed in its sorrows, unheeding its strife.
>
> One day, when quite little, I went on a *chore,*
> To borrow some shuttles (they used them of yore),
> My father commanded his plow-horse so loud,
> That *echo* responded away down the wood.
>
> Half thinking that *echo* and *ghost* were the same,
> I shouted, to test it, loud calling my name;
> It answered distinctly, as though it had sense,
> Which startled me somewhat; and yet, in suspense,

Still louder repeating this name and then that,
I kept up with echo a rather shy chat;
Till timely bethinking myself in the case,
I asked why my tongue *utters* just when I please.

Then lifting my feet and my hands in a trice,
I found that they answered like echo precise;
My will but commanded, and they stirred at once,
And overtly acted a ready response.

'T was thus I perceived that I carried a soul,
The lord of my body, pervading the whole;
To claim such an essence as spirit must be,
Astonished me still more, and caused me to flee.

This all was in sight of the green, mossy spring;
The wood that it watered with echo did ring.
Which taught me, in sooth, the great science of mind,
Which tongue, feet, and hands then had caused me to find.

Life's lesson thus mooting, I labored to solve—
The soul's subtle essence in thought to revolve;
Majestic it rose, the vast lesson supreme,
Accorded by Sages in highest esteem.

Since science has taught me, imparting its lore,
What, verily, *Echo* had taught me before;
Resounding it came from my favorite wood,
In colloquy teaching, though artless and rude.

The thought of my soul and its value will bring,
To fond recollection the green, mossy spring:
The woodland below it, and life's natal hill
And cottage upon it, are visible still.

The worth of my soul, as its "Ransom" imports,
Brings fresh to my memory these early resorts;
The green, mossy spring by the sycamore-tree,
And soul-touching Echo, how sacred to me!

Gray-haired, and failing, the thought still employs
My mind's largest efforts, and hope's richest joys;
Revolving the lesson that came from the wood,
Suggested by Echo, as life's utmost good.

> A little of life yet remains to be told,
> My soul's final glory I prize as its goal;
> This lesson so early echoed from the wood,
> I'll love and pursue it as life's *endless* good.

The reader may add, "Large streams from little fountains flow!" Still it is no despicable work to trace thought in its leading strings as well as in its ampler developments, and more mature toil. The identity of the pigmy philosopher and the hoary poet may, it is hoped, satisfactorily explain the liberty here taken in this narrative. If it has been the habit of the writer to deal in metaphysics, it can be pleaded in extenuation that he commenced it early in innocent life, and first impressions are hard to be overcome. His sins perpetrated in *euphonies*, have less excuse, since he was forty-eight years of age before he fell into the *number-building* reveries.

I have a vivid recollection of the first *death* I ever witnessed. It was that of my mother's oldest sister. I may have been about eight years of age. She was crippled by accident, and died of a "mortified" limb. She triumphed gloriously in the conflict, and exhorted her children to meet her in heaven. She stated to my mother, with her latest breath, that she had the power to see her deceased friends as vividly on one side, as her living friends on the other side; and, like Stephen, she had visions of her Savior's cheering presence. How my young heart melted at the recital of these events and the sorrow of the parting scene! I saw one more funeral up to my fourteenth year; it was that of a schoolmate, who died of "cold plague" in 1815, a lad of thirteen years. This affected me much, and by this time I could appreciate the solemnities of death, and felt the call to me to prepare for the awful event.

MY FATHER'S REMOVAL TO INDIANA—MY CONVERSION AND CALL TO THE MINISTRY.

My father's strong opposition to slavery caused him to leave North Carolina and remove to Pike County, Indiana. This he did in 1818. The country was new, and times exceedingly hard, and privations many and great. The people were generally poor, and there were almost no schools then in the country. I am sure there was not a grammar-school in the county from the time I came into it until I commenced traveling, a period of six years. Of books we had scarcely any. That was the time to get an education for you!

In February, 1819, 'I was deeply impressed by God's Holy Spirit that I ought to seek religion. I felt, on a Sabbath in that month, greatly drawn to God, and contrite before him. Suddenly a temptation intervened, and put off the time of my repentance until summer. I boldly said to myself: "I will do so." I was darker than ever in my views, and far harder of heart than before. I plunged into sin with a presumption and progress unequaled before. August came and found me indifferent and willful— far from God by wicked works. Perhaps the first Thursday of August, 1819, I went, in the twilight of the evening, to seal my vows with God. I seemed to have no contrite emotion, and no power to pray, till I said: "I will, by the grace of God, now covenant to pray till I die!" That instant I felt some ground of hope beneath my sinking feet, and a ray of light darted athwart the impending gloom which had settled down upon my soul. I felt a faint spirit of prayer swell my heart and move to my tongue. But deep upon my guilty conscience an untold load oppressed. My fear of hell was strong, my shame and remorse indescribable. O how I desired the subdued, tender frame that I had sinned away during the previous winter! The following Saturday I felt the blessing of a tender heart return. The evening of that day I went to my father's cabin, and seated myself at the north door, and lifted my eyes to the north star, and it seemed that the divine justice pried into the recesses of my guilty, anguish-stricken heart. Then I felt "the spirit of bondage to fear." With much ado I refrained from crying aloud for mercy. Repentance was now doing its mighty work within, and soon the fruits meet for repentance were visible in my conduct. One evening, late, I was in a dark wood, agonizing with God for a blessing. I heard a hasty footstep approaching, and my brother spoke— supposing me to have been bitten by a snake. I confessed to him that I was praying for religion. As soon as he was gone, however, a frightful temptation came over me about the publicity that would now be given to my religious purposes. I ran home as if Satan were at my heels.

The following Sabbath, at meeting, I trembled and sobbed under the word of truth till all present could see that I was anxiously seeking salvation. I sought God day and night. Often my sorrows were so great that I felt little like eating, or attending to the business of the farm. One time the temptation followed a season of prayer to vow that I never would pray again. This, however, I speedily repelled, saying: "I will pray till I die!" I was much beset with carnal conceptions of the gracious work of God. I would fancy, when I was drawing to a decisive point in my supplications, "This is not the time and place," and all again was dark confusion, painful anxiety, and uncertainty.

The second week in September, when at work in the field gathering fodder, I was revolving in my mind why, being so anxious for salvation, and Christ so willing to save, I was not blessed. I commenced singing a spiritual song, the chorus of which was:

"Jesus, Jesus is my friend, O hallelujah!"

The perception that Jesus was indeed my friend filled me with inexpressible rapture. It was enough! Still I did not profess religion. Ten days afterwards my second brother was converted upon a sick-bed. He called in the neighbors to tell them what God had done for his soul. My feelings were not characterized by a sense of guilt; still they were extreme. I became helpless; my flesh tingled all over me, and I was crying to God for the abiding witness of his salvation. It came, and I exhorted my young companions to seek religion. From that time I retained the witness of the blessing which I had previously obtained in the field.

The following Sabbath I went to hear my father preach the funeral of an infidel. I thought with horror of his departure in unbelief, and then with joy upon my own recent conversion. That evening, before sunset, I took my hymn-book and New Testament, and hastened to the secret place with a glad heart, to pour out my soul to God in prayer and praise. I ascended a high bluff south of my father's cabin, a quarter of a mile. As I neared the chosen spot to pray, a sudden horror seized me, and a mighty quaking made my frame shiver "as the aspen in the breeze." I stood astonished and overwhelmed by a dread solemnity, such as I had not felt before, and never will be told; it was unspeakable. My cry was: "Save, Lord! I can not speak, for I am a child." Then a question as inly spoken came: "Will you do your duty, and enjoy this blessing, or refuse and lose all, and be worse than ever?" I replied: "Here I am, send me." I knelt and prayed, and rolled upon the ground, and shouted, and felt a greater blessing far than when I was converted. As the sun went down I walked calmly through the new corn-field, and did stop at times to ascertain if my feet touched the plowed ground. I passed through the cabin, and my mother caught my eye, and I saw her countenance beam with emotion. I dropped into a chair, and just then my father called me to assist in securing the sheep. My mother beckoned with her hands, and all was still. God that hour called me to go to the lost sheep of the house of Israel, to preach Jesus and the resurrection.

The work of the ministry became the one central idea of my life. In it all the plans of the future converged, and from it alone any comfort of heart was derived when looking toward the future. I joined the "Christian Church." My father had been a minister of that Church from about the time of Mr. O'Kelley's schism. In June of 1821 I was licensed to preach the gospel. With fear and much trembling I undertook the solemn task. At the angle from which I now survey this period of my life, I adore, and yet tremble. God led me in a way that I had not known.

EARLY MINISTRY—ARIANISM.

Not a year after I took license to preach I was betrayed into the errors of Arianism. This occurred from reading the writings of Plummer and Stone. The Socinianism of Plummer unsettled my faith in the divinity of Christ and the doctrine of the Trinity Mr. Stone's bland manner seemed to win my assent; yet I hesitated, with great conflict of feeling, to yield up the lofty doctrine of the Bible to his deceiving sophistry. This occurred in 1822. From the time that I gave myself to the delusion of these errors a kind of hazy light seemed to gleam upon my spiritual vision. The system, dealing mostly in negatives, tends more to unsettle than to confirm enlightened faith in God's holy Word and plan of salvation. My parents, who had ever been substantially Methodists in doctrine, had great solicitude concerning my Unitarian errors. They sometimes talked with me, and advised me kindly, and I regretted much to be the occasion of such concern to my parents.

In the fall of 1822 I went to a Cumberland Presbyterian camp-meeting in Dubois County, Indiana. I was soured toward the *sectarians*, and my mind was overcast with gloom as to the bright call to the ministry which I had received. Saturday night a *Mr. Lowry*, a prominent minister of that Church, sent for me, to have a friendly conversation with me about turning *Arian*, as he said he had heard that I had. I replied: "I am what you call that." He then stated his kind intentions in striving to convince me of my error. I answered him in monosyllables for awhile, and listened to his *orthodox harangue*, as I then viewed it. But when he came to expand his ideas of the twofold nature of Christ, there suddenly passed a power of conviction into my mind, and I gladly cherished it. All my hostile feelings instantly vanished. I could not refrain from shedding tears, for Mr. Lowry was making touching references to my ministerial prospects. On that subject I could not but feel. I confessed the convictions of my mind, and gladly hastened to pour out my soul in prayer. I saw my clear call to the ministry in its wonted light, and again entered into the sentiments of Christ's atonement and intercession as once I had seen and felt them. I lay upon the earth, weeping profusely the tears of gratitude for the return of the gospel faith to my heart. The disk of the sun of Christ's divinity grew bright and ample, and still broader; the light and heat of his salvation greeted me as it had not for twelve cheerless months previously. My whole being yearned and quivered to the mighty impress; and then my fellowship was truly with the Father and the Son, to orthodox measure. My heart and my head were alike Trinitarianized. 'T was done! And thirty-three years have since flown, and

I have not doubted of Christ's divinity one hour of that time.*

The next week I went to a Newlight camp-meeting in Daviess County, Indiana. Brothers Hughes and Rodgers were in attendance from a distance. Mr. Hughes was a good preacher of that faith and order. In the forenoon of Sabbath I preached on the gospel as "the power of God unto salvation to every one that believeth." I endeavored to show how the redeeming offices of Christ implied his divinity. That the gospel was verily "the power of God," because Christ was *truly* God. This was argued from various considerations, such as his creating and upholding all things. I felt much blessed in setting forth these lofty, central ideas of theology. Though in my nineteenth year, I trust, with the divine assistance, I was enabled to present these truths in a light that brought honor to the cause of Christianity.

Mr. Hughes followed in the afternoon with a sermon on the Divinity of Christ, as he called it. His text was the first verse of the third chapter of Hebrews, where Christ is said to be worthy of more honor than Moses. He went on with a wondrous list of Scriptures, "without note or comment," as he said,

---

* This sainted man, Mr. Lowry, lived to a very advanced age; and many years afterward he and Hargrave met on board one of those magnificent Ohio River packets, and enjoyed a day's journey together, exchanging mutual congratulations upon their faith and works. It was only "hail and farewell;" but now they are enjoying together that eternal friendship,

"Where congregations ne'er break up,
And Sabbaths have no end." —W. P. H.

to tell us all about his faith on the subject of Christ's divinity. Certainly it was more amusing than convincing to hear the effort of his two hours' sermon, showing that Christ made the worlds, and upheld them by the word of his power; and yet, as to the question of his proper Godhead, he would say: "That is *manism*—it is blasphemy! Jesus Christ is the *Son* of God!"

At the close of the service, I sought to have some conversation with him. He seemed shy and reticent. I asked him how we were to understand the sense in which "*Christ created and upheld all things by the word of his power.*" If actively and efficiently, then there was no power in any one else equal to the acts of creation and preservation. I next inquired how Christ came in possession of divinity. If by *delegation*, then God the Father was left devoid of the power conveyed to another being, and this would make Christ, at least temporarily, greater than the Father! This was more than Trinitarians themselves would allow. On the other hand, if Christ was merely *passive* in creation, he was not a creator at all, but the Father was the efficient agent; and Christ, in that case, only a *patient*. And to ascribe creation to him in such a case was a trifling farce. Or if Christ really did possess creating and conserving power, and the Father abstractly held the same power, then there would be two co-ordinate gods, or two powers equal to the act of creation, divided! In this way I felt for the pillars of his theological fabric, so as to cast down his castle built in the air for effect. He said, as he indignantly rose up to retreat: "I have seen as shrewd a fellow as you a *deist* before to-day."

Arians looked somewhat confused, and Methodists seemed right well pleased with the arguments of the newly-converted Trinitarian; and none but Mr. Hughes himself seemed apprehensive of my becoming a deist!

When I returned home I told my parents of the change in my views in this regard. They were "exceeding joyful," and my mother used all her influence to get me to join the Methodists. Little effort, however, was now needed to induce me to take that step. During the winter of 1823 I joined the Methodist Church, under the ministry of Rev. E. F Webster, since of the Ohio Conference. The following spring was a time of great religious excitement in the O'Kelleyan Church, of which my father was pastor. God owned the labors of the writer, giving him seals to his humble ministry.

DEATH OF A BROTHER.

I here record a great trial which befell us in 1822. My older brother, William Ellis, left home in May of that year, to go to Vandalia, Illinois, on some land business. It was a time of high waters, and when he got to the Okaw River, in attempting to get to the ferry, he was drowned in the backwaters. The heavy tidings full soon arrived, at which moment I was in the field some distance from the house. I heard the outcry and hastened to the scene, and witnessed what, to me, was the darkest tragedy of my life. My dear mother lay on the ground in an almost expiring condition, and sisters and brothers, wild with sorrow, were gathered around. My father seemed more calm than the rest. I strove to lift my heart to God in prayer for aid, and found the grace that did comfort me, even then, and helped me "to rejoice in tribulations also." This was the brother who had been converted the day that I professed religion. One of the sisters, Mrs. Martha Niblack, was not present. She gave birth to a son on the day the news reached her, who was named WILLIAM ELLIS, for the lost brother.*

MY ENTRANCE INTO THE ITINERANCY—ITINERANT LIFE.

Thirty-two years and a few days have elapsed since,† when seated in my father's cabin, confined indoors by poor health, my attention was called to a gentle rap at the door, which I proceeded to answer. A grave, serene, feeble, intellectual-looking old gentleman came in, with saddle-bags on his arm. He approached me with a beaming countenance, shook my hand, and said: "My name is Beauchamp." My surprise was a little painful, as I conjectured rightly the object of his call. He said: "Brother, I have come to employ you as a helper on this circuit; it is too large for one man to do the work." After a few minutes spent in settling preliminaries, I was fully

---

*He subsequently became distinguished as a lawyer; served as State senator, as judge of the Circuit Court, as member of Congress from the First District, Indiana, and as judge of the Supreme Court of Indiana.—W. P. H.

† These sketches must have been written when the author was about fifty-three years of age.—W. P. H.

committed to make an adventure in the traveling ministry. This day thirty-two years ago I left the home of my youth to trace the weary tracks of itinerant toil. Then I had to ask my father's leave to start; till now my Heavenly Father has not given me leave to stop. Each successive year between then and now has been controlled by others, and not by my own election, except that, in my call to God's holy work, I chose to give all things to him. Around this central idea of my life has since revolved my all of active effort and weary toil. As the trying, stern realities of the itinerancy have passed, what alternations have I witnessed, both in condition and feelings! None, I thank Heaven, in my one purpose. This calling has had its sunshine and cloud, its smile and frown, its flattery and censure, its joys and sorrows, its perils and God's defense and gracious stay.

I have seen God's way in the storm and calm, in affliction and in health, in poverty, not wealth. It is mine to inherit little beneath the skies, that I may learn duly to estimate that "better and enduring substance" which is on high. If I may but enjoy "the earnest" of so vast recompense, surely then life will be cheered with the disclosures of a glorious future, and death will be triumphant, which brings me to its possession. Till then, it is mine to toil on, "enduring as seeing Him who is invisible."

My first circuit was Patoka, in Indiana District, Rev. William Beauchamp presiding elder, and William Medford preacher in charge. This circuit included and touched upon the following counties: Pike, Gibson, Posey, Vanderburg, and Warrick. It required six weeks to make the "round," there being thirty appointments. Settlements were sparse in many instances, travel was hard, and accommodations generally rough, but somewhat smoothed by ardent friendship and deep piety. There was not one finished meeting-house on the entire circuit. We preached in cabins for the most part. I descended the peninsula to the neighborhood of Mt. Vernon, Posey County. Near this I found quite a number of the converts of the eccentric *Granade*. They were of the name of Ashworth. They told some vivid stories of his wonderful meetings. They had his revival songs, and seemed pleased always at an opportunity to relate something concerning the *great Granade*, as they called him. One amusing incident I can recur to. Old Thomas Milligan, from Ireland, was his colleague one year, and Granade had preached a wonderful sermon on "Appii Forum and the Three Taverns." The people were telling Father Milligan of the glorious sermon. He asked them what the text was. They told him, and he said: "O, he might as well have a hickory stump for his text." In the same neighborhood there was a sister of Thomas Milligan, the wife of a Brother Templeton. She could recollect Mr. Wesley in his travels in Ireland; and I had great pleasure in her recital of Old Country events, for she excelled in conversational abilities, in which she used a spice of wit when anything did not suit her.

Here my plan of travel said "ride-day;" and sure enough it was thirty miles to my next appointment, up in Vanderburg County, some ten miles from Evansville. On my way, at the instance of my colleague, I was met by an old man, who was to be my guide through the wilderness part of my journey. At sundown we came to his cabin in the woods, where I was to stay all night. After supper the question of our nativity was raised, and the old lady asked if I had ever heard of Captain Anthony, who was killed at McFarlan's defeat. She then continued: "I am his sister, and when the Indians killed him his brains spouted out onto my feet. My husband, a Mr. Cord, was killed by my side. When the work of death was done, five of the company were reserved as prisoners, who were myself, a son and daughter, and Mrs. Anthony, the wife of the captain, and her infant child; but it being too small, was soon killed. My children being able to ride upon ponies, were preserved. I have no recollection of any more that were spared."

They started from Cumberland Mountains—the bloody spot—and steered for Detroit. She said she suffered much on her way, having to wade streams to her chin. Her fatigue was fearful, and her sufferings from hunger and otherwise indescribable and extreme. When they got to Detroit, the prisoners were all separated and placed in different Indian families. The old lady said that her children were taken, she knew not where, till Wayne's Treaty brought out the prisoners for release. Thus she was doomed to two years and six months servitude in an Indian family. Sometimes she was beaten cruelly by the savages when they were drunk. Her Indian mother, however, showed her some kindness in the midst of her sorrows and great sufferings. Four months after they reached Detroit, a British merchant, on the Canada shore, heard that there was a beautiful young female prisoner among the Indians, and succeeded in purchasing her for rum and blankets. He being a bachelor, soon married her. The prisoner was Captain Anthony's widow. They were living happily and doing well the last time she heard from them.

The old lady said that when the time came for the prisoners to be forthcoming, according to the terms of Wayne's Treaty, she grew exceedingly anxious about her son and daughter. When she got to Detroit she kept a keen lookout, till at length she found them. They were little papooses in garb and speech; still she could identify them as her fatherless loved ones in tribulations. Then she fainted, and came near dying from the extreme emotions of her heart, in alternations of joy and sorrow; of joy over the living, and sorrow for the slaughtered dead. She told me that her son and daughter were both married and doing well, and members of the Church. She was married to a Mr. Simpson, and seemed contented and happy.

In Posey County I found one of Benjamin Abbott's converts, who gave me a rather graphic account of a love-feast in New Jersey, where he was *struck under conviction*, as he styled it. His name was Robinson. He said that at the commencement of the love-feast Abbott was not there. At length he saw an old man with a shaggy black coat come into the house; he ascended the pulpit, looked awfully around a minute, then lifting his hand and foot, he exclaimed in a loud voice: "The devil is in this house! My

God, drive him out!" He stamped, and continued to roar, "Drive him out! My God, drive him out!" until the people began to fall like men on the field of battle; or, as the old man had it, they fell like timber in a whirlwind, in the gallery and on the lower floor. It was twelve o'clock before the people could be quieted. Then Dr. Phœbus preached, and it was still enough, the old man said. He added that "the wicked said that Abbott raised the devil, and Phœbus laid him." Doctor Phœbus was Mr. Abbott's colleague, and was opposed to his great excitements.

Here, at old Brother Robinson's, I met with a strange fanatic of the *Liveforever* sect, as they were called. This man preached that he would live forever in the body. His chief text of Scripture in proof of his doctrine was: "He that believeth on me shall never die." He told awful lies about how much ratsbane some of his brethren had eaten, and he had killed the poison by his faith. He staid all night at Brother Robinson's, and kept up an annoying gabble about his own immortality I concluded to *sing* him into an "expressive silence," and put all my soul and voice into the following verses:

> "My days, my weeks, my months, my years,
>   Fly rapid, like the whirling spheres,
>   Around the steady pole;
>   Time, like the tide, its motion keeps,
>   And I must launch through endless deeps,
>   Where endless ages roll," etc.

The old barbarian actually looked crestfallen and plagued, for I sung "with a vengeance." To augment my perplexity, they told me that I must sleep with him. I lay down—all the time tempted not to—and about half an hour afterward, the old man roared out: "See here, young man, you can tell everybody you see that you have slept with one man who is going to live forever without dying!" I answered: "Hold your wicked tongue, for you will die soon!" He uttered a monosyllabic grunt, not unlike one of his bristled brethren, and I heard no more of him. They said that his best sermons were delivered in a still-house not far from there.

When I traveled Sangamon Circuit, in Elder Cartwright's district, I was telling him of my mishap on this occasion, and he gave me the following, as true, of himself and the founder of the "Liveforever" society. He said that old John McDaniel, who lived near Bowling Green, Kentucky, if I remember rightly, was a bachelor of gray hairs. A fever took out all his hair and beard, which came in again black as a raven. The remarkable phenomenon wrought forcibly upon the old gentleman's imagination, and, as he did not have far to go, he went crazy. He fancied that he was growing young, and soon would be twenty-five again. At that notch he would stay eternally—all by the main strength of his faith! He fell to preaching mightily, that he would rise to a proud defiance of mortality's most stringent laws—somehow like Adam would have done if access to the tree of life had not been interdicted. At one of Dr. Cartwright's camp-meetings in Kentucky, old John McDaniel said to him: "Peter, I have seen an angel, and have good news to tell you." "What is that?" was the inquiry

McDaniel—"Why, he told me that you would become a believer, and never die."

Cartwright—"That is fine; but did you smell him, Mac?"

McDaniel—"No, sir."

Cartwright—"Fie! fie! I know he smelt strong of brimstone."

Strange as it may appear, this old monomaniac collected quite a tribe of the weak-headed about him, and laid out a piece of ground as the favored locality on which the New Jerusalem, descending out of heaven from God, would compose its foundations and walls to quiet rest! Through its golden streets the immortal believers were to roam without let or hindrance. It is said that McDaniel built himself a booth upon the holy spot, and spent some time in pious waiting for the grand event. Not to prolong this narrative, the death of McDaniel himself soon put an end to this delusion.

The same year, 1824, I was on an adjoining circuit in Daviess County, in the family of a Mr. Chapman. His aged wife brought me a book, pointing me to a passage, and I read a remarkable circumstance, given by Bishop Asbury. It was concerning a Miss Borden, of New Jersey. It seems that she had been deeply convicted of sin, at the age of fourteen years, and under some strong temptation she had vowed that she would not pray, from which time she had no more power over the organs of speech. For two years and eight months she was dumb and in despair.

She heard of Abbott's preaching in some distant settlement, and by signs made her friends understand that she desired to hear the man preach, concerning whom she had heard such wonderful things. They took her to meeting, and during the introductory exercises, while Abbott was praying with the Holy Ghost sent down from heaven, Miss Borden began to pray, and suddenly the power of speech returned, and she shouted God's praise with a loud voice. When I had read the piece and shut the book, the old lady said: "I am Achey Borden." My emotions were indescribable. With a beaming countenance, she recounted the scenes of her despair and hope till the shouting spirit was not far from us all. She was then a feeble old lady; still she nearly always shouted in meeting, and, though her voice was weak, it had the pathos of old-style shouting about it. When her husband, Elijah Chapman, died they called on me to preach his funeral sermon. I also preached at her funeral. Brother W J. Forbes, late of our Conference, was present, and assisted, he having ridden Washington Circuit the previous year. Peace be to her memory!

NEW HARMONY.

My circuit came near to New Harmony, but it was then occupied by old Frederick Rapp. This was the year, however, if I mistake not, that Robert Owen visited the old German tyrant to negotiate terms with him to exchange the serfs of Rapp for the dupes of Owen, both to be herded upon the common-stock principle. While Rapp admitted the immortality of men, he treated them as beasts of burden. Owen held that men have no more claims to immortality than the beasts that perish. Rapp's domination over his countrymen was the blackest despotism that ever sullied the fair escutcheon of our State. Owen's stay in New Harmony was short, and is soon told, and well known. He was an infidel and a pseudo-philanthropist of large gifts, but more daring, without reverence for God or Christianity. He was indeed the implacable foe of both.*

EVANSVILLE.

This place was, in 1824, a small village, with not one good house in it. I preached in a little schoolroom to a small congregation on the Sabbath day. There were but a few members of the society; they were all poor, so far as I recollect.† This place is now ‡

---

* A glance at the "Debate of Owen and Campbell," which lies before me, will justify this severe characterization of him; for, while he is learned and courteous in debate, still he hangs upon the outer wall the banner of skepticism and Communism. The present quiet and beautiful town of New Harmony shows no traces of either Rappism or Communism—those twin monstrosities in her history. But, while Owen did not succeed in permanently impressing his peculiar views upon the community he founded, he left a distinguished progeny—Robert Dale Owen, scientist and publicist; and David Dale Owen, as State geologist, professor in the State University, etc. The former, as a member of the Constitutional Convention of 1851, was influential in the enfranchisement of the women of Indiana.—W. P. H.

† Robert Parrett, the "founder of Methodism in Evansville," had not established a residence there then, if we are correctly informed. Hargrave was honored with the life-long friendship of himself and his noble wife, as well as of the children, two of whom, John W and Richard, became successful ministers of the Methodist Episcopal Church.—W. P. H.

‡ Say 1856.—W. P. H.

a prosperous city, noted for the growth of its Churches and of Christian influences. What changes have occurred in that place within thirty-two years!

I remember Dr. F—— more distinctly than any man then in Evansville. I give the reason: One day, when "plodding my weary way" from a place called Sprinklesburg, down the Ohio River, I was overtaken by a sharp-looking man, who proved to be quite loquacious. Having seen me in Evansville, he said we would be company to that point. We had not proceeded far till he gave evidence of his entire skepticism as to the divine pretensions of the Bible. He lauded reason and deified nature, and did sundry other things that a sharp Yankee would do to shine, and to talk at the expense of a young, diffident preacher. He indicated how the poor story of the Flood could be falsified; and especially the idea that the clouds never wore a rainbow till the Flood made him laugh heartily at my expense, of course. But when he had spent his wit sufficiently, he informed me that there was a text of Scripture in the New Testament, which he believed for his own sake (not for the Lord's in particular). The text was the twenty-seventh verse of the first chapter of James: "Pure religion and undefiled before God and the Father is this, To visit the fatherless and widows in their affliction, and to keep himself unspotted from the world." He quoted the passage at length, and paraded his eulogies around it, saying: "This is the religion of nature; it is pure reason." He gave an exegesis of the text, dwelling upon its benevolent character—taking in its ample range the fatherless and the widow; but he touched lightly on "the flesh," whose pollutions are prohibited in the same passage.

I then congratulated the doctor upon his frank admission of the doctrines of his favorite text; that he had some affirmative ground to occupy as well as we Christians—some faith to defend against gainsayers. I proceeded thus: " Your religion being something positive, of necessity stands opposed to all that is its legitimate negation. As you say 'the text is reason itself,' then you infer that its negative is unreasonable in itself. Now, Doctor, I have you logically bound for the following consequences, viz.: That it is right to visit the fatherless and widows in their affliction, because it is wrong to neglect them. Now, Doctor, for your sanctions of reward for those who do these benevolent acts, and penalties for those who neglect to do them." "Hold there," said the doctor; "do you not know that it is in the line of my professional duty to visit and administer medicine to them in their afflictions? I am in for that all the time." I replied: "Ah, Doctor, their afflictions may mean much more than sick stomachs; and to administer to such afflictions, might be more than an emetic and blister; it might require food and raiment, and spiritual comfort in mental afflictions. But do you make your visits gratis?" Here he raised some quibble, finding that his affirmative was likely to grow too large on his hands. "Now," continued I, "we come to notice the inward grace of your admitted 'undefiled religion.' It requires that you keep yourself 'unspotted from the world.' This implies that it is wrong to be polluted by the world. So the 'religion of reason,' as you call it, prohibits such pollution. Doctor, do you keep yourself 'unspotted from the world?'" He replied: "I know that it is against me, but I can not do that." I replied: "So it comes to this, that you have demolished my religion at will, and spurned it all as unreasonable, and then you have adventured one of your own choosing; eulogized it as reason itself, and upon a moment's examination I find that it commands you to be what you can not be! Was ever a Christian in anything more unreasonable than even yourself—the censor of them all?"

The doctor seemed strongly inclined to get out of the class-meeting that I was taking him through concerning inward purity as a duty and an impossibility at the same time! Alas for these vaunting, doubting gentry, when they come to any well-defined affirmative ground on points of faith or morals! The doctor committed himself to an ignoble retreat before I could probe his theory about the sanctions appended to his "undefiled religion," especially the penalties for those who wallow in the pollutions of the world, despite the behests of his religion against such pollutions. I have known the glass house of infidels ever since; and before I will suffer them to pull down *my* house from over my head, I hurl a few smooth stones into their unfounded castle in the air, and they leave me to my preferences very soon. Try it, who will, and you will find it an efficient mode of defense—*reductio ad absurdum.*

The doctor invited me to dine with him, treated me with marked politeness, gave me some medicine for my indisposition, and invited me warmly to make his house my home when I came to town. I have always hoped that the short talk I had with him may have proven "a nail driven in a sure place."

ANECDOTES OF FATHER CRAVENS.

While in the neighborhood of Boonville, at the home of Brother John Baker, he gave me a highly-wrought account of a "two-days' meeting" held by Father Cravens in Baker's sugar-camp. The people came from far and near, some led by curiosity to hear the far-famed orator, and some to share the religious enjoyment of the occasion. The preachers from a distance came, and the meeting proved to be one of great interest. A revival broke out, and on Sabbath night they had a blessed time. The weather being fine, the night meetings were held in the grove. The old patriarch, fatigued, had retired to rest, and near midnight Brother Baker returned home, and the old man asked him how the work went on at the "stand." He said: "They have all got through, except the man who has two wives; he is having a hard time of it." "Two wives, eh!" shouted the old man. "Yes," said Brother Baker; "he has one wife and children in South Carolina and another here." "Did you not tell him he must go back and take up with his right wife?" "No," said Brother Baker. "You are a pretty doctor," rejoined Father Cravens. So saying, he got up, put on his clothes, gathered his staff, and said: "Come, show him to me." When they got to the mourner, he was lying with his head upon the lap of his second wife, crying loudly for mercy.

Father Cravens got down by him and said: "Are you very sorry for all your sins?" "O yes! yes!" was the reply. "Will you forsake them all if God will convert you?" "O yes!" was the response. "Will you leave this woman you have here, and go back to Carolina to your right wife? If you will covenant to do it, God will convert you on a credit. Say, will you?" "I can not do it," was the faint reply. "Get up and begone! You are as sure of hell as the devil!" replied Father Cravens. All was still, and the old man motioned to Brother Baker to return to the house; and when they were fairly on the way, added: "I fixed him!" Slaveholding, drunkenness, and polygamy had to "stand from under" when Father Cravens was about.

ITINERANT LIFE.

This year was not spent altogether in unavailing effort to do something for my Master's glory. Revivals extended throughout the circuit. At a meeting near New Harmony, aided by Rev. J. Shrader, a good local preacher, many embraced Christ. Among many others who were then received into the Church, was a young man by the name of Charles Bonner, who soon became a traveling preacher of our Church, and was for many years a useful member of the old Indiana Conference. I think he is now in California.

Our last quarterly meeting was a camp-meeting, at Old Shiloh, Gibson County It was a good meeting. Elder Beauchamp was there, in feeble health. He preached delightfully, and these were nearly his last pulpit efforts. He never returned home. Here I took my recommendation for entrance into the traveling connection. Doctor Beauchamp's death, however, prevented its appearance at the Conference. Still I was admitted, and appointed to Salem Circuit, Rev. Samuel Lowe preacher in charge. It was a month before I could learn where I was appointed. I walked five miles to gain information upon that point, and found the youthful Edwin Ray at one of his preaching-places. He that year traveled Vincennes Circuit.

INCIDENTS ON SALEM CIRCUIT.

After preparation, I started about the last of November for my new field of labor. On my way, I staid in Paoli all night. Early in the morning I passed the grave of the loved and gifted Beauchamp. Then not a stone told where he lay; but I had such information as enabled me to identify the spot of his sweet repose. He had met death far from home, while performing the duties of his sacred office. The survey induced emotions painfully pleasing. Since then I have stood by the tombs of full many a companion in itinerant toils, who have gone to enjoy the reward a little in advance of me. Heaven make me as ready as Beauchamp and others, who were the early partners of my ministry!

The day that I was twenty-one years old I preached my first sermon on Salem Circuit, in a little brick school-house. That day I rode twelve miles to meet my colleague, and got to his appointment before the preaching hour; and as he was unwell, I tried to preach as well as I could.*

Rev. Samuel Lowe, my colleague, was a convert to Methodism, and in his first love. I here give the account, as he gave it to me, of his experience. He was a native of New Hampshire, and had been a "Free-will Baptist" in his youthful days, but on marrying among Presbyterians, had become a rigid Calvinist. He was deacon of the Church. He was rather combative in his intercourse with the Methodists. Lewis Roberts, brother of the bishop, concocted the plan to convert him to Methodism. His last marriage was in a Methodist family, and he carried on the shoe business in the house of his father-in-law, Brother Lemon. Roberts asked Lemon if he did not want to read some very smart books. The old man was, of course, glad to get them. So he left all of "Fletcher's Checks" with him. Brother Lowe soon noticed the old gentleman poring over some strange sort of books, and finding that the writer "worked with sharp tools," to use his expression, he set himself to read the books. When Mr. Fletcher stated his positions so fairly on Calvinistic issues, he said to himself, "You have got your match with that!" but to his surprise in almost no time he cleared it up, and was dashing on at something else. So he became charmed with the vast acuteness of his logic, and never ceased till he got through the last volume. Then he said: "If this is Methodist doctrine, I am a Methodist." Roberts came over to see him, and found

---

* How often it happened so with him! "Always ready."—W. P. H.

him thoroughly established in the new faith. "Being crafty, he took him with guile."

Soon after Brother Lowe took license to preach, and made " a workman that needed not to be ashamed." He was a decidedly useful, popular preacher, and for a few years he traveled, but was compelled to locate because of ill-health. He went into the dry-goods business, and lived a useful local preacher till, in 1843, he died in Coles County, Illinois. His end was peaceful. His son informs me that, from local affection of organs of speech, he for some time previous to his death did not speak. But when "his eyes were set," he took the hand of his weeping companion, and pointed upward, to show by gesture his prospects of the future. Peace to his memory!

We had a good degree of prosperity that conference year—1824–25—except as to our pocket-books. I received twenty-four dollars for my year's hard work.

The Rev. William Shanks lived within the bounds of the circuit. Before the year closed, old Father Cravens came to stay in his family. At our camp-meeting, at the close of the year, I heard Father Cravens preach one of his strong, eccentric sermons. His text was, "Curse ye Meroz," etc.*

BISHOP ROBERTS.

Bishop Roberts lived within the bounds of Salem Circuit. It was a happy circumstance that I had his

---

* Here the narrative is broken by the loss of a leaf of the manuscript.—W. P. H.

wise and timely advice on several matters on which my mind yet remained fettered with O'Kelleyanism. These were mere questions of ecclesiastical polity, not doctrinal difficulties. The courteous and patient manner in which he heard my difficulties, together with his solution of them, inspired me with gratitude toward him, and convinced me that I could abide *episcopacy* when administered by so amiable a man as I found him to be. Till then I did not think of taking ordination in the ministry, but felt it a high privilege to remain merely a licensed preacher in the Methodist Church. My scruples arose upon the question of a second ordination; that is, I doubted whether the *deaconship* belonged in any way to the ministry proper; and because through it alone I could reach the eldership. I thought of waiving both because of my scruples about the one. He put "Bangs on Episcopacy" in my hands, and that, teaching the doctrine that bishops and presbyters are the same order, as Lord King and Mr. Wesley contended, I found no reasonable impediment left in my way to orders. As to trouble on the score of the deaconship, the bishop said: "Young brother, your private views upon that subject need form no impediment to your advancing to orders; for what signifies it whether we give you the ministry in two parcels or in one?" That sensible, central idea released my mind from its needless anxieties, and I was in readiness against the time to take orders.

Having been chaplain to Bishop Roberts's family for a year, I take the liberty to notice my valedictory services in his house. The bishop was not at home the day alluded to. The appointment was on Saturday, and but few attended. When the meeting commenced there were but eleven present who were not members of the society, but before it ended I took nine of them on trial into the Church. A general shout occurred at the end of the sermon, and I called for mourners—a good use to make of the bishop's summer-room. A goodly number came forward for prayers, and some were powerfully converted. Rev. Lewis Roberts, of our Conference, was one who joined the Church that day. He was a lad of fourteen summers. He was in my district a few years since, and referring to the occasion, he said: "I thought it the greatest meeting I ever was at; and it still seems to me that I never heard you preach so well as you did that day on 'Faith, Hope, and Charity.'" Mother Roberts shouted gloriously. To average the meeting, it was one of the most successful of my itinerant life, to take nine-elevenths of the sinners present into the Church.

HONEY CREEK CIRCUIT.

At the Charlestown Conference I was appointed to the Honey Creek Circuit. This work included the counties of Sullivan and Vigo, and touched upon Knox and Parke Counties. It lay up and down on the Wabash River, from the mouth of Raccoon Creek, in Parke, to the Shaker Prairie in Knox. By mutual consent of the parties concerned, Vincennes Circuit and Honey Creek were united, and made a six weeks' work. Rev. Aaron Wood being on that circuit, thus became my colleague. The two circuits thus united, embraced Knox, Daviess, Martin, Greene, Sullivan,

Vigo, and a part of Parke. The reader may readily perceive that we had but little idle time, and we did not desire it. Father Holliday was our presiding elder. When quarterly meeting came on, we had joyful times, listening to the pointed, practical, and impassioned discourses of that evangelical minister of Christ. He was then but little past the prime of life, and possessed an excellent flow of spirits, well understood his duty, and was in earnest in its performance. He was prepared to lead in the van of Israel's hosts, and to exemplify to young ministers fidelity and untiring zeal in the cause of Christ. I never had a more efficient, faithful presiding elder, and bless God for the good which I received from his holy example and useful labor. He was an excellent preacher, without vanity, and, although he never was a skeleton sermonizer, there were marrow and fat things in his sermons. On many occasions I have heard him preach great, original sermons.

The most remarkable meeting we had that year was in Knox County, at the house of Brother S. Teverbaugh. Sabbath day, Brother Wood preached a good sermon on the first four commandments. He generally had the spirit of preaching, but on Sabbath night he got the spirit of exhortation as I never saw him since. He thundered and lightened so awfully that some fell to the floor, and literally stopped up the passage to the door, and some young men who could not effect their escape from the scene of terror in that direction, lifted up the floor, it being loose, and vanished from the congregation with a sinking motion through the opening! This was the only time I could not keep pace with Brother Wood in zeal.

At the close of this year 1826, Brother Wood and myself attended Father Holliday to Mount Carmel and Shiloh camp-meetings. Shiloh was in Patoka Circuit, which I had traveled two years before. They were both good camp-meetings. There I had my first acquaintance with Rev. S. C. Cooper, of the North Indiana Conference. He was then an exhorter, and undergoing life's hardest trial—the loss of his beloved companion. Here, too, Brother Wood saw Miss Beauchamp for the first time, who subsequently became his worthy partner in the life of the itinerant.

Shiloh was a far more powerful camp-meeting than Mount Carmel. Father Holliday preached with more than his usual pathos, and Brother Wood was strung up to his best mood for pulpit work. Sabbath night and Monday morning of that meeting were occasions never to be forgotten by me and many others. Some professed the blessing of a clean heart, and I had never before verged so near to it. On Sabbath night, while engaged in the altar-labors, I was met by such a blessing as overwhelmed my physical powers, and I lay at length upon the ground, and I might say of some things which then occurred: "Whether in the body or out of the body I know not; God knoweth." Though not caught up to paradise, heaven then "came down my soul to greet, and glory crowned the mercy-seat." Brother Joseph Tarkington was junior preacher on the circuit, and shared largely of the overflowing salvation of God that so many felt. O, how good are God's ways! This blessing was, in some sort, my outfit of grace for a heavy trial impending over my next year's labors. From that hour my access to God was easy and sweet, and my desire to "pray without ceasing" kept me where I could almost "rejoice evermore." A visit to my parents followed, and I went to arrange for our Conference, which was held in Bloomington, Indiana.

BLOOMINGTON CONFERENCE—APPOINTED TO SANGAMON CIRCUIT, ILLINOIS.

Here I first saw Bishop Soule. A short time after I arrived in town, the day previous to the commencement of the session, some presiding elder sent me with a message to the bishop's room. Bishop Roberts arose, smiling, shook my hand heartily, asked after my welfare, and led me to Bishop Soule, who was sitting in a rocking-chair, apparently in a meditative mood. His bearing was dignified and somewhat awe-ing, and as Bishop Roberts said, "Bishop Soule, let me introduce to you one of our young preachers"— naming me—I thought I was entitled to a greeting. But judge of my surprise, when he uttered not a word, sat as before, cast his eye askance, let his elbow still rest on the arm of his chair, and slightly inclined the back of his hand toward me. I recoiled on Wednesday from the hand which, on the following Sabbath, was imposed upon my head in the ordination ceremony. I told some of my friends of the repulse, but they only said: "O, he was in one of his abstractions." I then thought, and still believe, that he was wanting in the kindness of heart that was exuberant in Bishop Roberts. Such acts look very like a breach of this precept, " Let none think of himself more highly than he ought to think;" and this again, " Be courteous;" and yet again, " Condescend to men of low estate." I record this as a warning to other great men not to lock themselves up in their greatness; since, as Massillon so powerfully said, " There is none great but God."

On Sabbath, Bishop Soule preached a mighty sermon in the court-house on " Justification by Faith." His text was: " But to him that worketh not, but believeth on Him that justifieth the ungodly, his faith is counted for righteousness." He was then in his palmy days, and surely he was a workman of no ordinary skill and logical powers. Arians quailed before him. When showing what Christ's divinity was to his redeeming virtues, and what the gospel is to our hopes, and what he does with our hopes who denies Christ's Godhead, he exclaimed: " Cursed be the lip and palsied the tongue which would detract aught from the divinity of my Lord! I should not wonder if some infidel should leave the house." The Arians rushed for the door in a hurry. He ordained the deacons after the sermon. I was one of the class. At the rise of the Conference I was appointed to Sangamon Circuit, Illinois. Joseph Tarkington was my colleague; Rev. Peter Cartwright, D. D., our presiding elder.

SANGAMON CIRCUIT.

We left Bloomington in company with Dr. Cartwright, and proceeded directly to our circuit. The weather was fine all the way, and we got on in good time. We commenced our work under fair auspices, and had good meetings generally and sometimes mighty shouts at family prayers.* O, how I felt the mighty blessing which I had received at Shiloh camp-meeting! "Effectual, fervent prayer" seemed to be the life and strength of my soul. I endeavored to give myself to exhortation more than I had done, and I felt fully enlisted, and had a "mind to the work." Just here my ability failed me. Dyspepsia took strong hold of my frame, and it withered, and my strength fast diminished under the starving life that I then endured. My labors with elder and colleague were agreeable and satisfactory in every particular, and it was no ordinary trial then to retire. I was compelled to do so, however, at my second quarterly meeting. To this my kind elder assented, and I took a long farewell of that interesting country!

On my way home I spent the Sabbath at Vandalia, and after preaching I requested any one who could show me the spot, to accompany me and show me where my dear brother, five years before, had been drowned. A gentleman kindly tendered me his services, and with a heavy heart I went to where he died alone. I then visited his grave; and what thoughts came crowding up to touch me with sad reminiscences of a loved brother, cut down in the twenty-second year of his age! How like this

---

* Those who ever heard Hargrave lead in family prayers, would not wonder if, under predisposing circumstances, the shout should arise at the family altar in the cabin of the early settler. And from what we know of his presiding elder and colleague, we would expect the same results.—W. P. H.

changeful, fleeting world does this event appear! How many blooming hopes have withered, and the bright prospects of coming life are here entombed! How many hearts have heaved a sigh at this tragical event, which consigned the high-minded and gifted youth to an early grave here in a distant land and a lonely place! I, your smitten brother, in feeble health too, and doubtful of earthly prospects, stand weeping beside a kind stranger, who can only say: "He lies in one or the other of these graves." Ah! could a humble stone but tell where he rests, how would it cheer this troubled heart! But five years, O Ellis, thou hast here reposed amid stranger graves, and none of the villagers can certainly say which in sooth is thine! Worse than I had anticipated! Such thoughts catechised my quivering heart, and the gentleman standing by me heaved sympathetic sighs, and tearfully pointed to a far shorter grave, saying: "In *that* sleeps my lovely blue-eyed boy of three years!" That brother's grave I have never again seen. But how many fresher ones have I wept over, near the spreading gum-tree, where parents and most of best earthly friends sleep, awaiting archangel tones to wake them to "ever-during bloom!" Lord, prepare me for my change, and for a place with the happy dead in the bright world of fadeless day! The following lines were suggested by the scene here narrated:

MY BROTHER'S GRAVE.

Far distant, I've found it at last!
 The place of a brother's repose;
A stranger points out the sad place,
 That place he imperfectly knows.

Full well I once knew the grand form,
   Reposing so quietly here;
Nor heeds he the loud-roaring storm,
   Nor the fall of his young brother's tear.

How jocund and glad did we rove
   Along in life's morning so bright,
Communing in brotherly love,
   Scarce thinking of Death's fearful blight!
But beauty, here faded, lies sere,
   And strength has forsaken my mate,
Since 'wildered in yon woodland drear,
   Alone he encountered his fate.

Humanity had not an ear
   That heeded, though loudly he cried;
No friend then attended to cheer;
   Alone and unaided he died!
His horse, which had borne him away,
   Remained, a dumb beacon, to show;
His hoof-prints bespoke where he lay,
   Beneath the mad current so low.

Till strangers reclaimed from the flood
   The burden that long he had borne,
That horse still prophetical stood,
   Methinks for his master to mourn.
And strangers conveyed my dead, where
   He rests 'neath the hillock I see;
Now calmly exempt from the care
   Which tells in its rigors on me.

At home, in a sorrowful mood,
   Both parents and lov'd ones did wait,
In passionate yearning did brood,
   Concerning our brother's dread fate.
Too soon the sad tidings came on,
   Revealing the fatal delay;
They told that the brother and son
   Would, alas! in *this* narrow house stay.

> Here rest, my dear brother, in peace,
>   Repose in this quiet retreat,
> Till Michael shall sound thy release—
>   Immortal, each other we'll greet!
> Like Jesus, who conquered, we'll rise,
>   Outshout the glad seraphs, and fly
> To meet our dear Lord in the skies,
>   And live where we never shall die;
>
> And range where we never shall weep,
>   And sing of redemption above;
> In sight of the Lamb we shall keep,
>   Through visions of glory shall rove;
> Eternally freed from all pain,
>   Eternally shut in with God;
> With Jesus eternally reign,
>   There make our celestial abode!

After a restless night, I started on the Vincennes road for home. The prairies were wet, it being the month of April. Night overtook me without a house to stay in, except a miserable hut, where there was a man in a dying condition. He told me if I could tie my horse, and put up with bad fare, he would be glad, for they, that night, had no company. I concluded to try it. After all matters were arranged, I seated myself, overcome by the toils of travel and the sympathies that had pressed upon me from the events of the day before. I spoke of my brother's fate, and that I had been at his grave. The man exclaimed: "Richard, is that you?" And I said: "Mr. Rogers, is it possible that this is you?" I had known him in the White River country, and he had gone to parts unknown; but saddest of all, he was not prepared for his fast-approaching doom. I prayed for him, and exhorted him to make the needed preparation. He wept much. The next morning I continued my journey. In two more days I reached home, and though I had written to my parents of my declining health, they had not thought of my being so feeble and emaciated. My mother wept tenderly, and said: "Son, I had fears that an Illinois grave might contain *you!* If you die, we will sleep by the gum-tree together!" O, the luxury of an immortal hope under these touching, trying scenes of life! I much expected to end my days that summer.

Charles Slocomb was on the circuit, and old Father John Fox was employed to aid him, as his health was poor. After my long confinement, in June Father Holliday's quarterly meeting came on at my father's. This was a welcome occurrence to me, for I was much depressed in spirits on some occasions, owing to my low state of health. That old patriarch preached on Sabbath, with the Holy Ghost sent down from heaven, and my last unconverted sister felt the shaft of truth that was hurled from the gospel bow. How I rejoiced! Within a few weeks afterwards, at a Cumberland Presbyterian camp-meeting, some miles distant, this sister was powerfully converted. For fifty hours previous to her conversion she took no nourishment, and some began to fear that she would die. Thank God, she found the heavenly manna, and all was well. This being the conversion of the last child, my mother rested with adoring, quiet ecstasy in God, and felt that she could say: "Now, Lord, lettest thou thy servant depart in peace, for mine eyes have seen the salvation of God!"

The following Sabbath night, two pious young

ladies were at our house, visiting my sisters, and after prayers—I was then barely able to lead in the devotions—while all was silent, my mother began to shout. My father, not perceiving the cause, asked an explanation. She said: "My last child is converted. Glory to God!" The victorious signal was well attuned, and our hearts well strung to the doxology; and above stairs and below "Glory to God!" resounded till neighbors heard the loud acclaim and came in. As soon as they entered, they caught the raptures of that hour. O, for a return of the old-fashioned family shouts! In my youth they were as common as household words. One of the predisposing causes was the old-fashioned family singing. Mere scientific singing will not do. We must sing by faith, " with the spirit and the understanding also;" then, with the reading of the Word, gospel power will revisit our firesides; our children will not backslide so easily; our class-meetings will become popular again; and our prayer-meetings cease to be merely a formal observance upon the part of many. By such means, adapting our work to the times, may we not return to the simplicity and spiritual power of the fathers? May God grant it!

That fall we held our Conference at Mount Carmel, Illinois, and in great feebleness I reached it. My weight was one hundred and sixteen pounds. I felt that *superannuation* upon my part was inevitable, though a gloomy alternative. I was pacing the porch before the door of the room in which the Conference sessions were being held; and Elder Cartwright moved my superannuation, and as some tender sympathizing allusions were caught, my emotions came near prostrating my little strength.

That afternoon Rev. S. H. Thompson preached, "Be careful for nothing." It was a word in season to my desponding heart. I returned to my room, and went then into a little ware-room of the merchant, and fell on some sacks, and wept and prayed till finally sleep came to my relief. After dark, Brother T. S. Hitt, of precious memory, came with a candle, and urged me to take a little refreshment. How grateful the reminiscences of such brotherly kindness!

The most interesting occurrence at that Conference was the sermon of Rev. John Strange, on Sabbath morning. His theme was based upon the expression: "Behold, I send you forth as lambs among wolves." He was in his happiest mood, and preached more than an hour. His eloquence beggars all description. One specimen alone is here attempted. When wrought up to the highest key, he seized upon the idea of what the disciples should say to melt and subdue sinners. He asked: "Is it to gird the ignited thunder-bolt upon his left arm, and to grasp the sword of wrath, edged with damnation, in his right hand? No! Mercy! mercy! mercy! is the burden of his theme!" His gesture and countenance when he used the expression "edged with damnation" were so unearthly, that it seemed that I saw scintillations of fire stream off the sword of wrath and sparkle through the aisle. I had a sense of vertigo, and the people all swayed from side to side as he did. A little more and we had all fallen to the floor. What screams and shouts followed all over the house!

At this Conference, Edwin Ray preached one of his sweet and impassioned sermons on the love of God to sinners. I though him the brightest young man among us of his day. But I reserve my remarks for a distinct chapter in his case.*

---

* Here end Hargrave's sketches of his early experiences. If they were ever resumed, they do not appear among his papers. It is a somewhat singular circumstance that he never mentioned them to any of the family. At the end of two years' superannuation, we are to behold him coming forth with abounding strength and vigor for a long life of usefulness. He probably had no further leisure for the work of the annalist. Yet we trust that in this fragmentary form these sketches will be acceptable to the reader, as containing a vivid account of his parentage, childhood, youth, conversion, and early struggles upon points of faith, in which he gloriously triumphed. Also the hardships and sufferings of those early days; methods of Church-work—the primitive camp-meeting era—characterization of some of the great leaders in the ministry, glimpses of society, etc.—W. P. H.

BIOGRAPHICAL SKETCHES.

REV RICHARD HARGRAVE, D. D.

BY WILLIAM GRAHAM, D. D.

THIS venerable man of God and minister of Christ was a member of the Northwest Indiana Conference. He closed his long and useful life at the residence of his daughter, Mrs. Campbell, near Attica, Indiana, June 23, 1879, in the mature age of his seventy-sixth year. He was a native of North Carolina; was born in Caswell County, December 5, 1803. He came to the State of Indiana, with his parents, at the age of fourteen years. He was converted at the age of nineteen, and was induced to unite with the "O'Kelley Church," sometimes called the "New Light Church." His conversion was spiritual and genuine; but he always regarded his first Church relation as a mistake, which he was not long in finding out. At the age of twenty he united with the Methodist Episcopal Church, and the following year he began to preach, which thenceforth became his lifelong calling. His first license is dated in 1823, though he preached before that date; in fact, he began to hold meetings and exhort from the time he united with the Church. Of his early life we have no written data. Though he was accustomed to talk freely about it, and sometimes would relate thrilling incidents of his childhood and youth, yet he left no notes to guide us in anything we might wish to say. This is to be regretted.* He had a remarkably retentive memory, and loved in his pleasant moods to talk about his early Carolina home and the colored people by whom he was surrounded; but he cordially despised slavery as from the impulse of his generous nature.

On March 10, 1829, he was married to Nancy A. Posey, with whom he lived in the tenderest love and harmony until God took her, June 12, 1871. This sad separation greatly chafed his spirit; no one felt the loss of a life-long companion more than he. And no marvel, for she was worthy of him in all respects, and just such a companion as his somewhat peculiar temperament and habits required. She was calm, patient, uncomplaining, and considerate; was by far a better manager of domestic affairs than was her husband; and always kept his home neat, cheerful, and inviting. She was one of those elect ladies, whom to know was to admire and love. How much of her husband's usefulness was due to her influence and care, only God knows.

The subject of our sketch left no record of his ministerial life,† but so far as we have any data, the following is an outline: In 1823, Patoka; 1824, Salem; 1825, Honey Creek; 1826, Sangamon;

---

*Subsequently to his death his autobiographical notes were found.—W. P. H.

† Except the first three years.—W. P. H.

1827-28, he was superannuated; 1829, Paoli; 1830, Franklin; 1831, Carlisle; 1832, Crawfordsville; 1833, Lafayette; 1834-37, La Porte District; 1838, La Porte; 1839, Shelbyville; 1840-41, Manchester; 1842, Ladoga; 1843, Crawfordsville; 1844-45, Newtown; 1846-48, Indianapolis District; 1849-52, Greencastle District; 1853, Lafayette District; 1854-55, Shawnee Prairie; 1856, Perrysville; 1857, Pine Village; 1858, Frankfort; 1859, Delphi District; 1860-63, he was superannuated; 1864-65, Thorntown; 1866, Battle Ground; 1867, Monticello District; 1868, Battle Ground District; 1869-70, Terre Haute District. In the fall of 1871 he was again placed on the superannuated list, and he continued in that relation until he died. But he by no means ceased to preach when he no longer had a regular charge assigned him; he averaged two hundred sermons a year during his last superannuation; and from his last Conference, in September, 1878, until the middle of the following March—when he was stricken down by disease—he had preached one hundred and four sermons in various places.

Richard Hargrave was a royal preacher. He is justly ranked with the first class of pulpit orators of his day, and deserves to be classed with Allen Wiley, John Strange, James Armstrong, and James Havens. In personal appearance, though not of majestic mien, yet he was impressive, and any one would have taken him to be a man of mark. In height he was about five feet, nine inches; of heavy, compact frame; round features; broad, high, and intellectual forehead; head bald, and hair light in color and thin. In his organic structure he was symmetrically developed, and presented a physical form of completeness. This description answers for the last thirty years of his life; when younger he was more spare. His face was florid, and his movements quick, indicative of a sanguine temperament. His countenance was expressive of emotion, frankness, and guilelessness. Nothing selfish, sinister, or scheming could be detected in his features, nor did anything of the kind find a place in his heart. His outward appearance was the honest, artless expression of his soul; planning for selfish ends was foreign to his nature, to his taste, and to his habits. He was an honest man—loved sincerely and hated cordially,* but deceived no one.

No inconsiderable element of his power as a preacher was his remarkable voice. It was rich, full, sonorous, and musical, ringing out from a pair of full, round lungs with the greatest apparent ease, and peculiarly clear, distinct, and melodious. Though his voice was naturally one of the best, yet it had evidently been cultivated and trained by long use, and he had it under complete control. It was never cracked nor husky, and never seemed strained. He never screamed, never reached for a key higher than nature had supplied him with, and he never spoke in low tones and whispers; and yet his modulation of voice was sufficient to make it pleasant to the hearer and easy to himself. His voice filled an auditorium, so that the remotest listener heard him as distinctly as those who were near him, and yet it was never

---

* "Hated the sin, but still the sinner loved."—W. P. H.

unpleasantly loud to any. It was like the tones of an organ—musical to the ear, whether near or distant. That voice rang out upon the air with wonderful power at camp-meetings, arresting the attention and captivating assembled thousands, and compelling silence by its melody and charm. Few of our great preachers have been gifted with such a voice, and we do not sufficiently appreciate the value of such a gift. It has been said of public oratory that " manner is matter ;" if so, then voice is matter. It is certainly a vehicle of thought, and an instrument of power that counts largely in the effects of speech.

The manner of our subject, when in the pulpit, was also greatly in his favor. Under the most exciting surroundings he was deliberate, and showed no perturbation; however animated he was, he acted with coolness. He was master of the situation when in the pulpit. His movements and gestures, though rapid, were graceful; never abrupt nor nervous. It was a marvel that so excitable a man could be so self-possessed and deliberate in the pulpit. Impassioned earnestness beamed in his every feature, and yet his sentences rolled forth like the measured waterfall; his sentences never crowded each other, were never abrupt, never unfinished, but always musical in measure and in tone. His periods were rounded, and the emphasis was deliberately placed. His eloquence was not the dashing, irregular flood, but the swell of the rolling waves; not the noisy cataract, but the harmonious measures of the swelling tide. He never seemed to labor hard in preaching, and hence he did not weary his hearers; they had no painful sympathy with him, but listened with delight. He made the impression that it was natural and easy for him to preach, that he enjoyed it himself, and so it became pleasant to them. In short, the message was in him, like fire in his bones, and it seemed a pleasant relief to give it utterance. He was not usually tedious, so as to weary his congregation; his sermons were commonly considerate in length, though, when the occasion demanded it, he could preach by the hour. The best test of an orator's real ability is found in the audience, which he attracts and holds. Tried by this rule, our subject was a great preacher, and great to the last; for, whenever he was announced to preach, he was sure of an appreciating audience. Some of our Churches clamor for the vigor, magnetism, and audacity of young preachers, but here was a man well up in the seventies who, for real effectiveness in preaching, outstripped them all.

His style was terse, chaste, pure, sententious, and poetic. His sentences were short and well rounded, and his language was never labored. He did not hesitate for the want of words; with him thought and language kept even pace. He used theological and ecclesiastical terms freely, and put them appropriately; but he employed the old terms of the fathers, and carefully avoided the new. Such terms as "eschatology" and "soteriology" he despised as being pedantic, and never used them in discourse. He also avoided long words and words rarely used, confining himself chiefly to plain Saxon terms, so that the children could understand him. He was indeed more simple in style than he was in thought, and he seemed conscious of this, so that not unfrequently he repeated his thoughts in varied language, but without any hitch in the even tenor of his discourse. His method of putting things, and of expressing the truth, was unique. It was artless as it was expressive and effective. He had evidently studied no models, had copied no one, and therefore his own genius and individuality appeared in his discourses; these he never lost by becoming a slave to other men's methods. He could not imitate any one; he had to be himself, and was just like no one else. We had but one Richard Hargrave, and we shall not have another, for he was a subject that no one can copy. He ignored the ordinary artificial rules of logic and rhetoric; was pre-eminently natural, and had methods of argumentation peculiarly his own. Any one could discover that he had learned to preach without many human helps; he had blazed his way through the intricacies of controversy, and never forgot the well-marked path. His soul was born into the household of faith in the tumult of Arian and Socinian disputes, and he delighted to the last in dealing those old errors, which had given him so much trouble in early life, vigorous blows. He seemed to enjoy nothing better than to hurl the shafts of Scripture proofs against these old enemies of his. He was very apt and happy in the use of Scripture proofs, quoting them freely, and applying them appropriately, and often in such an unusual way as to surprise and impress his hearers. He always emphasized the testimony of Scripture, which was to him the end of all controversy.

He was an industrious and even an ardent student, not so much of books as of subjects; of Scripture and theology, rather than of science and philosophy. Though he was prone to abstract thought, yet he was far from being a metaphysician; he lacked the nice discriminations and the clear definitions. His was the Hebrew, rather than the Greek type of mind; comprehensive and majestic, rather than minute and exact. He not unfrequently shut himself up in his room for hours and half days at a time, even from his own family, that he might grapple with some problem which engaged his thoughts. He was not so great a reader as he was a thinker and student, but he digested well what he did read. He rarely ever read a theological work without severely criticising it, sometimes justly, but not always so. He was constantly looking out for heresy, being sensitively jealous of the great Bible doctrines. In fact, he was no mean critic. Watson and Clark did not escape his incisive Scriptural criticism, and even Wesley came in for a share at times. Though he had not enjoyed in early life the advantages of a liberal education, yet this disadvantage was largely overcome in after years, and he was especially well schooled in theology. Most of his sermons were based on the writings of the Epistles, those to the Romans and the Hebrews being among his favorites. From the force of early training, he was prone to treat his themes controversially, and yet not in the ordinary and objectionable sense. One not familiar with the old schools of error, when Methodism had to fight its way into public recognition and favor, would sometimes wonder what he was driving at, but it soon became apparent that he was planting his Scripture batteries against some deep-seated heresy in the popular mind. His method was to make the Bible its own lexicographer—interpreting Scripture by Scripture.

His mind and style were poetic. It is not strange therefore that he dealt freely in verse. Dante, Milton, Pollok, and Young were favorite authors with him, from whose works he quoted largely in his sermons. Blank verse was his delight, as his favorite authors would indicate. It was in keeping with his own rounded style. He had an aptness for writing such verse himself. Besides numerous manuscript sermons, one volume of which has been published, he has left a large amount of poetry in manuscript, of very considerable merit, and some of which may find its way into print. In his later years he was in the habit of quoting to a considerable extent from his own verse, which was so like his general style as hardly to be distinguished. The writer of this sketch was charged some years ago with the duty of revising a volume of his sermons for the press, the most delicate task of which was to erase long passages of original poetry; omitted, not for the want of merit in itself, but because it was not properly any part of a written sermon. What is not always the case with our most eloquent preachers, our subject had the gift of song. Standing on the platform at a camp-meeting, and singing in his musical voice such songs as the "Royal Proclamation," waking the echoes of the woods by night, was a scene not soon to be forgotten. Those silvery tones still linger in the memory of thousands.

The themes of his preaching were usually textual and expository, rarely topical, and always spiritual and evangelical. Christ and salvation chiefly made up the matter of his sermons. And he had great variety in preaching, seeing that his subjects were kindred in their matter, having for their focal points Sinai and Calvary, Moses and Christ, the Law and the Gospel. He used no notes, either in or out of the pulpit. When he wrote a discourse, he wrote it out in full, but never read it from the pulpit. His sermons were wrought out by study and prayer for each occasion; and if at any time he repeated himself, it was with such variations as to make it a new sermon. He took up a theme and followed it out in a manner which to him was natural, or at least habitual, however his method might strike a critical hearer. When in some rare cases his preaching did not satisfy him, or when he thought he had made a failure, he felt more alarmed than mortified, and seeking some retired place, he would betake himself to prayer, and for hours would agonize before God and seek forgiveness. Going in the strength of his Master, his idea was that his message must be a success, and when he thought it a failure, he attributed the cause to some secret sin in his heart. He felt an awful sense of the responsibility in preaching the gospel of Christ, and was very severe with himself. He could forgive others for a poor sermon, but he could not excuse himself. His sensibilities were very acute, and he held himself to the strictest accountability to God. For the schools of science and philosophy he found but little use, except to criticise the vagaries of some of their theories.

The gospel of salvation absorbed all his attention, and he had but little patience for anything else. He rarely lost any time in proving that man is a sinner and needs the remedy of the gospel, but assuming that fact, he pressed the claims of the gospel upon all hearts with an earnestness, tenderness, and pathos which were hard to resist. He was an impassioned orator, and often poured forth a stream of eloquence that was absolutely overwhelming. Sinners yielded by scores to his pathetic entreaties, and he never felt more satisfaction than when his efforts produced a tempest of conviction in his congregation. Then he was master of the situation and knew just what to do, never ceasing his efforts until he had put in shock the ripened sheaves which his trenchant blade had cut down.

He loved to preach. It was a passion with him. And he loved it to the end of his long and eventful life. Years before his death, when he was disabled by a spinal affliction, so that he was unable to stand without support, he could not be persuaded to desist from preaching, but delivered his messages sitting in a chair. During his last years of superannuation he preached as many times as when he had charge of a work. Like a true evangelist, he went from place to place, preaching the everlasting gospel to the children and grandchildren of his earlier acquaintances. His name has become a household word in many a home in Indiana. Unheralded and unexpected he would come into a town or neighborhood, and ask to preach that same night; nor did he seem to care when, owing to his unannounced arrival, his congregation was small, only so he got to preach. He had a message, and was impatient to deliver it. Of rest he did not think until actual weariness came upon him. Like Wesley, when he was weary he could take a short sleep anywhere, after which he was fresh again for the work. This is the more noteworthy from the fact that he never enjoyed sound health, and nearly always carried medicines with him.

He was a holy man of God, and, with all his eccentricities, his whole life was blameless; not a flaw mars the purity of his character. For many years he enjoyed the blessing of perfect love. He did not treat the subject, however, as a specialty, and something separate from the ordinary experience of the Christian life. He had nothing to do with different schools on this subject. He accepted the doctrine of Christian perfection as a part of Methodism and the gospel; was never troubled about nice distinctions in the matter, but regarded this blessing as the common heritage of all faithful Christians, and not of a favored few. Of theories, he had none apart from the gospel of grace, and he believed that the mission of Methodism is to "spread Scriptural holiness" in the world. He challenged no one's position, but preached holiness to all. He was a man of deep piety, strong prayer, and constant meditation with God. No matter where he was—whether on his long horseback-rides, in the cars, or in the homes of his friends—in his religious meditations he would become oblivious to his surroundings, and when he was suddenly waked from his reveries he sometimes exhibited such a queer spirit as to subject himself to criticism. Sometimes he believed that he had answers to prayer, and premonitions which amounted to charisms that some might have denominated superstitions, but which he believed to be spiritual verities.

In his personal habits our subject was not singular. In dress he was neat but not fastidious, consulting comfort rather than fashion. In the social circle, when in his pleasant moods, he was a much better talker than he was a listener; and his active, varied, and eventful life supplied him with material to be an interesting talker, so that his monologues were entertaining to all. He had his friends whom he always trusted without the least suspicion, and whom he sometimes taxed severely, never dreaming that he was putting them to any inconvenience, but accepting their services as a matter of course. When he did not like a person, he simply shunned him, but never tried to do him any harm. He was for the most a hearty eater, but he had his dishes which he preferred, and did not hesitate to ask for what he wanted at the house of a friend as well as at his own house. Some articles of food he would never touch, except to move them out of his way when at the table, sometimes with a slighting remark not at all agreeable to his hostess. If he ever read Lord Chesterfield on etiquette, he could not have been very favorably impressed with his rules. He was not what would be called a good companion; he was too much occupied, and too abstracted in thought and feeling. Surroundings had less to do with him than with most men; he could pursue a train of deliberate thought in the confusion of a whirlwind or a fire. But when his mind did become engaged with exciting surroundings, he became intensely agitated. His was not the abstraction of indifference, but of intensity.

During much of his active ministry he filled the office of presiding elder, and in that work he succeeeded the best. It was the custom of our former bishops to put their strongest men in that office; men of age, ability, and matured experience, as well as of vigor; representative men, and equal to any emergency. By this means Methodism gained its strong hold on the popular mind, and made the Church what it now is. Those were grand old men; very Trojans and victors in controversial warfare, silencing the batteries of error wherever they went, and taking possession of the field by the right of conquest. The visits of these giants to a neighborhood were events not soon forgotten. Some of us can remember how Brother Hargrave, in his palmy days, came dashing through the woods, on the back of a well-trained horse, up to a log cabin or a camp-ground; ready to stand up and preach to the wondering people as soon as he leaped out of the saddle and tied his horse to a tree, striking up one of the songs of Zion while he was taking his well-worn Bible and hymn-book from his saddle-bags. He was loyal to his Church in all things; never became wiser than his Church, and knew nothing but to preach what was in the Bible, to sing what was in the Hymn-book, and to administer the Discipline of the Church to the letter.

Richard Hargrave was a great preacher, and had but few peers. In our sketch we have tried to describe him as a preacher only, for as such he has been distinguished; and his distinguished ability in the pulpit demands that his traits of character should not be lost to the Church when those who have had the pleasure of hearing him are dead.

If we are asked to describe the secret of his power and success as a preacher, our reply is, that beyond what is said in the foregoing notes, it can not be done. The secret of his power did not consist in any one excellency, but in the blending and combination of several elements. It was the product of all. He was fully consecrated to his one work, was enthusiastic in that work, and would not suffer himself to be diverted from it. And though his work on earth is done, his influence for good will live for generations yet to come. "And by it he, being dead, yet speaketh."

The last scene came. He preached his last sermon in West Lebanon, Indiana, the middle of March, 1879, and went home to die. He told his friends that he had preached his last sermon, and that he knew his work was done. And so it proved to be. For over two months he suffered very acutely; but grace enabled him to endure it, and to triumph with joy during the intervals of his paroxysms of pain. To a friend he said one morning: "I have been sounding the profoundest depths of death all night long." But in that lucid interval his soul found expression in Scriptures and hymns of triumph. On parting with a friend, the morning before his death, he said: "I hope to be dead before you return tomorrow evening." And so he was. Death had no terror to him; he was anxious only that his sufferings might end. His remains were laid side by side with his cherished companion in the cemetery of Bethel Church, in Fountain County, Indiana, where he had held a camp-meeting forty-seven years before.

The honorary degree of D. D. was conferred on the subject of this sketch by the Indiana Asbury University; but he repudiated it, and would never allow himself to be called Doctor Hargrave. He was also honored a number of times by his Conference with a membership in the General Conference of his Church.

BY REV. JOSEPH TARKINGTON.

GREENSBURG, INDIANA, February 20, 1890.

DEAR BROTHER HARGRAVE,—I have your request before me to tell you something of your dear father.

My knowledge of him commenced in 1825 at a camp-meeting in Orange County, Indiana. I then heard him on the Divinity of Christ. Billy Cravens, as he was called, cried out loudly: "That's right, Hargrave; the sheep will eat that!" It was a very clear sermon on that subject. That year (1825) he was sent to Honey Creek Circuit. I was sent to Patoka Circuit, in the bounds of which his father lived, at whose house I preached once in four weeks. The son came home to see them two or three times, and I would get him to preach for me. His father had been an *O'Kelleyite* (who left Bishop Asbury and formed a Church of his own); but that year, under the preaching of Brother Charles Holliday, presiding elder, he joined* the Methodist Episcopal Church.

---

* Rejoined.—W. P. H.

Your grandmother, Richard, and Lemuel, had joined the Methodist Episcopal Church before. Your grandfather was a very quick-motioned man, somewhat slender. Your grandmother was a large woman, would weigh about two hundred pounds; very fair, with light hair. Your father's complexion was like hers. She was a mother to me. I was but a boy on my first circuit. I met them in class every round.

In 1826, Hargrave was sent to Old Sangamon Circuit, in Illinois; I with him. There was but one cabin on the *trace*, after leaving the neighborhood of Paris, Illinois, till we reached the waters of the Sangamon River, for which our circuit was named; that one cabin was on the Okaw River. We, together with Peter Cartwright, our presiding elder, to lead, got to that cabin the first night after leaving the *settlement*. The house was very small. When the table was set, we had to sit on the bed. There was but one bed in the cabin; and when we lay down that night, Cartwright, Hargrave, and I were told to take that. I, being the little fellow, had to take the middle. Three other men, who came in later, lay under the bed, their feet sticking out. We (Cartwright, Hargrave, and myself) went to bed first, and those men last; but in the morning they arose first. The family lay on the floor after putting the table out of doors where the cooking was done. We were three days going through the prairie. I took the north end of the circuit, and your father the south. Hargrave and I soon after went to see a man who was condemned to be hung for killing his wife; and on the day of the execution we went to the jail. It was a pen of logs ten feet high, covered with grass. The man was brought out, and sat on the top of the pen. Your father made the greatest exhortation I ever heard to five thousand people. Hundreds of people said it exceeded anything they had heard. He had the man before him to point to. He was very popular on the circuit; but he took dyspepsia in the spring, and had to return home. For some time he was not able to resume the work. I took charge of the circuit. When his health returned, he took work, and his power in the pulpit returned. At a camp-meeting above Brookville, Indiana, he preached, and seemed to carry everything before him. Concerning a sermon of his at one of our Conferences at Terre Haute, Indiana, Bishop Baker said he had seldom heard such. It was extempore. He seldom used notes. I never saw him have any.

I have written this to you very imperfectly. I am in my ninetieth year. Excuse all imperfections.
  Yours truly, JOSEPH TARKINGTON.

BY REV. H. C. BENSON, D. D.

My acquaintance with the Rev. Richard Hargrave commenced at the date of my admission to the Indiana Conference, in 1842. He had been in the itinerant field seventeen years, having been received at the first session of the Illinois Conference, in 1825. All his fields of labor were in Indiana, except one. In 1827 he was appointed to the Sangamon Circuit, Illinois, with Joseph Tarkington as junior colleague, and Peter Cartwright as presiding elder. In 1832 the work in Indiana was separated from Illinois and organized into a separate Conference, Mr. Hargrave being one of the charter members. In the organization of the work he was a co-laborer with John Strange, Calvin W Ruter, Allen Wiley, James Havens, James Armstrong, Aaron Wood, Edward R. Ames, E. G. Wood, James L. Thompson, John C. Smith, and George M. Beswick. There were others, doubtless, equally worthy of mention in this roll of honor. These were rare men for the work of laying foundations deep and broad, and building up the kingdom of God all over the State. They were educated in the solid branches; men of studious habits, sound in theology, and of superior gifts in the pulpit. We doubt if in the history of Methodism an Annual Conference in its organization was ever supplied with a larger per cent of efficient ministers. No marvel that uninterrupted success and abounding prosperity have crowned the efforts of our laborers in Indiana from the beginning.

The preaching in those days was doctrinal. The cardinal truths of the gospel were set forth with emphasis. The trumpet gave no uncertain sound. There is not in all the West an evangelical Church of any denomination that is not, in a degree, indebted to the Methodist pulpit for its clearness and force in preaching the saving truths of the gospel, and for effective methods of work. The legitimate fruits of such expositions of the Word and evangelical labors in the Lord's vineyard are now seen in the imperative demand for the revision of Confessions of Faith that were formulated over two hundred years ago. Iron-clad predestinarianism and Calvin's *horribilia decreta* have been relegated to the shades, for which all Christendom is offering to Almighty God devout thanksgiving!

"There are diversities of gifts, but the same Spirit." Mr. Hargrave was endowed with the "gift of prophecy" in the New Testament sense. He had the physical, intellectual, and gracious endowments of a preacher. He was masculine in physique, with broad shoulders, deep chest, a voice of unusual compass and power, full of melody and thoroughly disciplined. His elocution was nearly perfect, his rhetoric was copious and fervid; and if "feeling is the essence of eloquence," he was richly endowed, for a fire seemed ever burning in his bones;* his emotion could scarcely be curbed. He was divinely called and anointed for his mission. With the apostle he would cry out with intensest pathos: "Woe is unto me if I preach not the gospel!" And with Charles Wesley he would shout and sing:

"Happy if, with my latest breath,
I may but gasp his name;
Preach him to all, and cry in death,
Behold, behold the Lamb!"

It was the joy of his life to publish the glad tidings of mercy to perishing men; the pulpit was his throne of power.

Mr. Hargrave's reputation as a minister of remarkable ability was so well established all over the

---

* It is a remarkable coincidence that both Dr. Graham and Dr. Benson use this same expression in characterizing Hargrave.—W. P. H.

State that I knew much about him and of him before my admission to the Conference. I first heard him preach at a camp-meeting near Russellville, in 1845. It was on Sunday morning, in a well-shaded grove. The congregation was immense. Camp-meetings in those days were great occasions. He chose as a text the third verse of the sixth chapter of the prophecy of Hosea: "Then shall we know, if we follow on to know the Lord. His going forth is prepared as the morning, and he shall come unto us as the rain; as the latter and former rain unto the earth." In his exposition of the text he was careful to state that all God's promises of grace and blessing are conditional. He emphasized the "if" in the text as of exceeding moment, and that he alone can legitimately claim God's mercy who duly recognizes the condition. In treating of the scope and richness of grace revealed in the prophecy, a wonderful baptism of the Spirit seemed to rest upon him. His emotion was intense, and the impression on the congregation was overwhelming. With sobs, amens, and shoutings, the service closed. Forty-five years have elapsed since we heard that discourse, and yet some of the illustrations used and the thrilling appeals made are distinctly remembered.

Of his method of preparation for the pulpit in his study I can not speak; but in the introduction of his subject, and in suggesting lines of thought to be pursued, he was unique, and not quite clear to those whose methods of investigation differed from his own. At a Conference session, Bishop Hamline having preached in the morning, it devolved upon Mr. Hargrave to preach in the afternoon before the ordination of elders. He announced his text, and proceeded to state several propositions, which did not appear to be germane to the subject; at least so thought one gifted young minister who sat in front and near to the pulpet; so taking his pencil he wrote on a slip of paper, "What does he mean?" passing the paper to a senior minister. The answer, promptly returned, was: "Wait a few minutes, and you will see what he means!" Mr. Hargrave, giving a few moments to each of his preliminary propositions, was soon developing the leading thoughts of the text. He was at his best. His face fairly blazed, his eyes flashed, and his utterances were rapid and vehement. The congregation were in heartiest sympathy with the preacher and his sermon, and before its close, responses were audible and earnest in all parts of the Church. The sprightly young critic was shouting his amens at the top of his voice. The morning discourse had been very able; and, judging from the tide of feeling and the enthusiasm manifested, the sermon of the afternoon had not fallen below the bishop's exalted standard.

There were those who thought Mr. Hargrave wanting in social qualifications. If there were a company of several persons engaged in conversation, he was rather reticent, and would not take a leading part in conversation.* But with one or two friends he would make himself exceedingly agreeable. His attachments for his friends were strong and abiding. He was a close observer, and quick to note that which was incongruous or ludicrous. He had a keen

---

* He, however, frequently led off in conversation.—W. P. H.

relish for wit and humor. He could relate an anecdote, or listen to one related by a friend, with rare zest. When he was presiding elder of Greencastle District I learned to know him more intimately and love him more than ever before. Calling at his study once, when he had just returned from a quarterly meeting in a country charge, I found him in a playful mood. He had been the guest of a plain old farmer, who was a devout and useful member of the Church— a man of solid sense, but without culture. He had such sterling qualities of heart that he was greatly esteemed in the community. The family dwelling was a log cabin, which was well furnished and comfortable; but the chimney smoked fearfully "Brother Brown," said the elder, "your chimney is not properly constructed. You should have it taken down and rebuilt."

Brother Brown replied: "O, the chimney is not to blame; it is built just as I told the mason to build it. It is just like one I had built when I lived in Buncombe County, North *Carliner*, and that one never smoked. It's all owing to the atmosphere we have in this country. It's the atmosphere that makes it smoke. We didn't have any atmosphere in North *Carliner*, and our chimneys never smoked!"

When asked if he explained matters to Brother Brown, he said he did not. "I thought of it," said he, "but concluded that it would be a *hefty chore* to educate him up to a comprehension of the subject, and I could not take the contract." So he left him in blissful ignorance of the simplest laws of natural science.

Mr. Hargrave did not despise the gifts of his brethren in the ministry. Once, when he was a pastor, a new presiding elder was appointed to the district, whom he had heard. He was plain, slow, and unassuming. Like St. Paul, his bodily presence was weak, and his voice was wanting in compass and force. Mr. Hargrave, in giving an account of the new presiding elder's first sermon in his charge, said: "All his movements were suggestive of feebleness, yet I noticed that there was unction in his prayer. When he announced his text, I scarcely hoped that I should be edified; but, as he proceeded, I was soon impressed by the chasteness and accuracy of his language. Then his utterances suggested the dropping of jewels from a casket; and for forty-five minutes his words of wisdom were more than 'apples of gold in pictures of silver'—they were genuine diamonds of the purest water. Brother D. is a rare preacher!"

It was sometimes said that Mr. Hargrave was ambitious! Possibly it was so. He was ambitious to excel, that he might win more souls for Christ. He earnestly coveted the best gifts. He studied to show himself approved unto God—a workman having no need to be ashamed—rightly dividing the word of truth.

In his intercourse with his brethren—both lay and ministerial—he was careful to regard the rights of every one, giving honor to whom honor was due; and, while not exacting, he would not quietly submit to be treated with indignity. His rights and the prerogatives of his office, in his judgment, were entitled to a measure of reverence. While presiding elder of La Porte District, in an early day, R. C. M., one of the preachers of the district, inadvertently crossed his path. He keenly felt what he regarded as an act of discourtesy. After the occurrence, they first met in a neighboring charge, to assist in holding a camp-meeting, a Brother B. being preacher in charge. The presiding elder and Brother M. were each on his dignity; no brotherly greetings were exchanged. On Sunday morning, Mr. Hargrave went to Brother B., and said: " I am greatly embarrassed; there are only three of us here, and I can not ask Brother M. to preach till he has apologized for treating me with discourtesy." "All right," said Brother B. "You, of course, will preach this morning, and I will provide for the next service." The morning discourse was one of remarkable ability; it was a profound discussion of the evidences of Christianity, deeply impressing the vast concourse of people who had been drawn to the meeting by the fame of the presiding elder. After lunch, the horn sounded as the signal for worship, and the congregation were soon assembled. Mr. M. conducted the service, preaching a most searching sermon to the membership of the Church; conviction seemed to reach every heart. The benediction was pronounced, and the people left the stand. Brother B. noticed that the presiding elder had sat with bowed head during the closing service. He went to learn if he were ill. "Brother Hargrave," said he, "what is the matter? Are you ill?" He lifted his head, and tears were streaming from his eyes. " Brother B.," said he, " *I do n't like Brother Meek;* he is forgetful of the proprieties in his intercourse with his brethren. But, whenever he preaches, he *conquers* me; I am *forced* to yield, for his word is in demonstration of the Spirit and of power. The unction of the Holy One rests upon him!"

Henceforth no apologies were demanded or given; perfect harmony and brotherly kindness abounded; and Brother Hargrave and Brother Meek ever afterwards loved each other with pure hearts fervently. They were both devoted ministers, who have gone to their blissful reward, where there is always clearness of vision.

BY REV. JOHN L. SMITH, D. D.

VALPARAISO, INDIANA, February 27, 1890.

REV. W. P. HARGRAVE, A. M.:

My Dear Brother,—My acquaintance with your honored father commenced at the session of the Indiana Conference held in Indianapolis, in October, 1840. I was then quite a young man, was at the Conference for admission on trial, and had nothing to do but to take notes of men and things. I there first met Allen Wiley, Aaron Wood, Enoch G. Wood, E. R. Ames, Matthew Simpson, and Richard Hargrave. On the evening of the first day of the Conference your father preached in the old church, which was densely crowded, with perhaps hundreds unable to gain admittance. The text and sermon I shall never forget. Then in his prime, with broad shoulders, massive head, as he arose in the pulpit I was reminded of the lion shaking the dew from his mane. His text was chosen from Peter's Epistle, and was read with a grandeur that deeply impressed me, and was as follows: "We have also a more sure word of prophecy; whereunto ye do well that ye take heed, as unto a light that shineth in a dark place, until the day dawn, and the day-star arise in your hearts." There was stateliness and sublimity from the beginning, which gradually rose as a cloud in the heavens, accompanied by such lightning and thunder as I had never before heard. Rev. George M. Boyd sat with him in the pulpit, and has often said to me that he made my acquaintance through my shouting "Amen!" during that wonderful sermon of your father's. I had the honor in after years to be your father's presiding elder; and becoming more intimately acquainted, my admiration for his unique manner and profound talents and power as a preacher, grew with the years.

When he was stationed at Frankfort, in my district, I took with me to one of the quarterly meetings a young man who had quite a good opinion of himself, and we were invited to a turkey-dinner at the parsonage. Your father and I fell into a conversation on the subject of the introduction of evil, or sin, into the world. Knowing well with whom I was talking, I was cautious in my expressions of opinion, but listened with reverence to the masterly manner in which your father treated the subject. Before he seemed to be quite through, the young preacher struck in with his views, evidently with the purpose for the enlightenment of both of us. We sat mutely and listened until the close of his effort, when your father, with a peculiar look and manner, said to the young man: "Who was telling you?"

At a camp-meeting, held at the Battle-ground a few years ago, Bishop Ames preached on Sunday morning; and, as chairman of the Committee on Public Worship, I requested Brother Hargrave to exhort, according to old Methodist style. "But," said I, "before you exhort, I want you to sing 'Hear the royal proclamation.'" "But," said he, "I have forgotten it." "Go on," said I; "it will all come back to you." And so it did.

Present on the occasion were the leading professional men of Lafayette, with a crowd of possibly near ten thousand people. Judge V——, who was much troubled with skepticism, said to me afterward that he had been accustomed to hearing the finest performances in the opera as well as the best church-choirs in the Nation, but nothing that he had ever heard anywhere affected him as did that song. For days and weeks, he remarked, he seemed to feel the swell of the music and the touch of the sentiment as your father with his sonorous voice and peculiar manner, came over the words:

"Jesus reigns, he reigns victorious;
Over heaven and earth most glorious,
Jesus reigns."

One other incident must suffice. At the organization of the Northwest Indiana Conference, in 1852, Bishop Osmon C. Baker made his maiden effort as presiding bishop in an Annual Conference. The bishop, your father, and myself were entertained at the home of Jacob D. Early. The bishop had a terrible dread of the Wabash fever and ague; and though it was dry, hot weather in the month of August, he wore his overshoes constantly. He was afraid to preach, he said, for fear he would get sick; and asked me whom he should have do the preaching on Sunday. I told him we had quite a number of men who preached fairly well, considering that they lived in the wilds of Indiana; and suggested to him that he have Lucien W Berry to preach on Sunday morning, and Richard Hargrave in the afternoon. After dinner on Sunday he asked me who Berry was, and where he was educated. I told him that he had grown up in the woods. "Why," said he, "I never heard such preaching since I was born. How will the next man be?" "O well," said I, "he can preach some." So in the evening the bishop proposed to take a little walk, and among other things said: "I thought the morning sermon beat anything I had ever heard; but the effort in the afternoon, for profound thought, uniqueness in manner, and effect on the audience, was far beyond anything I have ever seen or heard."

I will only add, I have heard many fine preachers, but in many respects, though not in all, I regard Richard Hargrave, as a theologian and for force as an orator, equaled by few, and perhaps surpassed by none. Please accept this brief, and humble tribute to the life and labors of the great and good man, and with it my earnest hope for the success of the work that the honored son has undertaken.

Truly your brother, J. L. SMITH.

BY REV. G. H. McLAUGHLIN.

My acquaintance with Rev. Richard Hargrave began in 1829. He was on the Fall Creek Circuit,* and there being no parsonage on the work, and houses scarce, he and his young wife came and occupied a part of my father's house—a brick, one-story, three-room residence, still standing, two and one-half miles southeast of Indianapolis. He and his accomplished and lovely young wife proved to be very satisfactory occupants. We felt that we were not entertaining angels unawares, but well aware of the fact. Rev. John Strange had been a frequent visitor at our house previously; but eminent as he was as a minister and a companion, we felt that in Mr. Hargrave we had a worthy successor. The nine months of their residence in our house is still a precious memory in the minds of those who survive. Here their first child, Sarah, was born. The coming of the little stranger drew the families together in a very close relationship, especially interesting my dear mother and sisters, thus laying the foundation for a lasting friendship between the families. This babe was a comfort to its mother in her loneliness, and a tremendous loadstone to draw the father homeward when duty

---

* The Minutes show that Richard Hargrave was superannuated 1828-29; but it would seem that during at least a part of 1829 he had work as a supply. The best opinion seems to be that he traveled the Fall Creek Circuit with Charles Bonner, preacher in charge; Allen Wiley, presiding elder, Madison District. I am indebted to Rev. John L. Smith, D. D., for important information upon this point.—W. P. H.

permitted. This child was held in very high esteem ever afterward, not only for her beauty and real worth, but because of the fact that she was born in our house.

It is a fact of mingled solace and sadness that in the same room where Sarah was born the venerable Wm. McLaughlin and his wife, of precious memory, years afterward, took their departure to glory. This place, where prayer was wont to be made, was the scene of a long and happy domestic life.

Notwithstanding all my commendation of Brother Hargrave, I got into one difficulty through my connection with him. His horse got lame, and he must needs have another, which was some miles distant in the woods to the southward. There was no road then—only paths and traces. I, a boy of twelve years of age, was sent along with him to show him the way to a horse he could get. I rode behind him on the same horse, and as he was a large, square-built man and I a small boy, I could not see my way clearly as a pilot, and we got lost; but, after some perplexity, we found our way to our destination.

Richard Hargrave was no ordinary man. Whatever he was, seemed to have been of superior mold. Such was his physical structure. His eye was perhaps his most striking feature; of a dark blue color, exceedingly penetrating in expression, and, when he spoke, lit up with every phase of thought and feeling. His brow was prominent, his figure very erect, and in his early manhood—the period of which I speak— he was the perfection of manly beauty. His mind was of the most sterling type; it was not only strong, but capacious. It was a wonderful compound of seeming contraries; it was strong, yet delicate; logical, yet poetic; complex, yet simple; capable of great abstractions in reasoning, yet marked by great common sense and practical good judgment, especially within the limits of his life-work.

Mr. Hargrave's social qualities were of the finest quality. His friendships were enthusiastic and enduring. Of this the writer had the fullest proof for more than forty years. You could feel the throbbings of a swelling heart in the clasp of his hand. These social characteristics gave a charm and value to his princely pulpit powers. And as, in social life, the charm came from within, so his preaching was from the soul—the love of Christ constrained. He preached not only what he knew, but what he felt. The result was that the people learned what he had learned, and soon came to feel what he felt.

There was nothing tame or prosy in his make-up; and, in addition to this, he was "baptized with the Holy Ghost and with fire." Mr. Hargrave preached much and for many years, but he always preached to save. His was not a chosen profession, but a "high calling." He was a drawing preacher, but not a sensational preacher. As he drew the people to him, they came to be instructed and healed—not to be amused. I never knew him to take a sensational text. He preached the Word. To be sure, like almost all, he had his favorite themes; and most prominent of these, as I recollect, was the Divinity of Christ. Christ the divine and Christ the crucified, he considered the foundation, other than which no man could lay and save. His early conflicts with Arian and Socinian tendencies, perhaps, made him more pointed and potent on this subject.

Mr. Hargrave was fully consecrated to God and to his work. He was a spiritually-minded man and minister. He truly walked with God for many years, and had the evidence that he pleased God; "and he was not, for God took him." Blissful life! Let my last end be like his! He went up through great tribulation; but he washed his robe in the blood of the Lamb, and therefore is he before the throne.

> "How sweetly parts the Christian's sun,
> Just like the summer monarch sets;
> 'Midst cloudless skies, his journey run,
> To rise in brighter regions yet!"

BY REV C. A. BROOKE, D. D.

My acquaintance with Rev. Richard Hargrave began when I was a mere boy. In 1842, while he traveled Ladoga Circuit, he bought a small farm three miles south of Crawfordsville, and moved his family to it. My father's farm was just one mile east of this place, and the district school-house was within a few rods of the Hargrave residence. Here I first met the children of the family in school. As there was but one Methodist family (that of Samuel Hays, father of Rev. S. M. Hays, of this Conference) nearer than my father's, there soon sprang up an intimacy between the families. At a very early date, after meeting the Hargrave children in school, William P., the oldest son, and myself became ardent friends. The friendship, at least on my part, began in this way: A boy, a little larger than myself, in the school, was threatening me, when young Hargrave, then almost a stranger in the school, interfered in my behalf, and together we were able to defend ourselves. From that time on we were as David and Jonathan. The friendship, thus begun, ripened with our years, and strengthened with our growth. I do not think that, by word or act on the part of either of us, there was ever a shadow cast on our friendship. Being almost of the same age, we were drawn very closely together. Our great attachment for each other helped to cement the friendship of the families more closely, and in a very short time we were on the most intimate terms of neighborship.

My first impressions of "Elder Hargrave," as he was soon called in the neighborhood (though in my father's family he was always called "Brother Hargrave"), were feelings of awe and reverence for the great man who had come among us. And through all the years of my acquaintance with him, I never entirely lost a sense of these first impressions. My boyish imagination had not overestimated the greatness of the man and preacher.

The family remained on the farm for three years, and during all these years the families were on the most intimate and friendly terms. William and I frequently exchanged visits, invariably staying over night, when our parents would permit it. This gave me an excellent opportunity to know his father in his home-life. Boys are closer observers than they are sometimes supposed to be. The country in which we lived, being a heavy-timbered land, in those days it was customary to cut the fire-wood in several lengths in the woods, then, when the snow was on the ground in the winter, to haul it to the house on low sleds, where it was prepared for the fire-place. I had a yoke of oxen, and was frequently employed by Brother Hargrave to haul his wood. William and I generally did the work, and those days were occasions of rare sport for us. Sometimes his father would help us load the heavier logs. But whatever he did, he did it with his might, and not being accustomed to manual labor, and especially heavy lifting, he would soon give out and retreat to his study, and leave William and myself to do the best we could. I remember on one occasion he came for me, and was especially urgent that I should be on hand early the next morning, saying he had a nice lot of logs chopped in the woods, and that he was going to help and get up enough to last several weeks. Consequently, I was there the next morning a little after daylight. He accompanied me to the woods, and we soon had the sled loaded with nice, large maple logs. But in loading the second time, he pinched one of his fingers between two logs, and, immediately stopping work, he started for the house, where he stayed for the balance of the day, leaving William and myself to finish the loading alone. He was in this, as he was in preaching, full of impulse. Everything had to move with him and about him, or he would have nothing to do with it. One day he was passing a field where I was planting corn; he rode up to the fence and called me, and tossed a half-dollar to me, saying: "Charlie, I did not pay you enough for hauling wood for me last winter."

One year, during his stay on the farm, he, with Rev. Wade Posey, traveled the Ladoga Circuit. Our family church-house was at old Pleasant Hill, afterward Finley Chapel, one of the appointments on this circuit. This gave me an opportunity of frequently hearing him preach. I well remember what a profound impression his sermons made upon the people. He was of a highly nervous temperament, and in those days was subject to severe headaches; but on these occasions he frequently preached his most eloquent sermons, so that it became a saying among the people, that when Hargrave came into the pulpit with a red bandana handkerchief around his head you might expect "a big sermon."*

One of the quarterly meetings for that year was held at Pleasant Hill. Thomas Brown was the presiding elder, a man of a rough exterior and brusque manner, but a man of very considerable ability. He preached on Saturday night, and Hargrave closed the service with the most wonderful prayer I ever heard. It was of unusual length, occupying about twenty minutes, and made such an impression that the people went away saying: "Hargrave's prayer was far ahead of the elder's sermon."

After he left our neighborhood I saw but little of him for several years. I occasionally heard him at camp-meetings. The announcement that Hargrave

---

*The handkerchief would, of course, be taken off before he arose to speak.—W. P. H.

was to preach at any of these gatherings of the people was sure to bring everybody for many miles, who could possibly get there, to the ground. And they were just about as sure to hear a great sermon. I was converted in the spring of 1852, and in the fall of 1854 was licensed to preach and recommended to the Northwest Indiana Conference as a "suitable person to enter the traveling connection." My license to preach and my recommendation to the Conference were given by the same Quarterly Conference, and both bear the the signature of R. Hargrave, presiding elder. I always regretted that he was never afterward my presiding elder. After entering the Conference I met him more frequently, and generally had the privilege of hearing him preach, at least once a year; for very few Conferences—I do not now recollect any—were held, but he was appointed to preach at some hour on the Sabbath; and almost invariably the verdict among the preachers was, that "Hargrave beat the bishop."

My most intimate acquaintance with him, however, occurred in the late years of his life. After the death of his wife, and when he was superannuated, it was my privilege frequently to entertain him in my home, and have him spend a Sabbath with me. On one of these occasions when I was stationed at Trinity, Lafayette, he preached for me in the morning, and was to preach at Ninth Street Church in the evening. In the afternoon I left him in my study, while I attended our Sabbath-school. On my return he said, "Charlie, let us have a season of prayer here by ourselves," and upon my assent we kneeled together, and he led in a most earnest, fervent, and touching prayer.

Among the things for which he most fervently prayed was that his brethren of the Conference might be led to open the way for him to preach to the people.

He was passionately fond of preaching. At another time, some months after this, he was at my home, and in conversation about his preaching, said: "It seems that my very heart will break if I do not get to preach." At the session of the Conference at Crawfordsville in 1871, when he asked for the superannuated relation he said, while the tears fell over his face, "Brethren, this is the hardest trial of my life," and then touchingly referred to the recent death of his wife, and said: "Since her death, more than ever before, my work is my companion. I do n't know how I can live without it." The Conference immediately passed a resolution welcoming him to their pulpits, and from that to the day of his death he traveled at large in the Conference, was everywhere made welcome, and preached more frequently than if he had been in the regular work. He preached with all the fervor and power of his younger life, and his presence and ministrations were everywhere a benediction to the people. He was a born preacher. If I were asked wherein his wonderful power lay, I would say, first, he was a natural orator. He possessed in an eminent degree all the elements that go to make up an orator. While not tall in physical stature, yet his presence was commanding, his features were marked and prominent, and he impressed a congregation by his very appearance with his strong personality.

He had a wonderful voice, combining strength, clearness, and melody. His highest notes never grated harshly on the ear. There was a wonderful pathos in his voice that melted and subdued the hearts of his hearers.

Secondly, he was a strong thinker. His logic was overpowering. He was a ripe theologian. He delighted in the great themes of Providence and Redemption, and was perfectly at home in the mysteries and intricacies of each. He possessed a strong logical faculty. His presentation of a theme was unique, emphatically his own. As no one else could preach his sermons, so he preached no one else's sermons. He was neither in manner nor matter a copyist. He was deeply emotional, but it was the emotion born of great thoughts. It was not the rippling of shallow waters, but rather the surging of a mighty ocean tide. It had in it the grasp of unsounded depths. As its pulsations struck you, you somehow felt that there was a mighty engine of power behind each heart-throb.

In his greatest efforts and highest flights of oratory, the whole man seemed intsinct with life. Eyes, hands, voice—the whole man seemed to be speaking, and the entire system trembled and swayed under the mighty impulse that possessed him.

Thirdly, he was deeply religious. His Christian experience was clear and full. He preached a gospel whose power and sweetness he had fully tested. The great truths he presented were not only thought out, but had been tested in the deepest and richest experiences of his own heart. Gospel themes to him were no cunningly devised fables, but blessed, living verities. Neither were they cold abstractions, glittering like icebergs before the mental vision, but they were living forms, full of warmth and sunshine. Every great truth he uttered had been verified by the test of a personal experience. He was familiar with the "Tabor heights" of experience.

More than once he had, by spiritual vision, gazed on his "transfigured Lord," and felt folding about him the drapery of a "bright cloud." The gospel he preached had taken hold of the deepest foundations of his own great nature, so that it had become a part of himself, as real to him as his own conscious being.

BY REV. GEORGE W. STAFFORD.

I saw Rev. Richard Hargrave the first time at a camp-meting held in the vicinity of Bethel Church, in the fall of 1832. Rev. James Armstrong and Rev. Samuel C. Cooper were in attendance at this meeting. I was but a boy; but having been raised to know and honor ministers of the gospel, I was very greatly and favorably impressed by Rev. Richard Hargrave and Rev. James Armstrong. An exhortation delivered by the former was of great power, almost of majesty. My father was present, and thought he had never heard it exceeded in effectiveness and power. Brother Armstrong was a man of quick apprehension and of great tact. He made the most of Brother Hargrave's sermons, and especially of his exhortations, as the presiding elder. In the ensuing summer, 1833, Brother Hargrave visited my father's family near Attica, and received their Church letters. They (father and mother) had been members of the Methodist Episcopal Church from their early life in Southwestern Virginia, their former home. They gladly welcomed the ministers of the Church in their new home, in this then new country. Ever after this time Brother Hargrave was at all times a welcome guest and a spiritual adviser of my father's family. In the spring of 1836 I went to Virginia on business for my father. I remained there two years, during which time I was converted to God, joined the Church, was licensed to preach, and received on trial in the Holston Conference, and appointed to Asheville, North Carolina. I came home to make my arrangements to go to my appointment, was taken sick, and was not able to be from my bed until Christmas. In the meantime I advised Rev. David Fleming, the presiding elder, of my condition, and asked him to supply the charge, which was done. The ensuing fall of 1838, the Indiana Annual Conference was held at Rockville. The Quarterly Conference of the Bloomington Circuit recommended me to Indiana Conference, to be received on trial. I was appointed to the Newtown Circuit. From this time forward I was continuously acquainted with and on intimate terms with Rev. Richard Hargrave. I ever found in him a trusted friend and a father beloved in the gospel of Christ. In 1853 and 1854 Brother Hargrave was the presiding elder of Crawfordsville District. I was stationed at Crawfordsville. We had very pleasant associations, and had good success in preaching the gospel, and especially in raising the money to build the brick church, which was erected in 1855 and 1856, on the same lot on which now stands the more modern and costly building. The family of Judge James Stitt, my father-in-law, were members of this congregation. The judge died some years before, when Brother Hargrave was stationed at Crawfordsville, and he preached at his funeral. He was a very dear friend of this excellent family ever afterward. In 1861 I located my family at Crawfordsville. Ever after this time Brother Hargrave was a welcome guest at our humble home, whether I was at home or absent. We had a prophet's room, which he occupied, it being made as comfortable and convenient as possible by my dear companion. The last time he visited Crawfordsville, and but a short time before his lamented death, we had the honor and privilege of entertaining him, as a life-long friend and a messenger of the Lord Jesus Christ. Our children loved and reverenced him, and we all mourned his departure as of a father in Israel.

Brother Hargrave was held in public estimation as among the most able ministers of his day. Indeed I have often thought that his equal was not in Indiana in his palmy days. His voice was of wonderful compass; very musical, majestic, and attracted the public attention wherever and whenever he was the speaker. I have known his audiences moved and swayed as the forest by a mighty wind. On great occasions he was the favored orator. When the people were uninterested, his presence in the pulpit was sure to collect them together, and held them spell-bound to the close of his discourse, however prolonged. His personal presence, his wonderful voice, his extensive and accurate knowledge of the Word of God, his poetic language and impassioned eloquence, all contributed to make him one of the greatest men of his time.

BY REV. J. W. GREENE, D. D.

I was acquainted with Rev. Richard Hargrave from the time I entered the Conference, in 1856, till his death. He was at one time my presiding elder, and I had a good opportunity to know him well, as he frequently spent several days at my house, spending part of his time with the family, and part in his room in reading, writing, and singing.

It was not an unusual thing for him to repeat his poems and sing until the fire would be kindled in his soul, and he would walk the floor and shout, as you know he could, his " Glory to the Lamb!" There was considerable difference in age between us, and of course I could not claim that intimate friendship that his colleagues of about his own age would enjoy. I had great reverence for him as a true "man of God" and as a preacher of the gospel. Few, indeed, were his superiors. I have heard him preach at times when his congregation would be thrilled and moved in a way that showed that he had the people entirely under the influence of his wonderful logic and eloquence, while his great power of voice, argument, and persuasion seemed to bear them whithersoever he would. To his natural and acquired abilities, which were so superior, we must add, if we would know the secret of his power, his unfaltering trust and his unwavering faith in God. It was this that gave him such influence with men and has so embalmed his memory in the hearts of his brethren.

BY REV ALLEN LEWIS.

Dear Brother Hargrave,—Your kind invitation to me, to write some reminiscences of your dear father, starts a train in my mind of very tender reflections. Although he was considered an old man when I was a boy, and when I first knew him, I feel as if I could write a biography of him, I loved him so.

When I first became acquainted with him was when he was sent to our district as presiding elder. I was then a young layman in the Church. Many a mile have I ridden, through the mud, to hear him whom I then regarded as the best preacher I ever heard. I now believe he had no superior in the pulpit in his day.

When I entered the traveling ministry, in 1873, "Father" Hargrave was a superannuate. While in my first charge—the Bellmore Circuit—he came to our place to take treatment for a cancer on the neck. He staid at our house during the time of his treatment, and, notwithstanding his bodily suffering, preached in our Church with great power. The thought, to him, that he was nearing his end, seemed to give effectiveness to his sermons.

But it was the years 1878 and 1879, while at West Lebanon, when Father Hargrave endeared himself so much to our hearts. I say *our* hearts, for my wife loved him much as she did her father. During this time he was much at our house. It was about the year 1878, I think, when an incident occurred, which I suppose I shall never forget. There was a camp-meeting at Pine Village, some twenty or thirty miles north of West Lebanon, and I, with several other young preachers, attended, and undertook to "run the meeting." Father Hargrave was at this meeting. Well, any one could guess how the "management" came out. We all preached a sermon apiece, and the longer the worse; that is, the meeting went down instead of up. Toward the last of our preaching, we began to look to the old hero to come to our rescue, for if he did not it was a flat failure; but he seemed to enjoy our discomfiture, till we made an appeal to him in a body.

I have forgotten just the conversation in words, but the substance of it was: "Are you all done? If so, I'll try." The patriarch went "into the stand;" he was at home there; he had been there often before; he was just a fit in a camp-meeting stand. His text was Hosea vi, 3: "Then shall we know, if we follow on to know the Lord." And he *did* preach. That sermon is reverberating in my soul yet. The people were subdued, melted under it. Poor ministry! Shall we ever hear the like again?

Well, it was the following year, 1879, that this patriarch—this man of God—came to our house for the last time. It was spring-time. An "old settlers' meeting" was held on the Fair Grounds of Warren County. No one of the large assembly present on that occasion, who listened to his address, will forget the tender pathos of the old man as he referred to his recollections of his dear mother, his childhood, and his friends "gone before," leaving him so lonely. I have often thought, since that time, that he was under the influence of a sweet and tender sense of nearness to his heavenly home.

I hold it dear to myself as a privilege to have heard the last sermon this mighty preacher delivered. It was not many days after the time referred to above. It was quarterly meeting; Dr. Gee was presiding elder. The Doctor invited him to preach on Sunday morning; it was his last. We noticed the trumpet was not as clear as usual; the preacher was failing. But O, what tenderness! what love! what evangelism! What is strange about this last sermon, I have never met any one that could recall the text. If I may be allowed to speak of one characteristic of his preaching, I will say it was eminently expository. I think, of the many sermons I heard him preach, I could give nearly every text; but the last text is gone, with the preacher who used it. They are not gone—they both linger in my soul! If I were permitted to make one request, do you know what it would be?—"Let a double portion of his spirit be upon me."

A LETTER FROM THE SAME.

DEAR BROTHER HARGRAVE,—I inclose to you a few words concerning your father—*my father in Christ.* I do not know whether it is what you want or not. You probably know how hard it is to write of one we love. Everything about him and by him was interesting to me. His influence over me, especially in the pulpit, was unspeakable. I could listen to him preach by the hour, and not weary. His preaching was inimitable, because of special endowment.

God has made preachers inferior—a few, perhaps, superior—to him, but he made just one Hargrave. So I could write a book of him, which you are to do, but it is hard to write just a few lines. For instance, what a conversion he had! How he used to tell it in his sermons! When he "got brushed," as he called it, how he would mourn and pray almost all night, thinking that possibly the Spirit was grieved of him on some account, unknown to himself!—and so on, and so on. Yours, ALLEN LEWIS.

BY REV W. J. SPAULDING, PH. D.

MT. PLEASANT, IOWA, February 10, 1890.

MY DEAR FRIEND OF LONG AGO:

I am pleased to hear that you are going to publish some of your father's writings. He stood among the few of the great spirits of the world. He was august—a man of a fathomless, measureless nature. He possessed wonderful spiritual insight, and a marvelous spiritual comprehension; great potentiality, and a sympathy broad as the universe.*

---

*Doctor Spaulding, the author of the above brief outline, is an alumnus of Indiana Asbury University (now DePauw), of the class of 1854, as was also the writer. He is a son-in-law of Rev. Lucien W. Berry, D. D., then president of the University, having married Miss Martha, a daughter worthy of her distinguished parentage. During a considerable part of his college course, Mr. Spaulding made his home in the family of my father, and thus added to his knowledge of him as a preacher the knowledge acquired of him in the home-circle.

BY REV. W. R. GOODWIN, D. D.

AUSTIN, ILLINOIS, March 6, 1890.

REV. W. P. HARGRAVE, A. M.:

My Dear Old Friend,—Your note in the *Western* concerning your sainted father has stirred me wonderfully, and the past has been coming before me with all its precious memories.

It must have been about 1847 when I first heard your father preach. It was at a camp-meeting, near Brookville, Indiana, and he and Augustus Eddy were in their prime, and they preached "turn about" at that meeting. I well remember your father's text on Sunday morning—"The wages of sin is death." I can never forget how his sermon moved the great concourse of people, and closed amid such shouting as this generation knows nothing of.

My father's house was his stopping-place, and I remember that one of us "boys" had to sleep in the room with him, in order to awaken him out of the nightmare that usually oppressed him.

A few years later, while at Asbury University, I became better acquainted with him at his home and in Church-work. Those wonderful sermons and more wonderful sacramental services will live in my memory always. He was at his best when talking of the

---

Dr. Spaulding is himself well known as an able preacher and educator, having been president of the Mount Pleasant (Iowa) College for some twenty years; from which important trust he retired some two years since. We regret that we have not been able to obtain a full sketch from him.—W. P. H.

passion of Christ, and at such times his eloquence and power were overwhelming.

His sermons were usually lengthy, and sometimes, for the first half hour, they seemed to be rather metaphysical or obscure; but as he warmed up, and his eyes began to flash, and his body to sink and rise, as if about to leap into the air, he would pour upon the congregation such floods of eloquence and pathos as we, in this day, never witness.

On one occasion, during an Annual Conference at Terre Haute, Bishop Simpson preached one of his wonderful sermons. But your father's sermon, in the afternoon, was considered by all to have been more profound and more overwhelming than the bishop's.

One of the elements, and the chief, was his deep piety; and it was seen and felt everywhere. One day he stopped me on the street, and taking me by the hand, said with a trembling voice: "I can scarcely endure this weight of glory that is resting upon me, and I have asked the Lord to stay his hand, lest I die!"

The last time I saw him was in Danville, Illinois, in about 1878. He preached for me, though he was feeble. There were occasional flashes of the old-time fire; but his work was nearly done.

I have always regarded Richard Hargrave as one of the strongest men that Western Methodism has produced. His voice, his intense earnestness, his poetic temperament, his familiarity with the Scriptures, and his complete consecration, made him a peer of any of his contemporaries; and "there were giants in those days."

I sometimes fear that such men as Hargrave, Eddy, Havens, and Berry took their mantles with them; for it seems hard to find those who now wear them. The times are changed, but it is hard for some of us to change with them.

BY REV. W. H. HICKMAN, D. D.

CLARK UNIVERSITY, ATLANTA, GEORGIA.

REV. W. P. HARGRAVE, Pine Village, Indiana:

My Dear Brother,—I have waited for an opportunity to answer your kind circular-letter, and now that a moment comes, I am at a loss to know what to say. If it were to write to you personally, I could truthfully say a great many kind things to you and of you—things that I know; but when it comes to writing of that grand old hero of early Methodism, Richard Hargrave, it is not so easy, for two reasons: First, he was just leaving the active ministry as I stepped in; and, secondly, he lived on a higher plane, and in an atmosphere of religious abstraction that made it difficult for a boy to approach. He was, to me, a great man, and, in many things, a splendid model. He called at my house frequently when I lived in Attica. He was gentle to me as though I were his own boy, but had but little to say of himself. His words were all in the direction of consecrated work to God. The things that I heard of him were known better to some of our older preachers.

I now remember one little incident, which was sarcastic philosophy. At the dedication of our church at Waveland, in the summer of 1867, Granville Moody was on the floor, telling his experience in rather extravagant terms, which seemed very much as if he was working for effect. He made some reference to your father that was not especially complimentary, when your father reached over and whispered to me: "He hammers too much to tinker well." It impressed me deeply, and I have thought many times over the deep philosophy of that sarcasm.

Another time he was at my house in Attica, not long before his death. When he came to leave, I followed him to the door, and as he stood on the step he turned his eyes toward heaven and said: "Brother, keep your eye on the kingdom; row for the harbor!" That picture is fresh in memory still. Cane in hand, long gray locks, a beaming countenance! It has been an inspiration to me many times since.

One of the clearest and most powerful sermons I ever heard on the doctrine of purity of heart was preached by him. His use of proof-texts was especially fitting and strong. He was one of the few men that could use poetry with telling effect. This may be accounted for by the fact that he had the genius of a poet in his own make-up. Indiana has had few Richard Hargraves; indeed, early Methodism has had few. It is not given to many men to impress their generation as deeply as did he, especially on certain lines of theology.

BY REV. NOAH LATHROP, A. M.

I became acquainted with Rev. Richard Hargrave about A. D. 1849, and the acquaintance continued until the time of his decease. The intimacy between us was that of members of the same family, as I was married to his eldest daughter, whom he greatly loved.

He at times talked with and wrote to me concerning his experience and inner life quite freely, sometimes saying that some of his experiences were so marvelous, so soul-inspiring, so much of a communing with God as friend with friend, that he dare not mention them except to those most intimate, and who could in some measure appreciate them.

His Christian experience was always very deep, taking hold largely of his entire being. As the years went on it deepened, and the expression of his letters indicated that he was proving in his daily intercourse the truthfulness of the divine declaration: "Draw nigh to God, and he will draw nigh to you." His exhortations to his daughter and myself in his letters were many times burning messages of affection and love, begotten of the Holy Spirit.

REMINISCENCES.

At one time at Greencastle, Indiana, when he was presiding elder and H. N. Barnes was pastor over the only Methodist Church then existing there, Brother Hargrave came into the house just as the love-feast was closing, and the doors were thrown open. There had been a season of great spiritual power, and the manifestation of the divine presence was very marked.

Brother Barnes was walking back and forth in front of the altar, clapping his hands and shouting the praises of God, and many others were in raptures. It was a very unusual occurrence for Brother Barnes to make any more than very quiet and orderly demonstrations of his religious joy. I observed the presiding elder as he stood beside the stove, in an attitude which those only can appreciate who have seen him in his best mood; his hand held out toward the fire, and yet not toward the fire, and he (though to one unaccustomed to notice and measure him, little moved) deeply thrilled—stirred to the depths. He went into the pulpit and preached one of the most beautiful discourses on Christian joy, or of "crying aloud and shouting, as an inhabitant of Zion," it was ever my pleasure to hear. I said to myself: "He has changed his text after he came to the house of God." So it came out, for as we were going toward home he said to me, "I had intended to preach such a sermon" (naming one of his able, powerful doctrinal discourses, that at times he delivered with such ability and success), "but it was no use in such a state of feeling."

He felt, after he got into the house and breathed the atmosphere, that it was not germane to the occasion. Happy the pulpit orator who can catch and breathe the atmosphere of his people, and become the medium of communication between them and the divine, and tell them the word from the Lord! My honored father said on reaching home: "It was the best defense of shouting I ever heard, unless it was that of Armstrong, as I once heard him."

Once in Greencastle, during a revival of great power, I saw him under the following circumstances The meetings had been in progress for some time, the pastor being aided in his work by the professors in the university and many other excellent workers, not to omit the almost matchless exhorter and preacher, Rev. Lucien W. Berry, D. D., president of the university; but it was now not deemed necessary to preach each evening, but some one would open the meeting with singing and prayer, perhaps also with a Scripture lesson. After this the pastor, or some one under his direction, would exhort, and invite sinners to the "mourners' bench." The presiding elder being present, was asked to deliver the exhortation and give the invitation. He rose in evident embarrassment, and said, in substance, that it was very difficult for one coming in casually where a meeting had been in progress some time to know the state of the meeting and to know what to say suited to the occasion—he was standing on the platform in front of the pulpit— "But that we may know what we ought to say, let us pray." He took hold of the top of the chair from which he had risen to speak, and turned it around gracefully, yet impulsively, like the spinning of a top, and knelt down quickly, and it was quite evident he was talking with God about the matter, and that God was talking with him. When he rose, his face beaming with joy and a sense of the divine presence, he delivered an exhortation I have seldom heard equaled in power and pathos. I do not know that I ever heard it excelled. His whole being seemed alive to the occasion and the opportunity.

It is difficult to estimate correctly the subject of this sketch. It may be best done by comparison, perhaps by contrast. I first heard him under peculiar and trying circumstances. It was at the quarterly meeting in Greencastle, Indiana. Rev. Matthew Simpson, D. D., formerly president of Indiana Asbury University at that place, then editor of the *Western Christian Advocate*, was in the city. Mr. Hargrave, the presiding elder, having lately arrived upon the district, preached at the morning appointment on Sabbath; Dr. Simpson preached in the evening. I did not think at the time that Mr. Hargrave suffered by the comparison with Dr. Simpson. The sermons, however, were very different indeed.

I have compared him, at times, with Dr. L. W Berry. Their manner was altogether different, but few men in the pulpit were superior to any one of these; and which was superior to the other, who can tell? A leading merchant in Lafayette, whose name I can not now recall, said to me, about 1854 or 1855: "I have heard Durbin, and Simpson, Olin, and many others of our great men, as I have gone East on business, but Hargrave is the ablest preacher on the Trinity and the Divinity of Christ I have ever heard."

I should say that his power consisted in his deep piety, thorough loyalty to God and truth; a clear apprehension of the great, vital doctrines of the gospel of Jesus Christ; a thorough conviction of the vast importance of the same, and a persuasion that he himself was sent directly from God as an ambassador to lost men. While with these things he possessed a full vocabulary of good language, an ability to reason clearly and cogently, an imagination that dressed his thoughts in beautiful array, and a fervor and pathos equaled by few orators of pulpit or forum. His voice also was one of the most wonderful, if not, taken all together, the most wonderful I ever heard; very powerful, yet never harsh; often most musical, while his command of it was, for one not trained in elocution, almost matchless. He could, and did, vary from the loudest to the softest tones almost with the grace of an organ under the hands of the skillful player.

In song he was sometimes a marvel. I have seen him come out of the pulpit in raptures of joy, and start, from his heart (not to show what he could do, but because the song was in his soul), some Christian hymn as the congregation was leaving the church, perhaps half of them out, and many standing in the vestibule. The people would pause, and stand in rapt and breathless attention, while there flowed forth from his full soul some grand old song. Among these songs were "Christ in the Garden," "I love the holy Son of God," "Of Him who did salvation bring," "The Sun-bright Clime," and others.

But how can I describe him? He was, in many respects, *sui generis*. He was alone among men, in some respects, as an orator, and, in some respects, none were superior to him.

BY REV. NELSON GREENE.

The length of time covered by my acquaintance with Richard Hargrave included the years between 1840 and his death. The greater part of that time the acquaintance was intimate, and always mutually cordial, so far as known by me. I had heard of his fame as a preacher previously to 1840; but my personal acquaintance began about that time, when I was a student of a select high-school in South Bend, Indiana, and boarding at David Stover's, who was in the cabinet business with his brother Matthew, a local preacher, with whom Hargrave was intimately acquainted. The latter had preached as presiding elder in that part of the State and in the southern part of Michigan, then included in the Indiana Conference. That year he was stationed in Southeastern Indiana, and his visit to South Bend was just before the session of Conference. He opened the door of the cabinet-shop, and, without any salutation, looked around and asked David, "Where is Matthew?" Receiving the answer, he closed the door and went away. A short time afterward he returned, shook hands with David, accompanied with fraternal salutations and inquiries. He then said: "I want to preach to-night. Will you take an umbrella and circulate notice of the appointment?" It was then late in the afternoon and raining, which continued until late in the night, causing the audience to be small. His text was, 2 Corinthians v, 7, "For we walk by faith, not by sight." The sermon was one of the most powerful that I had ever heard, or have heard since then. He seemed to be walking by faith beyond earthly visions, among the spiritual things of God, and looking upon the unnumbered multitudes who had been redeemed from earth, as they walked the golden streets and gathered about the throne and Him who sat thereon. The audience were in sympathy with the preacher, and were carried to a sublime height of grandeur and of power, where all were overwhelmed by the weight of glory which settled upon them! Such was the immediate effect of the sermon that, when it closed, some of the believers felt like Peter on the Mount of Transfiguration, when he wanted to remain with Christ, Moses, and Elias always. Some were unable to move from their seats. An old Christian lady and a non-professing physician had to be lifted from their seats by friends. The invisible and subsequent results of that remarkable sermon will appear when "the books are opened" for judgment, revealing the works of every man, whether they be good or bad.

Some reminiscences, incidents, etc., connected with him, are still bright in the light of memory. My acquaintance with him became intimate while he was my presiding elder for the term of three years, and so continued through all the subsequent years of his life. He made frequent visits to our home, and slept many nights under our roof, generally requesting me to sleep with him.

He had happy moods of mind, and the reverse; the latter being generally induced by physical derangement.* When in his normal state he was the attractive center of a surrounding group of interested and delighted friends; when in the reverse mood he seemed oblivious to his surroundings.

At a quarterly meeting on my charge, one of the prominent official members had made arrangements to

---

* Not infrequently by spiritual depression.—W. P. H.

have him, myself, and wife dine at his house on Sabbath. After he had preached one of his great sermons, we were all seated around a long and well-filled table, to the number of near twenty persons. At the head of the table the presiding elder sat, facing a good-sized, well-cooked, uncarved ham. All things being in order, he was asked to " give thanks," which being done in short meter, he gathered the fine carving-knife and fork, in conjunction with the dying echoes of " amen," and began to slice the ham (at which he was an expert), saying : " Now, this is too bad that, hungry as I am, I must wait till this ham is carved ; that should have been done before it was brought on the table !"—not observing the visible effects in the countenances of the guests.

My estimate of his ability as a preacher is that he had *but few* equals, especially on the Atonement and power of Christ to save unto the uttermost. But few, if any, excelled him in preaching " Christ, and Him Crucified," in the light of the " more sure word of prophecy, whereunto ye do well to take heed until the day dawn, and the day-star arise in your hearts."

I think his power consisted in superior mental and spiritual endowment, developed through the power of faith in the verities of revealed religion.

Hour after hour in the night I have sat and listened to his recital of those poetical productions of his, marveling at the wonderful gifts of the man, and believing that his verses were indited by the immediate inspiration of God.

BY REV. A. A. GEE, D. D.

My personal acquaintance with Richard Hargrave began at the first session of the Northwest Indiana Conference, held in Terre Haute, September, 1852. I had seen him several times before, but had always felt so awed by his great reputation as a preacher that I had not dared to approach him, much less to speak to him. I had gazed at him across the Conference-room, admired his splendid physique, his noble, manly port; I had felt the thrill of his rich, full-toned, matchless voice; but I had stood abashed as in the presence of one of the world's grandest and noblest of men, one of God's sceptered kings of men, as indeed he was. At that Conference he drew me to him and laid the foundation for a friendship that was cordial and ardent. It was a simple advance on his part, so easily and naturally made, that I almost wondered if we had not always known each other well. As if by accident, we met somewhere about the Conference premises, and as we came face to face he grasped my hand, gave me a cordial, heart-full, old-fashioned, Methodist-preacher greeting, with his soul so manifestly in his hand that no ice was left between us, and no place for any in the future. With manifest interest he inquired about things in which I was interested, entered into conversation in a way that drew me to him, and passing, left me with no less appreciation of, or admiration for his real greatness, but feeling that with all his greatness he was a friend and a brother. Since then I have studied the breadth and depth of the man, but never been able to fathom him fully.

To me he always seemed the peer in pulpit eloquence and power of any man that Methodism has ever produced. He was king among nobles, and yet he made himself as much the fellow of those just entering the kingdom of a royal priesthood as he was of those who were robed and mitered in the highest peerage of that kingdom.

At the time my personal acquaintance with him began, I had never heard him preach. I had heard much about his wonderful preaching, and was exceedingly anxious to hear him, and during that Conference I heard him preach as I had never heard any man preach before. Not only was his great reputation as a preacher justified in my estimation, I felt as the Queen of Sheba felt when she first saw the splendors of Solomon's reign: "The half had not been told;" nor has it yet been told, and I suspect it never will be told. Only those who have heard him preach as he preached that day, will ever have an idea of the majestic grandeur and sublime power of his preaching at times of his highest exaltation and deepest inspiration. His foot was on the steps, his hand was on the throne, he had the freedom of the City New Jerusalem; he took of the things of God found there, and gave them to us who were gazing upon his exaltation. He ascended to that sublime summit over a road of prayer and earnest pleading, through trepidation and trembling, which perhaps but few suspected. Meeting him after the announcement for the Sabbath services had been made, I said: "I am glad you are going to preach to-morrow." His quiet reply was: "Well, I am not glad, for I have to preach before the bishop." With surprise I asked: "Does it embarrass you to preach before the bishop?" He answered by asking: "Does it embarrass you to preach before your presiding elder?" I had food for reflection then. Humility abides with real greatness. Self-distrust dwells with the best gifts and the highest attainments. To me that Conference Sabbath was the Sabbath of my life up to that time. I had stood before the bar of the Conference, and received the solemn charge from the lips of the man of God who presided. I had assumed the holy vows of the Christian ministry as they pertain to the office of a deacon in the Church of God. I felt that I had given up everything to God; I was on his altar, waiting for the "altar to sanctify the gift." To me the Conference love-feast of that morning was replete with the divine presence. Veterans of the cross were there, exchanging reports from the various parts of the field of battle. The drum-beat of victory was in many a tremulous voice. The songs of triumph were full of sweetest melody. The laborers were bringing the "tithes into the store-house," and God was opening the windows of heaven and pouring out blessings till there was not room to receive them. The sermon which followed was by Dr. Berry, president of Indiana Asbury University, and was characteristic of the man, deep, massive, grand. A master-workman was building into the temple of God prepared material, great blocks of polished stone; gold, silver, tried in the fire, refined. The Conference and the entire congregation hung upon his lips, feeling his words as live coals from the altar of God touching their lips and hearts.

Bishop Baker, in his first episcopal visit to our Conference, found himself so indisposed in health as to feel that duty required him to excuse himself from preaching; but he sat in an easy-chair within the chancel, his back to the pulpit, and listened with deep manifest interest to the sermon, and closed the morning's service by the ordination of a large class of deacons. To-day, while I write, I seem to feel the hands of that sainted servant of God upon my head as I felt them that day, accompanied with the conscious presence of the Holy Ghost in my heart, representing the divine side in the mutual covenant that day formally consummated. To me it was a holy anointing. I felt the imposition of the hands of Osmon C. Baker as a kind of paternal benediction, for while I had never known him personally till that Conference, my childhood's home had been redolent of the fragrance of his name. He had been the associate of my father and mother in their youthful days, all of them having grown up together in the same neighborhood in New Hampshire. Perhaps Brother Hargrave was the only one who went from that most eventful Sunday morning service, burdened in spirit. The burden of the Lord was upon him, because He had called him to preach the gospel that day. At three o'clock in the afternoon he stood up in the pulpit. Looking across the years, it does not require much play of imagination to remember his countenance as radiant with a scarcely concealed glory. There certainly was in the tones of his voice when he read the hymn, and especially when he led the vast assembly to the throne in prayer, a tremulo that set the heart-chords vibrating like strings of the golden harps in the hands of the celestial choir. In that pulpit was a spiritual battery sending out currents of heaven-kindled fire, and touching with that fire and with the Holy Ghost the hearts of those within the divine circuit. That afternoon's sermon was to be the crowning glory of that Sabbath of wonderful privilege, and was to live in the memory of hundreds till death.

The speaker was self-contained, but manifestly with divine help. The exordium was calm, but with a transparency that revealed the pent-up lightning even then unfolding "its fiery wing" for loftiest flight. But a few moments passed till that lightning was in full play, now darting its fiery tongues to farthest space, now flaming out in one all-embracing sheet and sheen of dazzling splendor. "Like the voice of many waters and of mighty thunders," the word of the Lord was heard behind it all, dropping from burning lips of clay upon hearts aflame. Every eye was fixed upon the preacher as he swayed the multitude with a scepter of power. The clearest, most logical presentation of profound thought and Bible truth was accompanied with wave after wave of overwhelming emotion, each wave rolling higher than its predecessor, and lifting the hearer farther up the spiritual heights, till in the peroration it seemed as if the borderland had faded from view in the light of a rising sun, and saints and angels were coming, led again in the joyous triumphs of the Church militant. We had almost climbed the Mount of Transfiguration. At any rate, we were on Pisgah's summit. We knew that the glory of God was passing, and that while we were in the cleft and covered with His hand, redemptive glory was revealed to us. The preacher was guiding a chariot of fire through the skies, and we were passengers for heaven.

At the beginning of that service Bishop Baker was seated as at the morning service; but before Brother Hargrave had been speaking many minutes he had worked his chair around till he was facing the speaker, and, with head thrown back and eyes fixed, he never looked away from the preacher till the sermon was ended. The ordination of elders followed, and as the bishop walked to his lodgings, still apparently under a spell, he inquired of some one walking by his side, " Does Brother Hargrave always preach that way ?"

Subsequent to this Conference, I often met the subject of this sketch, and always his society was a great privilege. The second year after that Conference he was my presiding elder, and, living beyond the bounds of his district, he often spent nearly a week at a time at my house, where he was always a most welcome guest, for his influence was always a benediction. The perfect freedom with which he settled himself into the home-life of the family removed all feeling that he was a stranger, nor did he impress one in any unpleasant way with his superior greatness. At the end of that year our Conference met in La Porte. The Rev. W H. Goode was then beating up volunteers for " the outposts of Zion." I soon found that interviews he had sought with me on the subject were serious, and that the matter had been carried to the cabinet, as, meeting my presiding elder one day, who, shaking his index finger at me and familiarly addressing me by my given name, said: "Don't you go one step." At the close of that Conference, I was appointed to South Bend, which was considered a much better appointment than the one I left, and I suppose that Brother Hargrave was entitled to credit for the appointment, as he seemed to enjoy the promotion—as such things have now come to be regarded—fully as much as I did. During the rest of his life he was often an inmate of my home, and his coming was always a matter of enjoyment. During years of his superannuation, while I was on the East Lafayette and the Lafayette Districts, he often visited my quarterly meetings, and his visits were always seasons of blessing; for I always invited him to preach at the popular hour, and he always accepted, modestly but gratefully; for he enjoyed preaching apparently with a growing relish to the close of his life. The last sermon he ever preached was at a quarterly meeting I was holding at West Lebanon, at 10.30 o'clock, on Sunday morning, only a few weeks before his triumphant death. Brother Allen Lewis was pastor at West Lebanon at the time, and will testify that the last sermon of this "old man eloquent" was a "feast of fat things"—a pentecost of power. I saw him once after that, walking four miles from Attica to Jonathan Campbell's, his son-in-law, at Bethel, to see him during his final illness. I found him waiting calmly, patiently, triumphantly for the end. He was "full of faith and the Holy Ghost." It was a feast to hear him talk of spiritual things. He reviewed much of his past life; dwelt with ecstasy on the most sublime portions of his deep, almost marvelous, experiences. To listen to his conversation seemed almost like standing at an open window of heaven, listening to some crowned saint telling over to attentive angels the triumphs of redeeming grace and dying love. His conversion, call to the ministry, the early spiritual forecast of his life-work, as revealed to his faith, almost to his natural vision, were themes with which he was filled, and on which to hear him then was a privilege not often realized in this life. Such a review as was passing in his mind naturally arrayed about him the mighty men who had been his comrades. The thought that he was soon to join them in the grand review and crowning before the throne, thrilled and lifted him almost out of the body. While he held himself in patient waiting for the Master, it was plainly seen that he was listening eagerly for the footfalls of the summons-bearing messengers, for the rustling of angelic wings. He had reached the station. He was waiting anxiously for the train; nor was he in any danger of being left by that train. Sometimes in his strongest manhood he had been so preoccupied as to be oblivious to his surroundings.

Once I left him on the platform of the Salem Street Depot, in Lafayette, to take a train that was to be made up there and start in a short time for Greencastle. Two or three hours later I was greatly surprised to see him entering my front gate. Stepping hastily to the door, I inquired: "What is the matter?" Looking up with a bewildered expression, he answered: "I could n't comprehend that thing!" "What thing?" I asked. "That train," he replied.

"Why," said I, "the train left on time." "Yes, I reckon it did," he said, "but I was looking for a train to come in from the north. I did not know that the train that was just standing on the track at the platform there was the one, and so I just let that pull out before my eyes, without getting on as I saw others doing; and I did not know any better till I got tired of waiting, and asked if the train for Greencastle would n't be along soon, when I was told that it had been gone an hour or two, and asked if I had not seen it leave. Of course I had." He was in no danger of being left by the train for which he was waiting that day I sat by his bed, then in the atmosphere of heaven. No preoccupation with great thoughts could render him oblivious then. Every soul-nerve in him was at its utmost tension. Nothing could prevent his taking passage on the first train from that station. His transportation was all paid, and he was washed in the blood of Jesus, and robed in the clean, white linen of the saints.

His thoughts dwelt with admiration upon the closing hours of the life of Bishop Ames, who had recently passed away, and whose death he characterized as "so grand—so befitting the close of the great life of a truly great man." When I went out from this room after a few hours of this sojourn with him, almost in the Beulah land, I realized that there was soon to be a vacant place in our Conference ranks that never would be filled again. There are great men, always have been, always will be great men and good in the Conference, but never another Richard Hargrave. We shall never feel the thrill of that inimitable voice, see the flashing of that eye, or be swept on by the torrent of that eloquence again.

If I had been asked, when I first heard him preach, to account for the phenomenal character of his preaching, its depth of thought, its fullness and clearness of Bible truth, its transparent logic, its metaphysical penetration and advocacy, combined with the most melting pathos and overwhelming power to stir the soul's utmost susceptibility to feeling, I suppose I should have answered: "The secret of the Lord." That answer would not be out of place now. Although there was no attempt while under the mighty spell of that sermon to analyze anything, or to find out by any special insight the secret of the preacher's power, I now think, after years of acquaintance with and study of the man, it was the secret of the Lord—"the hiding of his power" in his servant. It was "the hiding of his power" in a man of might. Brother Hargrave was not only endowed with a mighty soul, with unlimited capacity of moral greatness, he was correspondingly endowed with intellectual capacity and greatness. His mental and spiritual forces were so evenly balanced that, while he was logically argumentative, even metaphysical in an unusual degree, he was a heated furnace through which the gospel flowed in molten streams, fusing the hearts of his hearers.

He was a doctrinal preacher, with greater power to move his hearers than is often found in the most popular and effective of those who ignore theological dogma, and depend wholly upon a most masterly play upon the feelings of their hearers. With him religion consisted of body and soul. The most minutely accurate doctrinal teaching of the Word was the body and parts, through which the indwelling, eternal Spirit sent the breathing fullness of a perfect spiritual life. Profound investigation made him as much the master of the one, as a deep and constant experience made him perfectly familiar with the other. With him the two were inseparable. God had joined them together, and he allowed no man to put them asunder. There was as much ground of hope that a living spirit would expand and thrive in a dead body, as there was that the soul of religious life would or could grow and expand in a body of false doctrine.

The essential unity and the personal triunity of the Godhead was his "pillar of fire." It led him out of the Egyptian night of Unitarianism, and was his flaming guide across the desert. He lingered with it at Mt. Sinai. With Moses, he stood unsandaled upon its rugged rocks, and made himself familiar with its law and with the glory of the dispensation it represented. That fiery pillar led him to the border of the land of promise, and wafted him over. He feasted on the rich fruitage of that land, and at Mount Zion bathed his soul in fountains of life. Calvary crushed him, but Jesus raised him up. He struggled under the cross with "the Man of Sorrows," but it was the God-Man that flooded his soul with a divine and eternal illumination. From that time, Jesus of Nazareth was not simply the Great Exemplar; he was his God and Savior—an all-sufficient Savior.

When the Second and Third Persons of a Divine Trinity came into his creed, they came with a flood of light, of personal illumination, that filled him with a Divine Presence as real to him as any fact of his being. Jesus Christ was as much a distinct Divine Personality to him as he was to Saul of Tarsus when the dazzling splendors of that noonday revelation prostrated him without the gates of Damascus. Nor was the Holy Ghost less distinct and real in his office as Witness and Comforter. From that day he walked with God. The desert pillar of fire was replaced with the Shekinah glory of the mercy-seat—the rigors of the law with the abounding fullness of grace. The secret of his power was a realizing faith—a faith that made God a real presence, whose power that faith evidenced.

BY REV. FRANCIS COX.

I have read Brother Boyd's letters on "Methodism in La Porte County, Indiana," with much interest and profit. When he referred to Emanuel, the Christian Negro, my mind took hold of it with such pleasure as is not easily described. I was sorry he did n't tell it all. No doubt he could have done so. I do n't know that I can, but I can tell more than he did. In order to do it in my manner and from my stand-point, I shall have to go back two years, and connect an interesting circumstance with it.

When the Conference met at Terre Haute, the first time after the division of the North Indiana Conference (and I am sorry we have not the Minutes and appointments of that Conference), Bishop Baker was with us. For some reason he did n't preach. Dr. L. W Berry was present, and preached what many of the old members of Conference called a wonderful sermon. His text was in Hebrews xiii, 13: "We have an altar." The bishop sat with his back to the pulpit, and faced the congregation. To me he seemed to be lost in thought while he was weighing the wonderful ideas that were being thrown up by the great quarry-man from God's greater mine.

In the afternoon Brother Hargrave preached, taking for his text Philippians i, 9–11: "That your love may abound more and more," etc. The bishop sat in the same place, and at the beginning of the service, in the same position; but he did n't remain so long. First, he turned his head and looked upon the preacher, who was opening up large doors and great windows, that men and angels might see to greater depth in the knowledge and love of God. Then he shifted his position, and turned quartering; then a little more. There he sat, gazing, it may be, into heaven, while there was perhaps somewhat of a transfiguration and translation going on; for the preacher seemed to have followed Paul to the third heaven "in abounding more and more," while tears were running down the bishop's face. I heard some of the brethren say, on Monday, that the bishop asked if that was a common sermon for Brother Hargrave? I will not give the answer, but his reply was: "He is a wonderful man. That was a precious day, if the bishop did n't preach."

Now, at the La Porte Conference, Bishop Simpson was with us. Dr. J. T. Peck, Agent of the Tract Society, was present. When Sabbath came, and I saw he was going to preach, instead of Bishop Simpson—in particular—I was disappointed.

But when he told us that his text would be Philippians i, 9-11, then I thought, we will see the difference there is in these two great men—Peck and Hargrave.

I was seated where I could behold the sea of faces. The preacher moved on and out with majesty and power, making good work, and squaring every stone to be perfect in the building which he was erecting—the foot on earth, the top in heaven. It was thrilling to the soul. The congregation looked on with amazement and delight. I saw Brother Hargrave, as he leaned forward on the back of the seat in front of him, while on his face was a large, open smile, and his countenance lighted up with a halo most beautiful to look upon.

In his rear about six seats sat our sable brother, noted for his piety and devotion to God. He who would sing on the streets, as he sawed wood for a livelihood, " Hallelujah to the Lamb who did pu'chase ow'-a paw'don!" feasted and regaled himself on the entertainment that was being provided for the audience.

Now, while the master of the Lord's hosts, the Moses of the hour, was going forth, rod in hand, to smite the rock, that the people might drink, the welldrilled and thirsty soul of Emmanuel was filling up, and when the rock was smitten, and the water of life gushed out, his cup could but run over. (Psalm xxiii, 5.) At once he sprang to his feet and turned round and round like a capstan, saying, as he turned: "Jory! why, jory! why, jory! It's all jory!" This came upon many in the audience as an action out of place. To treat Dr. Peck, the future bishop, in this way, was almost unbearable. And what made it so much worse, with some, was that that saint's skin was, for some cause or other, made black.

But with reverence I will say, the Master of assemblies was present. The panorama stopped for God's servant, even as the sun stood still for Joshua to honor God, while there on the mountain-side could be seen, in the beautiful sunlight, the golden fringes of Beulah land. While the pillar of fire thus stood over the camp, nothing could be heard but the breathing of a soul communing with God, while it bathed in the ocean of light, drinking largely of the wells of salvation. He ceased as in a whisper, and was seated. A profound silence for a moment pervaded the audience, when the master of the occasion stepped forward, straightening himself, and reaching out his great arm, said: "There is a practical illustration of what I was trying to give you as the theory!" This was the climax. It electrified the partially paralyzed congregation.

Thus ended a circumstance and a scene I can not, nor would I, ever forget.

WILLIAMSPORT, INDIANA.

NOTE.—This was a contribution to the *Indiana Christian Advocate.*—W. P. H.

BY REV. WILLIAM A. SMITH, A. M.

The place was old Pisgah Methodist Episcopal Church, eight miles west of Terre Haute, Indiana, while "Father Hargrave" was presiding elder of the Terre Haute District. It was during the year of the great drouth, say 1854 or 1855. It was quarterly-meeting day. The Sabbath dawned with a cloudless sky, the day was very hot, and the roads very dusty. The meeting was in the grove. I do not remember the Scripture lesson; but I see now that venerable form as he stands, and I never shall forget the hymn nor the influence produced on my mind by the reading of it:

"God moves in a mysterious way,
His wonders to perform," etc.

And the prayer that followed! His apt and peculiarly powerful way of putting the Scripture promises impressed me as I never was impressed before or since by an invocation. An allusion was made in the prayer to the parched and withered vegetation and the lowing cattle, which brought us face to face with our helplessness. Then followed a tribute to God's power and his unchangeableness; and from these he urged his plea: "Awake, awake! Put on strength, O arm of the Lord! Awake, as in the ancient days—as in the generations of old! Art thou not it that hath cut Rahab and wounded the dragon? Art thou not it which hath dried the sea, the waters of the great deep; that hast made the depths of the sea a way for the ransomed to pass over?" Then he further urged his plea: "Let the sound of the going forth in the tops of the mulberry-trees be heard!" And then he alluded to Elijah and the prayer that sealed the heavens; and to that other prayer, and the servant, and the increasing clouds, and the sound of much rain, and the hastening of the prophet down before the chariot of Ahab. And then, in that inimitable style and voice of his, he proceeded, until his spirit seemed to take possession of the vast congregation, and, boy as I was, I somehow felt that we would have rain.

He commenced his discourse; theme, "Baptism of the Holy Ghost." Not a cloud was yet to be seen in the heavens. Soon he made his divisions, and in that masterly way was beginning his discussion. A peal of thunder in the southwest is heard, and though loud and clear, yet his manner seemed as if he expected it, for he gave no heed to it; but as if deeply intent on his great work, he moved on. Soon the whole heavens were darkened, and, as Elijah and the servant had to hasten, so did we to get to the church.

Witnesses remember this event, and in some way associate Father Hargrave with the coming of the rain, as they do Elijah upon Mount Carmel with the rain that then fell in answer to his prayer.

During the two years, long afterwards, when he was my presiding elder, it was always a pleasure to myself and dear wife to have him with us. His theme was the gospel, his mission to preach, and it was more than his meat and drink to proclaim the glad tidings of salvation. With me it is "Father Hargrave, of precious memory!"

BY EZRA R. LATHROP, A. M.,
Of the Minnesota Conference.*

So far as relates to Richard Hargrave as a preacher, his great qualities were only displayed in the presence of a great congregation, when people were prepared to exercise patience to hear a man expound some great theme of Christian theology. I do not mean by this that he was a dull or tedious preacher, but that only on such an occasion will people have, or can they have, patience to listen to such an exposition, or a preacher have the necessary inspiration to preach a great sermon. No man can preach a great sermon in thirty or forty-five minutes. His written discourses do not give any one who did not know him any idea of his style or power as a preacher. Not long since I was thinking of him, and could imagine him in one of his impassioned passages, his clarion voice, his flushed face—the flush mounting clear up into his bald head—his small hand in those easy and graceful gestures, and the long sentences which characterized his style, the unconscious rhythm into which he usually fell at such times, and the waiting, expectant congregation, thrilled as he reached his climax. His sermons were ponderous, and always pervaded by a clear, evangelical tone. His trumpet gave no uncertain sound.

He was, of course, a preacher of a former generation—a race now extinct. The conditions are all changed. Then the questions in debate were largely

---

*Extract from a letter written to Rev. N. Lathrop, and kindly furnished us. The writer is a distinguished member of the Minnesota Conference, though a native of Indiana, and at one time a member of the Indiana Conference.—W. P. H.

between the different religious denominations. It was the controversy with Calvinism on the one hand, and with the mild form of Unitarianism, represented by the New Lights (Campbellites) on the other. The fruits of the victory won by our fathers are seen in the recent movement to revise the Westminster Confession in the Presbyterian Church—the only real "Simon Pure" representative of Calvinism in America—and in the growing evangelical tone of the Campbellites.

The man who defends the faith to-day must do it against Agnosticism (Atheism?) Materialism, and the pernicious Higher Criticism that threatens to undermine the very foundations of the evangelical faith, this trio producing an indifferentism that is more difficult to penetrate than the positive wickedness of fifty years ago. For the open sinner, who never considered himself anything else, could be attacked by direct assault, and, his main position captured, he had nothing for it but to surrender; whereas the modern sinner scarcely consents that he is a sinner. He either does not know, or believes that death ends all; or else he is waiting to hear the end of the debate as to whether Jonah was really swallowed by a large fish, or whether Job was a real person or a creature of the imagination of the poet. In this discussion there is not the opportunity for declamation, rhetoric, and pathos that there was in the old one. "*Tempora mutantur*" in theology as well as in other departments; and we change with the times as always. So I think that pulpit oratory has not only changed, but in the necessary change it can not have the effect upon the masses of men that it once had.

BY JOHN CLARK RIDPATH.

No man of our heroic age in Indiana has left in my mind and memory a more visible and vivid image than Richard Hargrave. He was, in every sense, one of the men of our dawn. His words and work have entered potentially into the woof and warp of our life here in the West, and the threads which he contributed to the fabric can never be withdrawn.

It requires no effort on my part to call up the complete outline of this remarkable man. There he is, as he lived and walked among us in the last years of his earthly pilgrimage. Behold the form and features of one not easily forgotten! In stature not tall, but massive; a firm-set body; limbs like pillars for support; a head erect, even to old age; face smoothly shaven and deeply marked with the ineffaceable lines of character; complexion rather florid, indicative of that nervous-sanguine temperament by which he was impelled as a living energy among the people; the slight remaining hair of a massive, gnarled, almost heroic head, grown white as the snow of winter; fierce blue eyes, shining like the sky, lighting and giving light; a bearing almost haughty in its humility; a step like the step of a conqueror; and that indescribable voice!—it is Richard Hargrave, who thundered from our primitive pulpit with a power not wholly of the earth.

I first knew him in the fall of 1862. As a young man, I lived for some months under his roof, sharing his table, and having every opportunity to know him as he was. The lesson was sufficiently impressive.

He was at that time superannuated, but the impairment of his health had in no wise abated his zeal or darkened his mind. It may even be believed that his enforced retirement had driven the tides of thought and will and purpose to a higher level in his brain than ever before. While he was not exactly impatient of his condition, he nevertheless chafed like an aged lion in captivity. His mind, during his waking hours, was constantly at work. His habit of public speaking was so strong upon him that he could not well think without utterance. His manner was to talk much to himself. I have seen him many times sitting for hours together at his window talking, with no audience but himself, with almost as much vehemence and gesticulation as though he were in the pulpit.

Few men had naturally a greater concentration of thought and intellect than Richard Hargrave. Your so-called average man distributes his attention and mental energy upon many things at once. He is therefore prudent and reserved. His mind hides in many coverts, and you scarcely discover the trend and purport of his thought. Not so Richard Hargrave. What he thought was always in process of revelation. All of his intellectual forces were accumulated at one point, and that was generally the point of speech. Language was with him as much of a relief as it was a necessity. The tongue of his fathers was a valve through which the stormy, almost volcanic, energies of his mind found vent and liberation.

The most manifest result of this mental habitude is abstraction. People are wont many times to smile at the moods and actions of the abstracted man, little considering the intensity of the fire within. He who saw Richard Hargrave, as I have seen him, walking up and down the garden, swinging his heavy stick, each footfall like the step of a warrior, preaching to himself with a large measure of the force and unction for which he was famous in the desk, might perchance smile at the mood of a man so completely absorbed and isolated; but at the same time he must stand in awe of that majestic presence, seeking in this manner to follow its wonted activities and to reveal its power to the universe.

I doubt not that others, better than I can do, will in the pages of this symposium analyze and weigh in critical balance the intellectual and spiritual powers of Richard Hargrave. Most of what I have to say is born out of the quick suggestion and inspiration of personal memories. I recall one thing which others may omit to mention, and that is the unevenness and inequalities of Hargrave's power. He was a man of many moods and tenses. The time and the season and the circumstance had much to do with inspiring or dispiriting this remarkable man. Notwithstanding his vast experience, notwithstanding the hard discipline of his life, notwithstanding the turmoils and vicissitudes through which he had passed, notwithstanding the fact that the wounds and scars of a hundred battles were on him, he was nevertheless as sensitive as a barometer to the warmth or chill, to the dryness or humidity, of the surrounding elements. He was as easily encouraged and almost as easily cast down as a child. To his dying day he was tender to the touch, rousing himself to the highest form of enthusiasm or sinking back and moaning under the assault of enmity or indifference. He almost lived by the will, the voice, and sympathy of his fellow-men.

In all this we can see the predominance of that poetical constitution of which he was possessed in so high a measure. In his youth, I doubt not, he had been a man of many dreams and reveries. His sense of the beautiful in expression was of the highest order. He delighted in the harmonies of language, in the rhythmic flow of verse, in the happy and exquisite development of imagery. It is clear that the great religious poets—Milton, Thomson, Cowper, and Young—had at an early period of his development made a powerful and lasting impression on his mind. The sonorousness of blank verse became to him like the music of the spheres. It was in this form that his imagination sought and found its most powerful and capacious vehicle of expression.* The thought also was in keeping with the form of utterance. There was something almost Miltonic in the majestic imagery and heavy tones of this pioneer harp of the Western wilderness. There was something touching in Hargrave's faith in the virtue and enduring quality of his poems. They were in some sense his children whom he loved and reverenced. Nor can it be doubted that, even with the changed spirit of poetry and the variable standards of criticism which are set up from time to to time, the poetry of this venerable apostle of our primitive commonwealth had in it the quality of life and the true spirit of the bard.

---

* In the final re-writing of his verses, however, they were nearly all turned into rhyme.—W. P. H.

Richard Hargrave was a man who, by the intensity of his temperament, the strength of his will, the mighty impulsion of his virtues, must needs impress himself most deeply on the age in which he lived. That the influence which he exerted was salutary in the highest degree, that his work was monumental, that his memory is still a blessing in these lands, can never be doubted. No man who once heard that pathetic cry which marked the climax of his appeal in the pulpit can ever forget the sound, or cease to tremble at its magic vibrations. Green be the mound where the aged hero of pioneer Methodism is laid to rest! Bright be the sunshine, gentle the showers of summer rain, and perpetual the song of the twittering birds that make vocal the spot of his last abode in earth! As for us who still survive, let us emulate his heroic example, and scatter and repeat the story of his virtues and his fidelity.

JOHN CLARK RIDPATH.

GREENCASTLE, May, 1890.

BY REV. H. N. OGDEN.

My acquaintance with Father Hargrave dates back to my boyhood, covering a period of at least thirty years. The first sermons that made a distinct impression upon my mind were preached by him at the camp-meeting near my father's house, on Battle Ground Circuit, away back in the fifties, at a time when he was so afflicted that he could not stand on his feet, but sat in his chair until near the close of his sermon, when he would arise and stand during the utterance of his last sentences.*

He visited me at Oxford, Indiana, in 1873, spending an entire week, including two Sabbaths. On his arrival he suggested that, if I desired, he would preach for us during the week; which arrangement I gladly made. And though he was in feeble health he preached grandly every evening during the week and twice on Sabbath. He was so careful about causing any extra trouble in the household that he insisted upon doing everything for himself that he could possibly do.

His last visit to our home was in Williamsport, only a few weeks before his death. Returning from West Lebanon, where he had spent the Sabbath, on the way to the house of his son, who had met him at the railway station, it was necessary for him to stop and rest several times. Calling at the parsonage, he sat and rested; and in reply to an inquiry as to his health, he said: "I have preached my last sermon. I had hoped to die in the pulpit; but now I see it is not to be so. But the will of God be done!" He seemed greatly affected as he realized that he was laying aside the armor.

He soon afterward repaired to the home of his daughter, Mrs. Campbell, near Attica, Indiana, where

---

*This was the enduement of the Spirit, enabling him to triumph over what then seemed a mortal weakness. Toward the close of his sermon he would arise from his chair, often shouting praises to God, entirely forgetting his weakness, only to sink back again into an almost helpless condition when the effort was over. This was during his superannuation.—W. P. H.

he spent the remaining days of his life.* I visited him there during his last illness, and, though suffering intensely, his mind was clear, and his utterances were in harmony with the sublime ideas he so often expressed in his sermons. I was present at the funeral services at the old Bethel Church, assisting Brother N. A. Chamberlin, the pastor, in the last sad rites. I think I was the only minister present, except Brother Chamberlin, but of that I am not sure.†

Richard Hargrave was a prince among preachers. I doubt if there was one in the State who excelled him in the presentation of the sublime doctrines of the Bible, which he made to live and move, as they are experienced by the sinner saved by grace.

BISHOP SIMPSON'S INTRODUCTION TO THE SERMONS OF RICHARD HARGRAVE.‡

Preaching is God's great instrumentality for the conversion of the world. The Word of God is the "sword of the Spirit." This the preacher should wield with all the power and skill of the veteran warrior. Christ in his great prayer for the Church

---

* Here he had made his home from the death of his wife, about eight years.—W. P. H.

† This is true. By previous arrangement, Dr. J. W T. McMullen was to have preached the funeral sermon, and was telegraphed for to Lafayette, Indiana, but for some reason could not attend ; and, owing to the state of the weather, there was no time to arrange for the attendance of a number of the ministerial brethren who desired to be present.—W. P. H.

‡ This tribute by the sainted Simpson is introduced here to show the estimation in which he held the subject of this biography, both as a preacher and a man.—W. P. H.

said: "Sanctify them through thy truth; thy word is truth." The living preacher, besides the truths uttered, has elements of power over his auditory. His intonation, emphasis, eye, and gesture may aid him in his work.

The written sermon has power only in the magnitude and interest of the truths conveyed, and in the choice and arrangement of words in which those truths are enforced. Nor can the style be so direct or hortatory in the printed as in the spoken sermon. The one is intended for the moment, with its peculiar associations and excitements; the other for the quiet of the lone and silent hour. The one may vary its illustrations, or even repeat its language; the other need only be forcible and clear as the eye may rest, if need be, or recur a second time to the printed page.

The printed sermon may have great power. It had been heard by a few; it may be read by many thousands. It had been preached to one generation; it may be read by children's children. In a moment of leisure it addresses the understanding and reaches the heart. Possibly the youth from home may read again the story of the Prodigal, and be made to return to his Father's house. The afflicted and sorrowing, confined to chambers of sickness, may be consoled as though they sat under the "droppings of the sanctuary."

The present volume will be gladly welcomed by thousands in the West, not merely as a volume of evangelical sermons which may be instructive and profitable, but as a remembrance of the past. Multitudes as they read will call to mind "the days of old," when on the camp-ground, or in the grove or cabin, they heard the same subjects discussed by the living, earnest minister.

Few men in the West have addressed larger audiences for a long series of years, or reached more hearts than has Rev. Richard Hargrave, the author of these sermons. Early in life, about the age of seventeen, he entered the ministry, in what was then known as the "O'Kelleyan Christian Church." His father was one of its ministers. The associations around him led him for a time into Arianism, but convinced of his error, he united with the Methodist Episcopal Church, and became a minister therein in his twentieth year. Nearly forty years have since passed away, and now, "though faint, he is still pursuing." Though superannuated and suffering much from pain, he sometimes addresses large audiences, though unable to stand. Like Bishop Asbury, sitting in his chair, he moves the people, by his story of the cross, to penitence and tears. At two annual conferences in the last year have I seen large assemblies thus moved under his preaching.

It will be noticed that the character and offices of Christ are the themes of many of these sermons. This, I think, has been characteristic of his pulpit efforts through life. Christ is, and ought to be, the Alpha and Omega. But to one who for a time was influenced by the Arian error, and then restored, so perfectly does the divinity of the Savior fill all the pages of the gospel, and present such firm foundations for the truly penitent, that it is not remarkable it should be the great theme of his preaching.

The writer has aimed at giving the substance and general form of his preached discourses. This he has done at the request of many friends—friends who desired to read what years since they had heard with profit and delight.

His life has been one of toil and sacrifice. In a private note addressed to me, he says: "I am now fifty-eight years of age, and never managed a year of my life for my own temporal benefit, having commenced to travel before I was twenty-one years old. And now I am unable to manage any temporal business. I 'preferred Jerusalem above my chief joy.' I have spent my time and strength in the cause of Christ. When I started traveling I was strong; now I am weak. Then I had zeal; and now I feel its unabated fire glow upon my heart. The spirit still is willing, but the flesh is weak. Ah! I have loved the cause for which I have toiled, and I love the men with whom I have toiled and suffered. Few earthly hopes remain to me; but the hope of glory still cheers me, and will, I trust, sustain me to the end. Let my friends pray for me till I shall change the trump of the gospel for the harp of glory—the sigh of suffering pilgrimage for the shout of final victory."*

While his friends recall his appearance and manner, there are thousands who never saw his manly

---

*Notwithstanding his apparently hopeless condition as to health at that time, he was not long afterward very unexpectedly restored to his usual health, and labored effectively upon circuit, station, and district till his final superannuation in 1871. His death did not occur till June, 1879, and he continued to labor actively until March of that year, and used to say that he "preached more than any of the boys."—W. P. H.

form, that almost seemed to swell with the truths he uttered, and who never heard that clear, musical voice, which could hold thousands in attention, who yet will be profited by reading the volume now presented. And many a Christian will be moved to aid in its circulation, both for the good it may accomplish, and for the purpose of cheering with the support thus furnished the evening hours of one who has given his all to the cause of Christ. May the Holy Spirit accompany these sermons, and make them instrumental in leading many to the Savior!

M. SIMPSON.

MAY, 1862.

LETTERS

CONCERNING

RICHARD HARGRAVE.

FROM REV W. W JONES.

CANDLER, FLORIDA, March 12, 1890.

MY DEAR BROTHER HARGRAVE,—I am very sorry that I have so long delayed answering your letter, but I wanted to take time to give correctly any items that I may send you concerning your dear father and my dear friend and brother.

My field of labor is perfectly new, so far as the Methodist Episcopal Church is concerned. I organized the society (twenty-eight members, including probationers). They are not able to support a pastor, so I have been compelled to work with my hands as well as attend to my pastorate. Please accept this as my excuse for delay—so busy, and yet doing very little.

The length of time since I first became acquainted with your father is, I think, fifty-seven years. In 1833, according to my recollection, he and a minister by the name of Griffith preached in my father's house, in Rob Roy, Fountain County, Indiana. I think it was then Covington Circuit.* I was but six years old, but remember him from that time. My acquaintance with him was, upon my part, very near life-long,

---

* Lafayette Circuit.—W. P. H.

and we were as intimate as could be, considering the difference in age. When I was a very small boy my father said: "Brother Hargrave is one of our very best preachers." Said my father: "Some say he is not social, but he must have time to study his sermons, in the family or out of doors in the cold." Houses were small, and he had no separate room. So when he commenced the investigation of a subject he held to it, notwithstanding the mothers talked to him and the children cried around him; but when he was through he was as sociable as any one. After I had a family of small children, your father, when at my house, would sometimes play with them. Once when they were spinning their tops upon a table, he entered into the fun with them; but when they were all tired and about to quit, he said to the children: "When we have danced our jig, we shall all fall over and die, just as those tops did."

After I was licensed to exhort, your father was my pastor on the Bethel Circuit, near Attica, Ind. I realized my weakness, and was afraid to talk before him; so I made my appointments at a school-house, away from the regular preaching-places; but the brethren at Bethel Church complained about it, and said that they did not license me to get rid of me. They wanted me to give them an appointment; so I selected a time when your father would be at the further end of the circuit, twelve miles away (it was a two-weeks' circuit). Your father heard of my appointment, as he afterwards told me, and thought he would hear his boy Jones talk, as he had no night appointment and the roads were good. The church was full; but I felt no great embarrassment, as I was accustomed to worship with them. After prayer I announced my subject and commenced talking; but just then the door opened at the further end of the house, and, behold, the one whom I had so anxiously avoided stood before me! It was like a clap of thunder in a clear sky, and I forgot my text and took my seat. But, notwithstanding this miserable failure of mine, afterwards, when he was presiding elder of Lafayette District, in March, 1860, he placed me on the Monticello Circuit. I was recommended by this charge to the Northwest Indiana Conference, and on the 15th of October, 1860, Brother Hargrave, at Terre Haute, Indiana, presented my case for admittance, and I was accepted on trial. Your father said to me, "Now, Brother Jones, this is my last official work;" but it was not, for he was my presiding elder after that.

In 1877, when I was pastor of Kewanna Circuit, he visited me, and staid with me about a month. While there, he spent a great part of his time in revising, correcting, and more especially re-writing his "Sacred Poems," and he finished this work while at my house, sewed them together, and said: "Now I am done; this work is finished. If, after my death, my children see proper to publish them, they can; but if they do not, I have done my part."

He preached quite a number of sermons for me while there; and on his last Sabbath with me, after he had preached, in about five minutes I raised from the congregation forty-three dollars. So he went away feeling that we appreciated him and his work.* He

---

* This was after his superannuation.—W. P. H.

preached grand and powerful sermons, as he always did. As a preacher, I considered him as one of the very best. As to wherein I think his power consisted, I would say that, in the first place, he was endowed by his Maker with extraordinary preaching talent. He improved his talent. But few men possessed such a voice as he had. Another, and the very greatest source of his power, was the divine unction. His preaching was in the demonstration of the Spirit. He was a man of prayer. He depended on his Master for his sermons, and He helped him and made him a power. Your brother in Christ,

W W JONES.

FROM REV. S. BECK, D. D.

SOUTH BEND, INDIANA, March 17, 1890.

DEAR BROTHER HARGRAVE,—I beg your pardon for this long delay in answering your letter. It is due, in part, to oversight, caused by sickness in my family, and to an unusual pressure of work during the winter months. I do not know that I can communicate anything that will be valuable to you in publishing your book.

I first heard your father preach in Bainbridge, when he was presiding elder on Greencastle District. (I think it was called Greencastle District at that time.) He lived in Greencastle. I think it was as far back as 1850; you know the date of his appointment to that district. I remember that his quarterly meetings were occasions of great interest. My father lived near Wesley Chapel, nine miles northeast of

Greencastle. In the summer, when quarterly meetings were held at that church, we would always go to the grove on Sunday. Crowds of people would come from other appointments and neighborhoods, and your father, occupying the rude platform erected for the occasion, with his unparalleled voice and wonderful power and eloquence, would sway the people as the forest is swayed before the mighty wind. Not unfrequently hallelujahs and shouts of praise were called forth by his perorations.

He was presiding elder after I joined the Conference, but I was never in his district. After he superannuated he visited me frequently in all my charges — Attica, Crawfordsville, Greencastle, and Thorntown—entertained at the parsonage, and preaching with great acceptability to the people. I was always glad to have him come, because his preaching roused and stimulated the Church.

I was well acquainted with him from the time I first heard him preach until his death. I regarded him as a great preacher, powerful, especially in his voice and oratory. Yours, faithfully,

S. BECK.

FROM REV. B. H. BRADBURY.

DE MOTTE, INDIANA, February 18, 1890.

REV. W. P HARGRAVE,—Yours is at hand, and in reply would say that I have neither the ability nor the memory to comply fully with your request. I have Hargrave's and Morris's sermons, and my practice is to read one sermon every night; and could not well do without them.

I was but little acquainted with your father, and that in his later days. Bishop Janes was heard to say that he had heard the best preachers of England, and your father was as good as any of them. I have heard him at camp-meeting when I thought that no one could preach with him. I have heard him at Conference; but it seemed to me it was not the camp-meeting Hargrave.

I commenced preaching in my nineteenth year, joined the Conference in 1839. I have been in the work fifty years—superannuated ten years—and, if a young man, would like to spend fifty years more in the service of my Master! The Methodist Church was small when I joined; but now she has the world in her arms, and we are splicing hands on the other side. At this I rejoice. I have seen the death of slavery, and I want to see Prohibition succeed in the overthrow of the saloon. Yours, as ever,

B. H. BRADBURY.

FROM J. H. HULL.

DANVILLE, IND., January 6, 1890.

REV. W P. HARGRAVE:

Dear Brother,—I reply promptly, as you request. I knew your father from the fall of 1838; intimately, for more than thirty years. I attended a camp-meeting with him in Tippecanoe County, about thirty years ago. He was not well, but preached Sunday morning with great power, most of the time seated in a chair. The late Presiding Elder Benjamin was present. I saw my opportunity to do him a kindness, and made an appeal for money for his benefit. (He was then a superannuate.) The crowd responded nobly, with one hundred dollars cash.

My wife was one of his greatest admirers. She entertained him for two weeks at our house in Lafayette, while he was being treated for sickness of some kind. Some years afterward she sent word to the bishop that if there was any difficulty in getting a good appointment for him, to send him to Battle Ground; she would take care of him for one year herself. These things are mentioned to indicate what we thought of him. My last interview with him was in Attica. We were at Sister Wilson's, and he spent two days with me at the meeting.

When in his prime, he was said to be equal to any preacher in the State. This is not overdrawn. It would be hard to separate his points of pulpit power without marring the whole. In prayer, in preaching, in exhortation, his soul and entire personality was in. His familiarity with the Scriptures gave him the advantage of some. From this source his sermons were made searching and wonderfully luminous.

He loved me much—I never could tell why. We experienced mutual pleasure on meeting. I am nearly seventy-two years old, and am expecting to see my dear old friend before long. I can not say anything about myself, only that I am the least of all saints, and have no hope but in Jesus. You have my best wishes for your health and peace. God bless you!

J. H. HULL.*

---

* A NORTHWEST INDIANA SEPTUAGENARIAN.—This is the seventy-second birthday of Rev. John H. Hull. His years have

FROM REV. J. B. DE MOTTE.

GREENCASTLE, IND., January 22, 1890.

REV. W. P. HARGRAVE:

DEAR BROTHER,—Your note and circular are before me. I fear I shall not be able to assist you greatly in your laudable undertaking. However, I am inclined to do what I can. I saw your father first at Rockville, some time in 1836 or 1837 C. M. Holliday was the preacher at Rockville, and I think your father was stationed at Crawfordsville. Of course he came on horseback. The occasion was a quarterly meeting, held in the Presbyterian Church, for we had

---

been replete with great usefulness to Methodism in Central and Northern Indiana. He entered the Indiana Conference in 1838, and has given it fifty-two years of earnest, consecrated labor. In the early days of the State he traveled the large circuits of Marion, Muncie, and Winchester, in Eastern Indiana. He has been stationed at Richmond, Centerville, Fort Wayne, Lafayette, Greencastle, Indianapolis, and his last station-work was at Danville, from 1884 to 1887. He was presiding elder one term on the Indianapolis District, North Indiana Conference; one term on Indianapolis District, Northwest Indiana Conference; two terms on Lafayette District; and one term on Terre Haute District. In 1882 he took a superannuated relation, but became effective in 1884, and was stationed at Danville, where he served three years with great ability and effectiveness. On the 10th day of June, 1887, he had a slight stroke of paralysis, which caused him to retire from the active work of the ministry, and he now holds a supernumerary relation, and makes his home at Danville. But his heart is aflame with love for Christ; and he exercises his gifts as his strength will allow. His presence is a blessing and a joy. E. G. H.

DANVILLLE, IND.

no church of our own at that time. He preached five times at the meeting—Friday night, Saturday morning and night, and twice on the Sabbath; that is, he did all the preaching.

The sermons were powerful, and the fame of the preacher great. Personally, I knew little of your father after this until about 1860. After the last date we met often, and were somewhat intimate. I regard him as one of the best preachers of what is known as the "giants" of the early days of Methodism in Indiana. He had a high and manly—I think, a holy—ambition to excel. There was perhaps, in his early days, something human in it.

As you know, the latter days of his ministry were deeply consecrated to God and to holy living. In the time of our more intimate acquaintance, his was a consecrated, a holy life. He had studied deeply the plan of salvation, knew well the way to the Cross, and always led his hearers to Christ crucified. He was at times, I think, subject to gloomy, or, rather, desponding spells. In such a spirit I remember he came to a quarterly meeting in my work, when he was presiding elder. The weather was very cold. I met him at the station, and asked him to follow me to the parsonage. He did so, almost without a word. When we arrived, the church-bell was ringing for service. He said, in rather a gruff tone: "Sister De Motte, I must have a cup of tea before I can preach." My wife hurried up the tea; he drank it hastily and in silence. The children stood amazed, for they loved Father Hargrave. When we got to the church there were only a few persons in the house—it was Saturday evening. He said, in the same harsh tone: "We will sing and pray, and if there are not more people here, we will go home." We sang; he prayed with great power. By this time there were more present. The cloud passed away; the sunlight came. He preached with great power and sweetness.

He came to the love-feast on Sabbath morning, but said nothing. He gave us another of his glorious and powerful sermons. We were a little behind with him in pay; I took a collection, and got what we called for. Some of the brethren on Monday morning added a small amount in presents. He was quite ready to preach again at night, and I never saw him in a happier mood. Of course, we made everything as pleasant for him as possible.

Another time he was holding a quarterly meeting in my work. The weather was cold. We had to hold the meeting in a school-house, and a great deal of the labor seemed to be like "seed by the wayside." After dinner, Saturday, as we sat by a warm fire, the wind whistling round the corners of the house and the snow drifting in clouds, I said: "Brother Hargrave, recite us some of your poetry." He began, and for at least two hours he entertained the company most royally with beautiful strains of poetry, flights of imagination, and bursts of eloquence worthy of any occasion. He also sang us some of his own composition. I shall never forget the time. We forgot the storm—were filled with the Spirit. You know, for sometime toward the close of his life, he did not like to sleep alone. I was easily waked, and a quiet sleeper; so he was glad to have me for a bed-fellow.

At such times he was fond of close talks on experimental religion, and always led off. His strong, impulsive nature made these interviews pleasant, often delightful, and always instructive.

One of the deepest wounds of his life was his superannuation. He could not see through this, nor at first be reconciled to it. But he went on preaching as often as he could get the chance. We made it a point, as often as we could during these years, to invite him to our house and to preach for us. Some of his very best sermons we heard and enjoyed in this way. Our children—they were small then—were always fond of him, and he was always a welcome guest at the parsonage.

Kindest regards, etc.   J. B. DE MOTTE.

FROM DAN YOUNT, ESQ.

YOUNTSVILLE, IND., February, 3, 1890.

REV. W. P. HARGRAVE:

Dear Brother,—Yours of the 20th of last month was duly received; but being somewhat unwell, and having many things to see to, I thought I would defer answering your letter until in better health and leisure moment; but I have concluded to write this as an apology for what you wish.

In regard to your father, I heard him preach many years before I had any personal acquaintance with him, and before I was a member of the Methodist Church, with pleasure and profit. I may say that I have had nearly forty years' personal and Christian relationship with him; and I esteemed him very highly for his personal piety, for his profound acquaintance with the Scriptures and their deep spiritual meaning. His strength lay in his peculiarly forcible pulpit illustrations of his texts.

I came to this place March 1, 1840. I was a member of the Society of Friends. Born November 3, 1807. Converted when fifteen years old. I joined the Methodist Church in 1842. In two or three weeks after I joined the Church, Father De Motte put a class-paper into my pocket, and in my poor and imperfect manner my Christian brethren and sisters would willingly be led, until in 1885 the infirmities of age compelled me to retire. I have done but little for the cause of Christ, but am thankful for the little I have been permitted to do. I recommend a religion that gives happiness to life and a hope of heaven.

Yours affectionately, DAN YOUNT.*

---

*Dan Yount, or Uncle Dan, as he has for many years been familiarly called, is a prominent layman, and one of the most remarkable men in Methodism. He emphatically walks by faith, not by sight. A man of large means, carrying on an immense business, gradually built up from small beginnings, all has been consecrated to Christ. He has given unstintedly and ungrudgingly to the support of the Church and her benevolences. He has been the mainstay of the Church locally. His loyalty to the cause and his love for the preachers and their families has been conspicuous. His smile was always a benediction to their hearts, as we knew full well by experience. But above all was the leadership of such a man in the Church. As a class-leader he was unsurpassed—thoroughly versed in Scripture, apt to teach, a sweet singer, an irreproachable example, full of faith and good works, a joyous Christian. Such is Dan Yount. May the Lord yet add to the years of his happy and useful life!—W. P. H.

FROM REV. PHILANDER WILEY, D. D.

Rev. W P. Hargrave:

Dear Friend and Brother, — Your favor received yesterday. I do all my writing, holding my paper in my lap. . . I was born after my father* entered the Conference. Our house was the preachers' home, and for years the church. I have known of, and personally known, all the Indiana preachers since the Indiana Conference was formed. Next to Brother Tarkington—and I knew him before marriage—my memory compasses the whole period of Indiana Methodism. In half-hour talks quietly I could give much personal and anecdotal history of nearly all the preachers. Half an hour is all my nerves can bear of any visitor.

I am not sure I ever met your father until I was a member of the Northwest Indiana Conference. He was my second presiding elder while I was on the Romney Circuit—in 1853 and 1854, I presume. You know he would rather preach than eat. I was tired, and there was such a contrast between his grand voice and mine that I could not read a hymn after his sermon. So it suited us both to have him come up and preach my quarterly meeting through. I had sent him home by railroad by Indianapolis, where he was going to start at midnight from near Lafayette and ride to Greencastle. I had raised half the money to buy him a horse. He was sitting silently with a family after the last quarterly meeting, when he sud-

---

*Rev. Allen Wiley, D. D., of precious memory.—w. p. h.

denly said: "Well, Brother Wiley has been kind to me this year!" Then the other side came to him, and he finished the sentence: "But he ought to have been, for I have done all his preaching for him."

Our Conference had adjourned at Valparaiso. We came over in wagons, and whatever we could find, to Westville in the late afternoon. We had to wait for the south train. It was determined to have Father Hargrave preach for us. O, how he preached! In the midst of his sermon, after telling of the stump where he was converted, his voice so full and round, he said: "I sometimes wish that when God shall create the new heaven and the new earth, he won't so change them but that I can recognize the old spot where my soul was converted!" He had reached a sublime climax.

I retain great interest in my Conference and in the preaching of Jesus. Philosophy and controversy never converted a sinner. Jesus alone antagonizes sin and unbelief. Therefore, preach Jesus! Look into his life and his own words and works; not in books, but in *The Book*. Be attentive and loving to the humble, the sick, the discouraged. Let no one be found too poor to merit a cheerful and hearty greeting and a kind word. The Lord make you wonderfully successful in winning souls!

As for me, "I shall be satisfied when I awake with his likeness." My doctor said: "You will go through the winter if you take care of yourself." Father only knows *the* time. My wife, God's best gift next the Redeemer, feeble almost as I am, sees I am cared for, and our Father has supplied all our wants and keeps us from worry. Your brother in great love,

PHILANDER WILEY.

2359 LOGAN AVENUE, DENVER.

FROM REV. J. J. CLAYPOOL.

MY DEAR BROTHER HARGRAVE,—I can not remember when I did not know your father. As to the degree of intimacy, I hardly know how to state that, I being so young in the ministry. The last three or four years of his life I was more intimately associated with him than before, from the fact that the store where I worked in Attica was a convenient place for him to stop when going off or returning from his preaching tours. Often he went home with me, sometimes spending the night. Often when with me he would give me a history of his meetings, and in some cases it was really amusing. I will give you one instance. I think it was the fall before he died. He was down near Hillsborough at a camp-meeting; was to preach on Sunday at 10.30. In relating the incident to me, he said: "The devil has often tried to drive me out of the pulpit, but never did it until yesterday." When he had barely commenced, the black Italian honey-bees seemed to be attracted to that white beard of his. As the first ones came he brushed them aside; but they returned with large reenforcements, until he was driven from the stand to a wagon in another part of the grounds; but soon the bees found him there, and he was compelled to surrender to them. The last time that I heard him preach was at the Huff school-house, three miles east of Attica. I had an appointment there. When I went, he was there. I asked him to preach for me, and he did so, from the text, "For God so loved the world that he gave his only begotten Son," etc. I thought at the time that I never heard him preach so well, though he always preached well. Many things may fade from my mind, but it surely can't be that I well ever forget the last time that he came into the store on his way home from his last trip out preaching. It was on Monday morning. He had come over from West Lebanon, and, as was his custom, came to our store to await an opportunity to get home. When he came in, I met him, took his hand, and said: "How are you, Father Hargrave?" He answered: "I am sick, I am sick. I want to get home." After some commonplace talk, I said to him: "Are you really sick?" He answered by saying: "Brother Claypool, my life-work is done. I have preached my last sermon." I asked where. He said at West Lebanon. "Yesterday afternoon," said he, "when I had only begun to preach I had the feeling that it was my last, and so said to the congregation. But," said he, "I never preached with such ease and power. There seemed to be a halo of glory about me, and I was so happy! Now I am done, and I want to go out home and die." I visited him often during his last sickness, and it was a great pleasure for me to sit and listen to him tell of the work, hardships, and pleasures of his life. Often, when in the midst of a grand history in which he would get so happy that he would shout "Glory to God," he would be seized with a paroxysm of pain that would wrench the tears from his eyes like an infant. But when the pain had partially subsided, he would say: "Glory to God! one less to endure; just a little nearer heaven!" He often told me that one thing he was thankful for was that he had never been accused of a heresy. My estimate of his ability as a preacher is that he was one of the strongest of his day. To me his power lay in his being a purely gospel preacher, with a sweet, musical voice, always preaching directly to the hearts and consciences of the people.

Autobiographical Sketch of Rev. J. J. Claypool.

As to myself, I have done so little that it is embarrassing for me to record the facts for any one to look at, but do so at your request, as they are easily looked up by reference to my memorandums.

I was born in Boone County, Indiana, August 7, 1842; was licensed to preach in Attica, August 7, 1876; entered the Conference 1880; ordained deacon September 5, 1880; ordained elder, at Attica, August 31, 1884; have received into the Church on probation, five hundred and ten; converted in my charges, five hundred and thirty; adults baptized, two hundred and thirteen; infants, seventy-four; funerals attended, two hundred and twenty-one; marriages, one hundred and twenty-seven. The work this winter is good, but we are not having as much revival as we had last year; the weather and roads are too bad. My Churches are all in fair condition, ready for work when the weather is so that they can get to the churches.

We all like our home and people very much. I

think in many respects this is the best circuit in the Conference. On this charge, Quarterly Conference means settlement in all things. They never have any deficit for anything. Parsonage good ; churches all good. I hope that you may find your work this year both pleasant, profitable, and be ready to take a work next fall again. I do n't like to see *our class* getting so small in the active work.

As ever yours in Christ, J. J. CLAYPOOL.

MONTMORENCI, INDIANA, February 5, 1890.

COPY OF A LETTER FROM REV. R. HARGRAVE TO HIS DAUGHTER, MRS. SARAH F. LATHROP, OF MINNESOTA.*

TERRE HAUTE, IND., June 22, 1871.

DEAR SARAH,—William's letter has before this informed you of the sad fact of your dear mother's death, as I suppose. She died the 12th inst., at four o'clock P. M. Sooner than this I have not felt as though I could write the painful narrative of my wife's sickness and death. Yes, Sarah, you are an orphan, and I am alone.

Her sickness was a complication of diseases. Hasty consumption took her off at last. Near nine weeks I watched in painful anxiety around her sick-bed. Three weeks before her death she called us to her, and gave us a parting address. The most intense utterances of parental affection she made in reference to all her children, present and absent. To those

---

*I need offer no apology for inserting this letter here, nor for the obituary of Mrs. Lathrop, which follows.—W. P. H.

who were present she said: "Be faithful! May the everlasting arms be around you all! Tell my sons to be true men, to be true Christians. . . I tremble for my sons; they are out in the cares of the world! Poor Sarah! I pity her in her hard lot in life! [The wife of an itinerant minister.] Tell her to be faithful!" To me she said: "My dear husband, you have labored long and hard to preach the gospel. Go on! Win many souls to Christ! You have been a kind husband to me."

Three different times she bade us farewell. The second time she prayed at the conclusion of her charge to us thus for herself: "Lord, pardon all my sins and shortcomings. Wash me in thy blood, and make me pure, that I may dwell with Thee, and with the holy angels, and the blood-washed saints on high. I want to be there! O, I shall be there!" Her speech failed, and she rested calmly until evening, when as a number of the friends were singing, she shouted, "Glory, glory, O glory! I never was so happy in all my life." Some present said they never saw heaven seem so near a dying bed as then. William got there four days before she died. Her utterance was very difficult then, but she could be understood as she recognized him as her "kind Willie boy."

When the final hour came, and she may have been within five minutes of her last, she began to cry so loud that I drew near, and one said: "It is glory that she is saying." I asked her, and she signed that it was. Her tongue had been paralyzed for some time. She made a sign for me. She kissed me, and passed her hand over my face and head with a quickness that indicated her ecstasy, and then said distinctly, "All is right!" These were her last words. A few more struggles, and her freed spirit took its flight. I believe she saw glory and bright forms in light when she spoke so loud. But I must stop. Dear daughter, there was enough to wring the heart with anguish, and also to thrill it with joy in your mother's departure. Let us be faithful a little longer, and we will land safe. Love to all. Pray for me.

RICHARD HARGRAVE.

MEMOIR OF MRS. LATHROP.

Sarah Francis, wife of Rev. Noah Lathrop, of the Minnesota Conference, died at Dundas, Minnesota, February 22, 1884. She was the eldest daughter of Rev. R. Hargrave, late of the Northwest Indiana Conference, and was born December 25, 1829. She united with the Church at Roberts Chapel, Indianapolis, in January, 1848, under the pastoral labors of Rev. S. T. Gillett, being the first one to start of a hundred or more gathered in at that season. She was married at Greencastle, Indiana, July 26, 1854, removed to Minnesota in 1856, and was with her husband in the itinerant ministry, part of the time on the very frontier, till her death. Indeed, she never had and never knew any other home than that of the Methodist itinerant minister. This home she graced by a life of singular beauty, purity, and excellence. Her father said, as he was giving her in marriage, at the age of twenty-four: "I never knew her to do a wicked thing." At another time he said: "She never gave me a moment's pain." One who was well acquainted with her says: "Her whole life was a psalm, her death a benediction." A brother minister, often her guest, writing to her husband, says: "Permit me to say a hearty amen to the universal verdict, which all her acquaintances unhesitatingly render, that among wives and mothers, friends and Christians, she stood the equal of any, and by those who knew and loved her best, the queen of all."

As she lived, so she died—quiet, patient, meek, strong in faith, giving glory to God. A few days before the last she said: "I was praying one day, and asked the Lord to give me an answer, and I seemed to hear a voice, saying: 'Wait, I say, on the Lord.'" She waited in patience and faith, maintaining to the last the liveliest interest in all the affairs of her family and the Church. She left a husband, six children, and two grandchildren. Her eldest brother, Rev. Wm. P. Hargrave, is laboring in the Northwest Indiana Conference, and the other brothers and sisters fill useful and honorable places in society. Funeral services, conducted by Rev. E. R. Lathrop and Rev. F. M. Rule, were held at Dundas, and she was buried at Northfield, Minnesota.

FROM REV. O. C. HASKELL.

FOWLER, IND., April 9, 1890.

REV. W P. HARGRAVE:

My Very Dear Brother,—I am not able to give you any facts concerning your father of which you are not already in possession from brethren who are older than myself, and who knew him longer and more intimately than I did. He was my presiding elder one year. This was the only time we were associated in Church-work. I admired him as a preacher greatly. I do not hesitate to say that he had the richest voice I ever heard; so full, so sweet, so commanding. His preaching was characterized by the presence of the Holy Ghost (which can not be said of all sermons); therefore it fell with power upon the hearts of his hearers.

You wanted me to tell you about myself. This is a more difficult task than the other. I was converted, baptized, and received into the Church under the ministry of John Leach, in 1853. I was received into the Conference on trial in 1860, at Terre Haute, Indiana, and appointed junior preacher with Father W H. Smith to Otter Creek Circuit. The next year I was appointed to the New Brunswick Circuit. In August of that year I volunteered in the Seventy-first Indiana Regiment of Infantry, and left my circuit before Conference. Not having passed my examination, consequently, not having been received into full connection in the Conference, I was discontinued. 1 served three years in the army as a soldier, the last year as orderly sergeant. The last two years our regiment was in the cavalry service, and known as the Sixth Indiana Cavalry.* I returned from my army service July 1, 1865, was married in August, and in September joined the Conference again on trial, and when this year is completed will have traveled twenty-five years without a break.

---

* Here we get a glimpse of the citizen soldiery by whom our flag was defended.—W. P. H.

It has pleased the Lord to give me some large revivals, as in the two years upon the Sanford Circuit, one hundred each year; and I believe some souls have been saved in every charge where I have been. My ministry, however, has not been characterized by large ingatherings, and what is called successful revival-work in a popular sense, so much as a building up and growth in spiritual life of the Church. I think my preaching is better adapted to the latter than to the former. On the whole I have succeeded in my ministry much better than seemed possible when I commenced, and God has fed me upon the "finest of the wheat" and the fat of the land, and I praise Him for His guidance and continual presence.

FROM A LETTER FROM REV. L. S. SMITH, A. M.

SHADELAND, IND., July 16, 1890.

REV. W P. HARGRAVE:

My Dear Brother,—I recall one occasion on which I saw your father. Once, at Greencastle, after his superannuation, he preached in Roberts Chapel, from the text, 2 Corinthians iii, 18: "But we all, with open face," etc. He sat, to begin, but became enthused and arose vigorously, by and by. I had never heard that he had an extraordinary voice, and was astonished at the full, deep, mellow tones of his voice. I was then a student at DePauw University. A number of us were taking lessons in elocution from a young professor from Wilbraham Academy, Joseph Carhart. At the next meeting of the class, the sermon and the preacher were both brought up. My recollection is that some member of the class requested the professor to criticise the sermon. He remarked that, "barring an occasional whisper, too low to be heard distinctly, it was one of the finest specimens of oratory I ever heard." One of the class said: "Professor, do you suppose he ever took lessons in elocution?" "He had no need to take lessons in elocution," replied the teacher.

My own ministry is so unworthy, I scarcely know what to say. I was licensed December 8, 1877, and in 1880 united with the Northwest Indiana Conference. Previously, I had preached more than the average local preacher, I presume, in school-houses and in neglected churches and neighborhoods, and on the Coatsville charge, where my home was from my birth, and where my aged and widowed mother still resides. My first appointment was Dayton, for one year; second, Bringhurst, for three years; third, Romney, for three years; fourth, Shadeland, for three years.

I have taken up appointments, either new or old and neglected, and added them to the charge, at every place except this. I have never left a debt on church property, or to individuals, unpaid by the Church. I claim no credit for this. I have been serving liberal and honorable people; and when I have been able to get their financial duty before them, they have met all their obligations. There have been valuable repairs made to the church property in every charge I have served, except the first.

I have been blessed with a few good revivals, but in the main have depended on the regular services of the Church for building up and maintaining the cause of my Master. And now, lest this tardy note prove a weariness to you, I add that the Lord has blessed me and my family abundantly, for which I am conscious that I ought to be more grateful.

I scarcely think I have penned anything that could have helped you in your labor of love, even if it had been sent sooner; but I wish you success in your efforts. I remain,

Sincerely your brother,   L. S. SMITH.

FROM REV. L. C. BUCKLES.

SOUTH HUTCHINSON, KANSAS, February 19, 1890.
REV. W. P. HARGRAVE:

Dear Brother,—Yours of the 11th inst. at hand. Am much hurried for time, as I am trying to get my affairs in shape to return to Indiana next week. Do not know whether I will succeed or not, but hope so. Will just give you the names of the pastoral charges served, and the time spent in each. Was admitted on trial in the fall of 1858, at Valparaiso, and appointed to Alamo Circuit; remained one year; then two years on Clinton Circuit (these were the only circuits I ever traveled); then Michigan City, two years; Rockville, two years; Perrysville, one year; Centenary, Terre Haute, one year; La Porte, two years; Plymouth, two years; Valparaiso, three years; Crawfordsville, three years; Michigan City, two years; Thorntown, two years; Terre Haute District, one year, when the form of the district was so changed as to include Greencastle, and the name changed to

Greencastle District; on this remained three years more. At the close of my term on the district, was appointed to Asbury, Terre Haute, where I remained two years, when my health entirely failed, and I was compelled to take superannuated relation, which relation I have now sustained two years.

The most extensive revivals of my ministry have been at Clinton, Rockville, Valparaiso, and Thorntown. In these meetings between four and five hundred were converted. Have never served a charge in which there has not been more or less revival, and in which people have not been converted and added to the Church. I do not now think of any other facts of interest, other, perhaps, than this one—at the time of my appointment to the district I had been more consecutive years in station work than any member of the Conference. There were others who had been more years in station work than I had, but not consecutively. Their time had been broken by district work, change of relations, etc.

The Church at Michigan City has now unanimously asked me to fill out Brother Harris's time, and if I can arrange my affairs here, will go there next Wednesday. Everything is uncertain yet.

With kindest regards I am as ever, your brother in Christ, L. C. BUCKLES.

FROM H. L. KINDIG.

WAVELAND, INDIANA, March 20, 1890.

DEAR BROTHER HARGRAVE,—Your circuler letter has been overlooked in the midst of my special meetings.

I do not know that my note is especially important, however, as I have come into the Conference so recently.

I was born near Eaton, Ohio, October 8, 1859; moved to Iowa in 1865; converted and united with the Methodist Episcopal Church in 1870; graduated with the degree of A. B. from Northwestern University in the class of 1886, and from Garrett Biblical Institute, with the degree of B. D., in the class of 1888. Served South Bend Circuit as supply during the years of 1886 and 1887; united with the Northwest Indiana Conference at Greencastle, in September, 1887, and ordained deacon at the same time, having been licensed as local preacher by the Evanston Quarterly Conference in 1883. I served South Bend Circuit a second year, and am now on my second year on Waveland charge. During my first year on South Bend Circuit we built a new church, with sixty-two accessions the first year and thirty-six the second. We have added a lecture-room to our church here this year. Had fifty-six accessions last year and twenty-eight this year since the Conference.

You are at liberty to use any or none of this, according as your space and purpose may suggest.

My wife joins me in kindest regards and the wish that you may have abundant success in your undertaking. Fraternally, H. L. KINDIG.

FROM E. R. JOHNSON.

CRAWFORDSVILLE, INDIANA, January 23, 1890.

BROTHER HARGRAVE,—Yours of 2d inst. at hand, and I have been very busy. I now attempt to comply with your request so far as I can.

I was acquainted with your father from the winter of 1868 to the time of his death. I was not intimate with him to any great degree. He was at my home when I was pastor of the Wea Circuit in the year 1876, and was at Mace when I was pastor there in the year 1880,* and preached in my church each night for over a week, two or three times sitting in a chair while preaching. His sermons were powerful ones, and were prized by the people.

I have no letters of his writing, as we never corresponded with each other by post.

His ability as a preacher was, in my estimation, of a high order. I think his power largely lay in his clear understanding of Bible doctrine, and his plain and forceful way of stating his thoughts; and also his rich personal experience of conversion from sin. He told me of his enlightenment upon the subject of the Sonship of Christ, and his withdrawal from the New Light Church and· union with the Methodist Church shortly after this change of mind.

As to my own life: I was born in the town of Oswegatchie (now the city of Ogdensburg), in St. Lawrence County, New York, May 14, 1831. Was born again in Farmersville, County of Leeds, Ontario, Canada, November 7, 1847, at about 10.30 A. M., in

---

* Probably the winter of 1878-9.—W. P. H.

the coal-shed back of my father's blacksmith-shop. For twelve years I was living in a condition of unrest, because of my unwillingness to become a preacher. In the year 1857, I was sent by the Canadian Government to teach an Indian industrial school, and here I was licensed to preach by the Wesleyan Methodist Church. Came to this State in the year 1868, and supplied Oakland Hill Mission, Lafayette (now Congress Street). The church-building was completed during my administration, and dedicated by Dr. Bowman, now senior bishop. 1869, supplied Pittsburg Charge; fall of 1870, was admitted on trial at Terre Haute, and ordained deacon by Bishop Matthew Simpson. My labors have been, since my admission on trial up to the present, in Boone, Clinton, Montgomery, Tippecanoe, Fountain, Vermillion, Parke, Hendricks, and Marion Counties, for the past twenty years. Four persons who were converted under my ministry, through the blessing of God, are ministers, and have met with some considerable success. Some who are not ministers have done good work as evangelists. So that my labor has not been without results. To God be all the glory!

I was ordained to the office of elder by Bishop Simpson (who also ordained me deacon) at South Bend, September 14, 1873. I have much to be thankful to God for his goodness to me. I am

Yours, fraternally,   E. R. JOHNSON.

Recollections of my Father,
Rev. Richard Hargrave.

By Rev. William P. Hargrave, A. M.

As my dear and lamented father included in his autobiographical sketch, published in this volume, an account of his birth, parentage, childhood, boyhood, conversion, call to the ministry, and an outline of the first three years of his itinerancy, as well as of his failing health and superannuation, upon the threshold of his ministry, we are saved the labor, and the reader the time, requisite for relating these opening chapters of his career. We would remark, however, in passing, that in his brief narrative we are carried back to the primitive days of society in the great Western wilderness, and through that vista we have glimpses of the Southern hive from which swarmed, in the beginning of the century, so large a proportion of the best population of what is now the grand commonwealth of Indiana. We have a view of "Ellis's Meeting-house," the cradle of Methodism in Virginia, where the General Conferences were held, so often mentioned by Asbury in his journal, built by Hargrave's maternal grandfather on his own land, a prominent land-mark in the history of the Church. We see his maternal grandmother standing forth with beautiful prominence, laying aside the mere formalism which had characterized her previous religious life in the Church of England, and joining hands with Asbury in the first act of that mighty evangelism hailed by redeemed millions. We see his maternal grandfather freeing a large family of slaves, under the mighty impulse of that teaching of Wesley's that "slavery is the sum of all villainies." We see his own father turning his back upon the "Old North State" because he was not willing to raise his family in a slave State. We see also the birthright of the Wesleyan faith, which they brought with them as a panoply in their wilderness home, and how the first leavenings of that faith, through the prayers of pious parents, wrought a transformation in the heart of the youthful Hargrave and sent him forth—"The voice of one crying in the wilderness, saying, Repent, for the kingdom of heaven is at hand!"

We shall take up the narrative where he left it off, at an event, next to his conversion and call to the ministry, the most important to him—I mean his marriage. On the tenth day of March, 1829, he was married to Annie Posey,* of Knox County, Indiana. We shall pronounce no eulogy upon her, but leave her in the estimation of the reader, where she is placed by the tribute of Dr. Graham in his sketch of the husband. Her life-work was written in strengthening and tranquilizing influences upon her husband; a home ever made bright and happy by her presence, written in the lives of her children, in her life-long devotion to the interest of the Church, and in the tes-

---

* So baptized, but for some reason, subsequently called Nancy Ann.—W. P. H.

timony which, upon her departure, she left behind, that her "record was on high."

Of this marriage there were born eight children— Sarah Frances, William Posey, Caroline Indiana, Richard Watson, Mary Elizabeth, Martha Ann, John Wesley, and Lucy Ellen—five daughters and three sons.

SARAH, the beautiful, the amiable, the affectionate daughter, became the wife of the itinerant. She was married to Rev. Noah Lathrop July 26, 1854. He was a member of the Northwest Indiana Conference, and since of the Minnesota Conference. At the age of fifty-six years, after a life " as ointment poured forth," she died in great peace in her far northwestern home. She left a husband and six children to mourn her departure.

WILLIAM P., the writer, the eldest son, can only say that he sought to be the eldest in love and duty to parents, brothers, and sisters. It was his privilege to wait at the bedside of both parents in their last illness, and to receive the welcome plaudit, " You have been a good son." For the rest, he has been permitted to serve his country in war, the State in peace (in a judicial capacity), and the Church in the ministry. September 25, 1860, he was married to Miss Martha Erskine, of precious memory, who was to him a most helpful and blessed companion until her death, October, 18, 1886. He is an alumnus of Indiana Asbury, now DePauw University, 1854.

CAROLINE I., the gay, the joyous one, ever alert about the business of the household, fond of society, became, May 15, 1856, Mrs. Jonathan P Campbell, of Bethel, Fountain County, Indiana. It was at her home that both parents died, and from which they were carried to their last resting-place in the old Bethel church-yard. Thoughtful for their comfort, attentive to every want, she and her excellent Christian husband did all they could. Seven children—three sons and four daughters—bless this union.

RICHARD WATSON, personally resembling his father more than either of his brothers, served his country honorably throughout the War of the Rebellion, both in the volunteer and regular service, being lieutenant within four files of captain, Seventeenth Regulars, when he was wounded at Antietam and placed on the invalid corps, where he continued to do honorable service till the close of the war, first upon the staff of General Peck at New York City, and afterwards upon the staff of Governor Morton at Indianapolis, Indiana. He is now a prominent lawyer at Marshalltown, Iowa. He has been twice married—to Miranda T. Hooker, June 2, 1859, who died in early womanhood, leaving a beautiful little son, who soon followed his mother to the "sunbright clime;" September 1, 1864, he was married to Miss Augusta Beecher, of Fort Wayne, Indiana, a daughter of Dr. Beecher, for many years a prominent physician of that place. They have lived prosperously and harmoniously at Marshalltown, Iowa, during most of their married lives. Three sons bless this union.

MARY E., the gentle, the quiet, who, in the language of Mr. Wirt, had the "low, sweet voice of woman," after devoting a dutiful girlhood to helping her parents, both in the home and by her services in the school-room, married Hon. Elisha Little, of Warren County, Indiana, and spent a blissful life at their country home. To them were born three children—two girls and one boy. The mother died in great peace, June 24, 1875, and her body awaits the resurrection of the just upon one of those beautiful circular mounds not uncommon in that part of Indiana. Her stricken husband placed it upon her monument that, "Like that other Mary, she chose the better part." Her two daughters, aged respectively eighteen and sixteen, will enter DePaw University this fall, with the brightest of prospects.

JOHN W., the third son, also served his country through the War of the Rebellion, enlisting before he was eighteen years of age, re-enlisting and serving to the close; was prominent in "Wilder's Brigade." April 7, 1869, he was married to Miss Charlotte Erskine, worthy sister of Mrs. W P Hargrave. To them have been born seven children. Their first home was near Rensselaer, Indiana, where they resided a number of years, and buried a sweet little daughter. Some years since they removed to Kansas, there to bury a second little daughter, "dear as the apple of an eye." Parents and children surviving are prosperous and happy.

ELLEN, the youngest daughter, who in many respects was more favored in point of privileges than any of the daughters, having numbered among he instructors both Rev. C. N. Sims, D. D., now chancellor of Syracuse University, New York, and Professor John Clark Ridpath, LL. D., the historian. After graduating at Thorntown Academy, and successfully teaching in the common and high schools of Indiana for a number of years, she was married to Hon. Elisha Little, of Warren County, Indiana, October, 1876. To them have been born four children, two of whom survive—the elder, twelve years of age; the younger, six—both promising boys. Ella has the physique of her father, though combined with many characteristics of her mother. She is deeply interested in the work of the Woman's Foreign Missionary Society, and ever since her marriage has maintained an orphan at Bareilly, India.

The grandchildren above enumerated, twenty-six in number, having enjoyed the superior advantages of the present generation, give promise of abundant success and usefulness in life.

In looking back over the long and active life of my dear father, my regret is that I did not in some manner preserve the data from which could have been directly produced his biography. However, we have only one instance of such memoranda, persistently kept, with this end in view. I need not say that I allude to Boswell shadowing Johnson, picking up every word as though it had been a grain of gold; reproducing every gesture and tone of voice; photographing person and costume; writing down almost every conversation heard through a long series of years; and reproducing all with marvelous fidelity in that incomparable work, "Boswell's Life of Samuel Johnson." And we will here incidentally remark that Richard Hargrave strongly resembled Samuel Johnson in many respects—in enthusiastic devotion to life-purpose, hatred of shams and deceptions; in being, when in the mood, the autocrat of the circle in which he moved; in being master of the purest English; in having accomplished in his chosen department a prodigious life-work; and, alas! in being subject all his life to a malady which sat upon him like the "Old Man of the Sea."

Notwithstanding this last admission, my earliest recollections of my father bring to mind his splendid physique, his long absences from home, always on horseback, and the joy that pervaded the household upon his return home, "Father is coming!" Mounted upon his deep-chested, fast-walking bay horse, sitting erect, massive and imposing, as though he were a great general returning from battle; dismounting, surrounded by the whole family—all to be kissed and embraced, beginning with the mother; the baby to be taken into his arms, while the waiting horse must have his share of patting and caressing. Alas! never more shall the family see the joy we then knew till reunited in the home in heaven. How can I express it otherwise than to say that he was carrying into the bosom of his family the gospel of love which he preached? Welcome all the toils, sufferings, and privations of the itinerant! His are the rewards of the righteous—"an hundred-fold in this life, and in the world to come life everlasting!"

My first recollections of him carry me back to the time when my accustomed seat was upon his knee, where, with my head pillowed upon his deep-heaving bosom, I usually fell asleep after the fatigues of a child's little day. And from those earliest memories I am carried forward to one beautiful day in June, when, as I sat by the couch of the dying man, and while an ineffable smile lit up his face, he said: "My son, you do not know how much I have loved you!" I remember, too, how he used to labor to make home pleasant and comfortable, especially for the long and severe winters of the lake-region of Northern Indiana. I remember, too, the comfortable carriage, or spring-wagon, in which the family used to remove from one charge to another—all owing to his care and mechanical ingenuity; for he usually got out the wooden bows that covered the wagon, and prepared the oil-cloth which kept out the storm and sun. This was before there were any railroads in Indiana, and our journeys were often over bad roads and in inclement weather. The utmost solicitude used to be manifested for the comfort of my dear mother and the children. I am speaking now of the gentle and affectionate heart of this strong man. I remember, also, how we used to make our annual pilgrimages to the southern part of the State, where, in adjoining counties, were the homes of our beloved grandparents on both sides. These annual visits are among the bright spots in memory, as we were always received with that affection ever manifested for grandchildren. These homes of our grandparents were some of the prominent homes of early Methodism. In Holliday's "History of Early Methodism in Indiana," the author says: "Richard Posey deserves honorable mention among the pioneers of Methodism in Indiana." Richard Posey was my mother's father, and it was to his home we were welcomed by his surviving wife, Frances Posey, who also deserves equally honorable mention as one of the mothers of Methodism in Indiana.

Again, William Hargrave, my paternal grandfather, was a life-long Methodist preacher, and so "entitled to honorable mention;" and Joseph Tarkington says of Sarah, his wife, that "she was a mother to him when he traveled the old Patoka Circuit." So these were all worthy of honorable mention. My dear parents' affection for the old homes and the loved ones there was something beautiful to behold; and those annual visits never ceased till, by death, the old homes were broken up, and the old homesteads went into other hands. After that, there were uncles and aunts and cousins to be visited occasionally; and we were always taught to love our kindred. I remember how strangely that line of N. P Willis's from "Ambition" used to strike me. When describing the ambitious young man, he says: "His kindred are forgotten or estranged." I used, as a student, to pray that, whatever my ambitions might be, they might never carry me so far away from my early teachings.

All the best affections of mankind must have been wonderfully developed in my father. His friendships were life-long. He instinctively acted upon the advice of Henry to the prince: "When thou hast found a friend, grapple him to thee with hooks of steel!" Among his life-long friendships were those for his brethren in the ministry and for many distinguished laymen. His intimate friends were such men as Aaron and Enoch Wood, Edwin Ray, Joseph Tarkington, John Strange, James Armstrong, Bishops Roberts, Simpson, and Ames, Isaac Owen, Augustus Eddy, Calvin W Ruter, Allen Wiley, John Miller, John C. Smith, George M. Boyd, John L. Smith, C. A. Brooke, John Hull, and generally the rank and file of the brethren of the Indiana Conferences, together with lay brethren and sisters throughout the work; for wherever he was admitted into the household he left a delightful impress, and was ever welcome thereafter. First and last, he had traveled in all parts of the State, and in some parts many times over, and his name was a household word. His genuine sympathy, his largeness of heart, and his unflinching fidelity to the cause of God gave him a measure of success wherever he labored—often great victories in the name of the Lord. His manhood and his purity of character were absolutely without spot or blemish; and herein lay one great secret of his acceptability among the people. Among the confidences which he gave me, he once said: "My son, I never intentionally did a dishonorable thing in all my life." Priceless legacy to those who came after him! His affections were fixed first of all upon his God and the Church, and then upon home, friends, his country, and humanity at large. His commission included all these.

It seems to be the opinion of some that he was wholly engrossed by the duties of the ministry to the exclusion of everything else. On the contrary, he was deeply interested in public affairs, in the causes of education, of temperance, and generally in the elevation of the masses. Those who knew him well will not need to be reminded of his patriotic devotion to the Government. The unfortunate collisions which occurred in Kansas upon the first settlement of the State appealed strongly to his sympathies; and with voice and pen he cried out against the outrages that were then committed upon innocent settlers from the free States. And when the Rebellion broke out he preached for the Government. These sermons attracted great attention, for the reason, among others, that there was then a considerable proportion of the people who were practically opposed to the war. On one occasion, as we are informed, he was escorted to a grand mass-meeting near Danville, Illinois, in a carriage drawn by four white horses; and he preached a sermon which created a profound impression. This sermon, and others which he preached about that time, have been spoken of ever since by those who were so fortunate as to hear them.

During the war of the Rebellion his letters were full of this theme; and from the first he rejoiced in the hope and the belief—as it was the subject of his constant prayer—that the war would result in the abolition of slavery and the establishment of our liberties as a people. As all three of his sons were in the army, he spent much time in prayer for them and for the triumph of the armies of the Union; and to the very last he retained a deep interest in public affairs.

Referring to my inner knowledge of my father's life, a fact that impressed me deeply was his tireless application. His school advantages embraced the barest rudiments of an education; and yet he pushed forward his studies—among other things, studying Murray's Grammar on horseback—and reading the best authors, until he gained a remarkably clear and forcible style, as shown in his published sermons and other writings; while in his spoken sermons he towered among the masters of the English language. There was a difference. He once remarked to a ministerial brother, in speaking of printed sermons, that "it was hard to bottle up thunder."

He arose invariably at four o'clock in the morning, and read, and wrote, and meditated incessantly, when not engaged in pastoral or household duties. As to these last, the claims of home and family were never neglected; while in the discharge of his pastoral duties, although in *his* day they were not brought down to so fine a point as in these latter days, yet the sick, the suffering, the lowly, and the penitent were never neglected; nor was there wanting the word in due season, that is often so potent in bringing sinners to Christ.

His library was standard, and embraced all the classics of Methodist theology, and minor publications usually read and consulted by Methodist preachers. And in the early days he not only read the books himself, but followed John Wesley's injunction to sell them to the people. His Scripture reading was immense, extending to the memorizing, by "chapter and verse," of the greatest part of the Bible. As his memory was phenomenal, he probably acquired these stores of the Word gradually in the course of his systematic studies. I might indicate my idea of his proficiency as a Bible-student by saying that he had stored away in his memory a complete analysis, similar in all essential respects to " Hitchcock's Analysis of the Holy Scriptures"—embracing "Cruden's Concordance." His knowledge of the Scriptures was obtained at first-hand. The command came daily to him: "Search the Scriptures."

With reference to his prodigious memory, I will only add that it was, according to the classification of the mental philosophers, both *philosophical* and *circumstantial*. It retained abstract facts in their relation to principles and systems; and it retained with equal tenacity names, dates, persons, circumstances. I doubt if he ever forgot a name or a face which he had once known. A beautiful instance of this was given me by a lay brother at whose house Hargrave had stopped "away back." He was only there for a single night. There was a little daughter in the family. Many years afterwards, meeting this brother, after the usual compliments, he inquired: "And how is little Mary?" The answer was: "Little Mary is well; she has been married a good many years, and has a large family of children. " Wonderful!" was the reply; "it seems to me but yesterday since she sat upon my knee!" What an advantage for the man of God! The Master himself said: " I am the good shepherd, and know my sheep, and am known of mine."

This extraordinary memory was especially useful to him in connection with his singing, as he rarely forgot a hymn which he had once learned; so that in his special work he could always sing the right hymn in the right place. And this was half the battle to the early itinerant; as he was the leader of the people in sacred song—such men as Strange, Ray, Havens, John Miller, and a host of others. And who can tell how many precious souls have been "born into the kingdom" in the tented grove as these sweet singers in Israel voiced some consolation or some divine promise just suited to the case? A lady related to me how she had lain at the point of death for many days, with typhoid fever, and how "Father Hargrave" visited her as her pastor; and how she never could forget the sweet hymns which he sang for her; and how, in all the years that followed, till his death, she delighted to entertain him at the home which he had so brightened by his presence!

His knowledge of the sacred poets was remarkable—of Milton, Young, Cowper, Watts, and the Wesleys, and others; and they beautified and lent a charm to his sermons and to his conversation. But, notwithstanding the close application, the stern demands of duty, and the constant self-denial of his life, Richard Hargrave was no gloomy ascetic. He had a keen sense of the humorous, was a natural mimic, and almost inimitable in anecdote and incident—of which his long life among the people gave him an almost inexhaustible fund. There were not only those which powerfully illustrated his sermons, but which entertained and amused in his conversation. So, when in a happy mood, he was one of the best of companions. Being from a slave State, his knowledge of the Negro was very accurate, and he figured a good deal in his anecdotes. So, of the German, the Englishman, and the Irishman; and, with the story, the dialect was generally reproduced with the utmost exactness.

As much stress has been laid upon Richard Hargrave's remarkable voice, and upon the extraordinary effects produced by his peculiar style of pulpit oratory, we will be pardoned for attempting a brief description—first, of his voice; and, secondly, of his peculiarities as a speaker. In this latter portrayal, we shall assume, as a fact, the divine *afflatus*, which so often descended upon him, carrying both him and his congregation beyond the bounds of mere human oratory.

As to his voice, while it was a true *soprano* in singing, it always seemed a *barytone* in speaking. He used none but the chest-notes, making the vowel-sounds with that peculiar openness and distinctness that is characteristic of the best type of English orators. This may have been a matter of patient practice; or, on the other hand, a natural gift. The reading of the Scripture lesson and of the hymn was in the same voice, and was easily heard to utmost extent of the greatest congregation, especially to the vast out-door multitudes which assembled at camp-meetings. This voice was so peculiarly powerful and musical that no one who sat within its compass could get away from it. The only way not to attend to what the preacher was saying, was to get beyond the sound of his voice—which would have been a long way. In the introductory parts of his discourse, while there was the power and distinctness—the fascination of which I have spoken—there was a deliberation, an apparent husbanding of strength, as though for a possible emergency. The quality of the voice, if critically tested, would be found to be similar to that of an "E-flat" cornet—soft, though loud, and beautifully modulated. Standing very near him, when he was preaching to one of those immense, out-door congregations, I noticed that in breathing he took in great quantities of air, in an easy, slow inspiration, fully inflating his great lungs, and keeping them filled while he continued to speak.

The great orators of that era used their voices as a distinct instrumentality for accomplishing great results; while their successors of the present generation, as a rule, use the voice as a mere vehicle for the expression of their thoughts in a conversational way. The latter may have its advantages, but the former is the true Demosthenean method, and will remain so to the end of time. It was a peculiarity of the voice, also, that it adapted itself to the theme of the speaker. In the language of Doctor Ridpath: "No man who once heard that pathetic cry, which marked the climax of his appeal in the pulpit, can ever forget the sound, or cease to tremble under its magic vibrations."

Having endeavored to give some idea of the *voice*, let us now speak of the *method* of the preacher. The logical divisions and arrangements of the discourse, and the preliminary discussion, were such as to arouse the reasoning faculties of the hearer and to interest him at once in the subject. When the speaker was himself, there was nothing tedious in this part of the discourse, but there was cumulative force in the sermon as it proceeded; one position carried, invariably strengthening the whole line of attack. Pretty soon the preacher began to have his own way, as he multiplied Scripture proofs and drafted into his service poetical quotations and passages from the prophets, until from a comparatively cold process of reasoning and dissertation, the sermon was now becoming instinct with life and passion. Surprises were apt to abound; and while the wonderful voice filled the air with its pulsations, the throbbing heart of the man of God seemed to have conquered all hearts for Christ. The sermon was now a series of climaxes, through which his hearers were carried by a power beyond their control. Now the heart of the hearer begins to throb almost painfully; there may be a momentary effort to refrain from weeping at some pathetic passage, but in a moment the barriers are all carried away, and tears flow freely—often tears of joy. Not infrequently the whole congregation are shouting praises to God at once; and *sometimes* they all arise to their feet, and, with one grand acclaim, give glory to God. Gradually the congregation are lowered from this state of intense spiritual exaltation, and the sermon soon closes. But sometimes it is not easy to dispose of the congregation. They will not separate; a few there may be who can not now arise to their feet; but there is singing and shouting and shaking of hands, until it seems a very Pentecost. But if it be a camp-meeting or other revival service, a well-directed exhortation, perhaps by another preacher, often fills the altar with penitents; and erelong—O, how often!—the shout of new-born souls is heard.

Effects such as I have outlined were characteristic

of his efforts on great occasions, yet were not wanting on many ordinary occcasions; for here was a man who, by the Divine assistance, always did the best he could.

Besides his poems and sermons, Hargrave wrote but little. Perhaps I ought to say, in passing, that he wrote no sketches of sermons. I do not think he ever used one; it would have been in his way. Occasionally he wrote a sermon *in extenso*, but I never heard him read one. He was an occasional contributor, upon some practical theme, to the columns of our Church papers. He also wrote " A Treatise upon the Lord's Supper and Baptism, with a Specific Argument Deduced from the Signification of Baptism, in Proof of the Mode of that Ordinance. Also, an Argument in Favor of the Divine Influences of the Holy Spirit upon the Heart in Salvation: Founded upon the Character of the Holy Ghost. With Strictures throughout upon Campbellism." The date of this was 1844. The treatise covered fifty-nine pages, 12mo, and was published during the heat of general controversy upon that subject. It is powerfully and racily written. A small edition, in paper backs, was published, which was doubtless disposed of quickly; and mine is perhaps the only copy extant.

As but few of our readers have access to "Hargrave's Sermons," for the purpose of giving some idea of his themes, we give briefly the Table of Contents:

SERMON I. *Proper Attention to Gospel Truth.*—" Therefore, we ought to give the more earnest heed to the things which we have heard, lest at any time we should let them slip." (Hebrews ii, 1.)

SERMON II. *The Sure Word of Prophecy.*—" We have also a more sure word of prophecy; whereunto ye do well that ye take heed, as unto a light that shineth in a dark place; until the day dawn and the day-star arise in your hearts." (2 Peter i, 19.)

SERMON III. *Christ and Moses.*—"And of his fullness have we all received, and grace for grace. For the law was given by Moses, but grace and truth came by Jesus Christ." (John i, 16.)

SERMON IV *Love Fulfills the Law.*—" Love is the fulfilling of the law." (Romans xiii, 10)

SERMON V *The Christian Walks by Faith.*—" For we walk by faith, not by sight." (2 Corinthians v, 7.)

SERMON VI. *Obedience by Faith.*—"By faith Abraham, when he was called to go into a place which he should after receive for an inheritance, obeyed, and went out, not knowing whither he went." (Hebrews xi, 8.)

SERMON VII. *Following on to Know the Lord.*—"Then we shall know, if we follow on to know the Lord. His going forth is prepared as the morning; and he shall come unto us as the rain, the latter and the former rain unto the earth." (Hosea vi, 3.)

SERMON VIII. *Justification by Faith.*—" But to him that worketh not, but believeth on him that justifieth the ungodly, his faith is counted for righteousness." (Romans iv, 5.)

SERMON IX. *The New Birth.*—" Marvel not that I said unto thee, ye must be born again. The wind bloweth where it listeth, and thou hearest the sound thereof, but canst not tell whence it cometh and whither it goeth: so is every one that is born of the Spirit." (John iii, 7, 8.)

SERMON X. *Atonement.*—" Being justified freely by his grace through the redemption that is in Christ Jesus, whom God hath set forth to be a propitiation, through faith in his blood, to declare his righteousness for the remission of sins that are past through the forbearance of God; that he might be just and the justifier of him which believeth in Jesus." (Romans iii, 24, 25.)

SERMON XI. *Believers Admonished.* — " Looking diligently, lest any man fail of the grace of God." (Hebrews xii, 15.)

SERMON XII. *Sin and its Consequences.*—" For the wages of

sin is death; but the gift of God is eternal life through Jesus Christ our Lord." (Romans vi, 23.)

SERMON XIII. *Priesthood of Christ.*—"Thou art a priest forever after the order of Melchizedek." (Psalm cx, 4.)

SERMON XIV   *The Mediation of Christ.*—"Therefore, he is able also to save them to the uttermost, that come unto God by him, seeing he ever liveth to make intercession for them." (Hebrews viii, 25.)

SERMON XV   *The Sufferings of Christ.*—"Searching what, or what manner of time the Spirit of Christ which was in them did signify, when it testified beforehand of the sufferings of Christ, and the glory that should follow." (1 Peter i, 11.)

SERMON XVI.   *The Glory of Christ.*—"Searching what, or what manner of time the Spirit of Christ which was in them did signify, when it testified beforehand of the sufferings of Christ, and the glory that should follow." (1 Peter i, 11.)

SERMON XVII.   *Tabor and Hermon.*—"The North and the South thou hast created them: Tabor and Hermon shall rejoice in thy name." (Psalm lxxxix, 12.)

SERMON XVIII.   *Majesty of God.*—" In the year that King Uzziah died, I also saw the Lord sitting upon a throne," etc. (Isaiah vi, 1-8.)

SERMON XIX.   *God is a Spirit.*—"God is a Spirit; and they that worship him must worship him in Spirit and in truth." (John iv, 24.)

SERMON XX.   *The Triumphs of Truth.*—" I will cut off the chariot from Ephraim, and the horse from Jerusalem, and the battle-bow shall be cut off; and he shall preach peace unto the heathen; and his dominion shall be from sea even to sea, and from the river even to the ends of the earth." (Zechariah ix, 10.)

There is something peculiar in parental as well as in filial affection. To the parent, the child ever remains a child, and especially is this so during the closing scenes of the parent's life. With the child the feeling is reciprocal, and the parent ever remains the fit object of reverence and obedience. The broad mantle of charity is thrown over all defects and failings, and to the last, the old ideal, or to use the word in its best sense, the old infatuation is kept up. Having no children of my own, it seems to me that both the upward and downward currents of my heart's best affections met and centered in my beloved and now departed parents; not to the exclusion, however, of my angel wife, for whom my love was but little short of idolatry, and my grief upon her loss almost distraction.

I can not sufficiently reverence that grand Church which was my father's nursing mother, nor those altars where he ministered in holy things. And I stand as a witness between the living and the dead, to testify how, to the last, he loved the cause in which he had labored, and his brethren in Christ; and how mournfully he said, in the first stages of the appalling disease of which he died (dropsy of the heart), "I fear I shall never preach again!" Not to preach, with him, was not to live. Just then there seemed some trepidation. His *plan* had, for almost threescore years, been to *preach;* God's plan was, now that his work was done, that his should be the welcome plaudit, "Well done, good and faithful servant, enter into the joy of thy Lord!" He now called him to the top of Nebo, that he should look over the Promised Land, take a parting glance at the wilderness through which he had urged his way in joy and sorrow, leave his blessing upon his beloved Zion, and sweetly rest in Jesus. His trust was in God, and after he laid him down to die, he was perfectly peaceful, notwithstanding he was often called to "sound the profoundest depths of death," as he characteristically described to his pastor his sufferings during one night. As a general thing during his last illness he had the full use of his faculties, and the rich stores of the word of God were his abundant consolation. Also the sacred poets, Milton, Young, Cowper, Watts, and the Wesleys, seemed to minister to him. At one time he said: "Death is a mighty archer, and he hunts us all aground!" At another time it was, "I am the resurrection and the life;" and again, "Blessing, and glory, and wisdom, and thanksgiving, and honor, and power, and might, be unto our God for ever and ever. Amen." At one time he quoted a passage from one of Wesley's sermons, then from Watson, then from Clarke, then from Fletcher. Of the latter he said: "I have, in some respects, derived more light from the writings of Mr. Fletcher than from those of any other of our prominent divines. Others were, perhaps, more learned, but he was more spiritual."

Recently before his last illness, he had been reading Bishop Simpson's "Yale College Lectures" on preaching, and he now remarked that "Bishop Simpson was raised up to do a great work. I have always admired and loved him."*

Bishop Ames died during father's last illness, and we hesitated to inform him of the fact, lest the news might agitate him too much in his low condition. And, although when told, it seemed to be something of a shock, he said, after thinking a moment: "Thank God! I shall soon join him! We have labored to-

---

* It will be seen that this regard was mutual, by a reference to the introduction to Hargrave's Sermons, written by Bishop Simpson.—W. P. H.

gether for more than forty years, and soon the reunion will come!" He added he regarded Bishop Ames as one of our great bishops, and especially in point of executive ability, second to none. He then related how, on a certain occasion, Bishop Ames had preached a sermon of unsurpassed power and pathos. After all, he seemed to gauge both these eminent divines by their power to preach and their devotion to the cause of Christ.

For sixteen weeks he lingered before the giant of suffocation could conquer the giant who held the citadel of life. After one of the frequently recurring paroxysms of suffocation, he said to me: "My son, that would shake a giant." It was my privilege to be with him almost all his last illness, and to minister as best I could to his comfort, for which privilege I can not be sufficiently grateful. In this labor of love I was joined by my dear wife, and we but added our efforts to those of my dear sister Caroline, Mrs. Campbell, and her devoted husband, and the children, in the home where the father and mother both passed away. By our joint efforts, I rejoice to know that his sufferings were very much mitigated.

At one time I said to him: "Father, is there not some passage of Scripture that you would like to have read to you?" Knowing how much he loved the fifty-third chapter of Isaiah, I asked him if he would like to have me read that. He said: "O yes! It begins, 'Who hath believed our report?'" and going on, he recited *verbatim* every word of the chapter! By that time he was shouting happy. "O yes," said he, "the kingdoms are but one!"

His love for his children was conspicuous in these last days. At one time he prayed for his dear Sarah, the eldest daughter, the wife of the itinerant, whose home was in Minnesota, and who was in a low state of health; that she might be strengthened to bear the news of his departure. He then followed with a prayer for each of the children by name. When the ministerial brethren called, from time to time, he greatly rejoiced, and gave to them the testimony that the grace of God was sufficient. Owing to his somewhat remote situation, however, he was favored with but few of these visits. Rev. Dr. A. A. Gee, his long-time friend, walked four miles to pay this last token of fraternal regard, and it was doubtless a blessed season to both these veterans of the cross. On the evening before his death, a delightful holy Sabbath afternoon, he reclined quietly, and conversed in an easy manner with a Presbyterian brother, an old friend and neighbor, who, during his pastorate at the old Bethel Church, near by, had often heard him preach. Among other things he said: "I am so thankful now that I have been enabled to do what I have done for Christ!" He seemed so strong and so well that afternoon, that after consultation with the family, it was determined that I should return to my home, a few miles distant, as I was almost compelled to do, for a single day. I bade him an affectionate good-bye, not doubting that I should see him again alive. But, alas! he died in great peace, early the following morning, June 23, 1879, at eight o'clock A. M., in his seventy-sixth year. I saw him no more in this world! Hastening to the house of mourning, with my dear wife, we joined in the preparations for the last sad rites. Surely father was never more beloved by children than he. Nevertheless but two of us were able to be present at the funeral. Three resided in far distant States, and one was detained by circumstances beyond control. As he died within the bounds of a circuit which, years before, had been the scene of a successful pastorate, and as his life-work was well known there, the demonstrations of grief for his loss, and of regard for his memory, were marked and unusual.

At length came the moment when myself and my dear wife (who loved him much) were left alone with our dead. What the thoughts and emotions of that moment were may not be expressed in language; but as the grand career of the man, from a mere human stand-point, passed quickly in review before us, above it all was his love for us and for all, and his zeal for God. And we could then see, for the first time, as he lay in his coffin, as Macaulay said of Louis XIV of France, how the *grand man* had once been a small man physically. But the great soul that had inhabited the clay tenement, at one time feeble and emaciated, had strengthened and nourished it until the very name of Richard Hargrave became a synonym for strength and beauty, until the man became a hero and a gladiator.

On the twenty-fourth of June we proceeded from the scene of the last conflict and the last triumph to the old Bethel Church, where the last sad rites were paid. An arrangement had been made that the funeral sermon was to have been preached by Rev.

J. W T. McMullen, D. D.; but he was not able to attend, nor was there time, under the circumstances, to notify the ministerial brethren at a distance in time for them to attend the funeral, as many of them would have done. But the church was packed with old friends, brethren, and sisters in Christ—a sorrowing and yet a rejoicing multitude. The funeral sermon was preached by the faithful pastor, Rev. N. A. Chamberlain, from 2 Samuel, i, 27: "How are the mighty fallen, and the weapons of war perished!" It was an appropriate and powerful discourse. Rev. H. N. Ogden assisted in the services; after which Jesse Meharry, of precious memory, the Christian philanthropist, spoke of his long acquaintance with the deceased and of the great work he had done. He related how, forty-seven years before, he had seen Richard Hargrave and James L. Thompson enter the old church together, and from that time onward he had been a bosom friend to the one who now lay lifeless before us, and he had known him as a power in the ministry.

It was a sweet and comforting service. Then we took the last look at the beloved father, "sorrowing most that we should see him no more," but rejoicing that we should meet again "in the sweet bye and bye."

We then consigned the body to its last resting-place beside the dear wife and mother. Upon the granite monument, which has since been erected to mark the sacred spot, are the words, chosen by himself: "Remember the words which I spake unto you while I was yet with you." Upon the reverse side of the monument are inscribed the last words of our mother, "All is right."

THE OLD GUARD

REV. JOHN STRANGE.*

> "Lives of great men all remind us
> We can make our lives sublime,
> And, departing, leave behind us
> Foot-prints on the sands of time;
> Foot-prints that, perhaps, another,
> Sailing o'er life's solemn main,
> A forlorn and shipwrecked brother,
> Seeing, shall take heart again.
> Let us, then, be up and doing,
> With a heart for any fate;
> Still achieving, still pursuing,
> Learn to labor and to wait."

IN this chapter we introduce, first of all, the name of one who was greatest of all, because he was servant of all. We shall introduce him with but little ceremony, without the formality of titles. He had none. He despised them, as he despised the vanities of men.

He often sang, with seraphic sweetness:

> "I trample on their whole delight;
> I seek a city out of sight,
> A city in the skies."

To have called him a doctor or professor would have excited his ridicule or alarmed him, and he would

---

* Copied from "Early Methodism in Indiana," by Rev. J. C. Smith; for sale by J. M. Olcott, 103 State Street, Chicago.

have said, like Job: "God forbid that I should receive flattering titles, for then God would soon take me away." He was above titles; they were toys to amuse smaller men; before him they vanished like vapor before the brilliant sun.

We shall introduce him, then, simply in Scripture style, as John Strange. I need not ask you to rise and do him reverence. A moment's reflection will convince you that you are in the presence of no ordinary man; that a master in Israel is before you.

Rev. John Strange was born in Virginia, the home of Washington, Patrick Henry, William Wirt, and a galaxy of other distinguished men, whose memories are enshrined in the hearts of the American people. He first saw the light on the 15th of November, 1789. Of his early education and surroundings we know nothing. He emigrated with his father's family to Ohio when he was quite young. While yet a lad he was converted, and joined the Methodist Episcopal Church after his removal to Ohio. In 1811, then in the twenty-second year of his age, he was received into the Ohio Annual Conference, where he labored with great zeal and usefulness for thirteen years. Here his fame as an orator of great power and popularity began to be national; but, yielding to his disposition to hunt out the lost sheep in forest wilds, he emigrated to Indiana in 1824, and was placed in charge of a work in the southeastern part of the State, embracing Rising Sun, Lawrenceburg, Brookville, and other portions of the adjacent country.

While on this work, Indians still roamed those forests, and committed many thefts and robberies, and sometimes even murders, among the defenseless settlers in the sparse neighborhoods. Ten years afterwards, when I was on Lawrenceburg Circuit, I used to hear many remarkable traditions of Mr. Strange by the prominent Methodists, who seemed never to weary in telling of his eloquence and faith and self-sacrifice for the Church.

On one occasion he lost a fine saddle-horse, that died suddenly of disease. His friends were sympathizing with him over his loss, which they had no means, in their poverty, of replacing with another. He coolly replied: "Why, brethren, should you be disturbed about this matter? I am not. I know that my Father 'owns the cattle on a thousand hills,' and in his own good time and way he will give me a horse, or a dozen of them, if need be, to prosecute his work. In the meantime he has given me the power of speedy and easy locomotion, which I shall use without interruption to my work." So, packing up his knapsack, and shouldering his rifle as a kind of terror to thieving and murderous Indians and wild beasts, he pursued his way around his circuit of three hundred miles, often without a guide, without roads or even paths, and often without shelter at nights save the canopy of the blue heavens or floating clouds above him.

Mr. Strange's father before him was a minister who, like his son, was of a cosmopolitan spirit, despising the luxury and vanity of cities and of wealth. He often sought the solitudes of the forest, where he might preach the gospel to red men and lost sheep scattered into the wilderness places. In one of these solitary excursions he lost his life, no one knowing, to this day, the spot where he fell or the means by which he lost his life, whether by the hands of savages, by wild beasts, or by starvation.

The introduction of John Strange to Indiana Methodism was as sudden and mythical, almost, as the introduction of Elijah, the great prophet, to the tribes of Israel, in the reign of Ahab. Elijah came unheralded; and the first grand swoop he made on the kingdom of idolatry was in the presence of the king himself, to whom he said: "As the Lord God of Israel liveth, before whom I stand, there shall be no dew or rain these years but according to my word." If a thunderbolt from a clear sky had struck the guilty king, it could not have surprised him more. So John Strange came upon us in Indiana like a bright flash, and his first sermon was a new era in pulpit eloquence. I was then a boy, thoughtless and irreligious. I heard of his fame, and learning that he was to be at a camp-meeting some four miles from my father's residence, in Jefferson County, this State, I went there, with many others, more to see and hear the famed minister than for any other purpose. At the close of the service on Saturday evening, just before the benediction, there stepped suddenly upon the platform a man in neat but plain attire, tall, straight, and remarkably graceful in person and manner, and with a round, well-formed head, dark, piercing eyes, yet exceedingly kind and benevolent in expression. In a moment every eye was fixed upon him, and if an angel had stood there the hush and silence could not have been more complete. Surveying the crowd for a moment, he broke the oppressive silence by saying: "Brethren and fellow-citizens: I am a stranger to you all. I have come here from a distance to enjoy in this quiet grove the precious privileges of social intercourse and Christian fellowship and worship. I have learned to-day that there are persons on this ground who have threatened the peace of this encampment to-night and to-morrow. Permit me, brethren and fellow-citizens, to say, I do not share with you these fears. I have too much confidence in the good sense, patriotism, and love of order of this community, and can safely confide to you, as fathers, as husbands, and sons, the safe-keeping and order of this meeting. You all have a deep interest in the good name of this community, and you will preserve it with sleepless vigilance. Such is my confidence in you all that I am ready to be your surety that you will, every one, be a keeper of the peace. If any offend, set it to my account; I will pay the forfeit." Saying this, he lifted his hands and said: "Let us pray." And *such* a prayer, for calm dignity, simplicity, faith, and power with God, I have never heard since. Though fifty years have passed, its impression is still upon my memory and soul. That man was John Strange. The audience was spell-bound. The peace and harmony of the meeting were secured, and every man was ready to die for John Strange.

To show his deadness to the world and his faith in God, I will here relate a fact well known to early Methodists about Madison. While he traveled the Madison District, about 1828, he resided in Madison. The people of that city, knowing his poverty as to this world's goods, and appreciating the dependence of his family, offered to secure to him in fee simple a parcel of land in the bounds of the city, with a house upon it for a dwelling. This he persistently, though thankfully, declined accepting, always offering Scripture reasons for so doing. Among other reasons he said: "I would not deprive myself the privilege, for all the land in Indiana, of singing those grand words:

> 'No foot of land do I possess,
> No cottage in the wilderness;
> A poor, wayfaring man!'"

This was no mere hasty sentimentalism with him; it was his master passion, governing him to the close of life.

The question is frequently asked by those who had no personal acquaintance with Brother Strange: "In what did his power over men consist?" The answer is, that nearly all the elements that constitute human greatness entered into his composition. His was a well-balanced mind, quick perceptive faculties, sound judgment, strong memory and will-power, and a brilliant imagination, combined with wonderful power of eloquence and song. His moral faculties were even stronger than the intellectual. He took no lessons in elocution from the schools; he was greater than the schools. He was nature's orator, drawing his inspirations from nature and from nature's God. His invocations, like those of Elijah on Carmel, were for answers by fire; and fire always came upon him and upon all about him, quenching the water, and wood, and stone, and all gross material sacrifices, leaving only the residuum of the spiritual and divine.

His pure, ornate, and copious language not only glowed, but burned. It not only illuminated and elevated, but it warmed and transfigured the soul. He loved the sublime in nature, the solemn forests, the lofty mountains, the expansive ocean, the rolling thunders, the starry heavens, and the blooming spring; and from these he ascended by easy gradations to the awful and sublime in redemption, the garden of Gethsemane, the passion and bloody sweat, the crucifixion and resurrection and ascension of the Son of God. Amidst these awful scenes he loved to gaze and wonder, like Moses on Sinai, amidst thunderings and lightnings and terror; and like Elijah at the rock of Horeb, when God passed before him in the whirlwind and earthquake. And gazing upon these scenes he was often " changed into the same image, from glory to glory, as by the Spirit of the Lord."

I have seen him under these inspirations when his form and features, naturally serene and beautiful, seemed to lose the type of the earthy and assume the type of the heavenly; something like Stephen in martyrdom, when he looked up and said: " I see the heavens opened, and Jesus standing at the right hand of God; and all who beheld him saw his face as the face of an angel." This is no fancy sketch.

These gracious revelations of power were not vouchsafed to this holy man as an extra partial dealing of God. If, like John the divine, on Patmos, he was permitted to walk amidst the golden candlesticks and see and hear the myriad harpers before the throne, it was because he, like John, had forsaken all to follow Christ; hence the appropriateness of that beautiful song he often sang with such sweetness and power:

> "No foot of land do I possess,
> No cottage in the wilderness;
> A poor, wayfaring man.
> I dwell awhile in tents below,
> And gladly wander to and fro,
> Till I my Canaan gain."

I have often seen him step from the pulpit with a countenance radiant with light divine, and sing these lines with a pathos and power and sweetness that moved the hearts of thousands as the forest-trees are moved with a mighty wind. Take him all in all as a man of deep convictions, of holy and simple trust in God, of unreserved consecration to Christ, of eloquence and power in the pulpit, and of purity and simplicity of life, we shall probably not soon look upon his like again.

Mr. Strange's long rides, hard labors, and many exposures early developed in his slender constitution the seeds of pulmonary consumption, and it was seen in the summer of 1831 that his ministry was drawing rapidly to a close among us. But his life and preaching became more heavenly as he approached the golden shore.

We will here try, as far as feeble pen and words can do it, to describe a sermon we heard from him at a camp-meeting near Columbus, Indiana, in the summer of 1831, perhaps the last public effort he ever made, except to preach the funeral sermon of Rev. Edwin Ray and James Bankson that fall before the session of the Conference, which convened in the city of Indianapolis. They had died only a short time before Conference.

The sermon at Columbus was the most extraordinary effort of his life. Pale and emaciated and heavenly in appearance, he took the stand at eleven o'clock A. M. on Sabbath. The stand was full of weeping ministers, and a strange stillness brooded over the place. He read, in deep emotion, the opening hymn:

> "Come, let us join our friends above,
> That have obtained the prize."

Then followed a prayer of great sweetness and power, by which all hearts were subdued. He then read his text: "These are they which came out of great tribulation, and have washed their robes, and made them white in the blood of the Lamb." (Rev. vii, 14.)

Everything conspired to the solemnity of that occasion; the still grove, the somber clouds, the hymn, the text, and, above all, the dying minister. The ground on which we stood was holy. Never saw I a congregation so solemn, so awe-struck, as the minister passed through the sermon, sketching, as John Strange alone could do it, the white-robed multitude before the throne of God, and the tribulations out of which they came, and their happiness now in the presence of the Lamb, leading them to the fountains of living waters.

Just then, when every heart was full and every eye and face was bathed in tears, he drew himself up to one of his loftiest attitudes and stood in solemn silence for a moment, then said, in a voice and manner than can never be forgotten: "Farewell, world.

I leave you in the hand of the Redeemer. Farewell, beloved ministers. Farewell, brethren, all; I shall soon be with the blood-washed on that shining shore. Very soon I shall lift these feet, *all dripping* from the waters of Jordan, and set them on the golden streets. Soon I shall be with Paul and John, with Polycarp and Wesley and Whitefield, and all the martyrs and sufferers for the testimony of Jesus. But who are *these?* There stands one in the midst of the throne, brighter than all. It is the Lamb in his glory; he becks and bids me come!" Then stepping forward a little, and waving his hand, he said: " Get out of my light, ye crowding multitudes; I must see Jesus, I must take him in my arms!" These words were prophetic, and with them he sank back in the arms of one of the ministers, Brother James Havens, I believe. What followed this beggars description. The ministers in the stand were bathed in tears, and most of them had fallen flat on the floor. Multitudes in the audience lay as dead men, overpowered with intense emotion. Some stood in silence, awe-struck; some shouted for joy, and all wept.

The following year that great man, that sweet singer in Israel, that golden-tongued Chrysostom of Methodism, closed his life and ministry.

During the entire year previous to his death his physical energies rapidly failed, but his inward man was renewed day by day. His mental faculties became more vigorous, if possible, as the body of mortality was being removed.

At the session of Conference that year he was placed on the retired list, among the superannuates.

While his judgment approved this measure, his heart rebelled against it. It had often been the expressed wish of his soul to die with the gospel harness on, and if God willed it, to go directly from the pulpit to the tomb.

The few months of his superannuation were not idly or uselessly spent. He preached loudly in the sick-room, and illustrated beautifully the virtues of patience, resignation, and calm reliance on God, and proved the power of that faith which had grandly sustained him through so many trials and privations of the ministry. He often repeated, with a prolonged trill of the voice and with singular effect, the words with which he often entranced whole audiences during his public ministry: " Hail, all hail, the power of Jesus's name!"

He spent much of his remaining days in meditations and annotations on the past; in receiving also messages of cheer and affection from ministers and faithful laymen all over the land, and in returning answers and blessings to them. His ruling passion to die a poor, wayfaring man, dispossessed of earthly goods, was strong in death.

A committee of brethren from the Shiloh settlement, some ten miles west of the city, where he had often resorted for a little quiet rest and unostentatious sociability, waited on him one day, about two months before his death, to inform him that the house they had been preparing for himself and family in that vicinity was now finished all ready for occupancy, and praying him to accept and be removed into it.

He was lying on his dying couch when they entered his room and made their message known. Without the least agitation, he looked up and said in a calm voice: "Brethren, I need no further lands or houses here. Yonder," pointing heavenward, "I have a house not made with hands, eternal in the heavens. I am about removing into that." Then thanking these good men, he bade them each a final adieu. They returned home, "sorrowing most that they should see his face no more."

So lived and so died John Strange. His closing triumph was a fitting logical sequence to his glorious life and ministry. The generation in which he lived has mostly passed away, but fresh will be the memories about his tomb so long as one remains who knew and loved him here. And in future history his name will still be repeated with veneration, as one of rare eloquence, fervent piety, and self-sacrifice to the interests of mankind.

It is to be regretted that a full biography was not published at or near the time of his decease; then data might have been obtained for a full and interesting history of him.

It is now about forty-five years since his death, and most of his contemporaries have passed, like him, from the stage of action, so that what is written now must be gathered mainly from the pages of memory of a few. The marks he made while living were on the hearts of men with words of fire. Though respectable in literary attainments, he had not time to write. He wrote no sermons. A written sermon, or even a skeleton, would have fettered his genius and restrained the fire of his burning eloquence. A written sermon in his hands would have been like the armor of Saul on the youthful David, and he would have said, like that young champion in the fight of faith: "Take these things away." He met the enemies of Israel in his day with more puissant elements of warfare than written theses and lectures coldly read from pen, ink, and paper. His weapons of warfare were the sword of the Spirit and burning words of eloquence poured forth from the heart, filled with the love of God and with love for the souls of men; and these were his trophies everywhere.

We have before alluded to his sermon before the session of Conference in this city (Indianapolis) in the fall of 1831, in reference to the death of two young ministers who had died late that year. We refer to Rev. Edwin Ray and James Bankson, both men of great worth and distinction in the Conference. The former of these, for many reasons, was loved and cherished by Mr. Strange with an affection rarely equaled among men. Though he was very feeble, not being able to be in the Conference-room but a small portion of the time, yet it was deemed very desirable that he should preach the funeral discourse of these two beloved ministers, if possible; and the Conference passed a formal resolution asking him to do so, fixing the hour for this solemn service on the Sabbath, at three o'clock in the afternoon. To this Mr. Strange gave his consent, for the sake of those two beloved brethren, though he felt wholly inadequate to the duty in point of physical strength; and moreover, he felt, as he said in the beginning of the service, that he regarded *that* probably the last effort he should ever make before a public audience, as it proved to be.

When the hour came for the funeral service the church was excessively crowded. The whole body of ministers was there, and as many of the citizens as could find standing-room. All were anxious to hear of the beloved Ray, especially, who only three or four years previously had been the faithful beloved pastor of the Church in which they were then assembled; and all were anxious to hear the beloved and dying Strange, probably for the last time. Pale and trembling in weakness he arose amidst the breathless throng, and announced his opening hymn:

> "Who are these arrayed in white,
>   Brighter than the noonday sun;
> Foremost of the sons of light,
>   Nearest the eternal throne?" etc.

During the reading of the hymn, in the minister's inimitable way, many persons in the assembly were bathed in tears. There stood the dying Strange, weeping over our dead comrades in the ministry, the beautiful, the courteous, the pious, and devoted Ray, and the learned, eloquent, and promising Bankson. The hymn being sung, and a solemn prayer offered by one of the ministers present, Mr. Strange arose and announced his text: "They that be wise shall shine as the brightness of the firmament; and they that turn many to righteousness, as the stars for ever and ever." (See Daniel, xii, 3.) There was the same form, the same eye, that never ceased to beam with intelligence and love, and the same voice that for years had thrilled vast audiences all over the West with its seraphic notes of sweetness and song; but O, how changed now! They were putting on the last type of mortality, ready for the marriage of the Lamb. He spoke feebly of the wisdom of those who serve God, contrasting it with the foolishness of this world. He spoke of the luster that shall adorn the character of every faithful Christian, and especially of every minister, who, like Moses, refused to be called the son of Pharaoh's daughter, choosing rather to suffer affliction with the people of God than to enjoy the pleasures of sin for a season, having respect to the recompense of the reward. (See Heb. xi, 24, 25, 26.) He spoke of the moral beauty of those who stand on Zion's hill—

"Who bring salvation on their tongues,
And words of peace reveal."

Having drawn a beautiful picture of the faithful minister who turns many to righteousness—of his wisdom, his prudence, his purity, and zeal—he applied it to the beloved ministers above named.

While delivering the discourse he was often compelled to lean for support upon the pulpit. Sometimes the fires within his soul would break forth with their accustomed brightness and fervency, then again would die away like a lamp nearly exhausted. As he spoke of Edwin Ray; of his beauty, innocence, and charming eloquence; of the friendship that had existed between them, like that which bound David and Jonathan together, and of his lamented early death, he became deeply affected, and covering his face with his hands for a moment, he ceased to speak and wept profusely. Then gaining a little strength, he uttered aloud: "O, Edwin, my son Edwin, would that I had died for thee! But he hushed my murmuring, and he dried my tears. Soon shall I hail thee, Edwin, before the throne.

Having walked together along this mortal vale, soon shall we walk together along the banks of the river of life, and drink forever of the stream of life that maketh glad the city of our God." With this apostrophe, such was the baptism of power that came upon the holy Strange and upon the whole assembly, that further utterance was impossible, and he sank in the arms of one of the ministers behind him, and the service closed.

This, I think, was his last public effort. On the second day of December of the following year his words were verified, and he joined the assembly of the first-born in heaven, and walked with his beloved Edwin along the river of life, where they thirst no more.

The remains of this distinguished minister now rest in the old cemetery, in the southwest of the city of Indianapolis, near its western border. The branches of a tall pine-tree spread over the consecrated spot, which is marked only by a humble slab of stone, on which are inscribed the following words:

Sacred
To the memory of the REV. JOHN STRANGE,
Who departed this life
On the 2d day of December, 1832,
In the 44th year of his age,
And the 22d year of his
Itinerant ministry.

They that be wise shall shine as the brightness of the firmament; and they that turn many to righteousness, as the stars for ever and ever. (Daniel xii, 3.)

To this spot we often resort, as to a sacred Mecca, for meditation and for a renewal of our vows.*

---

* Would it not be well for Indiana Methodism to erect a suitable monument to John Strange?—W. P. II.

REV. EDWIN RAY.[*]

"His life was brave but mild ;
In him the elements so mixed,
That nature herself might stand
And point to him with conscious pride,
And say to all the world, Behold a man!"

In the early spring of 1828 there came a stranger on horseback to my father's house in the dusk of the evening of a chilly day in March, and asked for lodging for the night. My father then lived on the old Madison road, some twelve miles from the city, and kept a private inn for the accommodation of weary travelers, to which ministers of the gospel were admitted free. The stranger alluded to was invited in and cared for with the best hospitalities the house could afford. There was something about his appearance that at once commanded attention and respect. A young man about twenty-five years of age; ministerial in his appearance, neither grave nor gay ; a little above medium height; well proportioned, symmetrical in body and limbs; fine personal appearance; head finely shaped ; open countenance and generous expression; auburn hair ; dark blue eyes, large and full, surrounded with heavy, arching eyebrows, that seemed the index of humor; quick perception and strong intellectual powers ; in a word, a young man who would command the love and confidence of any judge of mankind. So he seemed to my young imagination, being then a boy of some eighteen years of age. I need

---

[*] From "Early Methodism in Indiana," by Rev. J. C. Smith, D. D. For sale by J. M. Olcott, 103 State Street, Chicago.—W. P. H.

not inform the reader that that young man was Rev. Edwin Ray, the subject of this sketch. He was on his way to a quarterly meeting some five miles north of my father's residence, on Graham Creek, in what was then known as the Needham settlement. Rev. John Strange was presiding elder of the district that year, but being unwell, had employed Mr. Ray, then stationed at Madison, to supply his place at the said quarterly meeting.

Soon after his arrival at our house, he informed us his name, his profession, and the object of his visit. All this we had surmised from his outfit—a good horse and a well-filled pair of saddle-bags; the usual accompaniments of a Methodist preacher in those days. Having inquired immediately about the neighborhood where the meeting was to be held, and the state of the roads leading to it, we gave him the requisite information; stating, also, that an unbroken forest of black-gum swamps stretched out between him and the point of destination, with scarcely a foot-path to direct his way. At all this he seemed nothing daunted, it being part of his experience for years past. Turning to me, he said: "You must accompany me to the meeting; so prepare yourself for an early start in the morning. I can not take 'No' for an answer." Though I was not then a member of the Church, and made no profession of religion, I was half inclined to accept his invitation, for already I began to feel the magnetism of his presence and conversation.

Next morning, after an early breakfast, though the weather was very disagreeable, we mounted our horses and plunged into the swamps and sea of mud before us, arriving at Needham's about eleven o'clock, A. M., where we found a good audience awaiting the preacher. I do not now remember what Mr. Ray's subject was that day, but I remember well that he made a very favorable impression on his audience—all being loud in his praise.

On Sabbath the house was excessively filled with earnest hearers. His text was from Acts xxiv, 25: " And as he reasoned of righteousness, temperance, and judgment to come, Felix trembled, and answered, Go thy way for this time; when I have a convenient season, I will call for thee." The preacher had not advanced far before we were convinced he was a master in the pulpit. He spoke of Paul in feeling and eloquent terms; spoke of him as a prisoner, in chains, for Christ's sake; portrayed his courage and eloquence in the presence of courtly power. He then analyzed his discourse before Felix; spoke of righteousness, in its application to rulers and to all men; spoke of God's righteous acts, and how he will judge all men in righteousness at the last day. On this item of the text he became very earnest, and made forcible and affecting appeals to the consciences of his hearers.

He next passed to the consideration of temperance, in its more practical bearings upon human conduct and human destiny. He showed how Paul, the prisoner, by a master-stroke of policy, made this theme effective on the judgment and conscience of Felix— his haughty judge—while he avoided direct personal attack and recrimination, which might have ruined his cause. He showed, by beautiful illustrations, the happiness of a life of temperance in all things, especially in our appetites and passions. From these themes Mr. Ray passed to the subject of the judgment to come. On this he put forth his greatest strength and pathos, and made it more effective by his tears, which often, during the sermon, suffused his eyes and ran profusely down his face, which never appeared more graceful and manly than when draped in tears.

I often heard Edwin Ray preach during the two years he was stationed at Madison, and I think I rarely heard him that tears did not attest the earnestness of his soul in the delivery of his messages from God to men. His style of preaching was always worthy of imitation—scholarly, argumentative, earnest, and pathetic; free from rant, from pedantry, and from cant phrases and all attempts at wit and levity. His points were always clearly stated, and forcibly maintained by sound logical reasoning, and rendered the more effective by a deep vein of pious emotion, and a rich, unctious style of delivery.

Under the sermon at Needham's, to which we have just alluded, there were many convictions for sin, and many wept, especially when he descanted on the language of Felix to Paul, "Go thy way; at a convenient season I will call for thee,"—showing that this procrastination has been the fatal pretext of men in all ages, and the cruel device of Satan to keep men from an immediate surrender of their hearts to Christ. "Ah!" said he, "how many of my hearers to-day have been ruined with this perilous delay 'till a more convenient season!' That more convenient time," continued he, "never came to Felix. He never saw or heard the faithful Paul again, but was soon after

called back to Rome in disgrace for malfeasance in
office, was degraded, banished, and died miserably in
exile; and probably," said he, "a more convenient
season than this will never come to many of you who
are here present."

That appeal, I remember well, came with great
force to my own conscience. I was compelled to admit that I had often sinned in the same way; though
young, I had often trembled under the mighty power
of God's Word, and promised to yield my heart to
him at no very distant day, and then went away and
sinned again and again.

I determined, under this appeal, to do so no more,
"the Lord being my helper." So when an invitation
was given at the close of the service for persons desiring salvation to come to the altar of prayer, for the
first time in my life I yielded. Tremblingly, I arose
and forced myself forward. It seemed to me that a
thousand demons of unbelief and carnality stood before me to force me back; but I said in my heart:

> "I'll go to Jesus, though my sin
>   Hath like a mountain rose;
> I know his courts, I'll enter in,
>   Whatever may oppose."

At that altar I met, for the first time, Williamson
Terrell, well known through Indiana in after years.
He was then a young man, probably twenty-two years
of age, of noble bearing, full of religious zeal, full of
love and sympathy. How cordially he met me and
welcomed me to the household of faith! How he
stood by me, and wept and prayed and taught me
how to seek Christ! I felt then that my soul was

bound together with him in the bundle of life. A friendship then began which no hostile influence ever dissolved, and death can never devour.

My conversion did not take place then, nor, in fact, till about five weeks afterwards, when, on the 11th of April, 1828, while kneeling in secret prayer near the spot which afterwards became the grave of my sainted mother, the Savior was suddenly revealed to my heart.

I ever after regarded Edwin Ray as my spiritual father, as it was under his ministry that day that I was effectually aroused from the torpor of sin to seek salvation; and, having received Christian baptism at his hands shortly after, I regarded him the more as my father in the ministry.

In the above narrative I have anticipated several facts that belong essentially to this biographical sketch. These we shall now take up in their proper order.

Rev. Edwin Ray was born in Montgomery County, Kentucky, July 26, 1803. He was the son of Rev. John Ray, an able and useful local minister of the Methodist Episcopal Church, a man of patriarchal simplicity of manners and modes of living, displaying both in life and in death an unwavering faith and devotion to Christ and his cause. Edwin was converted July 26, 1819, on the anniversary of his sixteenth year of age. His conversion took place at a camp-meeting in Clark County, Indiana. When his father, who was at the meeting, heard of the conversion of his son, in an adjoining tent, he became very happy, and then and there kneeled before God, in the presence of many people, and solemnly dedicated him to God for the work of the ministry; which offering the Lord accepted, and shortly after he thrust him out into his vineyard.

He entered the ministry in 1822, then in his nineteenth year, and was received on trial in the Kentucky Annual Conference. At the close of his second year he was received into full connection, and at his own request was transferred to the Illinois Conference, which then embraced the State of Indiana under its jurisdiction.

His first appointment in the Illinois Conference was to the Vincennes Circuit; thence, in 1826, on the Bloomington Circuit; and thence, in 1827, on the Indianapolis Circuit. In all these charges, which were very large and laborious, he preached with great zeal and usefulness, rising rapidly to distinction among the ministers and people.

While on the Indianapolis Circuit—of which Indianapolis, then a small town, was one of the preaching-places—the old Wesley Chapel, on Circle Street, was erected, mainly through his personal labor and oversight. I have been informed by an old citizen that he often saw Mr. Ray cutting timber in the woods with his own hands, and driving a horse-team, hauling material for the building. These acts, though in the judgment of some might have seemed secular and unministerial, stand greatly to his praise, showing his zeal for the Church and for the furtherance of the gospel. He deemed nothing low but sin, and nothing hard that might glorify Christ.

While on this circuit, he married, during the year

1827, Miss Sarah Ann Nowland, daughter of the widow Nowland, long and well known in this city as a lady of great energy and purpose of character.

From Indianapolis Circuit Mr. Ray was sent to Madison Station in the fall of 1827, where he remained two years. It was during his pastorate in Madison that I formed his acquaintance, and the foundations of that immutable friendship which existed between us were laid.

While in Madison Brother Ray acquired that enduring reputation for learning, eloquence, and usefulness in the ministry which raised him to the highest rank of Methodist preachers in Indiana. He was deeply versed in the knowledge of the Holy Scriptures, in Church history, and in theological knowledge generally. He was a great admirer of the writings of the early fathers; such men as Ignatius, Polycarp, Irenæus, Justin Martyr, Tertullian, Origen, Jerome, Chrysostom, Cyril, and many others, whom he could quote with great ease and fluency on all questions of theological discussion. I can not state with certainty that he was a regular graduate of any of our colleges, but he was well versed in the principles of a good scholastic education. His language was always ornate and classical, and his style, both in the pulpit and in social conversation, was scholarly, chaste, and perspicuous. He rarely indulged in anecdote or repartee. Weightier matters occupied his mind. He was a man of enlarged charity and benevolence, and he everywhere drew about him men of intellectual and refined tastes of all denominations and professions.

During the summer of 1829 his health began to

decline, being the result of two prime causes—overtaxed labors and malarial poison, which he had probably contracted while in the Wabash region and in the malarial districts of White River, which at that early day in Indiana were the great hot-beds of fever and its kindred diseases. He was compelled, therefore, to ask of the Conference, at the close of that year, a superannuated relation. This was a sad stroke to him and to the whole Conference. He, however, remained but one year in this relation. His ardent love for the ministry could not admit of rest, and he accepted a call about the middle of the year 1830 to Terre Haute, where our Church was struggling, under adverse circumstances, to establish herself against many oppositions. He entered with zeal upon his labors in that city, and by the close of the year had succeeded in making many valuable accessions to our Church there, both in the number and quality of the membership, and in other elements of prosperity. There being a universal desire for his return to the station the ensuing year (1831), he was placed on the supernumerary list, and returned accordingly by the Conference. To this, however, he consented against his better judgment, feeling himself inadequate to the labor expected at his hands. Though feeble in health, he did the work of an effective man, not counting his life dear unto himself if he could be instrumental in the salvation of souls. He had a year of prosperity. The Church was greatly revived and enlarged under his faithful pastoral and pulpit labors; so that, in fact, he became the father and almost the founder of the Methodist Episcopal Church in Terre Haute, having brought it to a higher platform of intelligence and respectability than it had ever attained before. But his labors in that miasmatic region, in his enfeebled condition, were too heavy for him, and he again sank under them. At the close of the year he started to meet the Conference, which that year met in Indianapolis, but had proceeded only twelve miles when he was struck down with a severe attack of malarial fever, and was compelled to stop at the house of his faithful friend, Father Barnes, and, after lingering eleven days in extreme pain and languishment, he closed his life and labors together. From the first he had but little hope of recovery, but his joy and peace in Christ were unshaken, and he said to his wife and others: "The religion which I have preached and enjoyed has sustained me through life, has comforted me in many afflictions, and now enables me to triumph in death." Noble words these, and he sent them to Conference as a message and token to his brethren in the ministry. He was conveyed back, I think, after death for burial at Terre Haute; but after remaining there for several years, his remains were brought to Indianapolis for final interment, and deposited in the old cemetery near the eastern gate of the entrance, where they await the resurrection of the just. His funeral sermon was preached by Rev. John Strange before the Conference on Sabbath, together with that of Rev. James Bankson, a young man of learning and promise, who also died that year. That solemn service closed, also, the public preaching of Brother Strange, who, in about a year from that time, oined his beloved Edwin in the promised Canaan of rest. The text was from Daniel xii, 3: "They that be wise shall shine as the brightness of the firmament, and they that turn many to righteousness as the stars forever and ever." It was a most impressive and solemn occasion.

Though Edwin Ray died young in years and young in the ministry, hundreds shall rise up in the day of final reckoning and call him blessed. No less than three ministers among the living and dead in Indiana call him their spiritual father, and several chapels of public worship bear his honored name. One of these is in this city (Indianapolis), and on it God has poured forth during this year a great and signal baptism of power as if to pepetuate the memory of his faithful servant. I have always felt that the death of one so young, so good, and so useful as Edwin Ray was one of the mysteries of Providence which we may not understand now, but shall know hereafter. When we recount the names of the glorious men who have left the militant Church here and joined the Church triumphant above, it adds a deeper sadness to earth but a brighter glory to heaven. The courteous Ray, the eloquent Strange, the earnest Griffith, the shrewd and laborious Armstrong, the patriarchal Bishop Roberts, the statesman-like Ames, the heroic Havens, the weeping and polite Ruter, the learned Wiley, the strong, pathetic Eddy, the legal Brenton, the fatherly Thompson, the evangelic Hargrave, the sweet-spirited and thoughtful Beswick, the magnetic and resistless Berry, the bold and aggressive Jones, the incisive and metaphysical Oglesby, and many others like them, once princes in the army of faith, but nerveless and silent now. We ask, is this the end of man? is this the extinguishment of faith, and hope, and love? O, no! All these died in faith of a better life. What a galaxy of bright stars! What a rich cluster in the crown of the Redeemer!

REV. JAMES ARMSTRONG.[*]

Rev. James Armstrong was a native of Ireland, and was brought to America when but a child. He was converted when about seventeen years of age, and attached himself to the Methodist Church in the city of Philadelphia. He was licensed to preach in the city of Baltimore in 1812. He emigrated to Indiana in 1821, and in the fall of the same year joined the itinerant connection, in which he continued an able and efficient minister till the close of life, which occurred at his own residence, in La Porte County, on the 12th of September, 1834. Of him, Hon. R. W. Thompson says, in his "Fallen Heroes of Indiana Methodism:" "Armstrong was a man of immense power—strong, logical, and conclusive. He threw his whole soul into his work; and if, sometimes, he was not altogether precise in his style, yet at others he seemed almost moved by inspiration, so completely were his words expressive of his correct thoughts. When he intended to strike a hard blow, he never failed to make it terrific, shivering the helmet of whatsoever adversary dared, in his presence, to assail the citadel of Christianity." (Indiana Methodist Con-

---

[*] From "Indiana Methodism," by Rev. F. C. Holliday, D. D.

vention, 1870.) Mr. Armstrong's ministry was very successful. God gave him many seals to his ministry in Indiana; and honored him, as an instrument in his hands, with laying deep and broad the foundations of the Church in this new and growing State.

REV. NEHEMIAH B. GRIFFITH.

Rev. Nehemiah B. Griffith* was a native of the State of New York. In the eighteenth year of his age he came, with his father's family, to the State of Ohio. When about eighteen years of age he was led to Christ, and into the Methodist Church, chiefly through the instrumentality of Rev. W H. Raper. He entered the ministry in 1832, and continued, with great zeal and efficiency, until the day of his death, which occurred in St. Joseph County, August 22, 1834. Mr. Griffith was a very successful preacher. He was a clear doctrinal preacher; and he preached the doctrines of the Bible so practically and experimentally, and withal with such an unction, that his ministry was generally attended with extensive revivals of religion. His last words were: "Sweet Heaven, I am coming!"

Griffith was, at one time, a colleague of Hargrave.—W P. H.

REV WILLIAM BEAUCHAMP.*

"During the preceding year, the Church in Indiana had suffered the loss of one of her ablest ministers, Rev. William Beauchamp, presiding elder of Indiana District, Missouri Conference, which event took place at Paoli, Orange County, Indiana, October, 1824, in the fifty-third year of his age." Mr. Beauchamp was a native of Delaware; was converted in early life, and in 1794 joined the itinerancy. His first appointments were: Alleghany Circuit, Pittsburg, New York, and Boston. He located in 1811. In 1815 he removed to Chillicothe, Ohio, and took the editorial charge of the *Western Christian Monitor*—the only periodical at that time in our Church. He discharged his editorial duties with conspicuous ability. Mr. Beauchamp had previously published a volume of "Essays on the Truth of Christianity," a work of considerable merit. In 1817 he removed to Mt. Carmel, Illinois, and superintended the formation of a new settlement. In 1822 he again entered the traveling connection, and was stationed in the city of St. Louis. In 1823 he was appointed presiding elder of Indiana District, which included Charlestown, Flatrock, Blue River, Bloomington, Honey Creek, Vincennes, Patoka, Mt. Sterling, Corydon, Indianapolis, and Eel River—eleven large circuits—embracing one-third of the territory of the State of Indiana. He was, the same year, a delegate to the General Confer-

---

*He was Hargrave's first presiding elder. (See Autobiographical Sketch, page 34.)—W. P. H.

ence, which met at Baltimore; and such was the impression made by him upon the members of that body, that he lacked but two votes of being elected to the episcopal office. Had it not been for the fact that so large a portion of his ministerial life had been spent out of the itinerancy, his name would doubtless have honored the history of our episcopacy. On his return to his district he was seized with an affection of the liver, and, after suffering for about six weeks, fell asleep in Jesus, in the full prospect of a glorious immortality

Mr. Beauchamp was one of nature's noblemen—a man of true greatness. He was often styled the "Demosthenes of the West." His manner was plain, and his style easy and natural. His sermons made a lasting impression. His standard of Christian character was high. Holiness was his favorite theme. When holding forth the promises and invitations of the Gospel, there was a gentleness and tenderness in his manner and in the tones of his voice that was sure to touch the sympathies of his hearers; but when he became argumentative and discussed doctrinal points, and especially when he denounced dangerous errors, his voice would become elevated, his whole system nerved, and the tone of his voice and the flash of his keen eye would startle his hearers like peals of thunder. On one occasion the force of his eloquence was fully demonstrated. It was on a subject of controversy. His antagonist, who had sat and listened for some time to his arguments—too powerful for him to answer—began to look as if the voice which he now heard came from another world through the shadow of a man. He arose—apparently with an intention to leave the house—but being overcome, he staggered, caught by a railing, and fell into his seat; and there sat, overwhelmed and confounded, until the discourse closed, when he quietly left the house. The death of such a minister is deeply felt; but God watches over his Church, and "the gates of hell shall not prevail against it."*

REV WILLIAM CRAVENS.†

William Cravens entered the itinerancy in connection with the Missouri Conference, and was appointed to Charlestown Circuit as junior preacher with Calvin W Ruter. Cravens spent his ministry in Indiana. He, too, was a man of remarkable physical strength and undaunted courage. A Virginian by birth, he was an uncompromising enemy of human slavery. He had sought a home in the "Northwest Territory" that he might be free from the blight and curse of the peculiar institution. Mr. Cravens had been a local preacher for several years in Virginia previous to his immigration to Indiana, and had ac-

---

*The above sketch from "Holliday's Indiana Methodism."

†This narrative is taken from Dr. Holliday's "Indiana Methodism." There seems to be some uncertainty as to the exact year when this eminent man entered the ministry. Dr. Holliday states that he and Havens began the same year. But there is a discrepancy of a year in his statement of the beginning of the ministerial life of the latter. (Compare pages 54 and 272, "Indiana Methodism.") Singularly enough Dr. J. C. Smith does not give the date of Havens's entry in the ministry. We incline to the year 1821 (in the absence of the bound Minutes).—W. P. H.

quired great notoriety from the faithful and fearless manner in which he denounced vice in all its forms. He had a special abhorrence for the sins of drunkenness and Negro slavery. Against these he was accustomed to declaim with a directness and force that made the guilty quail before him, even on slave territory and in the aristocratic parts of old Virginia. While residing in Virginia, Mr. Cravens had an infidel neighbor by the name of "F.," who was a slaveholder. Cravens had labored in vain to convert him, either to anti-slavery principles, or to the truths of Christianity. At length Mr. F was taken seriously ill, and it soon became apparent that he would likely die. The near approach of death shook his faith in his infidel principles, and he became deeply concerned for his soul's salvation. At length he sent a servant with a request that Mr. Cravens would call and see him. Judging correctly as to the cause of the invitation, he hastened immediately to the home of the sick man, whom he found dangerously ill, and deeply distressed on account of his sins.

"O!" said the sick man, "I am glad to see you. I want you to pray for me, and tell me what I must do to be saved."

"Ah, Mr. F., I thought it would come to this. What have you done with your Negroes?"

"I have provided for them in my will," said Mr. F. "I have divided them among my children, as I wish them to remain in the family."

"I can not pray for you," said Cravens. "God will never have mercy on you until you are willing to do justly. You will never get religion until you set your Negroes free." So saying, Cravens returned home. But in a short time another messenger came for him.

"Massa wants to see you immediately," was the substance of the request.

The sick man felt that his condition was a perilous one. Death was rapidly approaching, and the preacher, in whose honesty and faithfulness he had full confidence, had refused to pray for him. He needed mercy, and yet he had failed to exercise it. The will was called for and altered, and the minister again sent for. On his arrival he said:

"Well, Mr. F., how is it now?"

"Mr. Cravens, I want you to pray with me, and tell me how I can be saved."

"What have you done with your slaves?" said Cravens.

"I have altered my will," said Mr. F., "and have provided for their emancipation."

"I will pray for you now," said Cravens, "and more than that, God will have mercy on you too."

In answer to their united prayers, God did bless him with an assurance of pardon and a bright hope of heaven. Christian civilization is deeply indebted to the chivalrous and indefatigable labors of such moral heroes as James Havens and William Cravens. They were born leaders; and having that sort of magnetism that attached others to them, they were a tower of strength in any cause. They were just the men to lay the foundations of society in a new country; they were men of comprehensive views; they occupied no doubtful positions, and gave no uncertain utterances on questions of doctrine or morals.* Their style was perspicuous, if not polished, and their dauntless courage and cheerful self-sacrifice exerted an inspiring effect upon their co-laborers, especially upon their junior brethren.

REV GEORGE LOCKE.†

George Locke was born in Cannonstown, Pennsylvania, on the 8th of June, 1799. His parents were David and Nancy Locke. His great-grandfather and grandfather were both clergymen in the Church of England, and his father was educated in reference to the ministry of the Presbyterian Church, which design, however, he abandoned, and engaged in teaching. The mother of George was a lady of superior endowments, and a pious member of the Presbyterian Church. The family came to Kentucky in 1798, and settled in Mason County, but two years afterward removed to Shelbyville.

Young Locke was converted in a revival that occurred under the labors of a local preacher by the name of Edward Talbott. In 1817 he was licensed to exhort, and shortly after to preach. At the session of the Tennesse Conference for 1818 he was admitted on trial and appointed to Little River Circuit, and the next year to the Powell's Valley In 1820 he was sent to the Bowling Green Circuit, as the col-

---

*See incident related in Hargrave's Autobiographical sketch, page 46 of this volume.—W. H. P.

†From "Indiana Methodism," by Rev. F C. Holliday, D. D.

league of Benjamin Malone, and with Charles Holliday as his presiding elder. During the year he was married to Miss Elizabeth R. McReynolds, a lady of fine cultivation and deep piety, and belonging to one of the best Methodist families in the State; and the following year he located. But not satisfied in a local relation, his name reappears the next year in the list of itinerants, from which it is never after to be stricken until he is called to his reward. His fields of labor in Kentucky, after his return to the Conference, were Jefferson and Hartford Circuits, on the latter of which he remained two years. Beyond the Ohio River the country was filling up with remarkable rapidity. Not only from Virginia and Tennessee, but also from Kentucky, hundreds of families, attracted by the cheap and fertile lands of Indiana and Illinois, had sought homes within their rich domain. Mr. Locke, believing that a wider field for usefulness presented itself in this new country, in the autumn of 1825 requested to be transferred to the Illinois Conference, then embracing the States of Illinois and Indiana. His first appointment was to Corydon Circuit, where also he continued the following year. In 1827 he was appointed to Charlestown Circuit. His labors on Corydon Circuit had been crowned with signal success, but on Charlestown Circuit he was privileged to witness one of the most remarkable awakenings with which Southern Indiana had ever been visited. He remained, however, on this circuit but about six months. The General Conference of 1828 elected Charles Holliday, then presiding elder of the Wabash District, Agent for the Book Concern at Cincinnati, and George Locke was appointed to fill the vacancy on the district. This district at the time extended from Shawneetown, on the Ohio River, up the Wabash, on both sides, above Terre Haute, some twenty or thirty miles, embracing an area of territory in Indiana and Illinois of at least a hundred miles from east and west, by two hundred miles from north to south. He traveled this district for four years, receiving much of the time scarcely enough to pay traveling expenses. His wife, who had been engaged in teaching from the time he re-entered the traveling connection, supported the family, and rejoiced that, in so doing, she could enable her husband to preach the unsearchable riches of Christ. His slender constitution gave way under the labors and exposures endured upon that district, and though he completed the usual term of service, it was about the last of his effective labor.

Sometime in the winter of 1831-2—one of the severest winters ever known in the West—Mr. Locke was returning home after an absence of several weeks. When he reached the Wabash River he found it gorged with ice. He and another traveler waited at the house of the ferryman three or four days for a change in the weather or in the condition of the ice; but no change came, and as they were impatient to proceed on their journey, they resolved on breaking a channel through the ice for the ferry-boat. Accordingly, the next morning, they addressed themselves to the work with all diligence, and at sunset found themselves within a rod or two of the opposite shore. Mr. Locke was standing on the bow of the boat, fatigued and tremulous, breaking the ice with a rail. Striking a piece with all the force he could command, it suddenly gave way, not making the resistance he had anticipated, and precipitated him into the river. As he rose, and was just drifting under the ice, his companions rescued him. Though the shock was a fearful one, and he was not only thoroughly drenched but thoroughly chilled also, he resolved to persevere in his work ; and actually did persevere till the shore was reached. He then mounted his horse and rode ten miles to the next house; but when he reached there he was frozen to his saddle, and speechless. The horse stopped of his own accord, and the family coming to the door and perceiving his condition, lifted him from his horse, and cared for him very kindly until, after a day or two, he was able to resume his journey.

Mrs. Locke had, for days, been anxiously awaiting the return of her husband, and finally yielded to the appalling conviction that he was frozen to death. A friend who was with her tried to assuage her grief by inducing her to look more upon the hopeful side; but she refused to be comforted. When he suggested to her that he should not be surprised even if she should see her husband that very night, she besought him not to trifle with her feelings by endeavoring thus to make her credit an impossibility. He scarcely had time to assure her that he was far from trifling with her feelings, when the latch of the gate was lifted, the well-known footstep of her husband was heard, and instantly she was well-nigh paralyzed with joy in his arms.

Amidst all his manifold and self-denying labors he never abated his habits of study. He redeemed time, not only for the study of systematic theology, but for general reading. He acquired some knowledge of Greek and Latin, and made considerable proficiency in the higher branches of mathematics. He continued his studies until a few weeks before his death, and had his books brought to him even after he was confined to his bed.

The General Conference of 1832, of which Mr. Locke was a member, divided the Illinois Conference, and constituted a separate Conference of the State of Indiana. In the autumn of that year he was transferred to Indiana, and was returned to Corydon Circuit. Here his health became much reduced, which led him to remove to New Albany, and engage with his wife in school-teaching.

In the autumn of 1833 he took a superannuated relation, and, on the 15th of July, 1834, he died. He never recovered from the cold contracted from falling into the Wabash River. He died of consumption, after much patient suffering, and in the full confidence of being welcomed into the joys of the Lord. His last words, which were uttered with his last breath, were: "Glory! glory! glory!" *

---

* Sprague's "Annals," p. 610.

REV JAMES HAVENS.*

Few names are more familiar in Methodist circles in Indiana than that of James Havens. He entered the traveling connection in the old Ohio Conference in 1821. He came to Indiana a few years later, and settled in Rush County, two miles west of Rushville, where he raised a large family, and where the family continued to reside until the children were all grown. Notwithstanding his family were located, Mr. Havens was emphatically an itinerant, traveling large circuits and districts, and often absent from home for weeks at a time. Mr. Havens's early education was defective, and he could barely read when he joined the Conference; but he had an energy that no obstacles could break down, a perseverance that never abated until its end was reached, and an ability for both mental and physical exertion that enabled him to accomplish what, to most men, would have been impossible. He arose to a front rank in the ministry, and made an impression upon general society that has been abiding. His knowledge of human nature was wonderful. He read the character of those with whom he came into contact by a sort of intuition, and he rarely ever made a mistake. His reproofs were scathing; and in the early settlement of Indiana he was for many years emphatically a terror to evil-doers. The stories of his encounters with the rowdies and roughs that were wont to disturb the early camp-meetings, and his uniform victories over them, would

---

* From "Indiana Methodism," by Rev. F. C. Holliday, D. D.—R.

constitute a volume of thrilling interest. And, although fearless as a lion in the presence of danger, he was, nevertheless, a man of the tenderest sympathies and warmest friendships. The results of his labors are seen in the social order and the general respect for religion which everywhere prevails throughout our State, as well as in the multitudes that were converted to God through his ministry The fathers labored, and we are entered into their labors. Mr. Havens secured a good general education, and was well read in theology and Church history He was a delegate to several sessions of the General Conference. His sermons were well prepared, though never written. When asked why he did not use the pen in preparing for the pulpit, his reply was: " Do n't you think the devil can read writing? I do n't intend that he shall either forestall me or flank me." During a large part of his ministry he filled the office of presiding elder, and exerted a commanding influence, both among preachers and people.

REV. ALLEN WILEY.*

Allen Wiley entered the ministry in 1818 in the Ohio Conference, but Indiana was the theater of his ministerial labors; and from 1818 down to 1848, the time of his death, he was closely identified with the interests of the Church in Indiana; and he, perhaps more than any other man, molded the character of Indiana Methodism. He looked more to the future

* From "Indiana Methodism."—R.

than most of his associates; and he organized and planned and worked for the future. His literary attainments were remarkable for the times in which he lived. He was a good Latin and Greek scholar, and everywhere recognized as a profound theologian. As a minister, his sermons, while presiding elder, made a profound impression. They were usually lengthy, seldom on the Sabbath less than an hour and a half in length, but always listened to with interest. He was one of the projectors of Indiana Asbury University, and early saw the necessity for denominational schools. He was a remarkable student, and retained his habits of study to the close of life.

REV. CALVIN W. RUTER.[*]

Calvin W Ruter was admitted on trial into the traveling connection in the old Ohio Conference, in 1818. His ministeral labors were spent in Indiana. Upon the organization of the Missouri Conference he was a member of that body, as also of the Illinois Conference while it included the work in Indiana. During his long ministry he was several times placed either on the supernumerary or the superannuated list, but with returning health was always found in the active itinerant ranks. He was for many years secretary of his Conference. He was an early and zealous friend of learning, and was one of the founders of Indiana Asbury University. He was a superior preacher, and one of the honored fathers of Indiana Methodism.

[*] From "Indiana Methodism."

REV. AUGUSTUS EDDY.*

Augustus Eddy was licensed to preach in 1821, near Xenia, Ohio. He was admitted on trial in the old Ohio Conference, at its session in Zanesville, in 1824; and here commenced that grand itinerant career which continued to the close of life without a blot upon his character.

His first appointment was to the old Miami Circuit. He continued to travel large circuits till 1831, when he was appointed presiding elder of the Scioto District, where he was continued two years. He then traveled two years on the Columbus District. In 1835 he was stationed in Cincinnati, Western Charge, with Christie and Hamline as co-laborers. In 1836 he was transferred to the Indiana Conference, and stationed in Indianapolis. His next appointment was Indianapolis District; then Whitewater District. He was next stationed at Wesley Chapel, Madison; then presiding elder of Madison District; and from Madison District he was appointed in charge of Lawrenceburg District. In 1848 he was transferred to the Ohio Conference, and stationed at Chillicothe. He was successively stationed at Hamilton and Xenia, and was then appointed presiding elder on West Cincinnati District. In 1855 he was transferred to North Indiana Conference, and stationed in Richmond. His next appointment was Indianapolis District, where he remained four years. He was then stationed at Ko-

---

* From "Indiana Methodism."—R.

komo, but a vacancy occurring on the Richmond District, he was appointed in charge of it, and served until the middle of the ensuing August, when he was appointed post chaplain in the United States army, at Indianapolis; which position he continued to fill for about four years. He was then returned to the Richmond District, where he labored for three years. He was then appointed presiding elder on Anderson District, where he continued to labor until smitten down with disease.

He closed his active work at Greenfield, where he held his last quarterly meeting, January 15 and 16, 1870. His disease was malignant erysipelas, which terminated fatally on the 9th of February, 1870.

He was permitted to die at home, surrounded by his children and friends, in full possession of his mental faculties, and in the triumphs of Christian faith.

Mr. Eddy was an instructive and entertaining preacher; his social qualities were fine; he was happy at home and delighted in the society of his friends.

He was three times elected to a seat in the General Conference. His life was grand and heroic. In the vigor of early manhood he buckled on the gospel armor, and he never laid it off. His manly voice was a trumpet-blast that gave no uncertain sound; and when his Captain called he was at the post of duty, ready to obey the summons. The workman is removed, but his work remains.

REV. AARON WOOD, D. D.

Rev. Aaron Wood, D. D., of the Northwest Indiana Conference, was born in Pendleton, Virginia, October 15, 1802, and died at his home in Yountsville, Indiana, August 20, 1887, having attained the age of eighty-four years, ten months, and five days. He was brought to Ohio, by his parents when three years of age, and united with the Methodist Episcopal Church at the age of sixteen years.

At the age of eighteen years he became an exhorter in the Church, and was licensed to preach by John Strange, on Mad River Circuit, August 24, 1822. He was recommended by the Quarterly Conference in due form to the traveling connection, and was received on trial into the Ohio Conference the fall of the same year. His official record is as follows: 1822, London Circuit, Ohio; 1823, Connersville, Indiana; 1824, was received into full connection in the Ohio Conference at Zanesville, ordained deacon by Bishop Roberts, and appointed to Madison, Indiana; 1825, Vincennes; 1826, Bloomington, ordained elder; 1827-8, Mount Carmel, Illinois; 1829, Corydon; 1830, Vincennes; 1831-33, located, taught school at Mount Carmel and preached on Sabbaths—made necessary to support his family; 1834-35, readmitted, and presiding elder of Vincennes District; 1836, agent Indiana Asbury (now DePauw) University; 1837, New Albany; 1838-42, South Bend District; 1843, La Porte District; 1844, Lafayette District; 1845-46, agent Indiana Asbury University; 1847-51, agent American Bible

Society; 1852-53, Terre Haute Station; 1854-57, Terre Haute District; 1858-60, Indianapolis District; 1861-2, agent Indiana Asbury University; 1863-4, Perryville; 1865, Ninth Street, Lafayette; 1866-67, Michigan City; 1868-70, chaplain Northern State's prison; 1871, agent Preachers' Aid Society, and supply on Argos Circuit; 1872-73, Delphi; 1874-75, Williamsport; 1876, Stockwell; 1877-78, Dayton; 1879-81, chaplain Soldiers' Orphans' Home, Knightstown; 1882-85, Yountsville.

In the fall of 1885, at the session of his Conference at Valparaiso, Indiana, he made the following request:

"DEARLY BELOVED BROTHERS,—At the close of the eighty-third year of my natural life, the seventy-second of my spiritual life, and the sixty-third of my itinerant life as a Methodist preacher, I respectfully ask the Conference to grant me the superannuated relation. Respectfully, AARON WOOD."

The request was complied with promptly, and the Conference joined in singing, as Methodist preachers can sing when their hearts are touched by such an exhibition of royal heroism as presented by this venerable man of God, in his graceful surrender of the furbished weapons of the active itinerant for the unpretentious sling and shield of the retired warrior. In the spontaneous strains of praise that blended in harmonious numbers, the fountains of love and immortality were unsealed, and old age, and severe sacrifices, and toil and sufferings were submerged by the rising tide of joy. It was a scene of victory over the forces of depression and unbelief, won grandly on one of the chosen battle-fields of these enemies to a genial old age; and none waved brighter plumes than the retiring veteran, who, even in his surrender of the itinerant field to others, gave a farewell shout that stormed the citadel of despondency and gloom, and gave freedom to the prisoners.

Since his retirement from the active ministry he lived at Yountsville with his estimable wife, loved, honored, and respected by all who knew him. And yet, even in the fullness of his advanced years, he could not be restrained from attending Conferences, revisiting his old-time battle-fields, and preaching as he had strength. Only a few months before his death his voice rang out in Meharry Hall, DePauw University, in strains of wonderful vigor and cheer.

He summed up his long career of active work thus: Fourteen years on districts, fourteen years on stations, thirteen years on circuits, twelve years in agencies, six years in chaplaincies, and three years in teaching and preaching on the Sabbath—sixty-two years in the active ministry.

He was honored with the title of Doctor of Divinity by the Indiana State University, without his seeking, though he evidently enjoyed the compliment (?). He was a member of five General Conferences—in 1840, at Baltimore; in 1844, at New York; in 1864, Philadelphia; in 1868, Chicago; in 1876, Baltimore. He was also elected reserve delegate five times, showing the esteem in which the Conference held him.

Dr. Wood was twice married—first to Miss Laura Beauchamp, daughter of Rev W Beauchamp. Three children were born to them—two sons and a daughter, when the mother died, in 1835. The three children are now dead. In 1839 he was married to Miss Maria Hitt, of Urbana, Ohio, who survives him in feebleness of body, but in the spirit of Christian resignation. She has been an efficient leader in the missionary work of the Church.

Of this latter union there were seven children—six sons and one daughter—only three of whom survive: Thomas Wood, D. D., superintendent of missions in South America; John S. Wood, M. D., a physician, located at Charna, New Mexico; and Joseph R. Wood, A. M., formerly missionary in South America, but now traveling in the Northwest Indiana Conference. The last two named were present at their father's death, as was also Professor Jesse M. Hitt, a nephew and adopted son of the deceased.

Dr. Wood died as he had lived, self-possessed, hopeful, and satisfied. Of the change coming upon him, he said: "I am ready." Friends at Youutsville, Crawfordsville, and Lafayette vied with each other in kindly attentions to the honored hero. The remains were interred in Springvale Cemetery, Lafayette. There were about thirty preachers, from afar and near, present at the funeral. "For he was a good man, and full of the Holy Ghost and of faith; and much people was added unto the Lord."

Of Brother Wood, as a man and a preacher, little need be said here. His life was contemporaneous with the history of Indiana, and his ministry covered the entire history of Methodism in the State. He personally knew the leading men of both Church and State, and he had a rich fund of incidents and anecdotes of their characters and deeds. It is doubtful whether there is another person living possessed of an equal knowledge of the men and history of the State of Indiana for the past sixty years. He had a retentive memory, and was a walking cyclopedia of events which occurred in his life-time; was the historian of Indiana Methodism, and could recall names and incidents of years gone by with the utmost clearness. He was among the pioneer preachers of Ohio, Indiana, and Illinois, when the settlements were few and far between; when the Indians lingered and were jostled upon the advancing wave of Christian civilization, and disputed their rights with the onward tide of white settlers. The Methodist itinerancy at that time meant threading forests and prairies on horseback, by blazed trees and buffalo-paths, wading swamps, swimming rivers, and exposure to heat and cold, hunger and want. Like most of his class in those days, Dr. Wood was a splendid horseback-rider. He read, studied, prayed, and sang in the saddle, sometimes starting herds of browsing deer by preaching and shouting through the woods on his long rides. A happy, heroic class of preachers were our pious fathers! Some of these early habits never left Brother Wood. Traveling the Yountsville Circuit on horseback, through all the winter storms, when over eighty years of age, was a rebuke to the softness of some of our young preachers.

He was a man of strong native mind and fair education. He gathered knowledge from books and contact with men and the outer world, was always eager to read the last books published, and kept abreast with the times to the last. Though an octogenarian, he was still a student, fresh and vigorous. He was open, frank, and honest, and, like most candid men, he did not suspect others of dishonorable motives. He was no schemer for place and position, but accepted cheerfully what at the time seemed proper, without fearing the loss of rank or position. He was of a cheerful spirit, never despondent, always hopeful, and never worried; was true as steel to his convictions, to his friends, his Church, and his country. Upon his moral character, during all his long and successful life, there was not a blot nor stain. His name is like "ointment poured forth" in thousands of households in the wide West. As a preacher he was earnest and effective, rather than ornate; dealt less in rhetoric and logic than in facts and Bible-truths; was familiar with Scripture, Wesleyan theology, and Church polity, and could defend his Church against all forms of assault. He had a strong, clear voice, and spoke with readiness and ease to himself, never ranted, and rarely shouted. He was emphatically a preacher, rather than a writer. His letters were in fewest words and to the point. A prince in Israel has fallen!—*Conference Memoir*

REV. DANIEL DE MOTTE.*

It has been said by an eminent political economist that the man who causes two spears of grass to grow where only one had grown before, is a benefactor to the race. This saying is beautiful in theory and true

---

*From "Early Methodism in Indiana," by Rev. J. C. Smith, D. D.

in practice. We see it often verified and illustrated among men. The reverse of this is also true. Many men not only do not produce the additional spear of grass, but even destroy the one which they found springing from the earth. These are cumberers of God's husbandry.

He whose name heads this article was an eminent example of the first-named class. His life was a benediction to the world. Thousands were benefited by his life of active benevolence, and thousands more are still being blessed by the influence that follows him. "Being dead, he yet speaketh." He caused life and freshness to spring up along every pathway in which he trod. Nature seems to have designed him for activities. Being of a "sanguine-nervous" temperament, he could not be still. With an active mind and an independent will, he was no slave to the conventionalities of society, unless these were founded on principles of practical usefulness and common sense. He chose sometimes to be singular, rather than obsequious to the despotism of fashion. Dealing trenchant blows at the fallacies of fashionable society, he chose methods of his own—methods in his way of living, of thought, of preaching, of travel, and general modes of life; though not so unique in any of these as to give offense, yet enough so to show his independence of them all.

I remember a specimen or two, which will illustrate my meaning. When I traveled the Crawfordsville District, in the summer of 1842, he traveled in the bounds of the district, and I often enjoyed the pleasure of his society. I remember distinctly a sermon which I heard him preach, during that year, on the text: "Train up a child in the way he should go, and when he is old he will not depart from it." It was wholly original. He said: "Now I am not going to talk to you to-day about questions of finance, how to get rich, or how to raise stock, but how to raise your children; not how to make them Cupids or demigods, as though they were descended from a race of fairies; but, being descended from flesh and blood, how to train them for usefulness here, and for happiness hereafter. In the first place, permit me to say that your children, though beautiful little creatures, are sinful and depraved like ourselves, and need severe discipline, and it can not be too soon applied. Their bodies are depraved, and need something more than sweetmeats and fine clothes to make them healthy and good-looking, and acceptable to God and to man. They need the elements of what I shall term *physical Christianity;* that is, the brush and comb, and profuse applications of soap and water and the crash-towel, and solid food, and often, perchance, the birch rod; for the *wise man* hath said: 'Foolishness is bound up in the heart of a child, but the rod of correction bringeth it out of him.' The rod is often more efficacious than medical nostrums in family government.

"Three-fourths of the urchins of society need these physical elements far more than they need school-houses just now, and lessons in algebra and *belles lettres.* Many of the girls, just now blooming into womanhood, need lessons in the kitchen how to make good bread, more than they do lessons on the piano and from the French dancing-master. The piano is good, and the French master is polite and good enough in his place; but common sense is better, and to know how to be useful is best of all."

Then, appealing to the young gentlemen present, he said: "Perhaps some of you are beginning to look around for suitable wives. Let me present you with two examples, and then make your choice. Here is a very pretty girl, neatly attired in silks, pearls about her neck, her fingers all sparkling with diamonds and gold, sitting in the parlor. The piano is before her, and she is thumping it in the most approved style of art. Beautiful music seems to be proceeding from the instrument. But what are the words of her song? Listen: 'O, what is home without a mother?' O, what a pious sentiment that! What a noble daughter! you say. But now let us turn away our eyes for a moment from this enchanting scene, and look to another apartment of this *home*. Who is that pale, feeble, care-worn woman there, sweating and toiling over the wash-tub, with one or two fretful children teasing her life away? Why, that is the mother the young girl was singing about! Sure enough, what would that home be without such a mother? Very soon filth and rags would cover it. Now, I ask, would not that mother and that home be much happier if that daughter would cultivate more the stern duties of the culinary department and the wash-tub, and think less of the piano and her French master and the drawing-room? Is this the girl of your choice? Nay, verily.

"Now let us present you with another example— a woman trained in the right way. She is described by a master in language and in human nature. Hear what he says: 'Who can find a virtuous woman? for her price is above rubies. She secketh wool and flax, and worketh willingly with her hands. She riseth also while it is yet night, and giveth meat to her household. With the fruit of her hands she planteth a vineyard. She girdeth her loins with strength, and strengtheneth her arms. She stretcheth out her hand to the poor and to the needy. She layeth her hands to the spindle, and her hands hold the distaff. Strength and honor are her clothing, and she shall rejoice in time to come. Many daughters have done nobly, but she excels them all.' Now," said he, "*this* is a *wife;* the other class are painted dolls. 'Look on this picture, then on that,' and choose between them." That was a bold and fearless sermon; but to have appreciated it fully, you should have heard it and witnessed the irony often expressed in his eye and voice.

From the Minutes of the Northwest Indiana Conference, of which he was a member at the time of his death, we extract the following from the report of the Committee on Memoirs: "Brother De Motte was born in Kentucky, March 19, 1789, and being left an orphan by the death of his father while he was very young, had a hard struggle to earn a support for his widowed mother, himself, and other members of the family. He was converted in the twenty-eighth year of his age, and witnessed a good confession to the close of his life. From the altar of prayer, where he received first the evidence of pardoned sin, he went directly to his home, and at once put aside the glasses and bottles, and placed a family Bible in their stead, and began family prayer. The next morning a neighbor, calling early and expecting the usual glass of 'bitters,' which was everywhere indulged in in those days, was amazed to be asked by Mr. De Motte to join in family prayer. The reader may imagine the integrity and firmness of moral principle displayed in this act. It was characteristic of the man in all his after life. Shortly after his conversion he was licensed to exhort, and then to preach as a local preacher, which offices he discharged with acceptability and usefulness. He removed from Kentucky to this State, and settled in Parke County in 1831; in 1835 was admitted to the Indiana Annual Conference as a traveling preacher, and for eighteen years cheerfully and faithfully filled the appointments assigned him, generally remaining two years consecutively in each pastoral charge, which was the full term then allowed by the Discipline. This shows that he was useful and acceptable in every place. In 1853 he was appointed by the Board of Trustees of Indiana Asbury University to act as a general agent to solicit and collect funds for the institution, in which capacity he continued for nine years, till the agency was abolished. His long continuance in this office shows his efficiency in this department of the service. Indeed, he was a most active and successful solicitor and collector; often exhibiting not only great industry and courage, but skillful diplomacy in allaying prejudices and healing disputes, which of necessity occur in the fiscal operations of the Church.

After the expiration of his college agency he was appointed by the managers of the Preachers' Aid Society of the Northwestern Indiana Conference to act as their agent, which office he discharged faithfully and efficiently for three years. At the close of this service he received a superannuated relation to the Conference, in which he continued nine years; thus giving him forty years' service as an itinerant minister in the varied relations of preacher in charge of circuits, college agent, agent of Preachers' Aid Society, and superannuate. "He was a man," says the report of the committee, "of rare judgment, large endowment of common sense, and of cheerful trust in God, and goodwill towards mankind, which all admired who knew him."

His first wife, the mother of his children, was an amiable Christian lady, plain in manners, of excellent understanding and sound piety, domestic in her habits, and patient in the endurance of the privations and hardships which wives of the early itinerant preachers were compelled to encounter. Having raised several sons and daughters, who revere her memory and bless her for her maternal love and care, and served her generation, at length she fell asleep in the maturity of age and in the triumph of Christian faith.

In 1867, Brother De Motte married a second wife, an estimable lady, worthy of him, and esteemed by his children. At an advanced age she still survives him.

The death of Father De Motte occurred February 2, 1875, after a lingering sickness. His end was peace, "calm as summer evenings be." His last words were, "All is well, all is well, blessed Jesus!" How fitting such a death after such active toil and care for the Divine Master! How full of hope the future to the weary pilgrim!

REV. WADE POSEY.

We regret that we have not all the data for our brief sketch of Wade Posey, but we have been unable to obtain them in time for present use. He was born May 10, 1810, and died October 16, 1861, aged fifty-one years. He entered the ministry in 1836. He was the second son of Richard and Frances Posey, elsewhere in this volume shown to have been eminent in the annals of Indiana Methodism. He was consequently a brother-in-law of Richard Hargrave, and between them there existed the utmost fraternal regard; though at the antipodes from each other in point of temperament, yet by that fact only supplementing each other's work the more effectually.

In person Posey was remarkable, as he stood six feet one and one-half inches in height, in young manhood very erect, of fair complexion, weighing about one hundred and seventy-five pounds. Reared on a farm and inured to hard work from his boyhood, he was in early manhood a giant in strength; and there is a tradition at Bruceville, Indiana, where he was raised, that in the old-fashioned art of cradling wheat or other small grain he surpassed all. He was also a splendid axman, and among his other achievements in that line was the clearing and fencing of a farm for John Hull Esq., of Houey Creek Prairie, Indiana.

Here, like Lincoln, he became known as a rail-splitter. This was the last work of the kind which he did, as he there received a call to preach the gospel, having been converted in his boyhood. He conferred not with flesh and blood, but at once joined the old Indiana Conference, and henceforward knew nothing among men save Jesus Christ, and him crucified.

As Wade Posey's manhood was of so marked a type, so his was an earnest Christianity. Like the apostle Paul, he labored first of all to keep his body under. In this regard he was a worthy example for the imitation of the rising generation of preachers. In all his ministerial history, every Friday was kept as a fast-day. This meant total abstinence from breakfast. On that morning he never went to the breakfast-table. How many of us can say as much?

When about twenty-five years of age he married Miss Calista Aligree, of an old Methodist family, a lady of great energy and decision of character, who was doubtless very helpful to him in his life-work. To them were born (so far as known to us) four children—three daughters and a son, the latter of whom died in infancy. The eldest daughter, Mary Frances, was graduated with honor from the Thorntown (Indiana) Academy, and subsequently became the wife of Rev. Fred. Woodcock, formerly of the Southeast Indiana Conference, now of the Southern California Conference. The second daughter, Martha, became Mrs. Champion, of Thorntown, a lovely woman, but died young, leaving two sons and a daughter, the latter of whom did not long survive her. The third daughter, Hattie, is Mrs. Brown, of

Brownsburg, Indiana, the happy wife of a prosperous mechanic.

Wade Posey thus, in all things, measured up to the apostolic standard. In his work for Christ, as in his previous life, he was a "stalwart." If a new church or parsonage was to be built, it was likely that he would be sent to build it. He never stuck in the bark, never flinched at hard work. No work seemed to be hard to him. His industry and heartiness of manner were infectious. With him it was "come boys," and the structure arose—the work was done.

Socially he was a sunbeam. There were few men so genial. He always appeared among the people mounted upon or driving a good horse; and he was always clad in a garb neat and becoming for a Methodist preacher. He was accessible to all, interested in the welfare of all, laboring for the salvation of all. His return for a second year (then the limit) was usually welcomed by his people. As a preacher he was plain and logical, rather than ornate or eloquent; and being a true minister of the gospel, he *spoke with authority.* "The common people heard him gladly." His work was generally accompanied by revival influence. He was one of the "sweet singers in Israel," and in this regard he had a special qualification for a Methodist preacher in those times. We trust the day will never come when our preachers will cease to cultivate gospel song.

Wade Posey was a close student of theology, and a general reader. His library was, for those days, large and well selected; and what time he could honestly redeem from the cares of the pastorate was spent in his library, communing with the fathers of Methodism, who have left so deep an impress upon their sons in the ministry and upon the Church at large. But his reading was not confined to these. He could say with the poet:

> "'Mid books and papers in my study pent,
> If this be exile, sweet is banishment!"

Posey was also a zealous friend of education and of educators—of such men as Simpson, Larrabee, Downey, Wheeler, and others of the faculty of the "Old Asbury University." He used to co-operate effectively with Isaac Owen and Samuel C. Cooper, so long useful and successful agents in building up and endowing that institution. And out of his slender means as a Methodist preacher he purchased a perpetual scholarship in that institution, upon which the writer attended the university for five years; and it will never pass from memory with what evident pleasure he proposed to me (not I to him) that when I got to be old enough to attend college I should have the benefit of his scholarship.

But we must hasten. His splendid physique may have been the indirect cause of his early death. For a number of years his work was in Northern Indiana, where the winters were intensely cold; and in the exuberance of his strength and spirits he, to some extent, disregarded the necessary precautions as to wrapping in encountering the heavy weather. In fact, he used to laugh at Hargrave, who wrapped like a Laplander in the northern winters. At the age of about forty years he suffered a severe attack of pneumonia, from which he never fully recovered, although he remained *effective* a considerable part of the time. A broken leg also interfered with his usefulness during the very last years of his life. But he "died with the harness on." He had just preached as usual at one of the appointments of his circuit, and afterwards rode to the farm-house of one of the members not far away He was seen sitting upon his horse at the gate, and upon going out to him he was found to be paralyzed. He was kindly taken into the house, but died in great peace within twenty-four hours, leaving messages of love for his absent family and for his ministerial brethren.

He lies buried beside his beloved wife in the old cemetery at Thorntown, Indiana; and upon the cottage monument that surmounts his grave is the following inscription: " The grave of Rev. Wade Posey, an itinerant minister of the Indiana Conferences for twenty-five years. He walked with God, and was not, for God took him." (No dates.) Upon a similar monument to the wife is the following inscription: " Calista, wife of Rev. Wade Posey. Died February 20, 1879, aged fifty-nine years, eleven months, and twenty-eight days. 'I know that my Redeemer liveth.'"

W P H.

MORE RECENT COADJUTORS.

REV. WILLIAM GRAHAM, A. M., D. D.

THE subject of this sketch was born in a log cabin in York County, Pennsylvania, November 9, 1821. He remarked, humorously, that he was "born in a hurricane;" insisting that he "*saw* the uprooted trees, blown down on the night of his birth," not pausing to explain *when* he had seen them. A fearful tornado had swept through the valley on that night, and subsequently his father showed him these huge prostrated trees and their upturned roots. His father was a Scotchman, and traced his ancestry to the Earl of Montrose, of the same name. He was born in the north of Ireland, and was brought by his parents to America when he was a child, settling in the State of New York. His mother—Martha Shugh—was a native of Chester County, Pennsylvania, and a descendant from a German father and a Welsh mother. The Grahams, of York County, were, at the time, one of a very few English-speaking families of the neighborhood, the county having been settled chiefly by Germans, whose descendants retained the language and literature, as well as many of the customs and traditions, of the fatherland; so that the Graham children became familiar with both languages, though the parents never ventured to speak the German. It was a religious family, the father adhering to the Scotch

Presbyterians and the mother to the Quakers. They were, however, liberal in their Church views, attending religious services wherever they had opportunity, until later in life, when they both became members of the Methodist Episcopal Church, and died in that communion. The family was poor, and, as is common with poor folks, they were rich in children, having eleven in number. These had to shift largely for themselves, working out among the farmers when of sufficient age, attending school more or less in the winter, and working during the summer. The country schools, in that early day, were poor in character, chiefly for the want of competent teachers. The current humorous accounts of the primitive log schoolhouse and its methods are applicable here, but need not be repeated.

The subject of our sketch worked on farms until he was seventeen, when he went to the city of York to learn a trade, and where for a time he attended school at the York County Academy, which he greatly enjoyed and zealously improved. This also brought him in connection with a lyceum, and gave him access to a well-stocked library, of great advantage to him during his stay in the city. He learned the trade of a house-carpenter, and, according to usage, had to serve four years for his "victuals and clothes," in order to get the trade. He thought himself fortunate, for it was not every youth that could get the chance. The custom had some advantages—it taught young men industry, patience, and subordination, and made them skillful mechanics.

His religious culture was by no means neglected

from the beginning. His father was a man of intelligence, above the average of the neighbors; he was an extensive reader, well-informed, of strong religious predilections, and competent to give his children good advice and the reasons therefor. His mother was a cheerful, hopeful, devout Christian, who made it her *first* concern to teach her children the lessons of personal, practical religion, reading the Scriptures to them, and praying with them separately. The result was a whole family of Church members, without a prodigal among them. He insists that his earliest memory, at the age of about three years, was when, before retiring for the night, he kneeled at his trundle-bed, with his mother's hand upon his head, repeating after her the Lord's Prayer. At the age of eight years, while sitting on a stool before his mother as she read and commented upon a lesson in the Gospel by St. John, one bright Sabbath morning, his young heart was "strangely warmed," he could not tell why. When dismissed, he went out from the pine-log cabin, tenderly weeping, and in a secluded thicket, alone with God, he prayed and rejoiced in his new-found love. It was a genuine, conscious, spiritual conversion! When he went to York, the time for walking barefooted four miles over the chestnut hills, to a country Sunday-school, was ended, and he embraced all the privileges of the Church with a glad heart. He gave his name to the pastor of Beaver Street Church, and began anew the Christian life. It was months, however, before he regained his "first love" of that memorable Sabbath morning. Not that he had been wicked, or prayerless, but somehow he had allowed the precious experience to slip from him. After a long and bitter struggle, on September 24, 1840, while working alone at the bench, the light and joy came back to his troubled soul. The Church at York was then within the bounds of the old historic Baltimore Conference, and it is remarkable how the name "John" figured in the pastorate at that time. Our subject joined the Church under John Gibbon, was baptized by John Poisal, who was followed by John C. Lyon; he was appointed class-leader and was licensed to exhort by John A. Henning, and licensed to preach by John Bear, the presiding elder. He was never formally received into full membership in the Church, but insists that he got there, nevertheless, by good behavior.

Meanwhile he became strongly impressed that it was his duty to preach, and the conviction kept increasing in force; but having other plans formed for life, his feelings rebelled, and he strove hard to suppress the conviction. It was the oft-repeated story of a struggle with conscience and God. He had a widowed mother to care for, and tried to shelter there; the Baltimore Conference was crowded, and there was no room for him, and he tried that subterfuge; preachers were dependent and poorly supported, he had a good trade, and was not going to submit to such humiliations; and his spirit rebelled more and more. After awhile, however, he waked up to the consciousness of spiritual darkness and wretchedness, and the expression of the apostle Paul—"Woe be unto me if I preach not the gospel!"—came to him with peculiar force. At last, on a memorable May morning, the struggle ended by a full surrender of himself to the will of God, and a season of unspeakable happiness followed. The change was marvelous. Now everything that he engaged in had to him a new interest. He had interposed one condition at his surrender which the Lord seemed to accept—"whenever the *Church offers* me work." That was not long in coming.

An older brother, Rev James Graham, A. M., was then a traveling preacher in Texas—the "Lone Star"—having gone to the Southwest nine years before, and begun his work as a missionary among the Cherokee Indians. He kept writing and calling for help. That summer a fellow-townsman, Rev. Andrew Hunter, D. D.—brother of the poet, Dr. William Hunter—revisited his old home, and took a wife in the person of Maria Jones, a class-mate of Mr. Graham. He set himself zealously to work to obtain a new recruit for the Arkansas Conference. In short, everybody, except himsef, seemed to think that Mr. Graham ought to go.

Application was made for license to preach, and John Bear, the presiding elder, required the candidate to preach before him and the Church on Friday night, preparatory to the Quarterly Conference on Saturday. If there is any "starch" in a young man, such an ordeal will take it out. It was called a "trial sermon," but, in the nature of the case, could not have been a specimen sermon. After a lengthy examination, he was licensed to preach, July 20, 1844. At the subsequent Quarterly Conference he was recommended to the traveling connection, September 14, 1844.

On October 8, 1844, he set out on his long journey to the far Southwest, which, at the time, was considered as great an undertaking as it is now to travel round the world. The journey was made by almost every method of travel—canal-boats, steamboats, stage-coaches, by wagon, camping out, on horseback, and on foot. Little Rock was reached in time for the opening session of Conference, the recommendations were accepted, and Mr. Graham received his first appointment from the hands of Bishop T. A. Morris, November 25, 1844, in the Arkansas Conference.

Fort Smith Circuit, which was his first work, extended along the line of the Indian Territory on the west, from the Arkansas River southward to the Fouche-la-fane. The appointments were wherever there was a settlement, from six to twenty-four miles apart, in private houses, unoccupied cabins, brush arbors, and a few log cabins called churches. It was literally a circuit—a ride and a service every day in the week; and the preacher did not cross his path until he got round in three weeks. The distance traveled each round was about one hundred and seventy-five miles. The people were poor, and lived in primitive style, and paid their preacher that year for his services forty dollars. The country was mountainous and picturesque, and the work was not unpleasant, especially as the inhabitants of every class came to the appointments and greeted the "parson;" some hungry for the bread of life, and all anxious for news and to break up the monotony of their isolated lives. Some souls were saved on the work that year.

The next two years his work was "Fort Coffee Academy," a mission-school among the Choctaws, in the Indian Territory, and in the bounds of the then recently formed Indian Mission Conference. It was a manual-labor school—rather two schools, male and female, five miles apart, under the same superintendency—where, in addition to the school-room exercises, the boys were taught farming and gardening and the girls sewing and household work. The mission was supported in part by the Church, but chiefly by Government funds allowed the Indians for educational purposes. This mission had been organized a few years before by Rev. W H. Goode, D. D., of precious memory, and Rev. H. C. Benson, D. D., now of California. Preaching and religious instruction were, of course, made prominent, and the work was interesting, successful, and promising for the future.

But in the meantime the unfortunate division of the Church occurred, and the Indian Mission Conference became identified with the Church South. After taking counsel of his friends and some of the bishops, Mr. Graham decided that the Church South was not the proper field for his life-work.

Accordingly, in the summer of 1847, he came to this State, and that fall he became connected with the work of the North Indiana Conference, there being at the time but two Conferences in the State. Owing to the want of provision for transfer papers, and the necessity for his location in the Church South, his name does not appear in the Minutes of the Conference until 1848, but a vacancy was left for him by Bishop Janes.

For the year 1847-48 his appointment was Independence Circuit, with James Johnson as colleague and preacher in charge. Rev. S. C. Cooper, one of the noblest men the Lord ever gave the Church in Indiana, was the presiding elder. The circuit was large in area, extending from the Wabash River to the State of Illinois, on which are now located at least six distinct charges. The year was characterized by some excellent revivals. That summer a destructive thunder-storm passed over Independence, where he lived. Two women were killed by lightning, at whose funeral he was called to officiate the next day, with the two coffins before him in the church. The text chosen was: "The Lord reigneth; let the people tremble."

In the fall of 1848 he was appointed to Goshen Circuit, at the time covering considerable territory outside of the county town, which is now quite a city. That year his wife had a severe attack of lung-fever, and was brought near to death's door, but through Divine mercy was spared.

His next pastorate was two years in La Porte Station. The first of these years was signalized by a wonderful revival of religion in the charge, in which there were over a hundred conversions, and the interest was so great that standing-room in the crowded church was accepted as a privilege. One Sabbath afternoon he baptized thirty-nine converts, four of whom were immersed in Clear Lake, when the ice was over a foot thick, an opening having been cut through the ice for the purpose, and teams being driven up to the spot as though it were on a field. Besides, the weather was extremely cold on that day. Stronger reasons than money were the inducements to go "down into the water" that day. The second year in the charge, the present more capacious brick church was built under many difficulties, but triumphantly completed by the end of the Conference year.

His next pastorate was one year at Eastern charge (now Ninth Street) Lafayette. That year the present house of worship was erected and inclosed, but the interior was not completed. The last part of the year the pastor was attacked with the distressing disease called "milk-sickness," and for a time was believed to be past recovery, but he improved in time to reach the Conference at Terre Haute by the easy conveyance of a canal-boat.

The following year he served the charge called Delphi and Pittsburg. That was in all respects a very successful year, not without some romance. He preached twice in Delphi and once in Pittsburg each Sabbath, and held prayer-meetings in each town every week. He walked between the towns, and the ferryman at the Wabash allowed him the free use of a skiff to cross the river at will. Thus he passed and repassed by day and by night. One exceedingly dark night, when the river was at flood-tide and out of its banks, on returning from a meeting at Pittsburg, his landmarks were lost, and after rowing a long time amid drift-wood and currents he landed on the same side of the river he had started from, quite a distance down the stream. Nothing daunted, however, he worked his frail craft up to the proper starting-point again, adjusted his visional apparatus more carefully, "pulled for the shore," and landed safely. After reaching home, his wife remarked dryly, "You must have had a long meeting." In those times it was not always best for preachers to tell their perils by sea and land to their wives. Their nerves were quieted by keeping some secrets from them, right or wrong.

His appointment, the fall of 1853, was Rochester District, of which he had not the slightest suspicion until Bishop Ames read it at the closing session of the Conference. He was secretary, and was taking down the appointments, and he barely succeeded in keeping the pen from falling out of his hand. It was cruel. That district seemed to have been made up of the odds and ends lopped off of other districts along the Kankakee swamps, and it could not survive more than one year, when it sunk to "rise no more forever." The incumbent, however, barely survived. He lived that year at Plymouth, and at first planned to travel his district in a buggy. He soon met with an accident, out of which he came with the fragments of a broken vehicle and a spoiled horse, narrowly escaping with his life. He got through the sloughs and quicksand bogs some better on horseback, though he came near losing his horse at one time, and got home in about the sorriest plight he was ever in. On the whole it was the most ill-starred appointment he ever had. There was *experience* enough in it for a life-time.

In the fall of 1854 Bishop Simpson appointed him

to the La Porte District, which he traveled four years. This proved to be a pleasant and very successful work. The preachers of the district were faithful in their work and loyal to their young presiding elder. Extensive revivals of religion prevailed. One winter in particular the whole district was in a blaze of religious enthusiasm, and hundreds were added to the Church. For the first time in his ministry the incumbent's salary was raised to seven hundred dollars, including house-rent and traveling expenses. Up to this time his "allowance" had been three hundred and fifty dollars, one hundred dollars "quarterage" for himself, one hundred for his wife, and a hundred and fifty dollars "table expenses." Nevertheless, in those days the preachers fared well, adopting the policy of "cutting the garment according to the cloth." Few preachers ever went in "debt," for there was no "probability of paying" if they did.

In the fall of 1858 he was appointed to the pastorate of Strange Chapel, Indianapolis, where he remained a full term of two years. It was not a first-class charge in the city, but the church was improved and the work was successful. California Street Church, in that city, has now taken the place of the former Strange Chapel.

His pastoral charge in 1860-61 was Fifth Street Church, Lafayette, now Trinity Church. At that time the war of the Rebellion broke out. Camp Tippecanoe was established, where regiments of soldiers were recruited for the army, and the times were exciting. Much was expected every way of the pastors of the churches, and there was little rest day or night at this center of action. A deportation of rebel prisoners, taken in the battle of Fort Donelson was quartered in an old warehouse, and between the recruiting camp and the prison quarters, where there were sick and dying, there was constant demand for Christian sympathy and kind offices. The prisoners were afterward removed, and the pastor's term of two years, which was still the limit, expired.

In 1862-63 he filled a pastoral term at Crawfordsville. It was difficult to make progress in Church-work there, the war being the all-absorbing theme. It required more care, skill, and effort to maintain the Church organization than at other times to extend its borders, but with vigilance and work the fort was held. A number of prominent Church members were bitterly opposed to the war and the administration of the Government, others denounced them in no measured terms, and the charge had a miniature war of its own on hand. The utmost care and prudence alone prevented serious clashes; but it was done, and that without any compromises with the spirit of rebellion. Outspoken sermons were preached in defense of the Government and the Union on the special occasions of National thanksgivings and fasts, and at the funerals of soldiers who fell in the field of battle, while at the Sabbath services the gospel only was preached, with appropriate prayers for the preservation of the Government, and the success of the armies and navy; that is, the preacher prayed for the Union, leaving it to politicians to curse its enemies. Financially, the pastor had to use his best skill and economy to keep up the Church, and to keep the wolf from his own door. Some thought they were doing right to "stop the feed" of "Abolition preachers," prices of living had risen to war rates, and to make ends meet on less than six hundred dollars a year was no easy task; but it was done. There was a better feeling at the end of two years, and a murmur of dissatisfaction that the charge was not allowed the new policy of a three-year pastoral term.

His appointment for 1864-65-66 was Asbury Chapel, Terre Haute. Taken all in all this was the most successful pastorate of his life. Years before, a mission church had been built in the north part of the city, known as the Sibleytown Church, which for some years had been fairly prosperous, but owing to the fact that the population of the city had turned in another direction, and other causes, it ceased to be an eligible point for the nucleus of a second Church. Meantime, the city was growing rapidly, and tending eastward, while Asbury Chapel was becoming numerous, and the mission Church was dwindling. After one year's pastorate in Asbury, the pastor asked that the entire city, including the mission, be put into his charge, which was done. The second year he interested the leading men in Asbury Chapel to purchase a lot and build a new church on Seventh Street. All agreed that such a measure was desirable, and they looked into the matter no farther than the good of Methodism, and leaving the plans chiefly to the pastor. A subscription was gotten under way, under the inspiration of the Centennial of Methodism, a Board of Trustees was appointed, a lot purchased, the mission property was sold very cheap, and the proceeds applied to the new church. The result was the present Centenary Church of Terre Haute. Of course, all this involved much labor and difficulty. Some of the neighbors and property-owners of the mission church wished it retained. A great many men in this world are selfish; but a more generous class than the members of "Old Asbury" will be hard to find. Owing to the extensive labors of the pastor, and the attention he had to give the new church enterprise, the official members employed Rev. Hillary A. Gobin—now Dr. Gobin—who was then a student of the university at Greencastle, and whose father then resided at Terre Haute, to assist the pastor during his college vacation. From books taken from the pastor's library, and under his direction, this young divine began his theological studies. By the close of the second year the Centenary Church was inclosed, and the basement so nearly ready for use as to justify an appointment from the Conference, and in the fall of 1866 Rev. Leander C. Buckles was appointed the first pastor of the Church. The membership was divided about equally between the two Churches. Everybody seemed pleased; but as most of the money for the new church came from members remaining in the old church, the pastor was often rallied on his tricks of inducing them to build a better church than their own for their neighbors to worship in. Besides this work, there was much spiritual prosperity. Asbury Chapel had one of the finest Sabbath-schools in the State, and each of the three years the charge was blessed with a precious revival of religion, in which over three hundred souls were converted. The reports of the ensuing Conference, in the fall of 1867, show that the property of the two Churches was equal, and in three years Methodism in Terre Haute had practically duplicated itself.

In the fall of 1867 he was appointed to Lafayette District, which was his field of labor for four years. While on this district he built himself a comfortable home in West Lafayette. In addition to the ordinary work of his office, he gave much time to the building of churches. He assisted largely in the financial plans of Trinity Church, Lafayette, which was erected at this time; and, after an address from Dr. Bowman—now Bishop Bowman—he laid the corner-stone of Trinity Church, June 22, 1869. He also managed the erection of the Chauncey Church, in West Lafayette, acting as one of the original Board of Trustees. That Church was dedicated by Dr. Granville Moody, January 23, 1870. The Church at Fowler, the county-seat of Benton County, was built entirely under his management, there being as yet no pastor there. He contracted with the builder personally for its erection, having first found safe backing for the enterprise. The fall of 1870 he was prostrated with a severe and prolonged spell of sickness—typhoid fever, followed by a low grade of nervous fever, the result of too much exposure and too little rest.

In 1871-72 he traveled the Terre Haute District; in 1873, the West Lafayette District; in 1874, the Crawfordsville District; in 1875 he was appointed to Asbury Chapel, Terre Haute, where he spent another year in the pastorate of that charge, but persistently declined a reappointment.

In 1876 he was appointed to Valparaiso, where he remained two years. The large normal school there made the charge especially interesting to him. He gained the good-will of the principal and professors, as well as of the students, by his attention to the school. They crowded his church on the Sabbath, and he was enabled to do some good work in defense of orthodox Christianity. The famous tabernacle meetings of Moody and Sankey at Chicago were held at this time, and soon thereafter the country thereabouts was overrun with imitators of the renowned evangelists. It would have been amusing, had it not been annoying, to witness their persistent audacity in pushing themselves before the Churches and the Christian people with their crude, shallow abilities. These irresponsible, self-constituted teachers of religion did the cause of Christ some harm, and then subsided.

The appointment for the fall of 1878 was Frankfort, where he continued two years. This was to him a new field, and he worked with a will to cultivate it, with good success. The Sabbath-school was especially interesting, and many of the young people were brought into the Church.

By this time the health of his wife, which was never the best, was so utterly broken down, that in the fall of 1880 he was obliged to take a supernumerary relation to the Conference. He took her to her quiet home in West Lafayette, where she seemed to improve in health. The last four months of that year he supplied the vacancy in the pastorate in Ninth Street Church, Lafayette. The following year he supplied Trinity

Church, Lafayette, over half the year. His wife, after enjoying nearly three years of quiet rest, one day in his absence from home was stricken down by apoplexy, and died in unconsciousness, June 5, 1883. For thirty-six years they had trodden life's pathway together, and the husband felt all the more lonely because he had no child to comfort him. His bereavement was most keenly felt.

In the fall of 1883 he was placed on the effective list, and was appointed to Dayton and Mulberry work. He filled that charge only one year, and under considerable embarrassment.

In 1884 his appointment was Chauncey and Congress Street, Lafayette. In the fall of 1885 his name was again placed on the supernumerary list, where it still remains. Since then he preaches and works wherever he is needed and called, and is always busy. On the 7th of August, 1889, his second wife died, to whom he had been married only a few years, and he is again alone in the world.

There are other points in the career of the subject of this sketch deserving of being noted. He was honored by his Conference as a delegate to two General Conferences—the one that met in the city of Indianapolis in 1856, when provision was made for the first missionary bishop; and the one which convened in Chicago in 1868, when the plan for the admission of lay delegates into that body was initiated. In this position, as in all others, he was active and faithful to the interests intrusted to his attention.

By application of his friends, unknown to him, the honorary degree of A. M. was conferred on him by Allegheny College, of his native State; and in 1868 he received the degree of D. D. from the same college.

He was a member of the Board of Trustees of the Northwestern University from 1854 till 1858, when that institution was in its infancy. Covering the same period of time, he served as a member of the Publishing Committee of the *Northwestern Christian Advocate*, which was the policy for its publication at that time. It was through his influence largely that Thomas M. Eddy was first elected editor of that paper, after the death of James V Watson.

From 1868 till 1872 he represented the Fourth General Conference District on the Church Extension Committee.

He was the secretary of his Conference six years, and was the first to publish its Annual Minutes in pamphlet form, in 1853. The Conference was not formed till 1852.

For nine years in all, from time to time, he served on the Joint Board as a visitor of the Indiana Asbury University; and he served the same institution nine years as a trustee, from 1878 till 1887 During this period the historic building burned, and a new one was erected on its ruins. At a later date the transition from Indiana Asbury University to DePauw University was planned and made. These changes involved many meetings and much labor on the part of the trustees and visitors.

Five years he served as Conference trustee, and was one of the Board who originated the plan for a permanent camp-ground at the Battle-ground of Tippecanoe. He was the active agent in organizing the joint-stock company which now owns and controls the property, and he is at this time acting as president of Battle-ground Camp-meeting Association.

There is another institution of the Church in which he has been, and still is, an active worker. The Preachers' Aid Society of the Northwest Indiana Conference was organized and incorporated in 1864. Of this he has been one of the managers and secretary of the Board from the time of its organization, and has also been secretary of the Society itself for years. Since 1881 there have been added to these duties the agency of the Society, so that he is fairly loaded down with its cares and correspondence. Still he works on, and makes no complaint in this work of benevolence; and no one asks to relieve him of his offices, since there is nothing in them but care and hard work. This quiet, steady attention to the wants of needy superannuated preachers and the widows and orphans of deceased preachers, he considers the crowning work of his life. Up to this time he has never missed a roll-call in Conference.

HENRY CLARK BENSON.

I was born near Xenia, Ohio, in 1815; sought the Savior and united with the Methodist Episcopal Church at Clear Spring Camp-meeting, in Union Circuit, Cincinnati District, in 1830. Rev. Augustus Eddy was preacher in charge, and Rev. J. F Wright presiding elder. Moved with my parents to Indiana in my sixteenth year. At twenty commenced to teach district school, studying privately to prepare for college. In 1839 entered the Indiana Asbury University in freshman class, though a little behind in some branches. Graduated with the third class in 1842. Entered Conference the same year at the session held in Centerville, Bishop Soule presiding. Appointed junior preacher on Mooresville Circuit, twenty-one societies in the circuit. It embraced four villages—Mooresville, Belleville, Monrovia, and Plainfield. United in marriage to Miss Matilda M. Williamson, June 7, 1843. In the spring of 1843 transferred to Arkansas Conference, and, with Rev. W H. Goode, was sent to found an academy in the Choctaw Nation, Indian Territory. Mr. Goode was superintendent of the mission, and H. C. Benson was principal of the academy, which was located at Fort Coffee, fifteen miles west of Fort Smith. The female branch of the academy was located at New Hope, five miles south of Fort Coffee. Taught in the male department. It was a manual-labor school, the pupils being boarded and clothed by the institution. The work prospered from the beginning. Remained at that institution till after the organization of the Methodist Episcopal Church, South, in 1845. Was ordained deacon at the first session of the Indian Mission Conference, held at Tah-le-quah, the capital of the Cherokee Nation, Bishop Morris presiding. There were two full-blood Choctaw Indian preachers ordained in the same class—John Page and Isaac Chuk-ma-bee.

In the month of August, 1845, was transferred to North Indiana Conference, stationed in the order following in the charges named : Rockville, Perrysville,

La Porte, South Bend; Berry Street, Fort Wayne; professor of Greek language and literature in Asbury University in 1850, 1851, and 1852. In 1852 transferred to the Oregon and California Mission Conference, and filled the charges following, in the order named: Stockton, Marysville, Stockton, Santa Clara, Placerville, Stockton District two years, Marysville District one year, Stockton District two years; a member of General Conference in Philadelphia in 1864; elected editor of the *Pacific Christian Advocate*, Portland, Oregon, and transferred to Oregon Conference; presided over the session of the Oregon Conference, in the absence of Bishop Baker, in 1866; a member of the General Conference in Chicago in 1868; elected editor of *California Christian Advocate*, and transferred back to California Conference; edited the paper twelve years, making a continuous service of sixteen years in editing. Was a member of the General Conference in Baltimore in 1876; visited the National Centennial Celebration. In 1880 appointed presiding elder of the Petaluma District; at the end of one year changed to the Sacramento District; served the full term; was a member of the General Conference in Philadelphia in 1884. In 1885 was appointed to Kentucky Street Church in San Francisco; served three years as pastor. In 1888 appointed pastor of the Church in New Almaden; returned to it in 1889. Have been greatly favored with the blessing of health. Have not been on the supernumerary or superannuated lists. Am not as young as I was forty-eight years ago, when I united with the Indiana Conference, and yet am able to render full service. But as the shadows lengthen, I am often thinking of the land of promise over the Jordan. "At evening time it *is* light."

REV. GREENLY H. McLAUGHLIN.*

The great-grandfather of the subject of this sketch was James, a native of Scotland, who married Nancy Rankin, and, emigrating to America, settled in Richmond, Virginia. His son William, father of the subject of this biography, was born in Virginia, December 19, 1779, and died March 26, 1836. He was reared in Kentucky, and later in life removed to Ohio. He married, December 31, 1812, Miss Elizabeth Hannaman. Elizabeth, their eleventh child, was born in Scioto County, Ohio, November 4, 1795, and died February 3, 1880. She married, as above, William McLaughlin, and had children—Susannah, Euphemia W., Greenly H., Nancy R., William H., Elizabeth J., and Maria G. William McLaughlin, who was a soldier of the War of 1812, bought the quarter-section of land two miles southeast of the courthouse, Indianapolis, Indiana, on which the subject of this sketch now resides, at the land-sales at Brookville, in July, 1821, before the lands of the "*New* Purchase" were subject to entry. There was then no road or trace through it, and it was regarded as not first choice; hence he was permitted to bid it off at one dollar and twenty-five cents per acre. This, however, nearly absorbed his entire capital, leaving

---

*This sketch is taken in part from "History of Indianapolis and Marion County."—W. P. H.

only a few dollars for the expenses incident to moving and fixing up. In September of that year he moved upon his purchase, and took up his abode in a temporary camp. This soon gave way, however, to a first-class cabin of round logs, eighteen by twenty feet, which for several years did the compound duty of kitchen, parlor, and bed-room, to which was often added the further services of tavern and meeting-house.

Greenly was at this time only four years old, having been born in Fayette County, Ohio, December 24, 1817, but remembers the peculiar trials and pleasures incident to pioneer-life in the midst of a dense forest. He remembers the abundance of game and of snakes, and to have seen Indians as they passed to and fro through the country. He recalls the primitive schools and the primitive school-houses, with the primitive teacher and his primitive rod and ferule. The structures were made of round logs, with doors of clapboards hung on wooden hinges, and with no light except what struggled through greased paper in the absence of glass. Nearly one entire end was devoted to the fire-place. Such, at least, was the one which stood on the identical spot now occupied by Mr. McLaughlin's elegant residence, and in which he obtained the knowledge of a, b, c, and other intricacies of the spelling-book. To the ordinary appointments of such houses, the dimensions being eighteen by twenty feet, was added a pulpit, in the end opposite the fire-place, in which the early Methodist, Baptist, and other preachers very frequently expounded the Word to the sturdy yeomanry of the country. And this school-house became so much of a religious center that it was followed by a neat hewed log and then by a frame church on the same farm, and the first camp-meeting ever held in Marion County was held there in 1826, under the management of Rev. John Strange.

The elder McLaughlin and his wife brought with them their membership in the Methodist Episcopal Church; and soon after their arrival the first class of that Church was formed in Indianapolis, of which they became members. His piety and talents were such that he became a leader and exhorter in the Church, and was extensively useful as such during the remainder of his life, which ended in 1836.

It is hardly a wonder that, under these circumstances, with such a home, a frequent lodging-place for the itinerants of those days, Greenly grew up a Methodist of the most pronounced type, nor surprising that four out of five of his sisters became wives of Methodist preachers.

As Greenly advanced in years, the educational advantages of the log school-house were supplemented by occasional attendance at some of the better schools in the town. He finally became a pupil at the "Old Seminary," adding frequent terms at teaching in the neighboring districts, both as a means of turning an honest penny and as further developing his own mind. In the fall of 1840, Mr. McLaughlin entered Indiana Asbury University, with the intention of graduating at that young institution. He was then nearly twenty-three years of age, with a religious character well established, and a fund of theological knowledge much above the average of men of his age just from the plow;

hence, when, the next year, he was licensed to preach the gospel, it is not strange that he at once took high rank among the student preachers of that institution. Such was the demand for his gratuitous pulpit labors, even at that age, that his studies were seriously interfered with, though he held a respectable standing in his class; and at the expiration of two years he yielded to the importunity of friends, and gave up his college life altogether, to enter upon the pastoral work in the Indiana Conference. His standing as a preacher may be readily inferred from the class of appointments received. He was welcomed to such places as Knightstown, Shelbyville, Brookville, Rushville, and Vincennes. While at Vincennes he was tendered the important work of chaplain to the port of Canton, China, under the auspices of the "American Seamen's Friend Society;" but his health not being sufficiently robust to justify such a mission, he declined. In 1849 he was solicited by Bishop Janes to take a part in the interest of the Methodist Episcopal Church at St. Louis, Missouri; but this he also declined for the same reason.

After seven years of successful pastoral labor, including one year as agent for Indiana Asbury University, he sought rest and recuperation by returning to a country life on the old farm, where he now lives. He immediately gave himself to the work of a local preacher, while engaged in the work of farming, and has been extensively useful and acceptable in that field. Meanwhile his health improved, but again relapsed, so that he never felt sufficiently strong to resume the work of a pastor.

Mr. McLaughlin is an industrious and successful business man, as he was, while so engaged, an industrious and successful minister. In these years of comparative retirement he has kept well read in the theological and general literature of his Church, often contributing to the columns of the Church periodicals valuable papers on theological and ecclesiastical subjects. He still lives on the farm purchased by his father more than sixty years ago, and to which he came when a boy of only four years. He is one of the few who have witnessed the growth of Indianapolis from the beginning. He was married, June 1, 1854, to Miss Mary M. Ball, of Rush County, Indiana, taking one of three daughters of the family, all of whom became wives of Methodist preachers. Mrs. McLaughlin has proved herself to be a worthy helpmeet to her husband, strong in the Christian faith, of a cheerful and happy temperament; their home is what every home should be, a type of the heavenly mansions. The children of this marriage have been four in number—Olin S., until recently a hardware merchant at Knightstown, Indiana; Wilbur W., a promising student of Butler University, Indiana, who died at the age of twenty-two years in California. The other two children died in infancy.

Mr. McLaughlin has been for more than twenty years enthusiastic on the subject of holiness, which John Wesley called "the great depositum of Methodism." He had from childhood been taught the doctrine of entire sanctification for believers in this life, and he believed it to be true, as he believed other doctrines of the Bible. But not until he had been preaching the gospel, including holiness, for more than twenty-five years, did he seek and find this as a present, personal blessing and baptism. So surpassingly blissful and glorious was his experience now, that he has often been heard to say: "O, that I had known this in the earlier days of my ministry!" By voice and pen and example, he is still promoting the interests of this cause. He now feels and says that every minister of the gospel should endeavor to come to his people "in the fullness of the blessing of the gospel of Christ."

SKETCH OF MRS. ELIZABETH McLAUGHLIN.*

Elizabeth McLaughlin was born in Scioto County, Ohio, November 4, 1795, and died near Indianapolis, Indiana, February 3, 1880, aged eighty-four years. She was the daughter of John and Susannah Hannaman, from whom she inherited a strong physical constitution and a good mind. Of the children, of whom she was one, there is only a single survivor—Judge Robert L. Hannaman, of Knoxville, Illinois.

When she was about seventeen years of age she was married to William McLaughlin, with whom, in sweetest Christian wedlock, she lived till his death, in 1836.

A few days after her marriage her husband went to the War of 1812, and served to the close.

For almost forty-four years she remained a widow,

---

*This sketch is copied from "Saintly Women," etc., by Rev. M. P. Gaddis.—W. P. H.

counting herself still the beloved wife of him who was the object of her first and only love.

She was the mother of five daughters and two sons, four of whom survive—Mrs. E. W. Robe, of Kalamazoo, Michigan; Mrs. E. J. Miller, and Greenly H. and William H. McLaughlin, of Indianapolis, Indiana. All the children she brought up to an adult age, and they all became religious. She gave four daughters to be the wives of Methodist preachers, and her eldest son entered the itinerant ministry. The other son has long held an official relation to the same Church. The deceased children all died in the faith in the Church of their parents.

In addition to her own family, she assisted in raising four orphan children, three of whom survive her—Mrs. Elizabeth Denny, of Indianapolis; Mr. Harrison McLaughlin, of Missouri; and Mrs. Martha Beck, of Greencastle, Indiana, the wife of Rev. Asa Beck, of the Indiana Conference.

Mrs. McLaughlin joined the Church and was converted in girlhood, and was devoted to God for about seventy years. She was a member of the first class formed in Indianapolis, Indiana. It is doubted if there be a single survivor of that class. They are now a complete class in glory.

From Ohio her family moved to Rush County, Indiana, in 1819, and thence to Indianapolis, in 1821. Here, on the same spot, for more than fifty-eight years, she lived and labored. For a number of years her house was a place for worship, until a church was built upon her own land; and her house was also the quiet resting-place for the preacher. The lamented but then young and gifted Richard Hargrave, in the first year of his married life, spent nine months in the same room where this good woman died.

Funeral services, at the homestead, were conducted by Rev. Thomas H. Lynch, D. D., who discoursed most appropriately from 2 Corinthians, v, 1–5—the very same text used by Rev. Calvin W Ruter, D. D., at Conference, in 1836, in Indianapolis, at her husband's funeral—Dr. Lynch knowing nothing about that service.

Mrs. McLaughlin's religion was not only of an aggressive, practical character, but it was to her a constant comfort and support. She rejoiced in God as her Savior from all sin, and for many years was almost constantly filled with the theme and experience of "holiness to the Lord." As may be inferred, her end was not only peaceful but victorious and glorious. She was permitted to have, as the answer of an almost life-long prayer, a clear mind in the dying hour. Nearing the end, she exclaimed: "I am so happy! Come and bid me good-bye!" And then—as nearly forty-four years before, in the same room, when a departing husband and father called his family about him for the last time, and bade them farewell—so she gives a good word and a good-bye to the remnant of her children and her children's children; and sending a last and loving message to some absent ones, she sank into a quiet slumber, from which none wake to weep.

REV. GEORGE M. BOYD, D. D.

BY REV. JOHN L. SMITH, D. D.

Rev. George M. Boyd, D. D., was born in Lewis County, Kentucky, March 9, 1814, and died at his residence in this city on Sunday afternoon, January 26, 1890.

He lost his parents in early life, and was taken charge of by his uncle, with whom he remained at Urbana, Ohio, until he was about twenty years of age. In his sixteenth year he was happily converted under the ministry of the distinguished Wm. H. Raper, of blessed memory.

When about twenty years of age, Brother Boyd was licensed to preach; and in 1835, when twenty-one years old, he came to Indiana and was employed by Richard Hargrave, presiding elder, as supply on Cassopolis Circuit, with Thos. P McCool preacher in charge. The session of the Indiana Conference for 1836 was held at Indianapolis, where Brother Boyd, together with twenty-three others, was admitted on trial to the Annual Conference, and appointed to La Porte Circuit.

For the next five years he traveled the following circuits, namely: La Grange, Elkhart, Goshen, Terre Coupee, and South Bend. His first appointment to a station was Fort Wayne, in 1842; and to the Fort Wayne District as presiding elder in 1843, where he remained four years.

His next work was at Fifth Street, now Trinity, Lafayette, for two years. Then, in 1849, he was stationed at Terre Haute, and for the next two years was presiding elder on Crawfordsville District. At the organization at Terre Haute of the Northwest Indiana Conference in 1852, one quarter of the city of Indianapolis was included in the bound of our Conference. Brother Boyd was taken from the district to organize the work and build a church, being entitled as the most suitable man for this work.

Upon the accomplishment of his work in Indianapolis, he was sent to the Eastern charge, Lafayette (now Ninth Street), where another church was to be built. Here he remained two years. After which he was placed in charge of Attica Station in 1855, serving two years. From there he went to Perrysville, remaining two years. His next appointment was for two years at Greencastle, and for the next two years after that in Terre Haute Station.

From Terre Haute, in the fall of 1863, he went to La Porte, and, under the change of rule by the General Conference of 1864, he remained there three years. He next served a second term of two years at Fifth Street, Lafayette; when in 1868, at the request of the leading members of the Church at Valparaiso, where the Annual Conference was being held, he was appointed by Bishop Thomson to the place. Closing his three years' term of service in this city, in 1871 he was appointed to First Church, South Bend, when, at the end of two years, he was appointed presiding elder of La Porte District, remaining in that relation four years.

For the next two years he was pastor of the Church at La Porte. Then for two years he served the

Church at Michigan City, and in 1881 was appointed for the second term to this place.

Going in 1884 from here to Westville, where he remained two years, he returned with his family to settle permanently in Valparaiso; and for the next two years preached at Salem Church and Malone's, now comprising parts of the Valparaiso Circuit; thus rounding up his work of fifty-two consecutive years of active ministerial labor.

At the session of our Conference, held at Rochester in 1888, a scene occurred not soon to be forgotten.

George M. Boyd, after his long years of active and faithful service, the formerly strong and vigorous man, now feeling that the infirmities of age were bearing down upon his hitherto strong physical frame, voluntarily, after a few touching and appropriate remarks, asked his Conference to grant him a superannuated relation.

His request, by a unanimous vote of the Conference, being granted, one of the brethren struck the key-note of feeling in commencing to sing the hymn "Blest be the tie that binds," in which all joined heartily—the whole Conference moving forward, many with streaming eyes, extending the hand of brotherly affection to the esteemed and honored fellow-laborer.

Brother Boyd was a born preacher. Though without many advantages of an early education, he was by instinct a gentleman; and largely gifted by nature and refined by grace with a kindness of heart plainly manifest to all, and with an easy dignity and grace of manner in the pulpit, he was always not only an instructive and useful minister of the gospel, but was everywhere loved and honored as a man of unflinching integrity and honor.

Brother Boyd was honored by his brethren of the Conference, in that he was elected twice as a delegate to the General Conference, and from time to time served as pastor in the leading pulpits of his Conference, and as presiding elder as well.

In looking through his fifty-two years of active service I find that he served the Church and the cause of his Master in faithful labors, eight years on circuits, thirty-four years in stations, and ten years in the office of presiding elder.

And I can point to no man among us who, as a Methodist traveling preacher, has made a more honorable record than George M. Boyd.*

REV JOHN L. SMITH, D. D.

Rev. John L. Smith, D. D., was born on the 24th day of May, 1811, in Meherin Parish—Parson Jarratt's—in the County of Brunswick, and State of Virginia. My maternal grandparents, Owen by name,

---

* Brother Boyd was among the very first of the ministerial brethren whom I can recollect seeing at my father's house, away back at the dawn of memory—my father's life-long friend, and in some sort his spiritual son. He also honored me with his friendship and fraternal regard. The very manner in which he smiled, pressed my hand, and spoke my name, was a benediction. In the midst of increasing bereavement and loneliness I felt that there was *one* left. But, alas! he too has *joined the innumerable caravan*. He was a large-hearted, sweet-singing, smooth-working man of God, of grand and beautiful person and benign influence. *Rest in peace!*—W. P. H.

were converted under the labors of Rev. Robert Williams, in 1773 or 1774, at Portsmouth, Virginia, and, with five others, constituted a class of seven— the first organized Methodist class in the State of Virginia; and on the next day after his conversion he manumitted all of his slaves, eighty-three in number. He afterwards moved to Brunswick County; and of his home Bishop Asbury says, in his journal: "Here am I at the house of Brother William Owen, the first place I have found rest for the sole of my foot in Virginia."

My mother was converted in the eleventh year of her age, and taken into the Church by Bishop Asbury; was married at sixteen years of age, in the year 1800; raised ten children to be grown, nine of whom died in the Lord, all members of the Methodist Episcopal Church; and "I only am left to tell the story," my mother having died in 1852. Of her children, there were three sons and seven daughters. I was her fifth child and first son.

In 1826 we moved to the State of Ohio, and settled on a farm in Greene County, near Xenia, about fifty miles north of Cincinnati, in the bounds of Union Circuit, with William H. Raper and George W Maley, circuit preachers. At a protracted meeting, held in Union Meeting-house, I was powerfully converted to God on the first day of April, 1827

I can not remember when I learned to read, as taught by my mother. I commenced going to school at about five years of age, and was in school most of the time for the following ten years, the last one of which, before leaving Virginia, I was sent from home to what was then called a grammar-school, or what would now be called an academy.

When we moved to Ohio my father bought quite a tract of land, with a double cabin on it, and about five acres cleared. He, while a good manager, had perhaps never in his life, performed one day's manual labor. He hired a strong young man, a cousin of ours, and he and myself, in about six years, cleared and fenced and brought into cultivation about one hundred acres.

My custom was, after working in the clearing all day, to gather a bundle of scaly bark from the shell-bark hickory, by which to study at night.

I was licensed to exhort by Rev. William Sutton in June, 1836, and to preach, by Rev. James B. Finley, in February, 1837, on Saturday, in Wellington, Ohio, and by him was placed on a circuit on the following Monday, and traveled as a supply most of the time until March, 1840, when I came to Indiana, and was admitted on trial at Indianapolis, in the Indiana Conference, in October of that year, and sent to Winchester Circuit, with John H. Bruce as preacher in charge. In 1841, Muncie Station; for the next two years, Cambridge City; and in 1844, to Indianapolis, where I preached one winter in the court-house; had over three hundred conversions, and during the two years we built Roberts Chapel. In 1846 I was college agent; the next year, stationed at Terre Haute; and, in 1848, appointed by Bishop Hamline to Lafayette District; there two years; then four years on La Porte District.

I was sent as a delegate to the General Conference of 1852, in 1860, 1864, 1868, and 1876. Also was a member of the General Missionary Committee from 1856 to 1860; and a member of the Book Committee from 1864 to 1868; and was again a member and chairman of the Book Committee from 1871 to 1880,* since which time you have known of my whereabouts; nor need I tell you more than simply to say I am a sinner saved by grace.

I am still working for the Master on the Valparaiso District. I never enjoyed the work more in my life. My friends say they think I am *improving* in preaching.† I do feel that I am growing in grace. My wife is an invalid, but submissive and cheerful. We have a temporary but a Christian home. We are happy in the Lord, stricken in years. We shall soon " shake hands with time;" but we have a home *over the river*. Ever your friend and brother, JOHN L. SMITH.

REV. CHARLES A. BROOKE, D. D.

I was born in Montgomery County, Indiana, October 24, 1831. My parents, Josiah and Mary A. Brooke, moved to Indiana from Miami County, Ohio, in the fall of 1827, and settled three miles south of Crawfordsville. My boyhood, until I was seventeen years of age, was passed on the farm, engaged for the most of the time in such work as I could do on a farm in the woods. Up to my seventeenth year I had attended school but a little. After I was old enough

---

 The degree of Doctor of Divinity was conferred upon me by the Indiana State University, in 1860.
† Dr. Smith has always been a great preacher.—W. P. H.

to attend, perhaps I averaged two months a year, and that was frequently taken in broken doses.

In the spring after I was seventeen I went to live with my uncle, who resided on Shawnee Prairie, near Shawnee Mound, Indiana. Here I remained most of the time until I was twenty-one years of age. I worked on the farm from seven to nine months each year. The balance of the year I went to school at Shawnee Academy, and paid for my board with my uncle by doing chores mornings and evenings, and working on Saturdays. My wages were always paid to my father. I never received a dollar of what I earned until I was twenty-one years of age. I never thought of claiming any part for myself. I was clothed by my parents like the other children, and with that I was content. As my uncle did not raise wheat on his prairie farm, I went home each year to help harvest.

As I was the oldest, and father was not strong, it fell to my lot to do the "cradling." Sickles were just going out of use, and the "cradle" the "great improvement," in use for gathering the harvests. I could soon make a "full hand" with any of the men of the neighborhood in the use of the cradle or scythe. In this way my time was spent until I was twenty-one years of age. My school advantages at Shawnee Academy were as good as the country then afforded, outside of the colleges. I now had about four months each year of uninterrupted schooling, and by the time I was of age I had pretty thoroughly mastered all the English branches as far as then taught in the best schools. My thirst for knowledge was intense. When in the fall of 1852 I had reached my majority, I determined to finish the entire course at the academy. So I entered with the opening of the fall term, and remained during the entire year, which closed in the following June.

In the winter of 1852 occurred the event in my life which changed and gave direction to my whole subsequent life. My parents were devout Christians, and members of the Methodist Episcopal Church. Family prayers were regularly observed, morning and evening, in my father's home, and when I went to live with my uncle I found the same state of things there. So that from childhood I had been under religious influence and training. When I was about twelve years of age I became partially awakened, and united with the Church, but was not converted. No attention was given me by the Church, and I soon lost my concern, and gradually grew into an easy-going and strictly moral life. I never swore an oath in my life, and had but little opportunity to find bad company, had I been so disposed, for I was kept too closely at work. I said my prayers — *The Lord's Prayer* — every evening as I had been taught to do, and sometimes of mornings during family worship; but by the time I was twenty-one years of age I had not only lost all my religious desires, but had drifted into a kind of semi-skepticism. I had become very fond of reading, and having but few books or papers of any kind within my reach, I found access to the *Phrenological Journal*, and some of the books published by Fowler and Wells and soon became a convert to their "Philosophy," if it is worthy of the title.

Under this teaching, I soon began to think that anything could be accounted for on "natural principles," and that the supernatural had no basis of truth in it. Thus I was led to question the reality of conversion and the genuineness of a Christian experience, as I had been taught to think of these from my childhood up. Rev. W F. Wheeler and Rev. Hezekiah Smith were the preachers on the Newtown Circuit, which, while it did not include the Shawnee Academy Society, where I lived and was then attending school, was near by, having one of its appointments at Sugar Grove, the neighborhood immediately east of the academy neighborhood. Under the labors of these two godly men a great revival occurred early in the winter at Newtown, the head of the circuit. Many from our neighborhood attended, and some were converted, and the neighborhood was filled with the reports of the wonderful work that was being done. I was frequently solicited to attend, but steadily refused, giving as my reason that I did not want my mind diverted from my studies. About the first of February they began a meeting at Sugar Grove, in a school-house that stood on Andrew Insley's place, and was also used as a church for the neighborhood. This was much nearer than Newtown, and most of the people of our neighborhood attended. Another great revival soon began here, and the whole country was aroused. I still resisted all solicitations to attend until about the twentieth of the month, and then, partly out of curiosity, and partly to satisfy some of my friends, I went on Thursday night. I got a seat in the rear of the congregation, and amused myself by speculating on the reasons for the great excitement. Brother Smith had charge of the meeting, and, as I had never seen him before, I watched him closely to detect the secret of the mesmeric influence, as I then thought, by which he moved his congregation.

After a brief sermon and earnest exhortation, penitents were invited to the altar, and soon it was crowded; and, to me, a strange bedlam of prayer, crying, song, and shouting began, which lasted for an hour or more. Several of my friends came to me, and urged me to go forward; but I refused, as I had no idea of allowing myself to become unbalanced, as it seemed to me many were. At the close of the services an invitation was given to unite with the Church, when Jesse Meharry* came to me, and urged me to start by uniting with the Church. I refused; but, as he urged, I finally said, "I will think it over until to-morrow night," thinking thus to get rid of him. Just about this time the congregation was dismissed, and "Uncle Jesse," as we all called him, reported to Brother Smith that there was a strictly moral young man in the congregation that said, "to-morrow night." Brother Smith, though the congregation were mostly out of the house, immediately mounted one of the benches and began to exhort that moral young man that said "to-morrow night." I had reached the door, but was arrested by this strange proceeding, and paused to listen. The

---

*Donor of "Meharry Hall" to DePauw University.— W. P. H.

preacher closed his exhortation by urging the young man to decide the question "*to-night*," for fear "tomorrow night might never come," and again gave the invitation to unite with the Church. A conviction seized me that *now* was my time, and in that instant I decided the question, and gave him my hand for membership in the Methodist Episcopal Church.

I went to my home *decided*, but not *sensibly* convicted; that is, I had no emotional conviction. I had simply *decided* to be religious—that was all. I went to the meeting the next night, and was among the first at the altar of prayer when the invitation was given. But the entire evening passed without the least feeling on my part, so far as I could discern. I left the service, however, with a firmer resolve than ever to go through with what I had undertaken. The next day, being Saturday, I assisted in hauling shock corn to feed a large herd of cattle. I remained in the field to help load, and as the young man who was assisting me took the loads to the feeding-grounds, I was left alone. These intervals I spent in prayer. A young men's meeting had been appointed at the school-house for five o'clock Saturday evening. I got through my work in time, and walked six miles to be present at that meeting. There were three or four of us present who had not been converted, and we were invited to the "altar." I immediately went forward, and the moment I knelt at the altar, the great deep of my heart was broken up, and I began to cry in deep earnestness for mercy; and, before the meeting closed, my "mourning was turned into joy," and my cry for mercy into a "shout of triumph." I immediately began to exhort those around me; and, as the people began to gather for the evening service, we adjourned our prayer-meeting to the grove near by, and there kept up our service until it was time to go to the service in-doors.

Two or three penitents were converted after we had adjourned to the woods, and we returned to the house with a shout of triumph. This was on the twenty-third day of February, 1853. Immediately after the close of the meeting at Sugar Grove, a number of the older brethren at the Shawnee Academy Society took it upon themselves to commence a meeting there. That society was then connected with the Attica Circuit, and Rev. Jacob Cozad was the preacher. He was sent for, and came, and staid a few days, but soon returned to his home, and left us to do the best we could alone. Those who assumed the responsibility of the meeting, frequently put me forward to exhort and lead the meeting. We continued these irregular meetings for some three or four weeks, and quite a number were converted, and united with the Church at Brother Cozad's next regular appointment.

Thus began my work of Christian ministry. God put his seal upon my feeble efforts before man had given me any authority to speak to the people. I remained in school that summer. I was licensed to exhort by Rev. Jacob Cozad before my probation had expired. A camp-meeting was held at the Cole Creek Camp-ground, near Hugh Meharry's, in the early fall; and, as I had not been received into full connection, an arrangement was made between Brothers Wheeler, Smith, and Cozad by which I was transferred to the Newtown Circuit, was received into full membership by Brother Wheeler, and immediately recommended by the Quarterly Conference of that circuit, which met on the camp-ground, for license to preach. This was entirely unsolicited on my part, and really was not desired, as I intended to go to school in the fall. Their purpose was to have me licensed to preach, and that I should immediately enter the traveling connection. But when my case came before the Quarterly Conference—after examination by Rev. George M. Beswick, the presiding elder—objections were urged against me by some of the members of the Conference on the ground of my youth and inexperience; and, after considerable discussion, my application was withdrawn, and my membership was transferred back to the Shawnee Mound Society. I taught school that fall at Walnut Grove, near New Richmond. About the first of January, 1854, I went to Eaton, Ohio, and spent the winter with my uncle, Rev. J. C. Brooke, and attended the Eaton Academy. In the spring I returned to Indiana, and spent the summer mostly on Shawnee Prairie.

At the last Quarterly Conference for the Shawnee Prairie Circuit, held at the Wheeler Grove Church—Shawnee Academy—I was again recommended for license to preach; and, after examination by Richard Hargrave, the presiding elder, I was licensed, and immediately recommended to the Annual Conference for the traveling connection. The Conference met that fall in La Porte. I was present, and on the recommendation from the Quarterly Conference and the indorsement of Rev. Richard Hargrave, who had known me from my early boyhood, I was received. I passed my Conference course of study satisfactorily, and was in the regular order of time ordained deacon and elder, and received into full membership in the Conference. My parchments as deacon are dated at Crawfordsville, October 12, 1856, and signed by Edmund S. Janes as bishop. My parchment as elder is dated Valparaiso, October 3, 1858.

By the help of the Lord I have continued unto this day in the regular work of the ministry, having spent a little more than thirty-five years in this work, without having turned aside a single day to any secular employment. In the good providence of God, I have been able to attend every session of my Conference through all these years, and answer to my name at the *first* roll-call, except in two instances, when, through sickness, I was not able to get to the seat of the Conference for two or three days. Including the present year, which is the thirty-sixth of my ministry, I have filled the several classes of appointments as follows: Circuits, five years; stations, twenty-three years; and districts, eight years. The stations I have filled in this Conference, in the order in which they were assigned me, are: Thorntown; Plymouth; Valparaiso; Roberts Chapel, Greencastle; First Church, South Bend; Asbury Chapel, Terre Haute; Trinity Church, Lafayette; La Porte; Valparaiso; Frankfort; and Monticello. At the close of my second year at Asbury, Terre Haute, I was transferred to the Cincinnati Conference, and stationed at Walnut Hills.

I remained there two years, during which time the present Walnut Hills Church was built, at a cost of about fifty thousand dollars. It is now one of the strongest and wealthiest Churches in the Cincinnati Conference. I became home-sick, and, at my own solicitation, was re-transferred to my old Northwest Indiana Conference, where I expect to spend the balance of my days, and in whose ranks I expect to die. Bishop Ames transferred me from the Cincinnati Conference back to the Northwest Indiana, and stationed me at Trinity, Lafayette. When I reached my new field I found the new Trinity Church-building inclosed, and the chapel and Sunday-school rooms under contract for completion. These were finished and ready for occupancy by the following spring. At the dedication of this part of the building we raised about twenty thousand dollars, and immediately began work on the main building. This was completed in a little over a year, and dedicated free of debt.

The amount raised toward this enterprise during my pastorate was about thirty-five thousand dollars.

Revivals of greater or less extent have been in every charge with which I have been connected. The most extensive were in First Church, South Bend, where over six hundred were converted and added to the Church. Among the number was Rev. H. A. Buchtel, D. D., now of Denver, Colorado. At Asbury, Terre Haute, two hundred and fourteen were received during my first year; at Walnut Hills, about one hundred and fifty; at Lafayette, over one hundred; at Valparaiso, during my last pastorate, about two hundred; at Frankfort, about one hundred.

During my last pastorate at Valparaiso a new and beautiful church, costing twenty-five thousand dollars, was built. This, I think, is the *best* church in the Conference, though not costing as much as some others.

I was delegate to the General Conference in 1876, which met at Baltimore. I was for five consecutive years elected on the Board of Triers of Appeals. The degreee of D. D. was conferred upon me, July 11, 1883, by DePauw University.

REV. S. T. GILLETT, D. D.

BY REV. JOHN H. HULL.

Rev. Samuel T. Gillett, D. D., almost the last of the fathers of Methodism in Indiana, died at his residence, No. 138 Massachusetts Avenue, at nine o'clock, January 27, 1890, the immediate cause of his death being a severe cold, from which he might have rallied had he not been enfeebled by extreme age.

He was born near Earlville, Madison County, New York, February 19, 1809, and was nearly eighty-one years old. His father emigrated to the West, coming down the Ohio River and up the Wabash to Fort Harrison, about four miles above the site of the present City of Terre Haute. The fort had lately been abandoned by the troops, but the county was still filled with Indians. Here Mr. Gillett took a bad cold, from which he died. The widow, on account of severe sickness breaking out here, removed with her family to a cabin near the present site of Rockville, Parke County, Indiana. Dr. Gillett was now eight years old; Indians plenty all around the widow and her little family. The Doctor's eldest brother (half brother), Napoleon B. Palmer, who was then living in Madison, came and took the family to his home. There young Gillett lived until 1826, when he was appointed to the United States Navy as midshipman, by President Jackson. In 1827 he was assigned to the war-ship *Lexington,* and made a cruise of three years in the Mediterranean. On the ship *Delaware,* a seventy-four man-of-war, he visited Egypt and the Holy Land. He visited the reputed tomb of the Savior, and this left upon his memory a scene that was never effaced.

In 1831 he was married, at Madison, to Miss Harriet A. Goode, sister to the late Dr. W H. Goode, of precious memory. Soon after his marriage he was converted, and resigned his commission as a lieutenant, and, in 1837, entered the Indiana Conference, and was ever afterward a man of one work.

He received the following appointments: 1837, Lawrenceburg Circuit; 1838, Wilmington Circuit; 1839, Rising Sun Circuit; 1840, Rising Sun Circuit, and to the Bethel, Louisville, Kentucky; 1841, Lawrenceburg Station; the same year, United States Navy; 1842, Lawrenceburg Station; 1843-4, Terre Haute; 1845, Greencastle; 1846-7, Roberts Chapel, Indianapolis; 1848-51, Centerville District; 1852, Asbury Chapel, Indianapolis; 1853-5, Connersville District; 1856-7, Centenary, New Albany; 1858, Bloomington District; 1859-60, Locust Street, Evansville; 1861, Evansville District; 1862-3, Wesley Chapel, Indianapolis; 1864-5, Bloomington; 1866-7, Indianapolis District; 1868-9, Asbury Chapel ; 1870-2, First Church, Greensburg ; 1873, Third Street, Indianapolis ; 1874, Edinburg; 1875-6, supernumerary ; 1877, Centenary, New Albany ; 1878, Grace Church, Indianapolis ; 1879, he was superannuated, which relation he sustained to the Conference until his death.

Dr. Gillett was a man of unusual vigor of intellect. To whatever his attention was turned he devoted himself with the utmost fidelity, whether in the pulpit or in business. In social life he was an ornament to the most intellectual and refined circles.

He was a clear and most instructive preacher. He never had to seek an appointment; was always wanted in more places than he could fill. He enjoyed the confidence of the bishops and all his brethren in the ministry, and is greatly missed and mourned by thousands.

The funeral services were held at Roberts Park Methodist Episcopal Church, under the direction of Dr. Van Anda. The Rev. Henry Day, D. D., of the Baptist Church, Indianapolis, and the writer of this took part, by request of Dr. Gillett. The Tippecanoe Club, of which he was a member, conveyed the body of the deceased from the residence to the church, where were assembled a large audience in waiting. There were ministers present from all the Conferences in the State. DePauw was represented by Drs. Martin and Curtiss. The casket being placed before the altar, the family were seated together on the second seat from the front aisle. The floral offerings were most beautiful and appropriate, suggestive of the pure life that had gone out and of the glorious immortality obtained. Dr. Van Anda read an account of the last hours of Brother Gillett's illness.

His mind was perfectly clear and peaceful—quoting passages of Scripture upon which his faith was founded and fast anchored to the cross. He triumphed gloriously, peacefully falling asleep in Jesus.

Looking at the life, from first to last, of this good and great man, we can say nothing less than, "Servant of God, well done!"

REV. JAMES WILSON GREENE, D. D.

BY REV. WILLIAM GRAHAM, D. D.

The subject of this sketch was born in Greene County, Ohio, February 1, 1829. He is the son of John and Nancy Greene, who were blessed with a family of twelve children—nine sons and three daughters—of whom James is the youngest child. They were a family of sturdy, enterprising, prosperous farmers, forming a little colony within themselves. In the year 1832 they emigrated to Indiana, and settled on Sumption Prairie, St. Joseph County, in the northern part of the State. Such a family in a sparsely settled country was quite an accession, and their influence was felt for good. The country was yet new, still inhabited by numerous Indians of several tribes, and South Bend, now the county-seat, and a large, prosperous city, was then a mere trading-post, chiefly for the Indians.

Mr. Greene's mother, whose maiden name was Jackson, was a devout member of the Presbyterian

Church, and though the father was not a Church member, he was in full accord with the Christian religion. In the course of time a Presbyterian church-building was erected two miles east of the Greene farm, and a Methodist Church was built about the same distance from the farm south. At both these Churches the family worshiped, and the fruit of the early religious training of the children, especially by the devoted mother, is seen in the fact that all who grew up to maturity became active, useful Church members—some in the Presbyterian and others in the Methodist communion, always, and till this day, in peaceful harmony. The tender sympathy for each other's welfare, temporal and spiritual, is the rich fruitage of early religious culture.

The subject of this sketch, though he first attended Sabbath-school at the Presbyterian Church, afterwards made choice of the Methodist Episcopal Church, with which he connected himself, March 4, 1853. He at once began the religious life and work, and in about a year was given license to exhort, under the ministry of Rev. John S. Donaldson. His reputation as an efficient, promising young man extended beyond his local Church, and in the fall of 1855 he was astonished one day about noon when the presiding elder of La Porte District met him in a lane near the homestead, and told him that the great Head of the Church had work for him in another field, and had sent for him. He was accused afterwards of turning pale, but he explained that he had been having chills, and was not well at the time. He was running a saw-mill in the timber-lands near by, at considerable financial profit, and when the persistent presiding elder saw the situation and the modest hesitancy of the young man, he began to doubt the success of his mission, but never once let up on the urgency of his plea; assuming that it was a foregone conclusion that he must go. In the midst of the conversation, Greene's sister called the parties to a bounteous farmer's dinner, which the presiding elder, after his long ride, hugely enjoyed, but for which the candidate showed but little relish. Being afflicted with the rigors, however, one would not expect him to have much appetite. The result of the interview was a promise to report at Rensselaer, November 1, 1855. He was on time, with horse, saddle-bags, and all the needed equipments of a Methodist circuit-rider, and he has been on time ever since. Promptness is one of his marked traits.

On December 15, 1855, he was licensed to preach in due form by the Quarterly Conference at Rensselaer. About four months afterwards a vacancy occurred at Michigan City, through the ill-health and resignation of Dr. J. G. Osborn, and Brother Greene was appointed to the pastorate of that charge the remainder of the year, greatly to the regret of the Rensselaer folks. At Michigan City, as everywhere else, the pastorate of Brother Greene was successful. The Quarterly Conference at the close of the year, recommended him to the traveling connection, and in the fall of 1856 he was received on trial in the Northwest Indiana Conference, held at Crawfordsville, and was appointed to Dormine Circuit, which was a part of the old historic "Union Circuit," of La Porte County. At the request of the Church at Michigan City, he was appointed to that charge in 1857 His appointments for 1858–59 were to Crown Point. There his labors were blest with a precious and extensive revival of religion, the charge was greatly strengthened, and during his second year there he managed the erection of the neat and commodious house of worship still in use in that charge. Altogether, it was a very successful pastorate. His next appointment, 1860–61, was Stockwell. There we had at the time a prosperous Church academy, and his influence over the students was very happy and fortunate. In 1862–63 his appointment was Delphi. In that charge were some of our most intelligent and enterprising Church members, but they were not numerous. The town was then too small to sustain the several denominations represented by its citizens, and all the Churches were weak numerically and financially. Besides, the country was at that time in the most intense period of our late war. Nevertheless, this pastorate was not without some good fruit. In 1864–66, Brother Greene was the pastor of Strange Chapel, Indianapolis. Though this Church at the time did not rank with the best of our Churches in that city, yet its pastor was the equal of any, and was respected by all. During his stay considerable spiritual interest existed in the charge, and quite a number of souls were converted and gathered into the Church, and they parted with their pastor in sorrow.

The next three years, 1867–69, he was stationed at Greencastle. In this university city he had a wide and appropriate field for his genius, and well did he improve it. His relations to the faculty were always pleasant, the students found in him a sympathizing brother, and the citizens were warmly attached to him. Each of these years was characterized by interesting revivals of religion. In 1870-72 he had pastoral charge of Centenary Church, Terre Haute. It was the trial period in the history of that new Church. It was without a parsonage, and a perplexing Church debt had been dragging along for years, discouraging some of its members, and threatening disaffection. The appointment of Brother Greene to the pastorate at this crisis was opportune, and gave him an opportunity to exhibit his financial ability, and his skill in harmonizing diverse plans among brethren. Under his able leadership the parsonage was built and paid for, and the annoying old church debt was wiped out. This Church did not entirely lose their favorite by the pastoral limit. He continued to live in the city, and traveled the Terre Haute District as presiding elder, 1873-76. In this new field of operation he was abundant in labor, and his preachers always became warmly attached to him. Jealousies and envies never found a place between the preachers and a leader of his modest, gentle spirit.

In 1877-79, Brother Greene served as pastor of Crawfordsville Station. In 1880-81 he was stationed at Asbury Chapel, Terre Haute. During 1882-85 he traveled Crawfordsville District. For the next three years, 1886-1888, he was assigned a new kind of work, the appointment of agent for DePauw University. In the adjustment of affairs between Hon. W C. DePauw and the trustees of the university, in which DePauw conferred his magnificent and much needed endowment on the institution, and the name was changed from "Indiana Asbury" to "DePauw University," the Northwest Indiana Conference—as did also its sister Conferences in Indiana—had assumed the payment of $15,000 each on the general plan. The field had already been largely canvassed, the undertaking was Herculean, and no provision was made for a salary. Brother Greene accepted this agency with great reluctance, and only after the earnest entreaties of brethren. The result proved the wisdom of the choice. He pursued the arduous, unpleasant task until every dollar of the amount was paid by him into the treasury of the university, himself advancing the money on some unmatured notes. The Conference is under lasting obligations to him for this self-denying work in behalf of our cherished university. After it was all accomplished, he said: "Taken all in all, these were the best years of my work for the Church." In 1889 he was appointed to Jamestown Circuit. (He found, as some of his brethren had done before him, that when he had dropped out from the front, the ranks had been closed up by others, leaving no place for him to re-enter where he had stood before.)

On December 25, 1861, James W Greene was married to Miss Catharine Elizabeth Organ, of La Porte, Indiana. She is the daughter of a leading Methodist family, who were prominent in the Church and of high standing in community. They had emigrated from the eastern part of Virginia to La Porte in an early day. Samuel Organ, her father, was a merchant for many years, and afterwards became a banker. Mrs. Greene is a graduate of Albion

College, Michigan, and is a lady of intelligence and polish, as well as a model housewife. Their marriage was blessed with five children, all sons, one of whom died in childhood, and four are now young men, an honor to their parents.

Brother Greene was ordained to deacon's orders by Bishop E. R. Ames in 1858, and to elder's orders by Bishop Matthew Simpson in 1860. He was a member of the General Conference in 1880, and was elected a reserve delegate in 1888. He has for a number of years been an efficient trustee of DePauw University, and is one of the managers of the Preachers' Aid Society of his Conference. In 1888 the DePauw University conferred on him the honorary degree of D. D., of which he is eminently deserving.

As a preacher, Brother Greene is modest and unpretentious, tender, earnest, and effective; never verbose or boisterous. His delivery is soft, smooth, and pleasant; speaks extemporaneously, and shows more than usual originality. A vein of sincerity and deep piety runs through all his pulpit efforts, impressing one with a solemn conviction of his integrity as a man of God intrusted with a divine message for his hearers. His themes are studied with an adaptation to the varied phases of human life; does not attempt display of oratory, nor deal in metaphysics, nor battle with men of straw, but addresses himself to the intellect and the heart. He seeks to profit rather than to please his hearers, and yet is always entertaining. Much of his success is due to faithful, personal, and pastoral work.

In person he is of medium height, compactly

built, rather heavy set, well proportioned, drawing on the scales about 180 pounds. His head is of intellectual mold, and he wears a pleasant countenance. In disposition he is sociable and friendly, amiable in manner, and frank and open in his demeanor; a man calculated to win favor and make friends wherever he goes; plain and unostentatious in his habits and manner. Let no one imagine, however, that he is a man who can easily be imposed on because he may not resent a wrong; there is mettle under that amiable exterior. He never quarrels with any one, as is the fashion of most men, nor does he seek to revenge an injury or a wrong, but simply chooses to travel a different road from those who deceive him or treat him meanly. He has a keen perception of deceit, fraud, and shams, and reads character as we read books; is shrewd to detect the false, and his rising indignation against the shallow attempts to cover a mean act is withering; but he prefers to leave the culprit to work out his own destiny. He is the kind of a man of whom it is sometimes said, "He has no enemies;" but that is a mistake. He may deserve no enemies; but any man of positive character and push in this world will run against the unprincipled, and excite jealousies. The designing and scheming, who think they have his favor, are very much mistaken. But to the honest and upright, who intrust to him their confidence, no truer or more reliable friend is found than James W Greene.

REV. GEO. W STAFFORD.

I, George W Stafford, was born in Giles County, Virginia, September 24, 1815. My father came to Indiana in the spring of 1832. I was converted September 6, 1836, in Giles County, Virginia; was licensed to preach at Stafford's Meeting-house, in Virginia, September, 1837; was recommended to the Holston Conference, received on trial, and appointed to Ashville, North Carolina. I was received into the Indiana Conference at Rockville, in the fall of 1838, and appointed to Newtown. The Lord favored us with great success on this charge. Four hundred were added to the Church. My next appointment was Frankfort; two hundred were added to the Church this year; at Rochester, the next year, one hundred and ninety-six.

Through a ministry of fifty-one years the Lord has been very gracious and kind to us. I have been on the supernumerary and superannuated list ten years, preaching when health and opportunity has favored us. I have seen the Indiana Conference enlarged into four Conferences, and the numerical and financial strength of the Church increased correspondingly.

The first division of the Indiana Conference made two Conferences—Indiana and North Indiana. I was a member of the North Conference. The North Conference was subsequently divided, making a Northwest Conference. I was stationed at Richmond at that time, but was transferred and stationed at Crawfordsville; afterward, at Frankfort, Valparaiso, Greencastle, and Rockville. From the latter I removed to Crawfordsville, where I still reside, and where I presume I will remain until I am transferred to the better home " not made by hands." The days of my pilgrimage must soon end. Now in my seventy-fifth year, I have no regrets that I have given my life to God and to the ministry. My chief regret is that I have not been more faithful, and that I have not done more for the Master and for the Church purchased by his own blood. May the blessing of God rest on my family, on the Church, and on the ministry, when I shall have gone the way from whence I shall not return. "God be with you till we meet again!"

REV. W. R. GOODWIN, D. D.

William Rees Goodwin was born in Brookville, Indiana, July 17, 1832. His parents were among the earliest and leading Methodists in the Whitewater Valley, and their house was for nearly sixty years a " Methodist tavern," at which all Methodist preachers and many of the early Methodists found a free and hospitable home.

After spending his youth in work on the farm, attending school during the winters, he entered "Old Asbury" in September, 1851, and graduated in 1856.

Immediately after graduating he married, and took charge of Goshen Academy, near Louisville, Kentucky.

In September, 1857, he entered the Southeastern Indiana Conference, and was ordained deacon by

Bishop Morris, having been a local preacher four years. His first charge was Edinburg; then Greenwood, Moore's Hill, and Laurel. In each of these charges extensive revivals were had.

In August, 1863, he became president of Brookville College, and remained there three years, and then accepted the chair of English literature and belles lettres in Illinois Wesleyan University, at Bloomington.

At the close of the year he took work in the pastorate, and served the following stations: Lincoln, Champaign, Quincy, Mattoon, Danville, and Decatur, and then for four years was presiding elder of the Quincy District. He then served Centenary Church, Jacksonville, for two years, and for one year was in California in the interests of Prohibition. He then transferred to the Rock River Conference, and served the charge at Park Ridge one year. He is now stationed at Austin, one of the finest suburbs of Chicago, and is having success.

He was a delegate to the General Conference of 1880, and first reserve in 1884. The degree of D. D. was conferred upon him, in 1872, by the Indiana State University. He was ordained elder by Bishop Baker.

Although he has written no book, some of his sermons are in print, and he has been a frequent contributor to the Church papers, and has had several articles in the *Ladies' Repository* and the *Quarterly Review*.

JOHN CLARK RIDPATH.*

Professor John Clark Ridpath, LL. D., the historian, was born in Putnam County, Indiana, April 26, 1840. His parents were from Virginia, near Christiansburg, on the summit of the Alleghanies. The father and mother began life under circumstances of extreme hardship, poverty, and discouragement. He was the first-born son. His birth-place was the humblest of log cabins. He had no advantages beyond those of the frontier subscription and common schools; but while yet in early boyhood, his mind began to display qualities that gave promise of future eminence. Even from childhood his appetite for books was insatiable. To the people of the neighborhood, his understanding and quickness to learn seemed marvelous. At seventeen he was a school-teacher in his native district. At nineteen he entered Asbury (now DePauw) University, at Greencastle, Indiana, and in June, 1863, was graduated from that institution with the first honors of his class. The rapidity with which he made his way through college became a memorable circumstance in its history. The course of study, including two years of preparatory work, was six years in extent. Young Ridpath began at the beginning, and completed the entire course in four years, doubling the second preparatory and freshman years, and also the sophomore and junior. At the same time he taught in a family for his maintenance, and during his senior year was, for the most part, engaged in

*This sketch is taken from the "Twentieth Century Review," February number, 1890.—W. P. H,

teaching in an academy. But such was his ability in the mastery of all branches of study, that he was able to reach the first rank at the end of his course. During his college career Mr. Ridpath began to display his powers as a writer. His essays, poems, and sketches were remarkable for their elegance of diction and solidity of subject-matter. Many of his college productions found their way into print, were favorably noticed by leading newspapers, and were read with interest outside of Indiana.

Already, before his graduation, Mr. Ridpath had been elected to an instructorship in Thorntown Academy. In 1864 he was made principal of that institution, and two years afterwards was chosen superintendent of the public schools in Lawrenceburg. The last named position he held for three years, his administration, both as a teacher and an officer, being regarded as one of signal ability and success. In 1869, Professor Ridpath was elected to the chair of English literature in his *Alma Mater.* Two years afterward he was promoted to the chair of belles lettres and history. In this department of teaching the larger part of his educational work has been accomplished. His career as professor in the halls of the university was one of conspicuous success. In 1879 he was elected vice-president of the university, and in the following year was honored with the degree of Doctor of Laws by the Syracuse (N. Y.) University. Meanwhile, his reputation as an author, lecturer, and public man had become widely extended, and his services on the platform were in large demand in most of the Northern and Western States.

Dr. Ridpath was the principal promoter and originator of those important measures by which Asbury University was put under the patronage of Washington Charles DePauw, whereby an endowment fund of nearly two millions of dollars was secured to the institution, and the name of DePauw conferred upon it. All the official correspondence with Mr. DePauw, relative to this great educational enterprise, was conducted by Mr. Ridpath, and to him the final success of the project was attributed.

Dr. Ridpath's work as an author began in 1874. His first books were the outgrowth of his historical studies in connection with his department of university work. In the year just mentioned and the year following he produced his "Academic History of the United States." The work was at once successful. This was followed, in 1876, by a "Grammar-school History," intended for use in the public schools. In 1877 the author published his "Popular History of the United States," a work which has reached the extraordinary sale of two hundred and sixty-five thousand copies. This was followed in, 1878–79, by "An Inductive Grammar of the English Language." In 1880 he published a "Monograph on Alexander Hamilton;" and in the same year became one of the editors of the "People's Cyclopedia." In the winter of 1881–82 he issued his "Life and Work of Garfield," which, in the course of three months, reached the sale of seventy-five thousand copies. In the following year he published a "Monograph on the Trial of Guiteau," which attracted much attention. He had in the meantime begun the preparation of his largest and most important work. This was a "Cyclopædia of Universal History," on which he labored assiduously for several years. This work was completed in three large volumes, and given to the public in the autumn of 1885. It has been received with wide popular favor. The demand for the work has extended beyond the limits of the United States, and the sale has reached seventy thousand sets. Such has been the success of the work, that the publishers have prepared and issued an *edition de luxe,* in eight volumes, imperial octavo, half-crushed levant, limited to one thousand sets—perhaps the finest single publication ever made west of the Alleghanies. Dr. Ridpath's "Popular History of the United States" and the "Life and Work of Garfield" have both been translated into German, and have met with much public favor in that language.

Meanwhile, in lighter literature the author has achieved similar success. His essays and articles for magazines and reviews are much read and admired.

In the last three years he has been engaged in the production of another large historical work on the "Great Races of Mankind;" being an account of the ethnic origin, the tribal migrations, and the historical development of the principal families of men. Upon this he is expending even greater labor and pains than on his former works. The publication is expected to appear in three volumes about the beginning of 1891. All of Dr. Ridpath's books, though mostly in the so-called dry domain of history, have had the peculiar merit of going directly to the people; and it can not be doubted that his works have been largely potential in producing a general taste for historical reading among the American people. To this popularity and general influence the author's vivid and brilliant style has largely conduced. Recent discriminating reviewers have not hesitated to declare his diction as elegant, refined, and picturesque as that of any American or recent English author. His ability also to seize the leading features of events, to generalize in an interesting way on the greatest of subjects, to deduce the principle of things, and in particular to be scholarly without being pedantic, has been much commended and dwelt upon as constituting an element in the success of his already voluminous writings.

Dr. Ridpath's home is in Greencastle, his college town. He has as yet scarcely reached the prime of his life. He is in full health and strength and vigor of spirits—ready for the greatest task and the most strenuous application. His career happily illustrates the ever-repeated but oft-forgotten lesson, that there are few, if any, obstacles which industry, energy, ambition, and intellectual force can not overcome.

REV ALLEN LEWIS.

I entered the Northwest Indiana Conference in 1873, at twenty-six years of age. Dr. J. W Greene was my first presiding elder. I was appointed to the Bellevue Circuit. I came very nearly being rejected by the brethren of that charge, because they said: "We have had supplies, unordained men, young men, and one thing and another, till we are tired of it." I did not blame them, so far as I was concerned. I was a poor prospect for a Methodist preacher. However, I staid with them, and they staid with me the full term, three years.

My next charge was West Lebanon, of which Dr. Aaron Wood said to me: "If you can make it there, you can succeed anywhere."

This Church, when I went to it, was in an "uproar." I used to think of it that about the best people of it were on the outside, and the other kind were on the inside. I remember the principal steward's report for the first quarter. He had collected nine dollars and a half, and meeting a man as he came to church, whom he owed a dollar and a half, he not having any money of his own paid him out of the preacher's money, but he would pay it during the year. I thought that was good in him all around. I remained with this blessed people three years, the full term. God gave us a glorious revival; about two hundred and forty joined the Church during one winter.

Thence I was sent to Burlington Circuit, having the village of Burlington, and the "regions roundabout," as its contents. There were six appointments, preached three times every Sunday, and every other Sunday rode thirty miles or more. I was glad I survived. Built two churches, a stable, and repaired the parsonage; left at the end of the first year; too much work to suit me; in fact, this has always been my trouble.

From this place I went to Winamac, where, some of the more superstitious say, the old Indian Chief Winamac is buried under the Methodist Church. Notwithstanding all this, the three years spent in this charge are the pleasantest to me, so far, of my ministry. The work is small, two appointments near each other. The people, while not more religious than others, are above those petty faults which give a pastor so much trouble.

My next move was to Lebanon, Boone County, where they used to say the people were web-footed, owing to the aquatic condition of the country. This condition of the country has greatly changed, and Boone County is one of the best counties in the State. Well, I remained in this beautiful little city the three full years. Had the usual "ups and downs." This was my first station, and here was my first Prohibition vote. I think my vote for Mr. St. John for President created more stir than any other one thing I did while I was there. God gave us revivals while here, and the church-building was remodeled.

The next turn of the wheel brought me to Brazil, Ind., the city of coal, dust, and saloons—a cosmopolitan city. In our Church here we have a Pentecost all the time, so far as "tongues" are concerned, sometimes a small "Babel" is more the condition. This is the "biggest thing" I ever had anything to do with. God has blessed the Church of this place so that it numbers about seven hundred. There are four Sunday-schools, having a membership of twelve hundred.

Here I must stop. How much more of the journey remains is not known to me. At present I am happy in my work, and would rather be a Methodist preacher on earth, blessed of God, than an angel in heaven. Yours, ALLEN LEWIS.

REV. J. H. CISSELL, D. D.

LAFAYETTE, INDIANA, February 18, 1890.

MY DEAR BROTHER HARGRAVE,—Your favor of the 11th received. I have grave doubts as to whether there is anything in my history that will in any way interest the general public; but of course, I am willing to comply with your request.

I was born of pious parents in Marion County, Ohio, July 9, 1840. When eight years of age my father brought me to Indiana, where, with the exception of about one year spent in Iowa, I have resided ever since. I was converted at a camp-meeting in Jasper County in 1856. Was licensed to preach and recommended to the Annual Conference by the Battle Ground Quarterly Conference in 1859, and was received on trial the same year and appointed junior preacher on Hebron Circuit. At the end of that year I discontinued, and was out of the work for one year. In 1861 I was again received on trial and appointed to Maxinkuckee Circuit; 1862–64, Kewana; 1864–66, Monticello; 1866, Door Village; 1867–69, Rochester; 1869–72, La Porte Circuit; 1872–75, Michigan Street Church, South Bend; 1875–77, La Porte; 1877–81, La Porte District; 1881-83, Lafayette District; 1883-86, College Avenue Church, Greencastle, 1886–87, Ninth Street Church, Lafayette; in 1887 I was appointed to Lafayette District, of which I am now the presiding elder. I was ordained a deacon by Bishop Morris in 1863, and elder by Bishop Scott in 1865. I was elected to the General Conference of 1880, and received the degree of Doctor of Divinity from DePauw

University in 1884. I was married to Martha Tarr in 1860. She died in 1867, and in 1868 I married Margaret White, my present wife. Three of the seven children whom the Lord has given us have gone over the river. Very fraternally,

J. H. CISSEL.

REV SAMUEL BECK.

With regard to myself I have but little to say I was born in Wayne County, Indiana, November 3, 1832. My father moved from that county to Putnam County in 1849. What little education I got I acquired in common and academic schools. My father made arrangements for me to go to Indiana Asbury University; but a short time before the time for me to enter he failed in business, and lost all of his property. I felt it my duty to help him rather than burden him with expense. And instead of entering college I commenced teaching, and taught common schools, including one year in Bainbridge, for fifteen years, in connection with farming. I was licensed to preach by Dr. Aaron Wood in 1859. I served the Church four years and a half as local preacher; was appointed by Brother Chenowith, presiding elder, to North Salem Circuit, in the spring of 1864, to fill out the year after Brother Mershon's death. That fall, 1864, I joined the Conference (Northwest Indiana) at Delphi. Bishop Baker ordained me local elder at that Conference. I was appointed to Covington Circuit; remained there two years, and was sent to State Line Circuit, two years; from there to Attica, two years; to Crawfordsville, three years; Greencastle, three years; Thorntown, one year; Thorntown District (name changed at the end of one year to Frankfort), four years; Asbury, Terre Haute, three years; La Porte District, to date, four and a half years. During my pastorates, the Churches at State Line City and Marshfield were built, and the Church at West Lebanon was inclosed while I was on the circuit. The Church at Attica was built while I was pastor, and the parsonage at Greencastle. I had good revivals at Attica, Crawfordsville, Greencastle, and Terre Haute, ranging from one hundred to over two hundred conversions at each of the places. The special feature of my work at Thorntown was the providing for an old Church debt of eight thousand dollars, which had been hanging for several years. I succeeded in getting it in individual obligations, paying about one-half of it actually, and the balance was paid within two years. My work as presiding elder has been pleasant, and I trust in a good degree successful. I am on my fifth year on this district, and I think, in some respects at least, it is the best of my presiding eldership. I was ordained elder by Bishop Thomson at Valparaiso in 1868.

If you will pardon what might seem to be a little egotism on my part, I will send you a quotation from a letter received last week from Chaplain McCabe. I will give his own language: "Your circular at hand. It is immense. Of course you will succeed. The way to raise the missionary collections is to find four hundred and fifty men like you, and put them into the eldership. If the bishops would only do that, the work would be done. Methodism would be soon giving two millions for missions."

Now Brother Hargrave, I have given you these dates and facts concerning myself. I have never thus written of myself before; I do not expect you to publish them *verbatim;* but if there are any points in them that will help you in making up your book, you are at liberty to use them. Hoping that this communication is not too late for use, and wishing you great success in your effort, I remain

Yours faithfully, SAMUEL BECK.

REV. HENRY MARSHALL MIDDLETON, A. M.

Rev Henry Marshall Middleton, A. M., was born in a little village known as Rapid Forge, located on Paint Creek, about three miles above Bainbridge, in the western part of Ross County, Ohio, on the 23d of March, 1849. His father, James Middleton, was the son of John Middleton, the eldest of four brothers, who moved from Pennsylvania in the early part of this century, all of whom were stanch members of the Methodist Episcopal Church, and pioneers of Methodism in Southern Ohio. Two of them were local preachers. Each of these families is represented by one or more traveling ministers of our Church, the subject of this sketch being the only preacher of his grandfather's family. His mother, Catherine Weller, was born in Germany, coming in her infancy with her parents, who emigrated to the United States, and settled in Ross County, Ohio. Her parents were members of the German Reformed Church, but con nected themselves with the Presbyterian Church in their new home in Ohio.

Henry was the fourth son in his father's family. Two of his brothers died in infancy. One still lives in California, and a sister, younger than he, lives in Ohio. When he was about five years old his mother died, leaving his father with three small children to care for. Being a man of humble circumstances, he was unable to keep the family together, and so looked out for them Christian homes in which they were brought up. It fell to Henry's lot to be placed in the home of Christian Iseman, near Bethesda, in Ross County, Ohio. Here he lived till he was eighteen years of age, working on the farm during the summer, and attending the district school about three months each winter, except during the latter part of the war of the Rebellion, when the entire care of the farm fell upon him. In this home it fell to his lot to be under the care of one of God's noble women, Mrs. Hannah Iseman, who, like the mother of Samuel, trained him for God. This noble woman still lives, at the advanced age of eighty-one years. At the age of fourteen years he was converted to God, and united with the Church at a gracious revival held at Bethesda under the pastorate of the now sainted Wm. McClintock, of the Ohio Conference.

When twenty-one years of age he came to Indiana and located in Benton County, in the vicinity of Boswell. He spent one year there, teaching school during the winter. In March of the following year, 1871, he returned to Ohio, and on the twenty-third day of the month, the twenty-second anniversary of his birth, he was married to Miss Ellie Hanawalt, at the residence of her father, near South Salem, Ohio. The summer was spent in Ohio in an unsuccessful attempt at farming on the old place on which he was brought up. In the fall he returned to Indiana, and taught school at College Corner, a few miles south of Boswell.

The following summer, under the pastorate of Rev Henry Vencill, he was licensed to preach, and recommended for admission to the Annual Conference, at the camp-meeting held that year at Pine Village. This course was taken under the urgent pressure of the pastor and presiding elder, Dr. J. W T. McMullen, but with great trepidation and reluctance upon his own part. He felt keenly the lack of qualification and scholastic training for this great work. He went to the ensuing session of the Northwest Conference, which was held at Thorntown, and not having prepared for the examination for admission, as it was wholly unexpected to him, he requested Dr. McMullen to withhold his recommendation, and permit him to serve as a "supply" for a year. This was granted, and he was sent to the Monon Circuit. He preached his first sermon in a school-house in Monon, in September, 1872, using as the text, "Commit thy way unto the Lord; trust also in him, and he shall bring it to pass." (Psalm xxxvii, 5.) The text is regarded by him as true, thus far, both to his life and ministry. In the fall of 1873 he was admitted on trial in the Northwest Indiana Conference at its session in South Bend, and reappointed to Monon.

His appointments have been as follows: 1872–73,

Monon; 1874–76, Battle Ground Circuit (now Lafayette Circuit); 1877, West Lafayette; 1878–80, Rolling Prairie; 1881–82, Michigan City; 1883–85, Brazil; 1886-88, First Church, South Bend; 1889, presiding elder Crawfordsville District. While on Battle Ground Circuit he attended and graduated from Battle Ground Collegiate Institute, then under the superintendency of Rev. G. W Rice, A. M., at that time a member of our Conference. He received from DePauw University the honorary degree of Master of Arts in 1886. He was ordained deacon at Greencastle in 1875 by Bishop Janes, and elder by Bishop Merrill at La Porte in 1877 At the Conference of 1877 he was elected recording secretary, which office he held till 1881, at which time he was elected assistant secretary. He served in this capacity, with the exception of one year, till 1887, when he was elected secretary, which office he still holds.

REV D. M. WOOD.

DANVILLE, IND., May 5, 1890.

BROTHER HARGRAVE,—Your letter came while I was in Florida, and on my return my wife was sick, and I have never caught up with my work. Have just got to your letter. Brother Hargrave, I candidly see nothing in my life worth printing. I was one year and a half at Wea; three years at Rossville; three years at Westville; three years at Shawnee; three years at Delphi; three years at Danville. I have staid my three years at all these places at the earnest request of the Churches served and the official boards. I have aimed at a plain gospel and thorough work. Have had good revivals in all my charges, and increase every year on Church benevolences in almost every charge, reaching the apportionments fixed upon my Churches. My wife deserves much credit for all my success. Cordially,

D. M. WOOD.

REV. T. F. DRAKE.

Tiffin Fletcher Drake was born in Fountain County, Indiana, December 11, 1848; united with the Methodist Episcopal Church at Crawfordsville, Indiana, at a quarterly meeting held by Rev. J. H. Hull, in 1868; joined the Northwest Indiana Conference at Brazil, Indiana, in 1878, on trial; and was appointed by Bishop Peck to Bringhurst, Indiana. Here he built one of the best parsonages in the Conference. November 3, 1880, he was married, by Rev. S. Beck, D. D., to Miss Alice Gilkey. He was ordained deacon by Bishop Foster, at South Bend, Indiana, in 1879. In 1881 he was appointed to Harmony and Knightsville. He was ordained elder at Michigan City, by Bishop Peck, in 1882. In 1882 he was appointed to Jamestown, Indiana. In 1884 he was appointed to Burlington, Indiana. In 1886 he was appointed to Winamac and Star City, Indiana. In 1889 he was appointed to Rensselaer, Indiana, where he completed Trinity Methodist Episcopal Church, which was dedicated by Bishop Merrill, January 26, 1890.

REV NOAH LATHROP, A. M.

The subject of this sketch was born at Spencer, Owen County, Indiana, November 9, 1828. He was of eminently Christian parentage; his parents were prominent members of the Methodist Episcopal Church. He was graduated in the regular classical course from Indiana Asbury University (now De-Pauw), July, 1854; and was married at Greencastle, Indiana, July 26, 1854, to Miss Sarah Frances Hargrave, eldest daughter of Rev. Richard and Nancy A. Hargrave. He received his first appointment in the Northwest Indiana Conference in 1854, from Bishop Simpson, to Romney Circuit. This was an old-fashioned four-weeks' circuit. Rev. Thomas C. Webb was his colleague. The work was hard, and there was not much time left for study; yet the Lord owned and blessed the work. Here the young couple buried their first-born child. His next appointment was by Bishop Ames, to Kingsbury Circuit, the same Conference. They had to move one hundred miles by private conveyance, and the journey was very dangerous on account of high waters. During that year he removed to Minnesota, and in August, 1856, was present at the organization of the Minnesota Conference; but not having procured a transfer as a probationer from the Northwest Indiana Conference, he took work under the presiding elder, Rev T M. Kirkpatrick, serving Cannon Falls Circuit. In 1857 he was stationed at Monticello. During this year the grasshopper scourge visited that country, and all suffered great privations. His next appointment was Osceola Mills, Wisconsin, where he remained two years. The salary was so small as to necessitate the sale of a quarter-section of valuable land, in order to live in comfort. Chatfield, Minnesota, was his next appointment. Stockton, Minnesota, the next. He lived that year in the house with his father, as there was no parsonage on the work. The next appointment was Plainview, Minnesota. Then at Anoka Station three years—a successful and happy pastorate. Next, St. Cloud, Minnesota. Next Paynesville Circuit, two years. Here he entered a piece of land—or settled a homestead—in the popple-woods. His next appointment was St. Cloud District, upon which he remained for three years. His subsequent appointments were: Northfield Station, Clearwater, Lake City, Zumbrota, Pine Island, High Forest, Dundas, Castle Rock, Clear Lake, Annondale.

While living at Dundas, February 22, 1884, he suffered that greatest of all losses, to the husband and father, in the death of his faithful and beloved wife. Their union was blessed with nine children, three of whom died in infancy. Those who survive are useful and happy.

October 6, 1886, he was married to Mrs. Marie Perkins, of Minneapolis, Minnesota; and, with his desolated home reconstructed, he is approaching old age brightly and cheerfully.

It may be said of Brother Lathrop that he has been a most useful and devoted minister. He has never affected the grace of oratory, but has always been regarded as an excellent preacher and pastor.

Endowed with strong common sense, good judgment, and fine social qualifications—" without spot or wrinkle or any such thing "—his charges have always been in safe hands. It may be said, also, that his eminent sense of justice and of right have always rendered him influential upon questions of public concern. He is eminently patriotic, and an outspoken advocate of every righteous cause. He was an original Abolitionist, being of good old Puritan stock; also an active advocate of *Prohibition*. In these regards his distinguished brother, Rev. Ezra R. Lathrop, of the same Conference, has a similar record. These men, together with many of their immediate associates in the ministry, are not to be misunderstood upon any question of right. *The trumpet gives no uncertain sound.* Such are the men whom God, in his good providence, sent to pioneer his cause and the cause of humanity in the great and prosperous commonwealth of Minnesota. Being *in at the start*, it was theirs to do a great deal of strictly mission-work, and, in the development of the Church, to keep pace with the progress of society, to keep the banner of Christ " still full high advanced," and to call the people up to the highest ideals of Christian living. Nobly have they performed these duties and met those obligations that devolved upon them! And it may be truthfully said that nowhere has the " religion, pure and undefiled," of Wesleyan Methodism been more fully exemplified than by many of these brethren, zealously laboring for Christ " away down among the zeros," upon the steppes of the great " Wheat State!"

It may also be said of Mr. Lathrop that he is a man of business, having been for several years secretary of his Conference.

REV. ALBION FELLOWS, A. M.

Rev. Albion Fellows was born in North Sandwich, Carroll County, New Hampshire, September 16, 1827, and was the seventh son of Stephen and Rachel Fellows. His paternal ancestry was of English descent, being descended from William Fellows, who came from England about the year 1640. His mother, Rachel McGaffie, was of Scotch-Irish ancestry.

When seven years of age his father moved to Dixon, Illinois. In 1840 the father died, leaving the mother and children to struggle with poverty and the hardships of pioneer life.

Albion was converted in 1846, entered Rock River Seminary, at Mount Morris, Illinois, in 1847, and remained as a student about two years. After teaching and working on a farm two years, he and his younger brother, Stephen, in April, 1851, entered the Indiana Asbury University, at Greencastle, Indiana, from which they graduated with high honors in 1854. During the junior and senior years he was a tutor in the university.

Immediately after his graduation, Brother Fellows was married to Miss Mary Erskine, a young lady of Methodist parentage, of remarkable force of character and deep religious experience, who became to him a helpmeet indeed. They were blessed with six children—four daughters and two sons. The sons died in infancy. The eldest daughter, aged thirteen, survived her father but a short time. The mother, with three daughters, remains. The latter are all happily married, and are an honor to their parents.

In 1854 the subject of this sketch joined the Northwest Indiana Conference. In 1854–55, was stationed at Valparaiso; in 1855–56, at Westville; 1856–58, professor of Greek in Fort Wayne College; 1858–59, in charge of Sumption's Prairie Circuit; 1859, transferred to the Indiana Conference, stationed at Boonville; 1860–62, stationed at Mount Vernon; 1862–63, presiding elder of Evansville District; 1863 to March, 1865, pastor of Locust Street charge (now Trinity), Evansville, where he died.

We are informed that Brother Fellows was sent to Evansville especially to build a church, as the congregation had outgrown "Old Locust Street," and the flourishing condition of the Church and the city would justify building. This plan resulted in the completion, in 1865, of the magnificent Trinity Methodist Episcopal Church. Brother Fellows, however, "only lived to see the church inclosed and plastered, and the lecture-room nearly ready for seating." He was succeeded in the charge by Rev C. N. Sims, D. D., now chancellor of Syracuse University, New York, under whose pastorate the church was completed, and the charge continued in a career of renewed prosperity.

With reference to the closing period of Brother Fellows's life, his beloved wife says: "No one but myself could believe how much of a martyr he was to the work of the pastorate, as well as to the soliciting and collecting of money, and superintending the whole work of building. He could not be persuaded that he must take rest, or relax his efforts in any part of his work, till it was too late. He had the most unbounded faith in an overruling Providence, and thought till almost the last that he would be spared to complete the work. On his return from what proved to be his last visit to the new church (he came home prostrated by the dampness of the walls), he rested awhile on the sofa, and then sat down to the organ and played and sang that hymn, 'Spirit, thy warfare's o'er;' then went to his room, not to leave it again alive."

Had Brother Fellows lived, it would seem that he must have had a life of great usefulness and happiness before him. With good general scholarship, and remarkable proficiency in the departments of education in which he labored, he was deeply grounded in theology, and continued ever to be a close student; also, deeply interesting himself in the public welfare. He molded his character upon the model of John Wesley. His self-denial was absolute; his energy and industry extraordinary; his life most methodical; his hungering and thirsting after righteousness insatiable; most exemplary in life; most genial and attractive in society; idolized in his own home; ever young in heart, the young thronged about him. As a pastor he was eminently successful; an excellent preacher, not aiming at the graces of oratory, yet striking in person, style, and manner; solemn, instructive, and convincing—" bringing in the sheaves;"

perhaps the sweetest singer of all. He was thoroughly cultured in the science of music, both vocal and instrumental. His voice was a pure and powerful soprano; and yet he was an equally good tenor. He was great in gospel song. Thus equipped for the work, his charges were in a constant state of revival and growth.

He died suddenly of *heart-failure,* in the thirty-ninth year of his age, "mourned by all the people."

We give in this connection a brief sketch of his brother, Rev. Stephen N. Fellows, D. D., eminent in the ministry and in educational work.

REV. STEPHEN N. FELLOWS, A. M., D. D.[*]

During the past thirty years no Iowa educator has been more public-spirited, nor labored more zealously outside the class-room to mold public opinion, wielded a greater influence in shaping the educational thought and movements of the State, than Dr. S. N. Fellows, so well known for twenty years as professor of mental and moral science and didactics in the Iowa State University. Stephen N. Fellows was born, May 30, 1830, in North Sandwich, New Hampshire. He is the youngest of eight sons of Stephen and Rachel Fellows, of English and Scotch-Irish descent. His ancestors were among the early settlers, coming to this country in the seventeenth century. When he was four years old his family removed to Dixon, Illinois, where, in the midst of the privations of a frontier life, his boyhood was spent. When Stephen N. was but ten years old his

---

[*] From the *Iowa Normal Monthly* for February, 1890.

father died, and the Fellows family were left to struggle with poverty amidst the trials and hardships of a pioneer settlement. He thus early learned to take care of himself, and he is a fair example of what may be attained under such circumstances by perseverance, industry, and energy. His early educational advantages were meager, but throughout boyhood he had a thirst for knowledge, which led him to read eagerly all books and newspapers within his reach. Hard work and hard fare on the farm developed a strong physical frame, and prepared him for the struggle for learning. At eighteen he entered the Rock River Seminary at Mount Morris, Illinois; but his means being exhausted, at the end of the fourth term he was obliged to discontinue his studies in school for a time. In 1851 he entered the Asbury (now DePauw) University, at Greencastle, Indiana, and by teaching, working on the farm, and boarding himself while at school, his finances enabled him to finish his course, taking the degree of Bachelor of Arts in 1854. During his junior and senior years he was tutor in Latin and mathematics. Just previous to his graduation, he was elected professor of mathematics and natural science in Cornell College, at Mount Vernon, Iowa. This position he held for six years—from 1854 to 1860.

In 1856, Professor Fellows joined the Upper Iowa Conference of the Methodist Episcopal Church. His chief desire in seeking an education was to become a minister of the gospel, and he only engaged in teaching in order to earn money to enable him to enter upon his duties in this field unembarrassed by debt. In 1860 he resigned his position in Cornell College to engage in the pastoral work, and for seven years he filled ministerial charges at Dyersville, Tipton, Lyons, and Marshalltown. Professor Fellows was married in 1856 to Miss Sarah L. Matson, daughter of Dr. S. G. Matson, of Anamosa, a lady of fine qualities and attractive ways. They have had six children, four of whom, two sons and two daughters, are still living.

In August, 1867, by unanimous vote, and without solicitation, he was elected principal of the normal department in the Iowa State University. In 1871 he received the degree of Doctor of Divinity from Cornell College. For twenty years Professor Fellows occupied his position in the university, and during that time was always its zealous supporter, and was thoroughly devoted to every interest of the institution. No man could have shown more complete devotion to every duty. He did excellent work for the university in the lecture-field as well as in the class-room, having worked in normal institutes and lectured in more than sixty counties in Iowa. A few years ago a prominent Iowa educator said through the daily press that he believed Professor Fellows had done more to unite the university and the public schools of the State than any other man in the institution.

In 1873, through the efforts of Dr. Fellows, the elementary normal department of the university was transformed, and became the chair of didactics, united with that of mental and moral sciences. For six years this was the only chair of didactics in any American college or university. This chair was founded on the idea of Dr. Fellows, that since a large number of the graduates of the university become principals and superintendents of schools, in the higher positions in the State, they should have some professional training in the last years of their university course, to fit them for their positions. It was found that nearly seventy-five per cent of the school principals and superintendents in Iowa, receiving salaries of one thousand dollars and upwards, received their education in colleges and universities; and of them the number educated in the State University "exceeds the number from all the other colleges and universities in Iowa."

Since the founding of the chair, in 1873, an average of more than one-half the number in the successive senior classes of the university have been enrolled in the didactic classes. This may give the reader some idea of the influence which has been exerted by Dr. Fellows in his class-room on the educational work of the State, the result of which will not be lost for generations to come. Outside of educational work, Dr. Fellows has exercised a wide influence in Iowa on the temperance question. His open letters on this question have attracted attention all over the land, and have been widely copied by the press. He is president of the Iowa State Temperance Alliance.

In 1887, Dr. Fellows's connection with the State University was severed. Since that time he has been in the regular pastoral work of the Methodist Episcopal Church. He is now stationed at Manchester, Iowa. He is still robust in health, and retains all the vigor, enthusiasm, and progressiveness of manhood's prime. It was a great loss to the University when his connection was severed therefrom. As a preacher in the pulpit he is thoughtful, fervid, and impressive, exhibiting great power of heart and brain.

SACRED POEMS.

The song of redemption is an ode to the Crucified, sung on earth and in heaven.

R. HARGRAVE.

OLD TESTAMENT SCENES.

CREATION BY "THE WORD."

SHALL I to muses reverently pray
    For flowing numbers to assist my song?
Or invoke the graces for a pleasing lay,
    To touch my bosom and inspire my song?
This were an idle, Pagan work, withal!
    With sacred awe I near God's throne of love;
For inspiration more divine I call,
    My thoughts and feelings graciously to move!

My theme so high demands the aid divine,
    To chase the shadows from my thoughts obtuse,
Which long have held them veiled from themes sublime,
    That poets in their inspirations use;
Aid for my heart touched by a glowing coal
    From off God's altar, that bright seraphs bring;
Grant to my humble muse her highest goal—
    The all-creating power of Christ to sing!

The praises of the great Incarnate Word,
    Who made and rules this goodly universe;
Jehovah's equal, equally adored,
    I magnify in melody of verse.
At his creative fiat, all divine,
    All things, in heaven and earth and sea,
Began to be, or see, or feel, or shine;
    At his behest they all got leave to be.

At whose command they all came teeming forth
    From chaos dark; the continents he founds;
He " o'er the empty place suspends the North;"
" He compasseth the waters with their bounds."
The planets haste them on their orbit-tracks,
    And keep the limits he for them ordains;
By force impelled, restrained by what attracts;
    As they began, till now, each course remains.

The bliss of beings sentient he means;
    His glory stands immovably secure,
Despite man's sin—too oft it intervenes—
    Yet still his laws immutably endure.
From cause so high, from Being so divine,
    Sprang principalities and mighty powers,
Unseen or visible, alike sublime,
    Alike dependent for their days and hours.

Most dignified amid terrestrial things
    Stands noble, godlike man, sublimely high;
His vision to his inward senses brings
    Delight from objects far remote or nigh;
And wide the empire that he holds at will,
    O'er fowls on airy wing that fleetly soar,
Or beasts four-foot that roam at large afield,
    Or fish that make their way with finny oar.

Man's body is a tenement well made,
    In which the tenant may in safety dwell;
His spirit is in holiness arrayed,
    The ends of being thus to serve full well.
A goodly instrument, contrived with skill,
    Man's frame is made to serve his nobler part;
To do the bidding of an inward will,
    And well evince the Maker's plastic art.

CREATION BY "THE WORD." 359

Man's organs, too, are set with just design,
  Most opportunely for the ends they serve;
The feet to walk, the hands their craft to find,
  And both, alike, the weal of life preserve.
Who built the *tenement*, the *tenant* sends
  To habitation fit for occupance;
Thus two distinctive parts man's nature blends,
  And both the blessedness of life enhance.

And must this twofold man anon be rent?
  Each part to its fit element return?
To keep them one, the "Tree of Life" is meant;
  Man lives if he forbidden fruit but spurn!
The *Logos* looks on man, well pleased to find
  His image on man's inward nature sealed;
There "righteousness and holiness" do shine,
  Ready for all God's holy will revealed.

Thus "wonderfully made" and Eden-blessed,
  Man seems well fit his Maker's will to do;
Was fit for abstinence, enjoined as test,
  And thus to escape sin's soul-undoing woe.
But O! our lustful look toward that tree,
  All laden with its tempting fruit, inspired
Inordinate desire—vile sympathy
  With Satan's lure; and innocence expired!

A cloud of hell-deserving guilt rose high;
  On man's transgressions came a horrid doom!
No "bow of promise" arched the angry sky,
  Nor ray of hope did shine athwart the gloom!
Dread thunder, with a soul-convulsing roar,
  Did iterate Jehovah's fearful wrath,
As man's transgression then came up before
  The Lord;—and out from Eden lay man's path!

REDEMPTION BY "THE WORD."

Jehovah sits majestic on his throne!
Bright glories manifold are all his own;
The right divine he claims to vindicate,
Nor inattent is he to man's lost state.
In his right hand, behold an awful scroll,
Of solemn moment to each human soul;
Externally affixed are "seven seals"—
Its contents none, the while, to man reveals.
God's angel challenges the One whose worth
Can set the secrets of that volume forth.
The prophet weeps for that no one is found,
On searching heaven, and sighting earth around,
Of dignity and worth to "take the Book,"
Its seals to break, and on its pages look!

The angel bids the prophet's tears be dry,
And silences each plaint and grieving sigh;
"Lo! Judah's Lion doth in strength prevail,"
While other worth than his could nought avail.
His eye he turns, to note the Lion's form;
"The Lamb" he sees, whose flowing blood is warm.
The Lion's form was not forthcoming then—
The Lamb, instead, did God's behest attend,
As, newly slain, and all in gory guise,
He confronts the throne, while hallelujahs rise!
The Lion did the wondrous gift obtain,
Incarnate in the Lamb, thus "newly slain."

Nor sooner doth redemption's plan decide
That Christ, in flesh, shall on this earth abide,
Than doth his glory on the throne grow pale,
To glitter in the "Tabernacle Veil."
To angel hosts that glory died away,
And stooped to earth, with fallen man to stay!

On mercy's plan the angels long did gaze,
To comprehend the meaning of the grace
Thus ratified to man, and free for all—
Denied the angels in their dismal fall!
But it was life from everlasting death,
That mercy deigned to show its glory, 'neath
Cherubic wings; to deck the "Mercy Seat,"
Replete with grace, true penitence to greet.

Lest guilty man, unfit for heavenly bliss,
Should taste immortalizing fruit, and miss
Life's boon supreme, and share immortal pain,
God cast him out "till dust be dust" again.
He sends him to a more congenial soil,
Till life should end, with all its sweat and toil;
Jehovah's *Justice* bids him there abide,
While *Mercy* can for all his woes provide.

Two cherubim their mission execute,
To drive man from the immortalizing fruit,
Thus shunning an eternal curse withal,
Involved in their undoing, primal fall.
Now bearing on the sinning pair, whose fate
Impels their flight to Eden's open gate,
They thrust at them their swords, whose angry flame
Pursues the culprits in their guilt and shame.

Nor sooner do the expatriated pair
Surcease from flight, and breathe awhile from fear,
Than hope springs up within the aching breast,
Though doomed to "vanity," at God's behest,
Where sweat exudes and mortal powers decay;
Yet do they hope, despite the debt to pay!
Creation all must share the flying woe,
And dying strife must visit all below!

The penal sword that drove them from their home,
And frowned upon their desolating doom,
Now calls its flames away from sinning ones,
To type His grace whose death for sin atones.
" On its own hilt the flames recoil," to show
How Mercy saves a guilty soul from woe;
How Innocence for guilty sinners bleeds,
To save them from their soul-undoing deeds.
They read the mild complexion of such love,
And come, in contrite penitence, to prove
Forgiveness free before the " Holy Place ;"—
To weep and pray, and ratify their peace.

ABEL'S FAITH.

Sad Abel nears " the presence of the Lord,"
To gain the comfort pardon can afford;
Full well he knows the dire defeat of Cain,
Whose bloodless gift no pardon did obtain ;
For gifts more excellent than Cain's he sighs,
And lo! hard by faith opportunely spies
The gentle lamb, whose streaming blood he brings,
Foreshowing richer grace and " better things."
Enthroned on high, the touch of faith God feels;
The Spirit sends and Abel's pardon seals.

Before " the presence of the Lord," in heaven
Glad angels shout when Abel is forgiven ;
They see the throne of God grow strangely bright,
And gently quiver in a softer light;
Justice appeared, God smiles in richer grace,
Through him who buys and ratifies man's peace.
Since man's first sin, the angels had not seen
God's throne so decorated with heavenly sheen.
" The Word of God" on high now reappears,
But manhood's meaner garb, it seems, he wears.

A voice of richer worth than Abel's blood
Beseeches mercy at the throne of God,
And far and near, Christ's sin-atoning love
Shows mansions bought for fallen men above,
While o'er the throne redemption's rainbow bends—
To all the firmament its luster lends;
And music chants far sweeter melodies
Than ever rang along the azure skies;
And robes were seen of fairer righteousness
Than angels ever yet had worn for dress.
They lovingly bespeak the task to serve
"The heirs" of grace, defend them, and preserve;
God makes them servants of his precious sons,
And in their hands they bear his "little ones,"
To keep them in the rage of battle's strife,
And shout them, victors, to their "crown of life."

THE CALL OF ABRAHAM.

'Mid Chaldee scenes idolatry holds sway,
Of sun-orbed fire or *Luna's* silver ray;
Or twinkling stars that shine in heaven's cope,
Which men adore, devoutly looking up.
The shrine wears rosy emblems of the sun,
And satellites that ever round him run.
Bright gods abound—all shining things are gods;
To them, with awe, idolatry still nods.
The sun-adoring temple glitters high,
The sun-adoring devotees loud vie;
To honor fiery objects their delight,
The sun by day, the moon and stars by night.
Here Abraham adores in humble plight,
Kissing his hand, extends it to the light,
To gain an absolution from his sin,
And renovation of his heart unclean.

Nahor and Haran mingle in the crowd,
Fire-gods adoring with wild orgies loud;
Enticed by fire, their hearts in idol-love,
Deny the only God, who rules above.
On Abraham there dawns a light divine,
Its uncreated glories on him shine;
Outblazes far the sun's effulgent face,
Shows sin's opaqueness, and its shades doth chase,
Enshrouds in darkness every idol bright,
Veiled in this disk of uncreated light!
The breast of Abraham imbibes desire,
That quenches all his love of sun-orbed fire;
From shining gods he turns with scorn away,
Charmed by the glories of Messiah's day.
Through vistas bright, lo! Abraham descries
The day of Christ, and laughs in ecstacies;
Sees nations with its peerless grandeur dressed,
Filled with its mercy, consummately blessed!
Sees Godhead glory blended with his "seed,"
Sees Godhead pity act redemption's deed!
Sees Messianic glories wide unfold;
Hears songs of chanting, melody untold,
That voice the bliss the nations shall receive,
Who on the *Seed of Isaac* shall believe.

Jehovah says: "Now get thee hence in speed
To unknown lands; thy journey I will lead."
His faith obeys, not knowing where he goes—
To all the "heirs of faith" a pattern shows.
His faith stands registered for after days,
The type for all of justifying grace.
Or ever Abraham in flesh received
The circumcision-seal his heart believed.
The faith of Abraham be ever mine!
Like him may I to holy deeds incline;

Like his, my heart be dead to earthly toys,
Like him aspire to ever-during joys.
With all his seed may I at last be blessed,
To lean my head on his paternal breast!

GOD'S COVENANT WITH ABRAHAM.

To Abraham, beloved, Jehovah says:
  "I am thy shield, and very great reward,
To cheer and keep thee all thy pilgrim days.
  Walk thou before me, heeding well my word."
Now Abraham, in agony of prayer,
  Implores a sign his failing hope to stay.
Quoth he: "This Eliezer is my heir,
  And childless I remain until this day."

"This shall not be thine heir," the Lord replies,
  "But from thy loins shall emanate thy seed;
Vast blessings from thy offspring shall arise;
  From nation yet unborn the Holy One proceed.
I am thy God, who called thee forth from Ur;
  This land I yield for goodly heritage."
The patriarch responds with trembling fear:
  "What token dost thou give me as presage?"

The Lord: "A heifer take of three years old,
  She-goat and ram, each split in twain;
A dove and pigeon dress, but leave them whole,
  And watch till thou the sought-for sign obtain."
Blood-seeking vultures come on drooping wings,
  Intent the holy sacrifice to taste—
To feast profanely on most sacred things;
  To drive them off the patriarch makes haste.

Now night-fall hovers o'er in gloom profound;
  The slumbering patriarch now quakes with fear;

All prone he lies upon the chilly ground,
    While God essays his aching heart to cheer:
"Thy seed shall dwell in stranger lands—not theirs—
    And cruel tyrants shall afflict them sore;
But I will note their anguish, heed their prayers,
    And bring them back to dwell as heretofore."

The sacrificial beasts are set in rows,
    And for God's sign is left an ample space;
"The smoking furnace" and the lamp that glows,
    Confirm sublime the covenant of grace.
The azure sky above seems diamond-lit,
    The seed of Abraham to signify;
Each starry gem foretells in manner fit,
    The children of his faith, remote or nigh.

"So shall thy offspring be the heirs of God,"
    Jehovah says, to reassure the Seer;
"In all the nations of the earth abroad,
    Shall thy glad seed in holiness appear;
Their faith imputed, too, for righteousness,
    All like thine own, when thee I first did call;
Shall all in Isaac's seed be fully blessed,
    And him they shall in reverence extol.

To thee and to thy seed I yield this land,
    From Egypt's River quite to Euphrates;
Thy heritage shall stretch, at my command,
    O'er Kenites, Jebusites, on to the seas.
Full seven kingdoms I assign to thee;
    Thus render thee and thine a rich bequest;
A goodly heritage the gift shall be,
    Where all thy seed in future time shall rest."

DESTRUCTION OF SODOM.

The cry of Sodom's sin ascends on high
To call God's anger down the frowning sky,
While justice brings Jehovah timely down
To curse the wicked with a woe profound.
Two angel forms attend him as he goes
To deal on wickedness avenging blows;
But mercy makes them halt at Mamre, where
The heir of faith doth offer up his prayer.
He looks, and lo! three seeming men appear;
He speeds, and greets them with most kindly cheer,
His face upon the ground in lowly mood;
Invites them to his tent for rest and food.
"Come, lave your feet, and cool beneath this bower,
And pass in quietness a restful hour;
Some bread I'll fetch you out in fitting haste,
And ye shall share a plentiful repast."

Quoth they: "So do, as thou hast kindly said,
While we abide beneath this cooling shade."
To Sarah now he says: "In haste prepare
The finest meal, and knead the dough with care,
And bake the cakes upon the heated hearth,
And make a banquet for these men of worth."
To bring "the fatted calf" he hastes afield,
This to the hand of the young man doth yield,
To dress it well with milk and butter blent,
To make a dainty meal is his intent.
All this he does to tempt immortal guests,
And sets abundance forth for them to feast.

When leisure serves, the angel asks to find
Famed Sarah's whereabouts, but asks it kind.
Quoth Abraham: "Lo! she is in the tent."

This Sarah heeds, with stirring thoughts attent.
Jehovah says: "I surely will return,
What time thy aged wife shall bear a son."
This, Sarah heard, as she, unseen, reclined
Near where the unknown angel guests had dined.
She laughs at fortune-telling, so absurd;
Nor did she think that thoughtless laugh was heard.
"Why laughed thy wife at things so good and true?
Is anything too hard for God to do?"
Quoth she: "I did not laugh." She was afraid.
"Nay, thou didst laugh," the angel gently said;
"The thing the Lord will certainly fulfill,
Thou shouldst accept with readiness of will."

The angels rise from 'neath the cooling tree,
And look intently at the sights they see;
Toward the cities of the Sodom plain
Their ear they turn, as if some news to gain.
Jehovah says: "Shall I conceal this thing
From Abraham?—the evil that I bring
On foul transgressors, for their evil deeds,
The hour of vengeance for their sin proceeds."
Their faces they in holy anger turn
To try if Sodomites shall *live*, or *burn*.

Now Abraham draws near in pleading prayer,
Aghast for that his kinsman doth dwell there:
"Wilt thou confound the good and bad in doom—
The evil and the good alike consume?
The judge of all the universe doth right,
In evil thou canst never take delight.
If fifty righteous souls, perchance, be there,
Wilt thou, for sake of them, the guilty spare?"
"If I in Sodom find the souls in quest,
I will on their account preserve the rest."
Quoth Abraham: "If there be lacking five,

Then wilt thou kindly save the rest alive?"
"If two score righteous souls and five there be,
On their account the rest shall all be free."
"If two score righteous men in Sodom live,
Wilt thou for sake of them all else forgive?"
The Lord replies, in plenitude of grace:
"For forty I will kindly spare the place."
And Abraham implores: "O, let the Lord
In mercy yet another chance afford!
If thirty righteous ones shall there be found,
Then shall forgiveness to the rest abound?"
The Lord replies: "If haply they be there,
For all the rest a pardon I'll declare."
Quoth he: "If one score righteous men there are,
Then shall they live in answer to my prayer?"
"If twenty righteous in vile Sodom dwell,
All else shall live my patient grace to tell."
"O, let not God be angry when I plead!
For kindred, all exposed, I intercede;
If in the place there chance to be but ten,
With righteous Lot, O wilt thou pardon then?"
"For sake of them I will the rest forgive,
And Sodom's guilty sons may longer live."
The angel ceased communing with his host,
And Abraham ceased pleading—all was lost!

To Sodom angels came at eventide,
Whom "righteous Lot" in charity espied.
He runs to greet them, in a cordial mood,
And makes them welcome to repose and food.
"Nay, rather we'll abide astreet," they say.
He presses them, and they turn in to stay;
To them he tenders hospitable cares,
And ministers to "angels unawares."
Now, citizens of heaven near hell are found;
Vile riot and debauch aloud resound;

Men brawl, and utter words that shame all speech;
Around Lot's house they toil " to make a breach."
The angels keep Lot's family secure
From ruffian hordes, with purposes impure,
Who vent mad cries, their shameless wishes tell,
And thus on earth enact the deeds of hell!

The morning dawns, the angels hasten Lot.
" Arise!" they say, " and leave this cursed spot!
The cities of the plain in guilt are doomed;
In haste escape, that ye be not consumed!"
They linger still, and loth they seem to go,
And leave the place consigned to utter woe;
In sweet, bewitching charms their home seems clad,
Thus summoned to depart they all are sad.
" More swiftly haste!" the eager angels say,
" For we can ne'er do aught while here ye stay;
We can not scathe these guilty heirs of hell
Till ye to mountain caverns flee to dwell."

Lot wails: " If now thy servant hath found grace
With thee, I can not flee to such a place;
Some evil will betide me that I die;
Yon little city, thither let me hie!"
The angel says: " I have accepted thee;
Fly quick to Zoar, and ye shall be free.
Look not behind thee—all are doomed to die!
'Scape to your refuge—still more swiftly fly!"

The sun rose bright, no evil yet appeared,
Men met astreet, and loud each other cheered;
They ate and drank without the fear of harm.
And lustily they laughed at Lot's alarm;
And brute desire each lustful bosom swayed;
Of evil less ashamed, lust louder brayed,
And mirth sang lyrics merrily and gay,
While all conspired to praise the rising day.

Meantime the angels are at work to blow
The bellows of God's wrath till ether glow,
And the omnipotence of ardent heat
Surcharges earth and sky with fuel fit
For decomposing flames that now dart up
From horizontal lines to heaven's cope.
Black clouds o'ercast the azure vault above,
And stormy vengeance howling winds commove;
The thunder roars along with deafening sound,
And earthquake jars convulse the solid ground.

The sun, erst very red, now paler seems,
Till sackcloth mantle shrouds his golden beams,
And dismal night ensues to gilded morn,
Of gloom profound and hopeless woe forlorn.
The clouds grow crimson, and sulphurous smells
Salute the nasal sense, and vengeance tells!
Now long, loud, bitter shrieks from all ascend,
While flaky drops of red-hot fire descend
On human forms, distilling death on all—
For Sodom's sins all Sodomites do fall.
'T was as "volcanoes vomiting their seas,"
That long had kept their contents ill at ease,—
Just so it rained in crimson drops the time
Upon the hosts accursed for nameless crime.

Far off doth Abraham now stand, just where
He pleaded long in agony of prayer,
For grace to screen the "Cities of the Plain,"
And lo! a cloud ascends of smoke and flame;
All like a furnace in an angry glow
Were Sodom and Gomorrah in their overthrow!

THE TRIAL OF ABRAHAM'S FAITH.

Jehovah strangely speaks to Abraham,
    To try his faith, who is Faith's promised heir;
"When sleep instructs the soul," the vision came,
    Presaging wonders that to him appear.
As if 'neath rose and amaranth shades reclined,
    His dreams are sweet, and lovely prospects rise;
To know the coming days his thought inclined,
    Whose scenes evolve before his grace-lit eyes.

"The heathen justified by faith" alone,
    Unveils, sublime, to his adoring gaze:
In virtue of His blood which doth atone,
    Whose all-redeeming merit loud they praise.
With joy he notes the heirs of his own faith,
    Who tread the path His holy feet do ply;
God speaks in love, and lovingly he saith:
    "As sea-shore sands, thy seed shall multiply."

What ample scenes unfold, what countless throngs
    Bestrew those mystic fields, extending wide!
He heeds their grace-extolling, grateful songs,
    As in the Father's love they safe abide.
From nations all they come in eager haste;
    From scenes of dark idolatry they speed;
Their idols loathing, glad they come to taste
    The feast of grace, prepared by "Isaac's Seed."

And Abraham they gladly greet as sire;
    Their filial claims most fatherly he owns;
Released from galling yokes of bondage dire,
    They share the liberty of God's dear sons.
Rapt scenes of softer glories glide along,
    Foreshowing better things, of richer grace;
They entrance the holy patriarch with song,
    As he descries Messiah's coming days.

Before his eager eye, next, Isaac stands,
  "In figure of the Lord," more decorate;
And, lo! they come in haste from Gentile lands,
  And humbly greet him in his high estate.
"What honors vast my Isaac now doth share!"
  Quoth Abraham, in gratitude untold;
"His fame resounds in nations near and far,
  And in all coming time shall it unfold!"

Anon, the curtain drops, and all is drear;
  Jehovah says: "Thy lovely son shall die!"
His heart is riven with convulsing fear,
  While he, upon his couch, aghast doth lie.
From out an Eden-sky dread thunder rolled—
  "Go, get thee to Moriah's distant height;
The sacrificial spot will there be told,
  What time obedient faith shall merge in sight;

There offer him a whole burnt-offering!"
  And Abraham from wondrous dreaming wakes;
God's dread behest doth all his being wring,
  While thus in fearful mood he greatly quakes.
With unaccustomed thoughts his heart is stung—
  Pierced through by griefs that Sarah must not know;
They inward writhe, unuttered by his tongue,
  While he to morning task doth sadly go.

And Sarah kissed her son, and gently placed
His silken ringlets, that his temples graced;
The balmy breezes, charged with odors sweet,
Their smiling faces with refreshing greet.
The father's brow is knit with boding care—
To tell the reason why, he doth not dare.
Quoth he: "Must all my hopes be quenched in night?—
My son be immolated in my sight?

Must I be deemed his murderer henceforth,
Whose life foreshows a son of priceless worth?
God's faithfulness must I thus falsify,
And at my hand the child of promise die?"
He lingers not to ply his feeble ken
To things too dark for him to comprehend;
He leaves the tent to Sarah and to tears,
And for his task, most onerous, prepares.

He goes with servants and his lovely child
To desert-scenes, most desolate and wild;
The lad beside him talks of things he sees,
Or birds' sweet warbling notes among the trees;
Sees mountain-slopes, where feed the hungry flocks;
The mountain-peak his dizzy vision mocks.
His heart is tuned to sympathies so pure,
That Abraham his grief can scarce endure!

Third morn the patriarch uplifts his eye,
And espies the place where Innocence must die!
The sign so dread, that now he fully knows,
Invites him up to soul-convulsing woes.
Quoth Abraham unto his servant-men:
"Stay here, while I yon mountain-height ascend;
My Isaac shall my weary steps attend,
And soon I will to thee return again."

This said, he takes the slaughter-knife and fire;
  The kindling-wood he lays upon the child.
To know the gift the victim doth desire,
  And asks its whereabouts, 'mid scenes so wild.
What question, this, for the believing sire!
  Perchance he "staggers," as the word he heeds—
"The Lord provides the lamb, and I the fire!"
  He keeps his feet, and on his way proceeds.

THE TRIAL OF ABRAHAM'S FAITH.

They both together move aloft, to find
    The spot in quest—to find the slaughter-lamb;
To know the secret, Isaac is inclined—
    He finds himself and the victim one, the same.
The father says: "Thou art God's lamb, my son!
    At his behest I bring thee here this day;
I nothing doubt but God will raise his own,
    Though thus commanded thee, my son, to slay!"

Now heavy comes the hand of Abraham
    Upon the limbs of Sarah's only child;
How he implores in a fond mother's name,
    In touching accents, passionate and mild!
His hands he yields to unrelenting cords;
    His arms are pinioned—on the wood he lies;
His doom he waits—its bidding is the Lord's—
    But still articulating plaints and cries.

His cries are heard on high—two angels stand,
    Who heard, attent, when God foretold his birth
At Mamre's Vale; now come at God's command;
    His guardian, too, as he sojourns on earth.
They heed his plea for life, and gently sigh,
    To set the note of grief for cherubim,
To chant the dirge along the yearning sky—
    Though unaccustomed to funereal hymn.

He lies like Him who shall for sin atone!
    The mount imbibes the flying sympathy;
The timid air complains in touching moan,
    That pleads for Isaac, that he may be free.
Kind angels sigh, as pitying whom they note,
    And fain would rescue from a doom so dread;
And far and nigh complaining dirges float,
    Imploring aid to save as from the dead.

And every tuneful harp that angels use,
    Or those unstrung around the throne above,
Resound with sighing odes that tell the news;
    Jehovah gently moves with saving love.
The air soft moves the curtains of the tent,
    Where Sarah lies, communing with her grief;
In melancholy frame her hours are spent,
    Till with returning Isaac comes relief.

There lies the lad, so very like God's Son,
    That all this grief is spent to type our day,
When "Isaac's Seed" for sinners shall atone,
    And in a bitter death their ransom pay.
The lad is fastened to the altar-wood,
    His cheek is whitened, and his neck is bare;
His father's bearing, in so earnest mood,
    The darling's death doth seemingly declare.

He stoops to grasp the horrid slaughter-knife,
    And Isaac shuts his tearful eyes to die;
His arms he nerves to take away his life—
    "Stay there thy hand!" resounds from out the sky!
He drops the bloodless knife with untold joy;
    His aided eye descries the ready ram!
He claims from death his *living, loving* boy,
    Triumphant in the all-redeeming Name!

"Jehovah jireh!" "Now I comprehend
    That God provides his offering the while,
The substitute most opportune doth send,
    And thus from death redeems my belov'd child.
In figure of the One who shall arise,
    And ope the charnels of the sleeping dead,
Now Isaac's offering stands before my eyes,
    As One who doth the gory wine-press tread!"

THE TRIAL OF ABRAHAM'S FAITH. 377

God, speaking, says: " Full well I know and own,
    Thy love to me surpasses all beside;
Thou hast surrendered up to me thy son;
    Rich grace shall all thy future days betide.
No longer shalt thou bear the name of *slave;*
    The dearer appellation take of *friend.*
My presence shall attend, defend, and save,
    Through all thy pilgrim-days till life shall end."

This said, and lo! the cloud of lovely hues
    Recedes aloft, and hides itself on high;
Entranced he stands, its golden glory views,
    Then on his Isaac casts a tearful eye;
As if a thousand harps were touched to lays,
    The serenade divine proceeds along;
'T was as ten thousand angels joined in praise,
    Did chant their wonder-stirring glory-song!

Transfixed, the patriarch aloft doth gaze
    Upon the azure sky, where glows the cloud,
That floats in ever-varying phase,
    Till the vaulted heavens its lambent glories shroud.
He heeds the fast-receding cadences,
    Whose rapture-stirring lays still ring on high;
His ravished heart, in holy ecstacies,
    With angel-hosts doth passionately vie.

He now unbinds the lad, and doth enfold
    His youthful form to his paternal breast,
That throbs emotional to bliss untold;
    Angelic tongues can never tell the rest!
With " perfect faith " and " perfect love " imbued,
    He hastens to his home in Mamre's Vale;
To ease his Sarah from solicitude,
    Recites to her the dread yet joyous tale.

The faith of Abraham be ever mine!
  My feet within his shining footsteps move;
To faithful deeds my ready will incline;
  My heart be filled with "perfect faith" and love!
My will may I surrender up to God,
  As he, his Isaac, in the days of yore;
Ascend the Mount along the steps he trod,
  And to life's end in holy faith endure!

JACOB'S DREAM.

Rebecca's darling son, by stealthy art,
Obtains a blessing costly to his heart;
From famished Esau his birthright did gain,
Who sold it at a meager price "profane."
To escape the vengeance of his brother's hand,
Aghast, he sped his way to Padan-land.
At Bethel he lays him down to rest,
His conscience with a guilty load opprest;
Soft slumbers gently come on downy plume,
To soothe him in his melancholy gloom.

The floor of glory o'er his head is rent,
Adown the opening glittering forms are sent.
He gains a prospect for his aided eye,
To gaze upon the glories of the sky,
And learn the lessons needful then to know,
To guide him on the journey he must go.
But O, the lovely scenes that now unfold!
Beget desire intensified, untold,
For mode most opportune on which to rise
On dazzling footsteps up the blushing skies;
Nor doth he vainly wish for ready means
To reach the soul-entrancing, lovely scenes.

A ladder of celestial make divine
Extends aloft, to where bright visions shine,
With golden rounds, on which Jehovah's host
Come tripping down on tasks they love the most.
Angelic songsters chant their sweetest lays,
And make the welkin vocal with their praise.
Refreshing was his sleep to weary limbs,
Inspired by melody of angel hymns.
How glad they were while Jcob in his sin
In earnest prayer the pard'ning grace did win!
His waking state how changed this happy morn,
From mood of the preceding night forlorn!
With awe he says: "The Lord was in this place!
But I could not perceive the timely grace,
Till my glad eye beheld those wondrous stairs,
That brought the angels to relieve my cares.
'T is God's own house—it is the gate of heaven,
Where late I found my many sins forgiven.
This goodly thoroughfare is mean sublime,
On which my prayer of faith can daily climb;
On which celestial friends can quick descend,
And their much-needed succor daily lend,
To aid and cheer me on my lonely path,
And save me from my injured brother's wrath."
A monumental stone did Jacob set,
To bring to mind where grief and mercy met;
Where feebleness and strength were sweetly blent,
When he, a pilgrim, on to Padan went.

JACOB WRESTLES WITH THE ANGEL.

One score of years had passed since Jacob fled
To Padan, where the lowing herds he fed.
The scorching heat by day his head did smite,
The chilly dews suffused his couch by night;

God's constant blessing rested on his toil,
And Laban's avarice did ten times foil;
His constant diligence did riches yield,
And multiplied his cattle in the field.
At God's behest he gets him on to Seir,
Where Esau dwells, whose ire he yet doth fear.
God says: " I am the God of Bethel, where
Thou didst erewhile, in agony of prayer,
Set up a pillar to confirm thy vows,
As God's own portals and Jehovah's house."
God's angel came, whom Jacob plainly saw;
He said, with bowing, reverential awe:
"This angel is Jehovah's mighty host,
Vouchsafed in mercy, else I had been lost.
He comes to pacify my brother's ire,
That I may not for former wrongs expire."
Devout he prays: " O God of Abraham!—
The God of Isaac and myself the same—
Returning now to friends and kindred dear,
I pray deliver me from boding fear!
Most kindly hast thou dealt with me erewhile,
Nor am I worthy of thy present smile.
With staff in hand I sped to Padan-lands,
And now, returning home, I am two bands.
From Esau's hand I pray deliver me,
My wives and little ones from perils free!
To me thou saidst: 'I'll surely do thee good—
Thy offspring make a countless multitude;
Like sands upon the ocean's winding shore
Thy seed shall be, and shall in grace endure.'"
Full well he feels his need of guardian hosts,
To keep him in the way his journey goes;
And shining hosts he sees on winged march,
Along the azure track of heaven's arch;
They on celestial plume of beauty come,

To guide him safely to his Canaan home.
Strange campaign this, that Israel essays—
To vanquish hate by friendship's soothing grace—
A pacifying touch on Esau's breast,
To win a brother lost by its high behest.
Peace-offerings are sorted out, and strung
In platoon order as they march along,
To bring them on to Esau's home in peace,
And gain his aching heart a kind release.
To herdsmen next he gives the orders fit,
When Esau's war-clad troops they needs must meet:
"If he shall ask to know the things he sees,
To him thus speak, his anger to appease:
'These gifts are thine; nay, we ourselves are thine;
All these are sent thee by thy brother kind.
Thy right he owns to rule from Hor to Seir,
Lo! now he comes but little in the rear.'"
At Jabbok ford the night-fall hovers drear,
And Jacob's bosom aches with dismal fear;
His wives and little ones he sends ahead,
While he remains behind in horror dread.
Full well he feels his need of pleading prayer,
To meet the dire events that now appear;
And suddenly "there comes a man," it seems,
While Godlike glory in his visage gleams;
Omnipotence now the feeble flesh imbues,
And strange the strife that presently ensues.
'T is God in wrestling strife with mortal man,
Who pleads in agonizing prayer to gain
A suit unprecedent; still man is spared;
His mighty faith avails, his prayer is heard
The stronger, who can tell—or man or God?
Omnipotence himself, or flesh and blood?
The morning dawns, nor is the man outdone,
To strength divine man's feebleness holds on.

His "joint" is strong, his "sinew," too, is tough,
To wage the conflict still, quite strong enough.
Behold the agonizing, wondrous strife,
That wins the meed of "everlasting life!"
The angel gently says: "Now let me go!"
The man omnipotently answers, "No!
For that I have not yet been fully blest;
Till then I'll strive, nor will I ever rest!"
The angel plies the touch—man's "joint" is rent,
"His sinew shrunken;" all his strength is spent.
Man's *feebleness* doth more than *strength* suffice.
To win the priceless, ever-during prize!
Strange conflict this, of man with God in strife!
Of love with love—the aim of both is life.
In mighty strife, as if to separate,
But closer still do they approximate;
By strong revulsion seemingly repelled,
Still by co-ordinate attractions held;
They do not, will not e'er consent to part,
Till man stands eminent, all "pure in heart."
If man do conquer God, and stand supreme,
'T is God's own might doth feeble man redeem.
Nor wonder why; for man himself is weak,
He can not pray aright nor fitly seek;
Unless an Intercessor aid his speech,
It never can the throne of mercy reach.
With "riven joint" and "sinew" paralyzed,
His inmost nature crushed and agonized,
All prone he lies before the Savior's feet,
Where strength and weakness opportunely meet;
Where "righteousness looks down" with smiling face,
And "truth springs out of earth" that takes the grace,
"And righteousness and peace each other kiss,"
And man receives the gift of heavenly bliss.
Though halting, Jacob walks with grander mien,

Fresh from his triumph at the Jabbok scene ;
Now with the better name of "Israel,"
With princely powers, full mighty to prevail,
To conquer malice in a brother's breast,
And free his bosom from a dire unrest.
Anon from Seir his brother comes in sight—
He speeds his way and falls in humble plight ;
While Esau feels a pacifying love
Impel his heart, that anger once did move ;
And peace o'er hate most sweetly doth prevail,
What time he pledges faith with Israel.
"An Israelite indeed," Lord, may I be,
Till I shall win earth's final victory !
Then Jacob's God I face to face shall see,
And sound his praises through eternity !

JOSEPH'S COAT.

Fair was the morn that smiled on El-Bethel,
    And nature seemed arrayed in her best guise ;
The breezes, redolent of grateful smell,
    The sense did cheer, as charming visions rise.
Sweet birds, embowered, did carol forth their note,
    And chanted echoes in a matin lay ;
And melody did iterate remote,
    Through spirit-soothing prospects, bright and gay.

Benoni stood by Jacob in his home,
    His hand enfolded in his grieving sire's ;
But nought could cheer, since Joseph had not come,
    Nor pacify his heart's untold desire.
In doleful state, presaging fearful news,
    He thinks of Joseph as in wilds forlorn ;
Dread shapes most terrible, his fancy views,
    Of Joseph 'wildered, or by lions torn !

Imagination hears imploring cries—
    With lion's roar his darling's moans are blent!
Or sights or sounds most dismally arise,
    Since Joseph comes not back the way he went.
He waits from dewy morn till noontide heat,
    To see the son of Rachel reappear;
Lo! Leah's sons his eager eye now meet,
    Who, mournfully, their grieving father near.

With well-feigned sorrow, and cheeks all bedewed,
    They come, their fabrication vile to tell;
One shows the darling's coat besmeared with blood
    (The father looks, and knows the coat full well).
Quoth he: "This coat we found near Dothan's plains,
    All rent as now, and gory as you note;
We sought, but found not any one's remains."
    And Jacob wails: "It is my Joseph's coat!

Through Hebron's vale I sent him down of late;
    Of ready will he went, to doom forlorn;
He kindly went that he might learn your state.
    An evil beast his tender frame hath torn!
Adieu! adieu! my lost and lovely son,
    That first I saw with fond, parental joy!
Was it for this that Rachel's weeping won
    Thee for me—O, my lost and darling boy?

I loved thee more than all my sons by Leah,
    And love for all did cost me ardent prayer;
What time I neared the Edom-mount of Seir,
    And Esau came, whose anger I did fear,
Jehovah's hosts in vision I did descry;
    Sublime they hastened on celestial plume,
Flew lovingly adown the azure sky,
    To save us from a dread impending doom.

When Rachel died she left thee with us still,
　To stay my heart in grief, sustain my age;
These tasks of duty thou didst well fulfill;
　Life's many nameless woes thou didst assuage.
Oft have I smiled to note thy gentle glee,
　With Benjamin, at morn or rosy eve;
Affection said: 'Thou shalt abide with me
　In age, its many evils to relieve.'

Hope painted thee in offices most kind,
　Revealing thee as ever near to aid;
In all thy acts to filial love inclined,
　I claimed thee mine till life's last debt be paid;
To straighten out my feet, mine eyes to close,
　Then lead the funeral march with measured tread;
To bear me to Machpelah's sweet repose,
　Where Leah sleeps among the lovely dead!

Ah! did my Rachel rear thee safely up
　To make a banquet for voracious beast?
Her matron love and my paternal hope
　Evanished at one dismal lion-feast!
No watchful eye of friend did thee descry,
　When chosen for a costly carnival;
No ear of friend did heed thy touching cry,
　When beast of prey my darling did assail!

This coat, so horrible, is sacred too;
　'T will make me think of thee, my lovely son;
While bending 'neath a load of heavy woe,
　I'll keep this relic as a precious boon!"
The dusty sackcloth round his loins he twined,
　Fell on the earth, o'erwhelmed with killing grief;
His many sons speak soothing words and kind,
　But fail to bring his bleeding heart relief.

LOST JOSEPH.

While El-Bethel resounds with saddest woes,
    Loved Joseph, sold, is in the merchant's hands;
And Rachel's first-born down to Egypt goes,
    O'er sultry deserts drear with scorching sands,
With saddest thoughts concerning whom he leaves;
    He thinks of Benjamin, and of his sire;
In doleful moods he passionately grieves,
    As on he winds his way to bondage dire.

Full soon he finds himself in Egypt's mart,
    Exposed for sale to many a bidder's gaze;
The crier's words he heeds with aching heart,
    And blushes as they pry him in the face.
To Potiphar the crier strikes him off;
    He homeward goes, a slave in servitude!
His single eye is fixed on things aloft,—
    Lust's fascinating charms does faith elude.

For purity he wins a dire reward—
    He goes as culprit to a dungeon bound;
His innocence illumes his prison ward;
    He wins the keeper's confidence profound.
His wisdom signifies *the baker's* fate,
    And tells, alike, *the butler's* quick release;
To whom he says: " Commiserate my state,
    While in the king's employ ye dwell at ease."

Yet, long forgotten, he in prison sighs;
    Ingratitude neglects his case forlorn;
The royal dreamer sees dread visions rise,
    And calls his council to his aid at morn.
The butler says: "I do my fault confess!
    For as in prison I abode of yore,
There was a Hebrew, who, in my distress,
    Foretold thou wouldst my office to me restore."

This lifts the Hebrew from obscurity—
    Arrays him royally at royal charge;
It coronates his peerless purity,
    And bids him go, by royal grace, at large.
To him the monarch said: "I had a dream—
    Since when my mind hath been in dread amaze;
Lo! seven kine came up from Egypt's stream,
    And in the meadows quietly did graze.

Well-fleshed, well-favored, they did all appear;
    No mart could boast of better-looking kine.
Then seven lean, ill-favored, came in the rear,
    So bad that none the like could ever find!
The famished kine the fat did quickly eat,
    But seemed as poor as they had been erewhile;
No better for their horrid feast of meat,
    They quickly disappeared beneath the Nile!

One stalk bore seven goodly ears of corn,
    And flourishing they did appear to sight;
And seven withered ears grew all forlorn,
    That ate the good, but bettered not their plight."
And Joseph says: "God shows his dread design.
    The goodly kine are seven plenteous years;
And seven famine years, the hungry kine;
    Though fed so highly, still no flesh appears!

The stalk where grew the sign for plenteous bread,
    Bespeaks the same the goodly kine did show.
The withered ears, that on the thrifty fed,
    Like the hungry kine, presage the famine's woe.
Let Pharaoh look him out a man discreet,
    And set him over all Egypt's fruitful land;
Let him control the revenue of wheat;
    Set helpers under his supreme command.

Thus food shall be in store for famine sere,
  That none may perish in the coming woe;
Thus all may live throughout the seventh year."
  And Pharaoh was pleased to have it so.
He calls in haste his ministers of state,
  Their deputies, with regalia proud—
To them, in conclave, now he doth relate
  His high behest, and speaks his will aloud.

Quoth he to all the magnates of his court:
  " Can e'er we find another man like this,
Of wondrous wisdom and of noble port,
  To do such work in manner all like his?"
To Joseph next he says in accent kind:
  " Thou shalt be o'er my royal house from now,
To teach my senators, my princes bind;
  And to thy chariot all knees shall bow."

Thus Joseph reigns, the second on the throne,
  To care for all, and succor all that want;
His wife, the daughter of the Priest of On,
  And to his Royal Highness minstrels chant.
" Now I am Pharaoh! without thy will,
  No man shall lift his foot, or raise his hand,
Except it be thy high behest to fill,
  Throughout the ample bounds of Egypt's land."

Thus speaks the mighty monarch of the Nile,
  And does unwittingly God's will supreme;
To elevate affliction's lowly child,
  Whose wondrous skill unfolds the mystic dream.
Thus he is prince o'er Egypt's ample store,
  To save alive a hungry multitude;
The herald of the Lord, he goes before,
  To honor him and do his people good.

JUDAH'S PLEA FOR BENJAMIN.

The second time the Hebrews came for food,
　Loved Benjamin, as hostage, came along;
Before the steward tremblingly they stood,
　Their money showing, clearing them from wrong.
With dread they say: "Who put it in each sack?
　We ne'er can tell—there must be some mistake;
The same we took, we honestly bring back."
　But still, in boding fear, they greatly quake!
The steward says: "'T was God who put it there;
　Think not of penalties, but go in peace;
Dismiss at once your every painful care,"
　He gently says, to set their minds at ease.
To Joseph's palace next they make their way;
　With gifts in hand, they reverently bow.
He speaks of one who did in Canaan stay—
　"This is the younger favorite, I trow."

Devout he says: "May God be kind to thee!"
　And hastens to conceal his tender grief;
Close in his chamber, where no eye can see,
　He hides himself for opportune relief.
His face he washed, his flowing tears he dried,
　Refrained himself, and said: "Set on the food."
They ate to full—were fully satisfied
　With viands royal, delicate, and good.

But why their seats accorded with their age,
　From Reuben down to Benjamin, the youth,
They could not guess, but thought it some presage;
　How anxiously they yearned to know the truth!
Why five times more for Benjamin was set,
　And yet each one had plenty in his mess,
They could not fully comprehend as yet;
　How much it puzzled them we well may guess.

They trace the number on their sacks, the same
    That told their pedigree in life full well;
But when the steward's inquisition came,
    To find the royal cup, they then could tell.
Refreshed and served, they hied them off with glee;
    But soon they heed the steward's stern behest;
Aghast they turn, the officer they see
    In hot pursuit, the Hebrews to arrest!

"O, why requite my noble lord with ill,
    Whose bountiful supplies did timely yield
Relief in want, and all your sacks did fill?
    Why steal his cup, within your sacks concealed?"
And Judah says: "Why speaks my lord this word?
    Sure he shall die, with whom this cup is found;
And we shall all be bondmen to my lord!"
    To test the case they cast their sacks aground.

With Benjamin the royal cup they spy,
    And sadly wail in all their bitter grief;
To Joseph's court they go, the case to try,
    If Benjamin be in verity a thief.
They fall before their brother Joseph now,
    As when he saw the harvest-sheaves of yore;
All broken-hearted in despair they bow;
    Judah essays their evil to deplore.

He now draws near, his brother's cause to plead;
    His thoughts are agony, his heart is wrung;
For Benjamin he disavows the deed,
    And claims that he is innocent and young.
Quoth he: "Let now thy servant speak a word,
    For thou art great as Pharaoh is great;
Let pity touch thy heart, most noble lord!
    While I recite our pitiful estate!

Thyself didst ask when at the first we came,
  If we a brother or a father had ;
We answered truthfully, as now the same,
  And plainly told thee of the darling lad.
Our aged father loves him tenderly,
  Close by his side he keeps him for his cheer ;
Thou didst protest thy face we ne'er should see
  Unless we brought with us our brother dear.

We pleaded then the sadness of our sire,
  That he could ne'er endure thy stern behest ;
That he would sink in grief—perchance expire—
  If thus his son were ravished from his breast.
He, youngest of a tender mother's love,
  And she no more ; his elder brother lost ;
These incidents we urged, thy heart to move,
  And save our anxious sire the pangs 't would cost.

To give his son a hostage to thy hand—
  A dire condition for a little bread ;
'T was hard to yield him then at thy command—
  To keep him now is penalty too dread !
'T will kill our sire should he remain a slave,
  So 'reft of all his earthly comforts here ;
His hoary locks will hasten to the grave,
  And bring on us the evil that we fear.

Our father's heart was stricken then and sad ;
  Sadly he wailed o'er memories by-gone :
' My wife did bear two sons—I then was glad,
  And now ye leave me stricken and forlorn !
The eldest one went out, and came not home ;
  His lovely face my eye hath seen no more ;
If this one meet a horrid, evil doom,
  'T will be more fatal far than heretofore.'

My lord, but think how sad must be his heart
    Ere now, while brooding o'er his dismal state;
Thus doomed with Benjamin so long to part,
    And Simeon, who has endured like fate.
And it shall be when he shall see us come
    Without the lad, that he of grief will die;
And I shall see his melancholy doom,
    Displayed, alas! before my tearful eye.

On penalties most dread I pledged my word
    For his safe-keeping and his sure release;
O, let me serve a bondman to my lord,
    But let my younger brother go in peace!
For how can I endure to see my sire,
    And leave the lad a hostage-slave in chains—
Lest I, perchance, incur my father's ire,
    Or see his anguish and expiring pains?"

Most passionately Joseph wails for grief:
    "Let no Egyptian stay to hear my speech!"
This gives his lacerated heart relief.
    Then to his trembling brothers, all and each,
He gives the Hebrew salutation clear:
    "I am your Joseph, whom ye sold a slave!
Draw near, my brothers, all draw near!
    God sent me here your precious lives to save."

Now Benjamin his arms of love enfold;
    Long time he weeps for grief and gladness blent,
Thinks of his exile and events untold;
    He thus his noble sympathies doth vent.
He takes his brethren all to his embrace,
    Weeps tears that tell his kind, forgiving love;
His brethren hide each blushing, guilty face,
    "But feel contrition all their bosoms move."

"And doth my father yet survive at home,
   Whose face I have not seen these many years?
His fondness robed me in my coat of doom
   That cost me banishment and sighs and tears!
Your faces, too, I have not seen till late,
   Since when I left you at the Dothan cave;
Where ye did sell me to a dismal fate;
   But God did overrule, and bless, and save.

Haste! get you up and bring my father soon,"
   Thus Joseph says. "The Lord hath made me great;
Come quickly down to share this goodly boon,
   And I will cheer you in your famine state.
Be near my side, and I will nourish thee—
   Come soon, lest all thy house may come to need.
Come soon! Egyptian stores shall all be free;
   In Goshen's fields thy famished herds shall feed."

MOSES.

The child of faith my lauding verse deserves,
Whose infant life parental faith preserves;
Despite the royal murderer's behest,
Safe in his slender ark the babe doth rest.
In tragedy his early life begins;
His tragic grief a royal mother wins.
Eventful life! O'ercast with saddest gloom,
But rescued, still, from Hebrew children's doom,
How fraught with incident! Attent, we note
Him launch the Nile in such a fragile boat;
Among the flags and willows, thus alone,
Without a foster-guardian—quite undone;
'Midst crocodiles that for their banquet roar,
He lies hard by the river's oozy shore.

'T was faith preserved him then, to bring
Redemption by the daughter of a king;
His plaints she heard, when all alone he woke;
His touching wails did royal grace invoke.
Faith interposed the maiden's heart, to sting
With kind emotion that relief did bring;
A royal tenure which should hence endure,
Which sends him home in loving arms secure.
Faith made the pretty, darling, foundling boy
The hope of home, of Israel the joy!
   The queenly mother claimed him for her own,
Intent to elevate him to a throne.
'T was thus a tender heart did timely train
The Hebrew child a royal crown to gain,
Impelled by *love* that in her bosom yearned;
Impelled by *faith*, her favor Moses spurned!
With scorn his faith abjures the shining boon
Of royal robes and Egypt's gilded throne.
The pleasing sins of princely courts arise
In fascinating charms before his eyes;
His faith a better heritage descries.
From kingly wealth he turns with scorn away,
Prefers the riches of Messiah's day.
   The groans of Israelites, attent, he hears;
With grief he notes their many woes and tears.
Afflictions come in dismal shapes apace
Upon his weary, much-enduring race.
He yearns o'er horrid scenes of bondage—woes—
Beholds the tyrant dealing on his blows;
He sees a Hebrew prostrate in his gore,
Relieves a brother from affliction sore;
He hides the slave-tormentor " in the sand "—
This mystic act should Hebrews understand;
Presaging thus God's vengeance on his foes,
And Hebrews, manumitted from their woes,

To claim, of right, their happy Canaan-land,
And conquer it betimes at God's command.
Next day he saw two Hebrews, as they strove,
And bade them change their enmity for love.
One says: "Who made thee arbiter and judge,
To settle quarrels and our hateful grudge?
Wilt thou kill me, as lately thou didst slay
The son of Ham, and hide his form away?"
Then hastily the Hebrew exile fled
To Midian, where Jethro's herds he fed.
Long time in painful exile he abode,
Till thoughts of kindred in his bosom glowed;
To bondage scenes he goes at God's command,
To lead the Hebrews to the "Promised Land."

THE FLIGHT OF ISRAEL OUT OF EGYPT

From Rameses the Hebrew hosts proceed
    To Etham, on the border of the waste;
To screen and guide them in their urgent need,
    A friendly cloud brings up their rear in haste.
'Tis van and rear guard on their dreary way;
    Its golden rays or darkling folds of gloom
Can guide the frighted hosts of God by day,
    Or bring on angry foes an instant doom.

It brings the "Angel of the Lord of Hosts,"
    The friend of Hebrews to defend and guide;
Or deal destruction on their hateful foes,
    Or, at his high behest, the sea divide.
In close defiles the Israelites appear,
    And mountains huge on either side arise;
Egyptian hosts are pressing on the rear—
    The raging sea in front their march defies!

Poor fugitives! so late from brick-yard toils,
    With borrowed jewels decked and strayed away;
Ill-clad for war, your failing hope recoils—
    Mad foes pursue in battle's dread array!
Your masters come in fury just behind,
    With warrior-ranks intent your blood to spill;
With steeds and scythe-clad chariots malign,
    To mow you down, or take you back at will!

Thus prudence chides, the hosts to intimidate,
    And only sees man's enemies below;
Jehovah smiles, his hosts to vindicate,
    And his omnipotence of love to show.
God's angel frowns severe from out the cloud;
    That look strikes through the guilty tyrant's soul;
His men of war, with their regalia proud,
    Are whelmed beneath the waves that o'er them roll.

One stroke from Moses and one beck from God,
    And the almighty work of wrath is o'er;
Smit by an angry, vengeance-dealing rod,
    Foes sink in dire defeat to rise no more.
Upon the shore glad Israelites descry
    The carcasses of men and dying beasts;
Wrecked, wheelless chariots glide swiftly by,
    Borne on the billows of the conquering seas.

Now Miriam, with harp and lute, essays
    To magnify the God of Israel;
They sing aloud his well-deserved praise,
    Exultingly their victory they tell:
"The horse and rider sink beneath the sea!
    The tyrant and his captains all are drowned!
'Tis Jacob's God who gives the victory—
    His foes are sunken in the depths profound!"

The cloud of fire leads on the hosts to Shur,
  Whose bitterness inspires the words of gall;
To pacify the angry hosts that err,
  A tree infuses sweet that quiets all.
To Elim next they go, whose dozen wells
  Invite the hosts 'neath cooling palm-leaf shade;
With *drink* replete, for *meat* the tumult swells,
  Till mutiny doth Israel's camp pervade.

While Aaron prayed, the glory of the Lord
  From out the cloud appeared, and thus he spake:
" I know the hosts; I heed their dire discord;
  At eve the flesh shall fall, that all may take;
At morn the bread shall lie for all their needs."
  And when the sun arose, the face of earth
Revealed the gift, like coriander seeds,
  Angelic food of life-preserving worth!

Ambrosial food they all may glean at will;
  Who gather more, have none, withal, to spare;
Who gather less, do have sufficient still;
  Thus all the mystic food may daily share.
Who anxiously the wondrous gift do hoard,
  Have tainted bread—not to be eat at all;
Those doubting minds, afraid to trust the Lord
  For daily bread that graciously doth fall!

On to the wastes of Sin the hosts proceed,
  The thirsty people murmur for supplies;
For them doth Moses strongly intercede.
  In plenitude of grace the Lord replies:
" Go, lead the people forth, and take thy rod—
  The same that smote the Nile with many a curse;
With strength begirt—thy strength is still in God—
  Go, smite the blessing forth, to quench their thirst!

Upon the Horeb rock, aloft, I'll stand,
    In readiness to yield the gift so dear;
Go, smite, what time I utter the command,
    And bring the blessing forth both cool and clear!"
'T is jubilee in Israel's camp the while,
    When all imbibe the cheer the waters give;
The drink—far more refreshing than the Nile—
    The Hebrews quaff with ecstasy, and live!

Dread bounds are set about the Horeb mount;
    The people Moses now doth sanctify;
If man or beast shall touch, on that account,
    They both for their profanity shall die.
The destined morn, the mount is all ablaze,
    And thunder-claps loud smite all the air around;
The people flee, impelled by dread amaze,
    Aghast to heed the soul-convulsing sound!

The trumpet waxes loud, and louder still,
    And Moses speaks, and God responds more loud;
Deep horror doth the great Lawgiver fill;
    While all is dark amid the smoke and cloud,
The people pray: "Let not the Lord thus speak!"
    Lest to such accents horrid death ensue;
For mediation they devoutly seek,
    As Sinai's glories stand aloft to view.

And when the Tabernacle is complete,
    And Moses sets its curtain to their sight,
From now it is the holy Mercy-seat,
    Where penitence may bow in lowly plight.
And now the cloud, descending, nears the door,
    And rests till all the people humbly pray;
Shekinah-glory gently hovers o'er
    The ark of strength, and graciously doth stay!

The man of God had well performed his task,
    And all seemed ready for their onward move;
But Moses passionately then did ask
    The gift omnipotent of saving love;
That unattained, all else had been a show
    Of empty ceremonial rites, sublime.
He prays: "O, let thy presence with me go;
    So shall I execute the will Divine!"

Full well he knows Jehovah's high behest;
    Already hath he seen his outstretched arm,
That screened the people in their dire distress,
    And instant saved them from impending harm.
He saw the frighted sea in haste give way,
    To make God's hosts a pass to march along;
He saw their enemies in dread dismay,
    And joined the Hebrews in their victor-song.

The cloudy pillar all day long had spread
    Divine defense along the way they went;
A cooling shade above their aching head,
    To foil their foes, their malice to prevent.
The fruitful trees of Paradise did shake,
    To yield ambrosial food in vast supply;
The Horeb rock did sunder wide and quake,
    And birds flew tamely down the evening sky.

There swings the ark, in its own curtains veiled,
    The emblem fit of Mercy's largest good;
With God in van, the Hebrews can not fail
    To vanquish foes and cross the Jordan-flood.
The guardian-pillar beckons on the host—
    Bids Moses march, and yet he doth not go;
And march they must, or Israel be lost.
    O, who can augur why he tarries so?

"O send me not, unless thy Presence lead!
 Thy Presence I implore!" he humbly cries;
"To go in van, our needy hosts to feed,
 And spread dismay amidst our enemies!"
God tenderly responds, to soothe his breast:
 "My presence shall conduct you on your way,
And bring you safely to your Canaan-rest;
 In travel-toil the fainting hosts shall stay."

God's Angel now more plainly appears in sight—
 Still nearer comes, and gently hovers o'er;
With love and pity blent in softer light,
 He takes the charge Divine to go before.
In their afflictions he's afflicted too;
 In love and pity he redeems their host;
He cheers them all their weary journey through,
 And screens them from the rage of angry foes.

His outstretched wings, omnipotent, upstay
 And carry them amid their travel-toils;
On loving wings doth tenderly convey
 The ones he loves; their enemies he foils.
As when the eagle stirs her eaglets dear,
 And bears them on her matron-wings with ease,
Just so doth Israel long time appear
 Upborne, till all their weary travels cease.

The presence of the Lord his people need;
 For it they should in supplication wait,
That he may go in the van, their hosts to lead,
 And guide them on to their triumphant state.
Christ is the smitten Rock, whose grace can yield
 The stream of life, and nourishment divine;
His saving strength doth all their weakness shield,
 Till they their Canaan-heritage do find.

MOSES CALLED TO DIE.

Jehovah says: "The time for thee draws nigh,
To leave the hosts, and get thee up to die.
Call Joshua, and then yourselves present;
And lo! The Pillar hangs above the tent;
It wavers down till streams of golden light
Converge above the ark, concealed from sight.
Diverging thence the coruscating rays
Gild all within the sacred Holy Place."
In solemn accents now Jehovah saith:
"The time draws nigh for thee to sleep in death.
Too soon the people will from me depart,
Misguided by an unbelieving heart.
My anger will wax hot, my face I 'll hide,
For that they sin by idols turned aside.
This song inscribe, their children timely teach,
And put it in their mouths to mold their speech:
My doctrine shall descend like gentle rain,
Till tender herbs and flowers its moisture drain.
To God, the Lord, ascribe omnific might;
He is the Rock whose far-discovered height
Bespeaks where pilgrims, on their weary way,
A shade may find at scorching noon of day.
His works are good, so perfect are his ways;
His equity and truth shall sweetly grace
His brow. Who to the Holy One but cleaves,
His faithfulness a recompense receives.
For else the souls, whose iniquities do tell
Their spot is not the spot of Israel.
A crooked seed to thus requite the Lord,
Thus spurn his mercy and abjure his word!
Consider ye far other days of old;
Your fathers ask, to them this truth was told:
When God admeasured earth by lots, they fell
According to the claims of Israel.

'T was in a howling wilderness, God found
His chosen ones by foes beset around.
He cherished them, and taught them truths divine,
He compassed them about with favor kind;
Through all their pilgrimage in days of yore
His mercy led them gently on, secure.
From Sinai's awful height Jehovah came,
Enlightened Seir and Horeb with a fearful flame;
From Paran's heights unveiled his excellence,
Attended by ten thousand of his saints.
From out his hand a fiery law he hurled,
Let loose his wrath to awe a guilty world.
His saints he keeps enfolded in his arms,
'Neath his pavilion secure from all harms.
 None else is like the Lord, who rides on high,
His chariots the clouds that deck the sky.
His excellence he writes on worlds above,
In characters of wrath or smiling love,
That all may read and fully understand
Rewards divine awarded unto man.
If good, they read their pleasing title clear;
If bad, their retribution of despair.
Or good or bad, God's excellence remains,
By angels read or devils in their pains.
 The everlasting God be thy defense!
His loving smile bespeaks thy recompense,
In his embrace shall Israel abide;
Near where Siloam's waters softly glide
His dews shall make the trees and fruitage glad;
With beauty shall the Sharon rose be clad.
Who else is like the people saved by God?
In all the pilgrim-journeys they have trod
He is their *shield* and *sword* and mighty *tower*,
Preserved are they by his omnific power."

MOSES CALLED TO DIE.

Then Moses ceased to bless the weeping hosts,
And from their ranks to Nebo's summit goes;
A shower of tears distills from weeping eyes,
A tempest swells, of wails that pierce the skies;
In eloquence of grief they loudly vie
To dirge their leader as he goes to die.
He slowly moves aloft, and there he turns
To view the scenes below, and sadly yearns.
What thoughts come stealing o'er his noble soul,
As touching visions to his eyes unfold!
The fortunes of the hosts he leaves behind
Weigh heavily upon his brooding mind;
The toils he bore for sake of others' weal,
His aching heart doth passionately feel;
The prayers he uttered and the tears he shed
He counts as through his memory they sped,
And by-gone scenes come up in solemn train,
And sounds long silent touch his ear again.
Ah! the sights he saw, the sounds he last time heard,
That suffused his eye, his yearning bossom stirred,
While thus the place of destiny he neared!

Jehovah says: " Now turn thine eye and note
The Canaan scenes near by or far remote.
Thine eye I cause to see the promised rest,
But ne'er shalt thou that heritage possess."
From Pisgah's top, lo! Gilead's heights arise!
Then Naphtali and Dan he eager spies.
Far off, next Ephraim's domain unfolds—
Adorned with Jacob's blessing, he beholds.
Manasseh's borders open to his gaze—
All Judah opes to view, quite to the seas'
Far south along the plains of Jericho
To balmy Zoar his searching sight doth go.

His head is dizzy, and his sight grows dim;
God's angel kindly stoops and kisses him,

His eyes are closed, and calm his quiet breast,
His spirit soars to gain Elysian rest.
Angelic choristers in anthems vie,
To bid him welcome to his home on high.
   Lo! Satan comes to canonize a saint,
With chorister and choir, his praise to chant!
This Michael espies and comprehends;
His task assumes, the body he defends.
Now Satan the archangel's right disputes;
Archangel might his mission executes.
His bearing high, no railing word he spoke,
The aid omnipotent did he invoke:
"The Lord rebuke thee!" Then he further said:
"Mine is the office to inter the dead."
This said, with strength divine, of noble mien,
He ousts the claims of the malignant fiend.
Hell's conclave hastily in dread adjourn,
And swiftly to their nether haunts return.
The mortal frame immortal strength inters;
God's will to Satan's, Michael now prefers.
A stroke he deals; wide gapes the solid ground;
The body is lowered to its tomb profound.
There, watched alone by the all-seeing Eye,
The dust of Israel's lawgiver doth lie!

JOSHUA AND THE CAPTAIN OF GOD'S HOSTS.

The noble son of Nun deserves my verse;
In humble measures I his deeds rehearse.
Great man! because his God had made him great;
He walked with Moses in his high estate.
What time God gave the law 'midst clouds and smoke,
He heard with awe the words Jehovah spoke.

He stood by Moses while the mingled sound
Of Apis' worship did aloud resound.
It sharply pealed upon the frighted air,
As Aaron in the idol's praise did share;
Before its shrine adoringly to nod,
And pay it homage that belongs to God.

Faithful 'mid vile revolt, sublime he stood,
When Hebrews murmured for their drink and food;
Unmoved amidst the faithless, dastard spies,
Whose unbelief to angry heaven did rise;
In faith he spoke to edify the host,
When multitudes were in the desert lost;
Till forty years did intervene to strew
Their carcasses in the way their march did go.
And firm he stood when Moses, too, did err,
And smite the rock, while God he failed to fear,
Or sanctify him in the sight of men;
And thus the Holy One did he offend.
And long he lived 'midst manifold revolts
Of Jacob's sons, whose God-offending faults
Did strew their forms along the erring way
They trod; who did their forfeiture thus pay.
He taught the rising race by faith to stand,
And valiantly to gain the Promised Land.

He saw the priest of God go up on high
To meet his Lord, and on Mount Hor to die.
He heard the parting words that Moses spoke,
As on the hosts he did God's grace invoke.
He gazed upon his slow and sad ascent,
As on to die alone he meekly went.
He saw the lingering looks he cast below,
As he to Nebo's height did calmly go.
Henceforth he stood in holy Moses' stead,
And in his footsteps faithfully did tread.

God bade him near the long-sought Jordan stream,
And when he reached its turbid, swollen brim,
Its floods recoiled, to ope the hosts a way
For Israel to cross unlet that day.
He saw the cloud, so long their kindly guide,
Recede aloft, and all its glories hide.
How sad a sigh he heaved when that dear gift
Did from their van its bright shekinah lift!
He saw the "manna" cease to feed the host,
When once they reached the long-sought Jordan coast;
They ate no more the sacred bread of heaven,
What time the coarser food of earth was given.
   Near Jericho they halt, on Jordan's plains,
Where Joshua a new commission gains.
And lo! it comes that he, in vision, spies
A form divine, arrayed in human guise.
With sword in hand he stands sublime to sight,
Intent to know what side he takes in fight.
Quoth Joshua: "Art thou for us or for our foes?
To me this secret graciously disclose."
"Nay, but the captain of God's hosts, I come
His friends to aid, and teach his foes their doom."
With godlike bearing high the words he spoke,
Then Joshua in awe did him invoke:
"What saith my Lord?" he reverently cries.
"Loose now thy shoes!" the Lord of hosts replies.
"This place is like where Moses erst did stand,
To take his ministry at my command.
To thee I this day give all Jericho,
The king thereof, with every hateful foe;
To thy victorious hand I yield their fate.
This order take and keep inviolate:
The city-wall encompass round each day,
With warrior-hosts, in battle's dread array,
Till seven days be fully overpast;
On this, the greatest and withal the last,

Full seven times that day surround the wall,
Then wait the signal for its final fall.
And seven priests the ark of strength shall bear;
The trumpeters shall march along in rear,
To blow the foe-dismaying signal strong;
The men of war shall shout it loud and long."

The white-robed priests the holy ark now take,
The men of war the battle charge do make;
And mute they march for seven days around,
And halt obedient ere they give the sound.
Quoth Joshua: "Now comes the welcome time
For foe's defeat and for our fight sublime!"

Meantime the Canaanites are perched on towers,
To note the foes that come, and what their powers;
What armaments they bring to fell the wall,
Or arms they use, or on what God they call.
They say: "A serenade of wind they bring
To overthrow our wall!—a feeble thing!"
They laughingly their gleeful scorn loud vaunt,
While music to their idol-gods they chant.
The warriors raise a shout both great and long,
The trumpets peal a blast both loud and strong;
Omnipotence that awful sound imbues,
That doth cheer God's host, their enemies confuse.
Dread earthquake makes their mighty bulwarks jar;
Loud thunder-claps assail the frighted air;
Strong shocks assault the foe-defying wall,
That nods assent to its undoing fall.
With sidelong force of terrifying sound,
Their massive battlements now strew the ground.
The stately palaces of kings give way!
Their inmates wail in frantic, wild dismay!
Ashtaroth's shrine convulsively bestirs;
The priests and devotees obey their fears.
Vile Dagon's temple rends from base to cope,
The fugitives resign their dying hope.

Huge Moloch, too, imbibes the flying dread,
Whose sooty throat with infant flesh is fed;
Who gulps the wailing dozens at his meals,
Now quakes convulsively and sidelong reels
To his terrific, desolating fall,
While frighted men on gods dethroned, loud call;
They utter prayers to oracles struck dumb,
To save them from their dread, approaching doom.
The city lies in heaps, and smothered cries
From dying thousands tumultuously arise.
   The victor-hosts, whose half-omnific shout
Had won the day and put their foes to rout,
Charge on, and God's behest of wrath fulfill;
And thus the fate of Jericho did seal.

¡DAVID.

The son of Jesse claims my humble lay—
  So meek and dutiful in rural life.
Behold the chances of his youthful day,
  Or with the lion or the bear in strife!
With crook and lute and soul-refreshing lyre,
  To melody and duty both inclined;
The tenderness kind nature doth inspire
  In pleasing alternations is combined.

And Jesse's care, and wakeful, tender love
  Enfold him closely, like a drapery;
Presaging then his mission from above—
  A giant slaughtered, and his country free.
With vast reverses interlacing youth,
  He stands aloft in the prophetic word;
The sire of Him "from Jesse's root," in sooth,
  And who adores him as his rightful Lord.*

---

* See Psalm cx.

When crime ingrate had rent the crown from Saul,
  And Samuel sought for royal regency,
On none of Jesse's sons the crown did fall,
  Till David's face the prophet's eye did see.
God kept his hand upstayed to bestow the grace,
  Till Jesse's sons all passed his scrutiny;
But when he saw the youthful shepherd's face,
  He poured on him the coronation free.

In David's house God sets salvation's horn,
  To ratify his promises most kind,
That men, released from bondage so forlorn,
  The mercy of God's covenant shall find.
In time of war the shepherd king is strong,
  While he the strength divine reveres withal;
O'er Jebusites his empire spreads along;
  Before his scepter kings and kingdoms fall.

Gilboa tells the meed of mystic love,
  In tones of sorrow, passionate and strong;
Its gentle touch doth all love's harp-chords move,
  And calms the grief that seeks relief in song:
"On places eminent for battle's strife,
  The Beauty of all Israel expires;
Vile foes, uncircumcised, bled out his life!
  From battle's rage his valiant soul aspires.

How did the mighty fall! And royal might
  And beauty then were stained with horrid gore;
'T was on Gilboa's lofty, bloody height
  He fell in front of battle's conflict sore.
The bow of Jonathan by death was stayed;
  Saul's thirsty blade imbibed full draughts of blood;
Nor empty, on Gilboa's height, that blade
  That drank from dying foes the crimson flood.

Gilboa hence shall taste nor dew nor rain,
    That drank the priceless blood of friendship up;
Thou didst thy thirsty bosom vilely stain,
    As there in pain expired sad Israel's hope.
With ceaseless famine shalt thou ever stay,
    Unclad with vernal dress and rosy wreath;
For there the warrior's shield was cast away
    What time my Jonathan did sleep in death!

Ye maids of Israel, for him lament,
    Who clothed you with your scarlet robes so gay;
Who decked you with each costly ornament,
    For him reiterate your saddest lay!"
Now *vision* comes to grace him more than war,
    And psalmody unlocks his tuneful soul;
Its numbers pour along the desert air,
    To Lebanon its touching accents roll.

And prophecy uplifts what intervenes,
    And dread futurity doth still involve;
Impelled by gifts of vision-yielding scenes,
    Redeeming grace he now essays to solve.
He stands where erst Melchizedek had trod,
    Sits on the stone that Abraham had set;
He feels desire to see his son and God;
    Typed when the Salem king and Abraham met.

Now vision decks the ample scene that beams,
    Till Zion basks in glory-wrought array;
Bright coruscations burst in lucid streams,
    Till earth is radiant with Messiah's day.
The visions from Jehovah's throne that shine
    Reveal a form most wondrous to behold;
Through manhood beam the glories all divine,
    Where truth and grace most lovingly unfold.

Jehovah speaks to David's Son and Lord,
In accents loud, that all may heed his word:
"My fellow-equal, on my honored right
Be seated on my throne of vision bright!
As wide unfold the portals of the East,
So shed thy light, as Zion's King and Priest!"
And presently Messiah's morn is dressed
Resplendent in the robes of holiness.

Each Sharon rose seems clothed in softer hues,
And herbs and flowers reflect the morning dews;
As starlit diamonds on the brow of morn,
So Christ all earth with glory shall adorn.
The Root of David and his Lord of right,
His offspring, and the Star of Morning Light,
The tender mercies of our God unfold,
Foreshown by types, by prophecy foretold.

In Isaac's seed omnipotence of grace
Shall save all saints, but Zion's foes shall chase;
Who will not own his rule and feel his love
Must taste his justice, and his judgment prove;
As potters' vessels, broken and undone,
Must fall before both David's Lord and Son,
Must yield a willing or unwilling praise,
To show his justice or evince his grace.

ELIJAH MEETS AHAB.

The sins of men had angered the Most High;
God's prophet prays, the heavens at once are dry.
Long time there fell no cooling dew nor rain;
Men sought for living verdure all in vain;
Through all the land the famine-dearth was sore;
The king and servant searched the land quite o'er;

This way and that the pasture-seekers went,
In quest of pasture, anxiously intent.
   Elijah meets the servant on his way.
Who, lowly bowing, doth obeisance pay :
"Art thou the man who curses Israel?"
" I am," quoth he; " go quick and Ahab tell,
Elijah waits his coming in this place ;
This message to thy master bear in haste."
" What have I done?" doth Obadiah say ;
"And it shall be when I shall go my way,
God's mighty Spirit shall transport thee hence ;
'T will cost my life to give the king offense.
As lives the Lord, there is no adjacent land
Where Ahab hath not sent to understand
If thou wert there, or ever there had been ;
If aught of thee had e'er been heard or seen.
Thy servant feared the Lord from early youth,
The thing I did was told my lord forsooth ;
How that I hid God's seers from Jezebel—
All this ere now doth Ahab know full well."
   Elijah says: "As God abides the same,
Before his face I stand, and in his name
I vow to show myself this very day."
To tell the king the servant went his way ;
To meet Elijah doth King Ahab come :
"Art thou the man, whose curse our land doth doom
To famine sore these three eventful years—
Who bring'st on us our many wants and fears?"
Quoth he : " Not I; but thou and thine have brought
This awful curse, and all this evil wrought.
Go gather me the hosts of Israel
On Carmel's height ; observe the mandate well!
The claims of Baal or the Hebrews' Lord
We there will test, and ample proof afford,

Whose is the temple and the valid shrine;
Thus try the Godhead excellence divine.
Four hundred priests of Baal, and more withal;
Four hundred *prophets of the groves* now call;
Myself alone, and they a host, and strong—
There, on the Carmel height, I'll face your throng."

In proud regalia the priests and prophets come—
Unwittingly to meet a dolorous doom.
To gods of groves, of hills, of vales, and seas,
They offer gifts their anger to appease.
To scandalize Elijah's God they vaunt
In praising idols, noisy orgies chant.
Elijah comes to make the awful test,
And settle claims divine at God's behest.
He notes the distance in a solemn mood,
As calm he comes to face the multiude.
With God's afflatus glowing in his heart,
His eye grows fearful as he acts his part;
In diction understood, and accent strong,
He says: "Why hesitate in doubt so long?
If Baal, in sooth, be God, obey his will;
Or if Jehovah, his behest fulfill.
This will I do to pacify dispute,
The case to try, and gain one God a suit:
Two bullocks take; the priests of Baal take one,
And lay it on the altar to atone,
The other will I take, and timely slay,
And place it on the altar-wood as they.
Thus all made duly ready by the priest,
The One who sends the flame to burn the beast,
Let him be God, in sight of all this day,
And all to him adoring homage pay."
They stipulate the signal to accord,
And settle thus who is the rightful Lord.

The priests of Baal first cleave the beast in twain,
Adjusting it aright the fire to gain;

And lustily to Baal they wail their cry,
To send the flaming answer from the sky.
No answer comes—long time they rave and fume—
No fire descends their bullock to consume.
What time Elijah mocks and quaintly says:
"Still louder cry till Baal impart the blaze!
He talks, perchance absorbed in other things,
And to your wants no kindly favor brings;
Or chases game, as he was wont on earth,"
Elijah says, with irony of mirth.
Their flesh they lance, and offer up their blood,
To timely gain the favor of Nimrod!
Till eventide they passionately rave,
Imploring Baal their sinking cause to save.
  "Draw near!" Elijah says.   With dread they come,
As culprits to their judge to hear their doom.
Twelve stones he sets, according to the claim
Of Jacob's sons, whose valid rights remain.
A trench he cuts around to vindicate
The holy offering inviolate.
And then he says: "Pour water on profuse"—
All this doth he their minds to disabuse.
He prays: "O God! may it this day be known
That thou art Jacob's God, and God alone!
Let it be seen that what I this day do,
Thyself hast done, thy arm divine to show!"
  Anon a red-hot stream comes darting down!
Consumes the gift—licks up the water round;
The worshipers of Baal it doth confound.
"Jehovah, he is God! The Lord is God!"
Resounds aloud, and spreads dismay abroad.
"Baal's prophets seize! and priests full soon
Haste with them to the slaughter of Kipon!"
Elijah says, with noble bearing high,
The signal for idolaters to die.

The terror-stricken throng in haste disperse,
Communing with their many dismal fears;
The frighted king goes up to his repast,
Elijah supplicates for blessing vast.
Full seven times he prays his suit to gain,
Till cheering signs arise, presaging rain.
Black clouds ascend, surcharged with needed showers;
On hills and valleys now the blessing pours.
The king pursues his way to Jezreel's vale,
To tell Queen Jezebel the horrid tale.
From palace colonnades she spies the race,
She sees the royal coach that comes in haste.
The rough-clad racer swiftly glides ahead—
More fleet than galloping steed in harness sped.
His shaggy beard and rustic mantle fly,
As in the race he strives, helped from on high.
He rides upon the raging storm at will,
And nears the queen without the dread of ill.
His grand day's work he grandly doth perform,
His Carmel-zeal doth still his bosom warm.
The angry queen, with malediction dread,
Now imprecates fell curses on his head.
By her gods she swears to take his life away
Before the close of the ensuing day.

ELIJAH FLEES BEFORE JEZEBEL.

Who late had stood sublime on Carmel's height,
And ordered battle when the Lord did fight;
Went single-handed 'mid his hateful foes,
And vanquished Baal when heathen shouts arose,
Grows chill of fear for what the queen ordains;
Beersheba he in speed and safety gains.
He leaves, the while, his faithful servant there,
And speeds him to the wilderness in fear.

A juniper invites him; 'neath its shade
He sat him down, and then most sadly prayed:
"O take my life away! My fathers were
As good as I, who did thy name revere."

Exhaustion hands him over to repose—
In sleep's embrace of peace his eyelids close.
An angel serves the one whom ravens fed;
He touched him gently, and he kindly said:
"Arise betimes and eat;" and when awake,
He sees upon the coals a well-baked cake.
The water-cruse most gladly he perceives;
He quaffs the water and his thirst relieves.
On angels' food he feasts with untold zest;
Ambrosial relishes regale his taste.
He yields himself again to sleep's embrace,
And Eden-like the dreams his thoughts did trace.
The angel interrupts his pleasing mood,
And bids him eat again of angels' food.
"Arise and eat, thy journey yet is great,"
The angel says; "'t is needful for thy state."
He eats, and finds full forty times the might
Of wonted food, to aid his rapid flight,
To reach the much-desired Horeb-cave,
That he his life from Jezebel might save.

"What doest thou, Elijah?" God demands.
Quoth he: "My zeal was stirred in Canaan-lands,
As men forsook their God, in recent years,
Threw down thine altars, and did kill thy seers;
And me they diligently seek to slay.
O take, Thyself, my useless life away!"
God says: "Go, stand before the Horeb-mount,
And note the wonders shown on thy account."*

---

* The remainder of this scene is mostly constructed from "Headley's Sacred Mountains."

Now sullen sounds complain along the air,
And louder swell, as swells Elijah's fear;
He speeds, but ere he gains the cave, a roar
Like ocean's waves that lash the groaning shore,
Assaults his ear, and sends the chilly blood
Recoiling on his heart; aghast he stood.
A blast ensues; it seems the chain that binds
The mount is riven from its old confines.
The rosy sun seems quenched in night and gone,
And all around is dismal and forlorn.
Old Horeb shivers, as in boding fear,
Lest it should quit its base and disappear,
And plunge old chaos with a fearful roar,
And be- as formless as he was of yore!
Elijah looks to see Jehovah's Form,
But finds it not amid the wreck of storm;
No God is found 'mid scenes of dread and fear,
Nor to the prophet doth he yet appear.

And all again is still; the winds no more
Assault the mount with soul-convulsing roar;
Huge spasms seize earth's very vitals now,
While rocks are trembling and the forests bow;
Earth's bosom parts with more than thunder's sound;
Convulsive throbs do shake the solid ground.
The fathomless abyss asunder gapes;
Dread precipices jut their haggard shapes
O'er yawning chasms beneath their yielding base—
Go thundering down the awful, dark abyss!
The prophet lies upon his cavern floor;
Aghast he heeds the grinding rocks that roar.
Quoth he: "Jehovah sure doth stand before
Me now." No God is at the cavern door.

The wild commotion ceases now its rage,
And nature's agitation seems to 'suage;

But in the silence, ominous, there seem
Presages new of awful sights that gleam;
And, suddenly, the heavens are all ablaze,
And streams of fire do each the other chase;
Adown they stream from angry heaven's cope,
Or dance fantastic down the mountain's slope.
The lambent glare lights up the prophet's cell,
And horrid things doth presently reveal;
And Horeb groans as if in tortures dire,
Involved in symbols of Jehovah's ire.
But God was not in malediction-fire.

 Three giant terrors past, what now remains,
To ease Elijah's heart from griefs and pains?
No God he finds in visions that have sped;
"What next?" quoth he, and pants in silence dread.
Now, in the breathless hush that calmly reigns,
That well succeeds to winds and shocks and flames,
A still, small voice falls gently on the air;
It pacifies his heart from anxious care,
And thrills his being with a deep delight.
He *looks*, but still God is not in his sight;
He *feels*, and God is in his peaceful breast—
Invisible—on whom his faith doth rest!
Though "small and still," the voice is strangely sweet;
It plainly tells where grief and gladness meet.
Its cadences how soft, and yet so clear
That all in heaven and sighing earth can hear!
O, who can syllable the tones of grace,
By which our God doth ratify our peace?
To soothe the anguish of a broken heart,
The antepast of heaven it doth impart.
It makes us gently drink compassion in;
It renovates and manumits from sin.
A ransomed spirit's harp can never tell,
And angel's lyre its bliss can ne'er reveal,

Nor hymn the joy Elijah then did feel—
Attested by salvation's ample seal.
And while his bosom quivers to the voice,
Exultant in such vast, ecstatic joys,
A sterner voice bespeaks his ear once more:
" What doest thou?" resounds, as heretofore.
Again he pours his sad complaints and cries;
Once more recites his many griefs and sighs;
The sins of Israel he tells in pain.
He leaves his cave to go to work again,
To oust vile Ahab and to make him feel
The condign punishment of Jezreel.
And Jezebel soon finds the curse of God,
That casts her down for dogs to lick her blood!
Elijah's God be mine! whose still, small voice
Will calm my fears, infusing heavenly joys
While battle's danger howls along my way;
Cheered by that voice I'll fight and win the day.
Then let me ride the chariot he rode,
To bear me to the excellent abode!
I'll see his manhood perfected on high—
Immortalized, with those who never die;
The body that he wore on Tabor's height,
So radiant, meanwhile, with the Spirit's light!
I'll vie with him to laud redeeming love;
Immortal, too—safe in my home above!

ISAIAH'S VISION.

God's throne of Justice stands securely high,
Adorned with light too bright for mortal eye;
Diverging thence, that light demands the shade
Of seraph's wings its luster to evade.
There Justice holds the even scales, to test
Man's acts overt, by motives in his breast.

A furbished sword hangs bright beside the throne,
To vindicate the acts the Lord hath done;
And Truth and Mercy go before God's face,
To try if Justice e'er can stand appeased;
To let Repentance take Compassion's seal,
And Gratitude its nameless blessing feel.
  Ofttimes had Justice frowned with darkling gloom,
And told the horrors of the sinner's doom;
And Mercy, crimson-vestured, stood between
The Lord and man, the guilty ones to screen.
Uzziah's crime Jehovah's wrath bespeaks,
Isaiah's penitence God's mercy seeks.
All heaven is astir; the Lord descends;
His dazzling train in majesty attends;
With harp and lute, and softer dulcimer,
They come, the sighing penitent to cheer;
To spurn the proud offender God appears,
Just as the impious king the altar nears,
In priestly robes arrayed, who has no right.
God's vengeance-dealing hand doth timely smite
The royal sinner, in his crime profane;
Who speeds in haste " the several house" to gain,
A guilty leper, there to die in pain!
  The flying terror spreads dismay around;
The Olive Mount its avalanche sends down,
That chokes the thoroughfare to Azel's vale;
Men flee aghast—with boding dread turn pale.
The storm of wrath is o'er; the smoky cloud
Now fills God's house, where angel-worship loud
Resounds in Christ-adoring, hearty praise;
They magnify Jehovah's saving grace.
Thrice holy notes they shout adoringly,
To sweetly laud the holy One-in-Three!
On man's behalf their mighty joys abound;
They bend in holy awe the scene around;

To see a sinner saved by Triune grace,
They carol forth sweet melody of praise.
   Soon as the angels from their praise do cease,
A sad, complaining moan floats on the breeze;
O! how unlike seraphic praise those cries!
Nor less acceptable the grieving sighs.
"Undone! undone! for that I am unclean;
I dwell among a people foul in sin.
My sinful heart and lips I loathe the most;
Mine eyes have seen the King, the Lord of hosts!"
The Lord imputes his faith for righteousness,
And saves him from his heart's untold distress.
While thus he lies in agony of woes,
The seraph plies the cleansing gift that glows,
And on his lips unclean the coal he laid;
Now purity his being did pervade.
"Thy sin is purged;" most tenderly is said.
Angelic hosts in ecstasy now raise
Their anthems, while the Lord approves their praise.
Isaiah feels the bliss their song implies;
In grateful praise the angels he outvies.
They sing in virtue of another's weal;
He manifests the rapture he doth feel.
But O! the touch of soul-refining fire
Doth love infuse, and grateful praise inspire!
He feels the gift unspeakable within,
Exulting that his heart and lips are clean.
   "And who will go for us?" the Lord demands;
"Who will obey my holy, high commands?"
"Send me!" the prophet says; "for here I am,
And tasks of duty anxiously I claim."
Jehovah says: "I send thee hence away;
To blinded eyes my light and truth display
In ears obtuse loud shout Messiah's day;

To hearts of stone apply the touch of love,
Though they impervious to that touch may prove.
Nor does the prophet guess the task he claims,
Or know the grace to compass all its aims;
What burdens he must bear to Israel,
What pains endure, his mission to fulfill!
His feet, unshod, must ply the rugged ways;
His half-clad form must travel in disgrace;
To Edom and to Egypt thus he shows
Their naked forms and feet devoid of shoes.
For two-score years and eight his vows he pays,
Till holy martyrdom concludes his race.

  The debt we owe to God we pay to man;
Nor is the work of righteousness in vain.
And O! to hear the final word: "Well done!"
To return from heavy toil, exulting home!
Return from fields where tears did fertilize
The precious seeds, that ripen for the skies.
Ripe sheaves we'll bring, in arms of faith upborne;
Exultant come, and wave them near God's throne.
Then 'neath his smile whose hand awards the crown,
With patriarchs and prophets of renown,
We'll gather with the shining victor-throngs,
And swell their shout, and aid to chant their songs!
Isaiah's God be mine! and mine the coal
Of soul-refining grace he felt of old;
And mine the nameless bliss that now he shares—
The spotless robe and golden crown he wears!

BABYLONISH CAPTIVITY.

Since slaughter hands stretched out to desecrate
  Loved Zion's scenes, and slew her noble sons;
Sad captives sighed in bondage desolate,
  To think of holy things and ancient ones.

Long years Jerusalem had dwelt in gloom,
  Her walls and temple desolate did lie;
Long years the Hebrews had endured their doom,
  And, grieving, for their native land did sigh.

Loved Home! 't was passion strong for thee that hung
  The tuneless harp on pliant willow boughs;
At thought of thee, sad lamentation flung
  Its plaintive notes where Babel's current flows.
The cruel conquerors did taunting say:
" Come, sing us one of Zion's cheering songs.
" O! how can we, in stranger lands, essay
The holy chants that moved our tuneful throngs?"

The prophet's heart is stirred in pleading prayer;
  Quoth he: " O Lord! the dreadful and the great,
Thy people, under thy parental care—
  Do thou redeem them from their sad estate!
To thee, O Lord, doth righteousness belong;
  To us, confusion for our wicked deeds;
Reveal thine arm, omnipotently strong,
  Thy wondrous grace our highest thought exceeds!

Incline thine ear; open thy gracious eye;
  Thy city see—for it is named for thee;
Thy goodness we implore, for this of old
  Did lead thy people through the crimson sea.
For sake of blood, thy covenant ordains,
  Send forth thy people from their bondage dire;
Their groaning heed, and sunder all their chains;
  Forgiveness send, and turn away thine ire!"

Now Gabriel, on ready wing, descends,
  And says: " O Daniel! much beloved of God,
His people he in holiness defends—
  His foes he crushes with an iron rod.

I come to give thee skill to understand
  The time, by grace, of sin to make an end
What time thy prayer was heard, was the command
  To build Jerusalem, and it defend."

At news so good, what rapture then did thrill
  The hearts of captives with ecstatic joy;
While cheering melody the air did fill,
  And every harp and every tongue employ!
"Jehovah hath wrought wondrously," they said,
  And tongue from tongue imbibes the flying sound,
All tongues were praising, and all hearts were glad,
  Throughout the Shinar bondage land around.

What thought of home did then each breast inspire,
  As Judah's sons returned to Zion's height!
With ready will, they leave their bondage dire,
  And come to Zion with untold delight.
The young, who saw thee not till then, were glad;
The old, who saw thy dreary state, were sad,
As o'er thy scenes they stood, subdued to tears,
At touching memories of by-gone years.

Full many urgent reasons then did weigh,
To make the youthful ones exult that day;
Full many weighed to make the ancients weep;
Who saw thy glory once, now see a heap!
No outstretched arm omnipotent appeared,
  As anciently, when Pharaoh was slain;
No cloudy pillar then to courage cheered,
  Nor cooled their path along the sultry plain.

No beams of golden light converge above
  Thy holy ark; no heaven-lit fire descends
To burn their sacred offerings of love.
  No angel form like Jacob's guide, attends!

Aloud the ancients weep, as well they may;
　Far louder still may younger ones rejoice.
A mingled sound from multitudes that day
　Commoved the air with loud-resounding noise.

With his prophetic habit girded round,
　With staff in hand, and look serene and kind,
The man of God the ancients to confound,
　Calls them to cast within their anxious mind:
" How seems this house before your tearful eyes?
　As nothing in your sight, although it seem,
Above the former house shall this arise,
　In glory more, by far, in God's esteem.

Behold I shake the heavens, and earth, and seas,
　And He shall come whom nations all desire;
Here will I show the sacrifice of peace;
　To magnify it nations shall conspire.
Zerubbabel, complete the house begun,
　And Joshua, resume thy offerings.
Through golden pipes shall holy unction run,
　His grace to praise who is the King of kings.

From Joshua remove the rags obscene,
Adorn him with a linen white and clean;
The miter fair—affix it to his brow,
The priestly badge inviolate till now.
Far more than priest to you this day I bring,
Whose mystic name is Branch, both priest and king;
Who builds the temple and the glory bears,
Who made the earth, and seas, and suns and stars.

By his omnific hand of plastic skill,
Creating all, adjusting all at will;
Upholding all, evincing all his power,
Whose glory shall from age to age endure,

Himself hath made an offering for sin;
Both cancels guilt and makes man's nature clean;
The right he holds to rule in wondrous grace,
The Lord of all—the holy Prince of Peace.

The corner-stone in Zion firm he lays,
The top-stone brings, with loud-resounding praise;
While heaven echoes with the cheering songs,
And earth, in ecstasy, the praise prolongs.
Grace, grace to Him shall human tongues proclaim,
And seraphim adore with tongues of flame;
Till shouting heaven and singing earth shall join,
To laud Messiah with a praise divine."

NEW TESTAMENT SCENES.

THE BIRTH OF CHRIST

THE sacred day, foretold by ancient seers,
Now hastens on—already it appears.
Prophetic diction speaks the time complete
When earth and skies shall the Messiah greet!
And anxious earth holds sympathy with heaven,
To seize the boon of endless life when given;
To accept the gift divine in manhood mien,
Made known by angels, and by shepherds seen.
   Long time did angels look with eager eye
Upon God's throne, but there could ne'er descry
The *Logos*, whom they saw before man's crime
Did veil the wonders of the scene sublime.
Perchance it cost a vast, adoring thought,
To know the cause or agency that wrought
The wondrous change that then they plainly saw;
To solve the case they searched with bowing awe,
Why guilty, fallen man—ingrate withal,
Found grace denied the angels in their fall!
   The eyes of holy men—a few there were—
Had looked for Jesus with an anxious care;
And some had sought in prophetic books to find
The needed grace to save the human kind.
Divine *afflatus* had in Zion ceased;
As time sped on, men's boding cares increased;
Angelic hosts had hid their dazzling plume,
And left the nation to their cheerless doom.

The *iron-footed image* seen of old,
On Zion proudly stands, with impious hold;
Strews Calvary with skulls of fated ones,
Denied a grave to hide their ghastly bones.
The shout of Pompey's warriors pealed along,
Where choristers had poured their chant and song;
The oath uncouth, invoking gods obscene,
Had brayed where throngs devout did last convene.
The Roman guard kept watch on Zion's height,
To awe the multitudes, bereft of night;
Their scepter gone, while tyranny holds sway,
And slaves their grinding tribute there must pay.
To Bethlehem, most anxiously we seek,
Among the downcast, lowly, and the meek;
For him we seek, whose going forth of old
Displayed his Godhead and his might untold.
From Bethlehem he goes, who is to reign
In Israel, and grace and truth proclaim.
The holy cherubim and seraphim
Descend, in awe of love, and worship him.
Creation once inspired their hearty praise;
Redemption now employs their sweeter lays.
The drowsy shepherds all are in the fields;
The shining, singing heaven to them reveals
Angelic forms on drooping wing above,
Or hovering down in offices of love.
A terrifying light flames lambent o'er,
Reveals the glittering throng still more and more.
The frighted shepherds hide their blinded eyes
From glory-visions sweeping down the skies.
Soft melody pervades the yearning air!—
Its distant chant more plainly now they hear.
"Fear not!" say they, and still more loudly sing:
" Good news of peace to guilty earth we bring!

THE BIRTH OF CHRIST.

In Bethlehem is born the Prince of Peace!"
Their music permeates the earth and seas—
Extending, swelling, shall the grace resound,
Till earth shall roll the glad hosanna round.
  The Magi sages from the far-off East,
In wake of wisdom's star follow in haste;
To Bethlehem it leads their searching eyes,
Bright-glowing in the azure-vaulted skies.
The gifted Magi never reasoned so,
Nor honor reason as just now they do;
Not in the schools where Zoroaster's lore
Was taught in venerated days of yore.
This star in vision appeared to Balaam's sight,
Confused his incantations with its light,
Rebuked his eager, hateful avarice;
O'er Jacob's Tents it hovered down in peace;
Smote Moab's corners with a slaughter-death,
And foiled the angry, warring sons of Heth.
The wise it guides to David's Lord and Son—
Its golden luster leads them gently on;
The brighter Morning Star of gracious hope
It types while smiling in the azure cope;
Star of the East guides to the humble stall,
Morn of the gospel-day sheds light on all;
Angelic hosts and sages come to praise
In holy mood, with glad doxologies;
They make unfeigned, grateful offerings,
And praise the Lord of lords, and King of kings.
  Through Herod's realm the worship echoes on;
So soon as Sage and Seraph home are gone,
Does Herod feign how glad himself would be,
To bend to Christ the reverential knee!
To kill the Holy Child is his intent,
His sacred claims divine to circumvent;

That heaven and earth in praising Christ should vie,
Makes Herod vow that infant sons shall die.
His edict reads: "All infant sons beneath
Two years of age, shall share a bloody death"—
Such death as butchers give their fatted herds,
When hungry mart but scant supply affords.

So soon comes sorrow on the heels of joys,
That Bethlehem resounds with Rachel's voice;
Complaining comes—how passionately sad!
Bewailing slaughter tyranny hath made.
Can mercy see, and not such woe relieve?
Can justice hear, and yet the sin forgive?
Patrolling butchers, cimeters in hand,
Pry out the infants in the sighing land,
Invade the couch of lovely innocence;
Not matron-love can interpose defense.
From darkling woods there comes a touching cry,
That tells where many sons of Rachel die.
Sad, doleful dirges wail along the air,
O'er infant sons, from mothers in despair.
In caves, on mountain-slopes, on craggy peaks,
The child expires, the frantic mother shrieks!
Full many a Rachel sees her son in gore,
All comfortless—"her children are no more!"

Egypt, ill-famed herself for deeds humane,
Preserves Messiah from the tyrant's ban;
Retains him till the infant-butcher dies;
An angel says to Joseph: "Up! arise!
For he is dead who seeks the child to slay;
In peace depart, for God shall keep thy way."
He turns aside in parts of Galilee,
Lest Herod's son enforce the vile decree;
All opportune, according to God's truth,
In Galilee the child abode till youth.

SIMEON AND ANNA.

Loved Simeon, devout, now seeks for Christ
In temple-courts, to fix on him his eyes;
Divinely guided, he believes the while
That he will live to see the holy child.
The Spirit leads him to the temple-scene,
To clasp *The Son*, the infant Nazarene;
According to the rites of olden days,
The parents offer up their gifts with praise;
The child he sees, and folds him in his arms!
The Spirit now unveils Messiah's charms.
Salvation in his arms and in his heart,
He prays: "Now let me, Lord, in peace depart!
For all my eager eye doth now survey;
The darkness flees before the approaching day,
Whose lucid rays shall gild the blushing morn;
Its beauties shall all Gentile lands adorn.
Coequal grace shall bless all Israel,
As from her worshipers rapt anthems swell,
To magnify the gift of priceless worth;
'T is God's salvation to the ends of earth!
  But O! a furbished sword mine eye doth see;
Of grief untold it is the mystery!
That sword will smite the shepherds, fright the sheep,
And make Judean matrons loudly weep;
'T will cleave men's hearts, their inmost thoughts unfold
And pierce with grief a yearning mother's soul!"
Now Anna comes, with accents sweetly mild,
Who timely worships the Messiah-child.
Of these she speaks, who for salvation wait,
To manumit them from their low estate.
In temple-courts for many anxious years,
Saints uttered pleading prayers and shed their tears.

They see Christ's going forth from Bethlehem,
And magnify his mission to redeem.
Penuel's daughter sweetly keys the note—
Still on the air its melting measures float;
Till time shall end the anthems shall resound,
And every harp Messiah's praise shall sound.

JOHN THE BAPTIST.

The Herald sent before Messiah's face,
Demands Elijah's zeal and sturdy grace;
On Zechariah's son the gift in quest
Descends, and animates his holy breast.
His rugged raiment, wove of camel's hair,
As costume meet, the prophet most doth wear.
He copies methods from old Carmel's height,
Where truth and error fought a bloody fight;
God's promise stood, that ere Messiah's day,
Elijah should prepare for him the way.
The honored gifts on John full soon descend;
Lo! multitudes his ministry attend;
Elijah's mode he takes to awe his foes—
The serpent's pedigree on some bestows.
To kingly lusts he reads a fearful doom;
To hypocrites he speaks of wrath to come.
Sublime he stands, Jehovah's lance in hand,
To strike repentance in; then gives command
To let the fruits appear unto the eye—
The inward grace his washings signify.
With mystic garb, and of abstemious mood,
Severe in speech, and eminent he stood,
Above the love of praise and worldly things,
And lust of gold, and dread of wicked kings;
He shuns the viands of the epicure—
Abstains from wine, is in his manner pure.

Great man! and great the work he comes to do;
How great he is grave scribes were fain to know.
" Is he the prophet drawn by steeds of flame ?"
Thus silence muses o'er his flying fame.
Men think, and ask : " Is he the very Son,
With claims authentic from the Holy One ?"
He says : " Christ must increase, and I decline ;
The herald star of morn, I only shine
To darkle in his uncreated light,
Whose rays can dissipate the shades of night.
My work is his, not mine, withal to choose—
Unworthy I to loose his sacred shoes.
The Bridegroom, he, whose mandatory voice
Inspires my breast with sweet, ecstatic joys.
My humble place is at Messiah's feet,
To heed his word, and all my vows complete."
 All things are ready ; lo ! the Lord appears !
Authority divine his mission bears ;
The rugged ways grow smoother still, and plain,
While heralds his sublime approach proclaim ;
High places sink, the low he raises high ;
To praise his name the shouting victors vie.
Let all adore, but none his might oppose ;
For they must fall who are Messiah's foes !
 The ancient types evanish now from sight,
While Christ, their Antitype, asserts his right :
The *all* of mercy and the *whole* of love
To those who do his full salvation prove.
To Jordan Jesus comes in lowly mien,
His steps majestic and his look serene ;
His errand there we have no need to guess ;
He comes to consummate all righteousness.
When from the stream the Lord of Life ascends,
As a dove the Spirit on his head descends.

This adumbrates his gracious mode to save;
In Jordan John the outer man did lave,
In figure of the Spirit's work within,
Whose renovation makes man's nature clean.

TEMPTATION OF CHRIST.

The tempting trial comes, and bears the Lord
To scenes that no supplies of food afford.
For two-score days he has a-hungered been,
So that, as man, he might succumb to sin.
His 'minished strength invites the Tempter's eye,
Who nears the Lord, his practiced arts to try.
Quoth he: "When flesh is weak, then am I strong;
This adage feasible has served me long.
That hungry One!—who can he be, withal—
Impeccable? or liable to fall?
Why this misgiving in my iron breast,
To approach this famished One, my might to test?
It thrills my wrath-enduring nerves with pain,
And makes me oscillate 'twixt loss and gain.
What strange alliance flesh may hold with God,
I can not guess; still anxious thoughts forbode.
Avaunt! I'll face it all; but should it prove
The power that hurled me from the realms above,
Humility will then to pride ensue,
And my most cherished plans I thus undo;
If otherwise, my triumph shall be grand,
And leave this lower world at my command."

He stirs his courage, and his thoughts he strings
To sophistry, and many a text he brings.
He makes his choice of *appetite* and *pride*—
Presumption and Apollyon deified.

He to his task addresses his best gift—
His *premise* claiming, lets *conclusions* shift!
" If Son of God thou be, what might is thine!
Why look so meager, and in famine pine?
Speak now these stones into angelic bread;
Quite good enough for gods who might be fed—
By thy omnific mandate feasted here.
Now feed to full, and yield faint nature cheer."
Christ says : " Man's nature claims unearthly food,
Of every promise from the mouth of God;
This better food let him receive with zest,
Nor bestialize God's Son to have him feast
His meaner nature by profanity,
To wield omnipotence for sake of thee."

On lusty wings upborne in rapid flight,
The Demon and the Savior gain yon height;
Upon the temple's pinnacle they poise,
And Satan now extends another choice:
"Be not afraid of this ascent, thou Son,
For if thou be Jehovah's darling One,
Thy feet are warranted against all harms,
Thyself enfolded in angelic arms.
They constantly have custody to keep
Thee safe; now make, in haste, the fearless leap!"
Christ says: "Thou shalt not tempt God's anger dread;
For should man's giddy heart aspire to tread
Presumption's elevated, slippery mount,
To turn God's holy word to vile account,
Then vainly shalt thou look and vainly feel
For angel hands to keep thee out of hell.
'Tis vain, in sinful lust, on God to call
For angel hands to save thee in thy fall."

Abashed the devil seemed, as he recoiled
From truth so apt; nor yet is he quite foiled.
Again he speeds his flight exceeding high,
Where prospects wonderful invite the eye.

"See there," the Tempter says; " nor be dismayed
To *look*, if *leaping* make thee so afraid.
Behold the glories vast this scene commands,
Of nations near, or in remoter lands;
These all are mine, and mine to give at will.
If peradventure thou my words fulfill,
That thou before my shrine adoring fall,
My right I 'll waive, and yield thee each and all."
Quoth Christ: " Thy God shalt thou adore alone,
And him obey, and render him his own.
Go! get thee hence! away!" the Savior says;
And Satan now the high behest obeys.
 Then, when the Tempter had his way pursued,
The angel bands the famished Savior wooed;
And to him heavenly manna gladly bring,
While they his triumph over Satan sing.

 Armed for the fight, and in the strength of God,
May we pursue the way the Savior trod!
Confront the Fiend with truth that Jesus taught,
And bear the Spirit's sword, with which he fought;
Thus learn the mind that was in Christ, our Head,
Strong in his might, well nourished by his bread;
Nor trust ourselves to guardian angels' hands,
Regardless of the Savior's high commands.
In sinful ways God's angels never keep,
But shield the just, whether they wake or sleep.
This needful lesson let all saints observe:
"*To worship God, and him alone to serve.*"
Let Satan tempt! though lion-like his roar,
In fury seeking whom he may devour,
With Christ, our Advocate, his rage we 'll scorn,
Kept by God's power, in angel hands upborne!

BETHESDA'S POOL.

Bethesda, with her beauteous portico,
Bespeaks where healing waters gently flow,
And for the impotent, and halt, and poor,
Unfolds her welcome, woe-relieving door.
She beckons multitudes in want to come
Beneath her gracious, ample, sheltering dome;
And test the virtue of her mystic font,
When by the angel troubled, as was wont;
Then one, in wretchedness, might take his chance,
Who to the yearning pool could first advance.
All else forestalled could only lie in grief,
And wait another chance to find relief.
  Thus partial was Bethesda's grace, and small,
While Jesus' larger grace is free for all.
With Christ 't is always *now*, and never *then*;
With Bethesda *then*, and oft long time between.
So marked the contrast, all may comprehend,
To Jesus come, and on his love depend.
Most wretched 'mong the ruined, sighing throng,
The aged cripple lies, has lain so long;
His stiffened limbs hang useless by his side,
Or lie extended motionless and dried.
One score and eighteen years had sped away,
And mocked the ruined cripple as he lay;
The chances that Bethesda seldom gave,
All failed the sighing sufferer to save.
Christ knows how long and weary hath been his state;
His bosom yearns with love compassionate.
Quoth he: " Wilt thou that I shall make the whole?"
The cripple doth his hopeless case unfold:
" What time the healing virtue is displayed,
And I am coming on devoid of aid,
Another comes between me and the cure,
And I, forlorn, my dreadful state endure;

Such sad defeats my many griefs enhance,
While I am doomed to bide another chance."
 The better grace of Christ's compassion yearns,
As to the paralyzed he gently turns:
"Arise and walk!" the Savior only says,
While through the withered limbs the fiat plays;
His ankle-bones and ruined limbs once more
Begin each office as in days of yore;
As all his being thrills with ecstacies,
From off his couch he instantly doth rise!
These Sabbath wonders Pharisees confound,
Who bid him cast his heavy burden down.
Not angry Jews can check his march sublime—
Thus nerved with strength and healing so divine,
They mutter their mad, Pharisaic zeal;
He voices forth the gladness he doth feel!

 Why lie a cripple, and your pain endure?
Come now to Christ and have a perfect cure!
Why wait for grace, long intervals between?
Approach Siloam's waters, and be clean.
They softly move, troubled by God's own love—
Unfailing stream, whose source is high above;
Through Christ, the channel, it doth freely flow,
To cleanse all sinners who to him will go.

CHRIST CALMS THE SEA.

 Loosed from her moorings, see yon ship essay
Her passage o'er the frightful, watery way;
With deafening roar the wind forbids her sail,
While thunders bicker, and mad sea-gods wail;
The raging tempest concentrates its force
Upon the bark, to whelm her in her course.

Perchance the Prince of air's resistless power
Assumes command this dark and dismal hour.
Fain would he sink that ship in ocean's deeps,
For sake of Him on board, who calmly sleeps.
Nor doth he duly estimate the might
Incarnate in the one he comes to fight.
  The ship is safe, her destination sure;
She'll stem the tempest, and each surge endure,
Though frighted seamen cease the storm to brave,
And yield their rudder to the victor-wave.
Imagination paints their fearful doom—
The deep-dug, yawning, all-devouring tomb.
They think of home, and many loving ones,
Whose griefs their fancies heed in touching tones;
Already hear their funeral dirges sigh,
Most passionate across the storm-wrought sky;
Themselves they feel descending into death;
"Lord save! we perish!" loud each seaman saith.
  Serenely Christ arose, and chiding said:
"O, ye of little faith! why all this dread?
Why all this agonizing, needless fear?
Regarding not my saving might so near."
He to the stormy winds but said: "Be still!"
The raging winds obey his sovereign will.
The warring waves from all their strife surcease;
On every hand there reigns a perfect peace!
Huge spasms that had convulsed the groaning deep,
Relax their giant grasp, and sink to sleep.
The angry waves their fierce contention cease,
And when the Master speaks are all at peace.
Calm is the sea, and beautiful it seems,
While on its bosom quiet heaven gleams.
The storm Christ throttles, and the seamen saves,
And foils the devil on the stormy waves.
Omnipotence incarnate saves the crew;
A placid sea and starlit sky they view.

Sweet, reverential thoughts their minds fill,
Who say: "See how the winds obey his will!
What man is this? His manner how serene!
Yet angry billows know what he doth mean.
'Be still!'—and that was all the Master said,
And ocean's storm-gods presently obeyed."
We praise omnific love, which timely saves
From howling dangers and from watery graves;
Safe landed on an Eden-quiet shore,
Life's stormy perils then forever o'er.

CHRIST RAISETH THE WIDOW'S SON.

The sad procession slowly swings its tread,
The dead in hand, to lay him with the dead.
The mother moves along in sad estate—
They opportunely near the city gate.
"The Resurrection and The Life" draws near,
The son to raise—the mother's heart to cheer.
Unwittingly they meet a God-like Friend,
Who comes his aid omnipotent to lend.
A mother's riven heart bespeaks the boon,
The Savior's yearning heart responds full soon.
Along the way, the mother goes in gloom,
She erst had trod to the voracious tomb;
Erewhile with part, but now she brings her all,
In death's embrace, beneath the sable pall.
  Her husband's death entailed sad widowhood,
But then her son beside her gently stood.
'T was sad to yield him up, whose manly arm
Did aid in weakness and defend from harm;
Thus yield her partner up, whose genial smile
Did life's inevitable woes beguile;
His love, the source of untold blessedness,
Her timely stay when heavy trials press.

CHRIST RAISETH THE WIDOW'S SON.

Of life's great ills he took his equal due,
And doubled all its joys in revenue.
Such inventory dread she counted o'er
What time she walked that dismal way before.
   But then her only child did gently tread
Beside her, to inter the beloved dead;
A manly mien he bore to mourn his sire,
And kindly soothe his mother's sorrows dire.
He, strong of arm and firm his supple tread,
Beside her kept his way behind the dead.
She gazed intent on one so kind and dear,
As hope's bright solace did her bosom cheer.
Quoth she: "Life's staff from me is roughly wrenched,
Life's gilded hopes in cheerless death are quenched;
My all is gone, save thee, my only son!
Be thou the staff that I may lean upon;
Be thou my light, to grace with pleasing cheer
My widow's home, so desolate and drear."
   That funeral, in sooth, was sad—*this* more,
Which now her steps describe, her cries deplore.
Behind the one on whom her hope was stayed,
She slowly moves, in sorrow's garb arrayed;
Her heart is stung with sorrow's keenest dart,
Thus doomed with all her earthly good to part.
There lies the form in death's embrace congealed,
Whose filial smile sweet solace oft did yield.
O, who can know her agonizing mood,
Thus left forlorn, in dreary widowhood?
Her friends are dead, and dead her earthly hope;
No star remains in heaven's cheerless cope!
Her heart now quivers to the touch of fate,
Its griefs her moans can ill articulate.
Her sad lament demands from all a tear;
It touches now the mighty Savior's ear.
"Weep not!" resounds, while Jesus stays the bier;
Pall-bearers halt with awe and trembling fear.

How vast the love that in his bosom swells!
Omnipotent the fiat which now tells:
"Young man, arise!"—and life resumes its beat
Along the nerves, infusing vital heat;
Dissolves the pitchy blood, expands the veins;
The arteries commove—volition reigns!
 The stir of life is rustling in the shroud,
The cry of wonder echoes still more loud;
To Christ, askance, revert all wishful eyes;
The widow's only son from death doth rise!
His eye, new-lit, descries a mother's face,
Which an unwonted luster now doth grace;
The last he saw, what time his sight grew dim
In death, and now all angel-like doth seem!
His tongue essays the sacred name to call;
She in his fond, embracing arms doth fall.
Fresh from his lips, the salutation given
Bespeaks the filial love that tastes of heaven.
All else he gently greets with manly mien,
Then worships Christ, and moves along serene.
His wonted strength doth now his form pervade;
With rosy health his cheek is now arrayed.
A mystic voice, resounding from that pall,
Proclaims the resurrection-life to all;
The lips that then did say, "Young man, arise!"
Shall speak our bodies to their paradise.

CHRIST RESTORETH THE NOBLEMAN'S SON.*

A stately castle overhangs the bay
Of Old Capernaum, while in it lay
A lovely boy in agonies of pain;
All healing remedies were tried in vain.

---

*This poem was constructed from a prose scrap found in newspaper. Author unknown.—R. H.

The unglazed lattices admit the air,
Which dallies with his silken ringlets fair.
His deep blue eye and lineaments of face
Bespeak him partly of the Ægean race.
Upon a cushion, spangled o'er with gold,
Reclines the child, fast breathing out his soul.
Above his couch a matron form doth bend,
Sustained by her own dearest earthly friend.
She grievingly exclaims: "What shall be done
To save from death our lovely, darling son?"
"I know no help," her husband doth reply,
While sorrow glistens in his downcast eye.

The sister says: "Were Jesus here, he'd save
My precious brother from an early grave;
The foster-mother told me so erewhile—
O, send for him and save the dying child!"
"And who is Jesus?" asks the stricken sire,
His bosom heaving with intense desire.
"A Prophet," one replies, "whose hand divine
Transformed the water into blushing wine;
At Cana now the prophet you may find."
"Prepare my coach and steeds without delay,"
The father saith, and hies in haste away.
The rush of wheels resounds along the shore,
To reach the Prophet ere the night is o'er.

Delirium comes on, dread symptoms rise—
The extremities are cold, with sunken eyes
Surrounded by a ring of livid hues,
That tells his doom; his brow breeds deathly dews;
His skin begins to spot—an omen dread
That soon he will be numbered with the dead.
Noon comes, alas! and he is sinking fast;
His pulse grows weaker—now he nears his last.
So near he comes to life's remotest verge
That watchers now prepare to chant death's dirge.

They lead the mother to another room;
The sisters follow, robed in sorrow's gloom.
Now all is still, save that a mother's cries,
Complaining, tell of heart-felt agonies.
Aghast they pause, to hear the accents swell:
"Jehovah! He is God of Israel!"
That dirge comes not, the while, but now
It plainly comes: "O, mother! where art thou?"
She screams, and bounding to her feet,
Makes haste her living, smiling child to greet!
An angel glides into her warm embrace,
With rosy tints of health upon his face—
The "honey-dew" of love upon his lips,
Sweeter than nectar, which wild fancy sips.
Now 'wildered vision says: "It is his soul!"
Now reason says: "It is my child I hold."
She praises God in ecstasy that weeps,
While rapture through her throbbing bosom leaps.
"What time?" quoth she. "The dial points to seven,"
The watchers say. "The Prophet sent from heaven,
Perchance, hath from a distance wrought this deed."
She to her servant says: "Up! go in speed!
Inform my lord the darling child is well!
How glad he'll be when you the tidings tell!"
Two chariots now appear in range, afar;
With headlong speed they each the other near.
The servant says: "Thy darling is alive!"
The sire demands: "What time did he revive?"
The servant answers: "Just at seven."
The sire replies: "The incidents are even."
They both, as silent as the fated dumb,
Make utmost speed to reach Capernaum.
To see the sire and mother and the boy
Embrace, inspires a moving, thrilling joy!

BLIND BARTIMEUS.

The beggared blind man sits by thoroughfares
   Where passers-by can note his sad estate;
And as the footfall of the throng he hears,
   He craves of them the gift compassionate.
He hears the sound of travel on that way;
   He asks and finds that David's Son draws near.
His heart is leaping and he now doth say :
   "What things hath Jesus done the blind to cheer?

Lo! they have gained the precious leave to gaze
   Upon the splendors of yon orb of light,
Not seen by me for many cheerless days,
   And gloomy years of unrelenting night!
An opaque wall seems arched quite o'er my head ;
   Its cruel ceiling is so dark and tight,
That on my gloom no pitying ray is shed,
   To sooth me in my melancholy plight.

How long since friendship's smile hath cheered my heart,
   Or shed its luster on my dreary gloom !
All nature's beauty and the charms of art
   Have fled, and left me to my dismal doom.
But O, if others would but lead my way!
   I have a gracious chance for sight once more ;
May see the glories of the king of day
   Adorn the world with smiling beauty o'er."

Such stirring thoughts their mighty office wrought
   Within the beggar's anxious, yearning soul;
Desire unwont intensified his thought,
   And his affections fused like molten gold,
When the refiner tests it in the fire ;
   Now comes the time for heaven-conquering prayer ;

Prompted by irrepressible desire,
   He flings it wailing on the yearning air!

The order-loving ones, with measured tread,
   And look demure, of visage long and wry;
With lifted hands and holy shake of head,
   Now bid him moderate his wild outcry.
He feels prevailing strength, unfelt till then,
   That lifts emotion to a higher key;
He brings his want to an Almighty Friend,
   And now prevails his God-like face to see.

Now Jesus pauses, nor will farther go,
   Until the beggar's suit is entertained;
He asks the thing that he would have him do,
   And full-orbed vision confident he claimed.
His eyes are eloquent with flowing tears,
   He brings his darkness to the light divine;
Clear vision now his new-lit eyeballs cheers,
   While cloudless day most beauteously doth shine.

All quivering, as the aspen in the breeze,
   His bosom yearning with delight untold;
His heart exultant with strange ecstacies,
   As to his vision scenes sublime unfold!—
Thus blest with sight, he mingles with the throng,
   And follows him who spake away his woes;
With shout impassioned and with joyous song,
   He magnifies Messiah as he goes.

CHRIST'S ENTRY INTO JERUSALEM.

The chariot of Ephraim is rent,
His battle-bow unstrung, his arrows spent;
The horse is slain on which gay kings in pride
Of pompous show and vanity did ride.

CHRIST'S ENTRY INTO JERUSALEM.

Their gaudy things, in which their souls did trust,
Are impotent—their honor trails the dust.
In grace he comes, whose right it is to reign;
Prophetic heralds all his love proclaim.
His signet bears authority divine,
His scepter rules o'er every land and clime;
He claims a world-wide, universal sway
O'er rivers' sources and from sea to sea;
And meekly he in holiness proceeds
Along the way his royal triumph leads.
In guise of man, lo! he salvation brings;
Both God and man—the mighty King of kings!
The horse he spurns, disdaining pomp and pride,
Upon the foal of an ass doth lowly ride;
The raiment of the great a carpet spreads,
To grace the way his royal triumph treads.
The palm-trees yield their foliage in haste;
Palm-wreaths in hand, exulting thousands praise.
They move ahead, each side and in the rear,
Hosanna doth the ringing welkin cheer!
To honor Davids Son they take delight;
Their tongues he fires, that they may praise aright.
On battlements and towers and porticoes,
Stand invalids, to note the throng that goes;
Augmenting still, as the vast concourse nears
The temple, where the faithful offer prayers
From hearts devout ascends the hearty praise,
Called forth by charms that Christ to all displays;
Not Tabor's song, nor Hermon's cheering voice,
Responding to each other's thrilling joys,
Could e'er excel the praise that Zion swells;
To honor Christ the glad hosanna tells.
Meantime, the innocent, in infant tones,
Shout to the triumph as it shouting comes;
The temple-gate, the walls, and colonnade
The mighty tribute to the Savior paid,

Till earth and skies conjoin in sympathy,
And celebrate Messiah's jubilee!
 Harsh discord mingles with the flying cheer;
One, chiding, says to Christ: "Dost thou not hear
This wild tumult and all this childish shout,
Resounding in the temple round about?"
Quoth Jesus: "Hast thou never read the psalm
Of old, composed to vindicate the claim
Of 'babes and sucklings' to their lisping praise,
Which God ordains to sing Messiah's grace?"
Emotions so divine, held in restraint,
Would sunder adamant in gaining vent.
Let human tongues the mighty anthem raise,
Or stones astreet will chant the holy lays.
The scene is o'er—Jerusalem gone home;
Christ turns from joy to mourn her awful doom!

CHRIST WEEPETH OVER JERUSALEM.

The all-perceiving eye melts o'er the scene—
Jerusalem undone—in culprit-mien!
Justice descends, with scroll in hand, and reads,
Articulate, man's God-offending deeds.
That scroll seems red with righteous Abel's blood;
And Barachiah's sons cry aloud to God,
To tempt the swift-descending wrath divine,
To smite the guilty with a blow condign.
All past is horrid, and the future dread
With vengeance, lowering o'er their guilty head.
The angry host of war in vision comes,
To desecrate the temple—strew its stones.
 The warrior's siege is planted in his view,
Who mourns the slaughter-work they come to do.
The Savior weeps! His cadences are slow
And tremulous, 'neath man's impending woe.

He wails, "Jerusalem! Jerusalem!
God's holy seers ye did in wrath condemn;
And stones did cast at messengers of love,
Authenticate, with mandate from above.
How oft would I have served your erring kings,
As chirping broods beneath maternal wings!
My outspread mercy, soft, and strong, and broad,
Had screened you from the awful wrath of God.
Ye would not let me timely save and bless—
Would choose anathema! All comfortless,
Your visitation-day is past and gone,
The things pertaining to your peace are flown.
Your house lies desolate before my eye;
Your scattered children piteously cry;
And me ye no more see—nor shall your race,
Till ye relent, and share redeeming grace!"

TRANSFIGURATION OF CHRIST

Mount Tabor, famed of old for ecstasies,
  That vied with Hermon, when the prophet sung,
As he descried through rolling centuries,
  The glories which upon that mountain hung,—
More cause of joy abounds this holy hour,
  More glory stirs the sacred place to praise,
As the inhering Godhead glories pour
  Their luster through Messiah's beaming face,

Three favored ones beside the Savior stand;
  Two others come, arrayed in brighter guise;
Three from the earth attend at his command;
  Two, once from earth, come glittering from the skies.
From earth and heaven they come in holy haste,
  The mortal and immortal saints attend,

To note the visions so replete with grace,
    Where grace and glory interlace and blend.

The orb of day, arrayed in tresses bright,
    When he his beauty and his strength puts on,
But faintly adumbrates the wondrous light
    Which in the Savior's face refulgent shone.
His manhood shows bright glories from within,
    Before which mortals fall and swoon away;
His vesture scintillating with the sheen
    That decks the mountain with a dazzling day.

Now Moses and Elias stand serene
    Beside the Lord, and talk of Calvary;
To timely know what such vast glories mean,
    And what Christ's final, awful agony.
Nor could the higher realms of bliss afford—
    Where saints and seraphs mingle in one throng—
The rapt delight they feel beside the Lord,
    Heeding the answers of his glowing tongue.

To Christ they say: "Thou art the source of love,
    Its price excelling, and its *way* and *end*;
Through thee the saints attain the joys above,
    On thee for grace and glory they depend;
Thy pledges of atoning grace have given
    Our tenure to the ever-during joys
Foretasted here, but fully known in heaven;
    Redemption all our grateful praise employs!

Thy name yields music for our lofty song—
    Our song, the praises due thy holy name;
Redemption moves each glowing heart and tongue,
    Sets saints and worshiping angels all aflame.
The time draws nigh, ordained for thy decease
    On Salem's Hill, to seal redemption's plan;
Which ratifies on high the terms of peace,
    In bitter death for every soul of man."

And Jesus says: "The body is prepared;
　　I wear it now, and now it wears the grace
So glory-like that by apostles feared,
　　They swoon, and ye can scarce endure my face.
This glory aptly comes in time to seal
　　My flesh for the atoning agony;
That penitence forgiving love may feel,
　　And wear white robes of spotless purity."

Their honors now they cast at Jesus' feet—
　　Prophetical or legal they resign
To Christ, in whom official honors meet;
　　Diverging thence, their full-orbed splendors shine.
The face of Christ more beauteous still appears,
　　With Godhead glories far more decorate,
Till Tabor quivers 'neath the grace it wears,
　　To shadow forth Messiah's coming state.

The glory-stricken three now lie entranced,
　　But Jesus touches them and they awake;
Now Peter's ecstasies are so enhanced,
　　He prays unwittingly three tents to make,
For occupancy human or divine.
　　His handicraft would rear the lodging straight;
His yearning heart and loving soul incline
　　To tarry within sight of glory's gate!

THE RESURRECTION OF CHRIST.*

Kind Joseph makes his humble suit to crave
Of cruelty for innocence a grave.
The right he gains with Roman seal and guard,
　　To lay the Savior in the tomb prepared.

---

*The "Passion of Christ" follows next in order, but is thought to be too rugged in thought and execution, and is therefore with regret omitted.—EDITOR.

The grieving few with gloomy thoughts oppressed,
Lay Jesus in a linen shroud to rest.
They haste away in solitude to weep—
Their Shepherd smitten, they the scattered sheep!
Their hope of immortality seems doomed—
"The resurrection and the life" entombed!
  At Joseph's tomb Rome's warrior troops convene;
Christ's claims they scandalize with jest obscene.
A monarch's grave they hold in custody,
Whose royalty they scout with witty glee;
And war-like feats perform to indicate
Their doom, who durst to break the seal of state;
How they would deal on them the slaughter-stroke,
Who chanced their warrior prowess to provoke.
They speak their raptures in the ear of night,
As *Luna* treads aloft her azure height.
  The jubilee of hell is in full blast;
To break their prisons angry fiends make haste.
One says: "Had Christ in Paradise but staid,
Where once authority most dread he swayed,
As erst we felt what time his vengeful ire
Did cast us down to punishment most dire,
Since when with chains of darkness we are tied—
The hateful badges of our humbled pride;
The hated signets of his hated power
Have we endured until this final hour.
But since he would his high estate desert,
And put on flesh, our purposes to thwart,
He finds a wondrous change; in Joseph's tomb
Himself fast folded in death's deepest gloom.
This time most opportune we now will take
To snap our chains, our prison-wards forsake!"
  They shout their joy—their croaking vespers chant,
Of hoarse blasphemy, and their triumph vaunt.
Through all the regions of the damned around,
The jubilee-music harshly doth resound.

The Jew, meantime, imbibes the flying joy,
And chants the notes that demon lips employ.
Hard by the Aramathean's burying-place
He stands agape, and sportively he says:
"How boots it now with Him who came to save—
But sleeps his last within a borrowed grave?
How goes it with his friends, whose tearful eyes
Pry wishfully, to see their Master rise?
Would they might now essay to steal their Lord!
Soon would they feel Rome's keen, death-dealing sword."
He vents his mirth with an uproarious glee,
And acts again the demon-jubilee.
While Jews and Romans each the other greet,
Down shines the signal of their dire defeat!
A mighty angel rolls the stone away;
Of visage bright, and dreadful his array.
Sublime he sits upon Rome's seal of state;
The keepers for fear of him do greatly shake.
Rome's brawny warriors, helpless, strew the ground—
Their bossy shields lie, useless, all around.

With God-like port the Savior leaves the grave,
His Godhead fiat prevalent to save;
Fills all the charnels which his death did rend,
And from their slumbers dazzling saints ascend!
They seem like morning stars, that brightly peer
From out empyreal depths with golden glare,
Too brightly habited for mortal eyes,
With glory-robes that deck them as they rise!
Imponderous and fleet as thought they move;
"Now skim the level, now they mount above,"
To meet bright angels in the middle air,
With heavenly melodies; and thus prepare
For the ascension-hour that now draws near;
And soon from mortal eyes they disappear.

The keepers flee as fast as limbs will let,
To tell the scribes and elders their defeat;

They, artless, tell it all in open court—
That Jesus left the tomb with God-like port;
An angel mighty had broke the seal of state,
And rolled away the stone inviolate;
How they could wield them neither sword nor spear,
But helpless pressed the earth, convulsed with fear.
With accent difficult and visage pale,
They tell the self-degrading, wondrous tale;
Each scribe is pallor-smit with deeper shame,
At very mention of the Christ's dread name!
They bribe the soldiers this affair to keep;
Quoth they: "Just feign that ye were fast asleep;
And while your rest profound was going on,
His disciples came and rolled away the stone,
And stealthily conveyed the corpse away,
A little while before the break of day;
And should the matter come to Pilate's ear,
We'll stand 'twixt him and thee; so have no fear."
This sorry fiction, poorly told the while,
The best they had, though fraught with silly guile,
And good withal, as infidels yet tell,
Who show their weakness and their shame reveal.

   Man's triumph is complete; now Christ doth rise,
And leave the tomb for an immortal prize;
Resumes his flesh, in which for us he died,
And cometh forth! Death's keys adorn his side,
And they shall open all death's charnels drear;
Then with their Lord shall rising saints appear.

CHRIST'S ASCENSION.

The Pentecostal feast doth mark the date
When Christ shall repossess his primal state,
And tread with pomp great Zion's courts above,
Replete with saving, sin-atoning love.

He moves serenely on to Bethany,
And speaks his parting words, how tenderly!
Two myriads of angels come in haste;
Twice-told that number deck yon ample space.
Of old, when Sinai blew his awful trump,
They came in haste, in robes of glittering pomp;
They saw vast glory when God gave his law—
O'er Bethany they pause with deeper awe.
They come to shout Messiah up to heaven,
Through whose ascent the Holy Ghost is given.
Glad saints, from out their dusty charnels, late,
The grand ascension triumph now await;
To meet Redemption's monarch in his rise,
And aid to laud him to his native skies.
They chant the psalmody of Jesse's son,
As Jesus rises to his Father's throne.
Omnific mandate voicing in their lay,
Bids heaven's portals ope Messiah's way.
The Porter of the skies demands his right,
Who claims a triumph through those portals bright.
It comes: "The mighty Lord from battle-strife,
Who died, and takes again immortal life,
Who drags his foes at his triumphal car—
Fly wide, ye gates! His royal way prepare!"
Obedient hosts in holy rapture wait,
To see the King of Glory pass, unlet.
The first-fruits from the dead attend his march,
All glorious they pass the victor-arch!
His glory hence is theirs eternally,
And they with him from death's dark prison free.

    To angel hosts the Son of God appears
More glorious for that he his manhood wears.
The *Logos*, blent with flesh, to all displays
A worth demanding higher meed of praise
Than o'er *creation* angels erst did raise.

But now, since God, in manhood's lowly mien,
Appears upon the throne, how changed the scene!
Attent, they hear a pacifying sound,
Which through God's courts doth, all divine, resound.
They hear with awe his all-prevailing prayer
To send the Comforter God's saints to cheer.
Nor sooner do they heed those accents mild,
Than things in heaven are sweetly reconciled.
More gentle sounds commove the air above,
And heaven basks in smiles of softer love.
Messiah takes his seat at God's right hand,
And angels worship him at God's command.
The Father on the throne now yields his Son
The coronation honors all his own.
He saith: "Thy throne, O God, abides secure!
Thy right to rule forever shall endure!
All earthly kings, after their little day,
Shall fade and wither, and shall pass away.
The heavens themselves, so glorious and so grand,
Shall also disappear at thy command;
But thou shalt stay, unchangeably the same,
And earth and skies shall join to swell thy fame!
On Zion's height sublimely take thy seat,
Thy friends to aid, thy enemies defeat.
Beside the way thy vanquished foes have fled,
Drink of the brook, and lift thy victorious head,
Till all are foiled, who will not timely taste
Thy saving love, and bow to thy behest."
This said, and all is love, and awe, and praise,
Inspired by the Messiah's saving grace!
  In quest of glory turn we now in haste;
But glory has from Sinai surceased;
To Zion all its mystic glories move,
Translated to "Jerusalem above."
Its glory darkles in his Godhead light,
Whose golden rays deck Zion's blushing height;

Converged in Christ its glory disappears,
In whom the Godhead bodily inheres.
His vesture, crimson with atoning blood,
Bespeaks him flesh, but still the Word of God.
A man upon the throne for man appears;
Above the throne the rainbow glory stirs,
Till all the firmament around grows bright,
And blushes in redemption's softer light.
The grace of Christ is fitly symbolized
By patterns yielded Moses from the skies.

MILLENNIAL TRIUMPH.

Loud swells the mellow chorus of the skies;
Echoed by earth, the ringing anthem flies;
Soft, dulcet sounds commove the yearning air—
Bright, drooping wings of cherubim appear.
Through golden ports God's tabernacle appears,
The *sea* of *glass* its blushing glory wears,
Till all its pavement scintillates with fire,
And sparkles in its glory-wrought attire.
The visitor saints on glassy flooring stand,
In joyful mood, with singing harps in hand;
Their victory they now essay to sing,
Won o'er the beast by their almighty King.
The beast they hated and did spurn his mark,
The number of his name, and ensign dark;
They walked with God in white, and now serene,
They stand arrayed in Glory's dazzling sheen!
  Messiah comes! a thousand years to reign,
What time the restless dragon gnaws his chain;
This time the earth, from war and strife released,
Keeps constant jubilee and perfect peace.
Thrice blest and holy they, who this day share
First resurrection grace, their bodies wear;

Above the second death and all its power,
Exulting dwell in light and life secure.
The wilderness puts on an Eden guise,
The heath with Sharon's rosy beauty vies;
And joy and gladness, sisters how sincere!
Like lilies of the vale the robes they wear.
Thanksgiving sounds with soul-impelling lays,
Till hill and valley echo to the praise;
Augmenting as it rolls its tuneful voice,
Till all the earth imbibes the flying joys.
   Dread warrior ranks, for horrid slaughter clad,
Surcharged with fury and with carnage mad,
Feel in their hearts the pacifying grace,
Cast down their arms, and ratify their peace.
The angry peal of battle notes has ceased—
All ranks disbanded, every heart appeased;
The victor's shout, the dying soldiers' wail,
No more the quiet ear of earth assail;
And mothers fond, and sisters mourn no more
Their sons and brothers, reeking in their gore.
The sword awards to human life its worth,
Wipes off its stains, and tills the fruitful earth.
The spear forbears to bleed the human kind,
And gently curves to cultivate the vine.
The lion fondles with the skipping lamb,
Lies down beside it equally as tame.
The leopard by the kid in friendship moves,
Then couches by the tiny friend it loves.
The lion huge obeys the little child,
Moves at its bidding, with a heart as mild.
The child weaves bouquets in the lion's mane,
Sleeps on his tresses, wakes and plays again;
Then moves at will among the serpent brood,
Which greet its coming in the trysting wood;
Plays at the portal of the cockatrice,
Nor feels one tremor of dread fear arise;

Nor aught to hurt, nor aught to fear is found,
In all the renovated earth around.
  "The woman" gets her up to her high estate,
In robes celestial, wondrously ornate;
Still upward moving, takes her lofty seat,
The sun her robe, the moon beneath her feet;
Her crown displays twelve mystic golden stars;
The Lamb's apostles Zion's glory shares.
Aloft she stands, adorned with ample grace;
Her wall the jasper's lucid hues displays;
Her base she garnishes to luster bright,
With sapphire, emerald, and chrysolite.
All interlaced, the twelve apostles lie,
In mystic honors 'neath her fabric high.
Twelve gates of pearl bespeak their honors too,
With Jacob's tribes their honors stand to view.
Twelve angels wait before her gates of praise,
Admitting saints who come with sacred lays.
Twelve stars that glitter on the woman's head,
Twelve stones that sparkle neath loved Zion laid,
Type the apostles of the holy Lamb—
Set high, laid low, in sooth import the same.
  How blest is earth in sight of Zion's grace!
Bright in her luster her redemption sees;
Gentiles behold fair Zion's glories rise,
Dwelling with Jews in sweet fraternal ties.
Kings laden with their golden gifts repair
In haste to Zion, make their offerings there;
Bring on her sons in tender arms upstaid,
Her daughters on their shoulders safe conveyed.
"What comes?" asks Zion as she lifts her eyes;
Who come as doves athwart the blushing skies?
These are her children in ecstatic haste,
Called by the signal of millennial peace.
The olive-tree in rich luxuriance grows,
Displays her foliage, her beauty shows;

Her Gentile branches flourish and are green,
Her Jewish tendrils drink her fatness in.
God's tabernacle still sojourns with men,
To cheer the meek, the lowly to defend;
The vengeful proud are held away in chains
The thousand years that God's Messiah reigns.

HYMNS.

TRUSTING IN GOD.

ON thee, O God, my hopes depend,
My Author, Way, and final End;
Myself I spurn, and to thee cleave.
O keep me, Savior! never leave!
The work of righteousness is peace,
Its quietness shall never cease.

Till thee I found, what pain was mine!
Since thee I found, what bliss divine!—
The bliss of perfect love to feel,
The inward life, the Spirit's seal;
Thou source and object of my love,
On earth below, in heaven above.

Return, my soul, unto thy rest!
In him thou shalt be fully blest;
The peace of God shall keep my heart;
From him O may I ne'er depart,
Till on the final day revealed,
My life with God in Christ concealed!

In sorrow's vale, in tempting strife,
This gift I ask—the hidden life;
This boon divine I humbly claim,
Through Jesus' all-atoning name.
Return, my soul, unto thy rest,
And lean upon thy Savior's breast.

When death's dread hour shall try my soul—
Its tempests howl, its billows roll,
If then I feel my Savior near,
Death's terrors shall not make me fear!
I'll scorn its power through perfect love,
And gain my Eden-rest above.

With blood-washed hosts I then shall stand
Beside my Lord, at his right hand;
And aid to swell their victor-song—
Its earth-born melody prolong;
The bliss ineffable then prove,
Foretasted here in *perfect love!*

A PRAYER FOR PROTECTION.

Savior, keep me, for me care!
   All my care on thee is cast;
Stir me up to fervent prayer,
   Keep and cheer me to the last!
While the tempter's lion-roar
   Makes the timid fear and quake,
Near thee may I dwell secure;
   Me thou never wilt forsake!

When afflictions shake my frame,
   When life's blasted hopes are sere,
Still relying on thy name,
   I will then no evil fear.
When the storms of death shall swell—
   Howling, dash with horrid roar—
In the vessel with me dwell,
   Guide me to the quiet shore!

Safely moored, life's perils done,
   I shall join yon happy throng;
'Mid them shout before the throne,
   Aid to swell redemption's song—
See the king in beauty arrayed;
   In the far-off land I'll stay,
Where no evil can invade—
   Pass a fadeless, endless day!

ZION'S GLORY.

"Glorious things of thee are spoken,
   Zion, city of our God!"
With each crimson type and token,
   Pointing to a Savior's blood.
Priests with sacrifices gory,
   Tread the inner court with awe;
Gazing on Shekinah's glory—
   Mercy sweetly blent with law.

And the ark contains the tables—
   Shows God's worshipers his will;
Better blood than sainted Abel's
   Speaks for us on Zion's Hill.
Strong the rock of her foundation,
   Firm her bulwarks stand secure;
Loved Siloam's consolation
   Runs divinely free and pure.

Their unsinning, perfect spirits
   Mingle with the shouting throngs;
Perfected through Jesus' merits,
   Chanting Zion's sweetest songs;
All their names inscribed in heaven,
   Bearing palms of victory;

All their sins through Christ forgiven,
   From all evil ever free.

Countless angels with them standing,
   Waiting for their tasks of love;
Thence to fly at God's commanding,
   Bearing heirs of grace above;
Four and twenty elders falling
   Prone before the throne in praise,
Loud the Lamb of God extolling
   For his sin-atoning grace.

We on Zion's heights will meet them,
   When probation's strife is o'er—
Shouting come, and gladly greet them—
   With them dwell for evermore!
There the Lamb shall gently lead us
   By the fountains of his love;
From the tree of life shall feed us,
   In our Zion-home above!

ACCESS TO GOD THROUGH CHRIST

O God, how boundless is thy love!
   How full of grace and truth is Christ!
By patterns yielded from above,
   Moses this better gift descries.

And Abel brings the gentle lamb;
   Its flowing blood bespeaks the grace,
Foreshowing Jesus' better name,
   To cancel sin and seal his peace.

On Jewish altars crimsoned o'er
   With blood of beasts, for sinning man;

The grace was typed in days of yore,
  To pardon sin and cleanse its stain.

When Christ doth ever intercede,
  We boldly near the throne of grace,
His richer merits there to plead,
  And offer up our grateful praise,

Thine utmost grace, O Lord, impart!
  Our utmost need we fain would know;
O make us, Savior, pure in heart,
  Perfect in holiness below!

CONSECRATION TO GOD.

Lord, I am thine, forever thine!
I would upon thy breast recline—
  As favored John of old;
Would feel the pulses of thy love
Impel my will, my passion move
  With ecstasy untold.

My consecrated soul would stay
Upon thy bosom night and day,
  And drink compassion in;
Would live a life of faith in thee,
And keep the law of liberty—
  Of liberty from sin.

Thy gentle precepts be my law,
And from thy bosom may I draw
  The grace to do thy will!
The aid divine on me bestow;
Where duty leads me, with me go,
  Till I thy word fulfill.

Love's pleasing toil will then be rest;
Sustained by thee and in thee blest,
　　Shall all be wrought in God.
My purpose—ever pure and true,
In all I think, or speak, or do—
　　Complete through Jesus' blood.

Grace I receive, God's will to do,
And keep the prize still full in view,
　　Till I the prize shall gain;
To suffer out my pilgrim years,
Till pity wipe my flowing tears,
　　And I with God shall reign!

THE MAJESTY OF GOD.

God sits enthroned in his own light—
　　Light unapproached by mortal eyes;
All things are open to his sight,
　　In earth below, or in the skies.

Before him cherubim adore,
　　Their faces veiling with their wings;
Adoringly they bow before
　　The Lord of lords and King of kings!

Thrice-holy notes they loud proclaim,
　　His praise they speak with tongues of fire;
They loudly magnify his name,
　　With sounding lute and praising lyre.

God's temple feels their mighty praise—
　　Its portals quiver to the sound;
While seraphim their anthems raise,
　　In reverential awe profound.

Shall earth-born man forbear to sing,
  Nor magnify redeeming grace?
Through Jesus' blood his faith can bring
  A richer meed of grateful praise.

And while he names a Savior's blood,
  And pleads its worth in humble prayer,
Love's rainbow decks the throne of God,
  And sheds its softer luster there.

Lo! God in Christ his love reveals,
  In sweetest grace and majesty,
When on repentant souls he seals—
  Through Jesus' blood—a pardon free.

SEEKING PERFECT LOVE.

I struggle with my sin,
  And look, O Lord, to thee!
I turn my anxious thoughts within,
  And yearn for purity.

Thy law demands my love—
  A perfect love to God;
This conscience gladly doth approve,
  When sprinkled with Christ's blood.

His blood for me was spilt,
  And still its grace remains;
The blood that canceled all my guilt,
  Shall wash away my stains!

The strength is all thine own,
  Which can the grace achieve;
Reliant on thy strength alone,
  I steadfastly believe.

My *being* I resign,
  My *all* I consecrate;
O for the blessedness divine,
  Of an unsinning state!

THE CHRISTIAN RACE.

With patience will I run the race,
On Christ will fix my steadfast gaze,
  And plead his timely aid;
The race of holiness fulfill,
Discard the weights of pleasing ill,
  For joys that never fade.

I'll think of Him, whose patience bore
The cross, for joys displayed before
  His tearful, pitying eyes;
The cross I'll bear, despise the shame,
And in his strength and through his name
  Will gain the heavenly prize.

A cloud of witnesses I note;
From regions nearer or remote,
  They gather to the scene.
Once they contended for the prize;
Now look they from the azure skies,
  Arrayed in dazzling sheen.

" Complete the race thou hast begun,
In patience all its distance run, "
  They say, to cheer me on.
I'll press along the mark to win
The victor's palm and raiment clean,
  And an unfading crown.

Once they were weary; now they rest
'Neath Eden-shades forever blest,
  Await my coming there;
In patience I will end my race,
And meet their welcome, kind embrace,
  And in their glory share!

FIGHT THE GOOD FIGHT OF FAITH.

Armed for the fight of faith I stand,
And heed, attent, my Lord's command,
  Firm girded for the strife;
My Captain's orders to obey,
And watch and reverently pray,
  Throughout my pilgrim-life.

My breast-plate take of righteousness,
The mind that was in Christ possess,
  And be in him complete;
Hope for a helmet will I wear,
And ever watching unto prayer,
  Peace shall defend my feet.

For sure defense I'll take faith's shield,
The Spirit's sword in battle wield;
  And thus equipped for fight,
I'll buffet life's impending woes,
And battle with mad, alien foes,
  Till they are put to flight.

Bold will I stand, nor beat the air;
With zeal that knows no let or fear,
  Deal on victorious blows;
Thus the Old Adam crucify,
And thus the angry fiend defy,
  Until life's conflicts close.

Then with a shout to Zion come,
From battle strife returning home,
  With songs of endless praise;
I'll ground my arms at Jesus' feet,
My recompense exult to meet,
  And loud hosannas raise!

THE REST OF FAITH.

Jesus, thou art all compassion,
  Tender, pitiful, and kind;
Melt my heart, and mold and fashion
  It, according to thy mind.
After all my faithless erring,
  Thou dost fold me to thy breast;
Death's dread terrors no more fearing,
  Now in thee I calmly rest.

Keep, O keep me through thy merit,
  Free from sin, in spirit pure;
Sanctified, may I inherit
  Grace to make my calling sure.
To thy righteous will and pleasure
  May I bow! O let me prove
Blood-bought riches, heavenly treasure
  All the bliss of perfect love.

May my will, in every action,
  Keep thy holy, high behest;
By thy sweet, divine attraction,
  Draw me to thy loving breast!
Clad in robes my Savior's passion
  Shall improve to purest white;
Like the Lord, in heavenly fashion,
  I shall dwell with saints in light.

PROSPECT OF DEATH.

In pain and weariness I sigh,
And languish for my home on high,
　Built by my Maker's hand;
A pilgrim I sojourn beneath,
Fast verging to the vale of death,
　To gain the promised land.

An earnest of that bliss above
I feel in a Redeemer's love;
　I taste the joys to come.
I'll suffer all God's righteous will,
Till I life's pilgrimage fulfill,
　Then gain my long-sought home.

And when I pass the vale of death,
Resigning up my fleeting breath,
　Be with me in the strife!
I'll shout to be released from pain,
Exult my recompense to gain,
　Of everlasting life!

There gaze upon my Savior's face,
There glory shall ensue to grace,
　And prayer shall end in praise;
There laud the risen Savior's love—
Safe sheltered in my home above,
　Loud hallelujahs raise!

LONGING FOR HEAVEN.

I languish my Savior to see,
　And dwell in the light of his face;
From sighing mortality free
　To share the fruition of grace.

His love cheers the city above
  With light that my vision can bear;
His smile of compassionate love
  Shall gladden and welcome me there.

How blest will the moment appear,
  That bids me ascend up on high,
When pity has dried the last tear,
  And sorrow has heaved the last sigh;
When Jesus beside me shall tread
  Death's dreary and shadowy road;
My body lie senseless and dead,
  Laid to rest in its charnel abode!

My spirit, upborne in its flight,
  By angels, its guardians below,
Shall speed to the regions of light,
  Escaping the regions of woe;
Shall escape to the city of God,
  Whose portals will yield to let in
My spirit, made pure in his blood,
  Who died to release me from sin.

My friends whom I love, I shall meet,
  Who wait for my coming above;
My coming with shouts they will greet,
  Beside me serenely then move!
The harp, and the lute, and the lyre
  Shall be tried to the praise-giving song;
All hearts and all tongues shall conspire
  To roll its glad numbers along!

GOD'S WORSHIP.

"Jehovah sits enthroned on high,"
  But bows his ear to humble prayer,
Attentive heeds the mournful cry
  Of all who worship in his fear.

The haughty soul he sees afar,
    Nor smiles on his self-righteous pride;
The humble share his tender care,
    Safe 'neath his strong pavilion hide.

To him who trembles at his word,
    Jehovah looks with pitying eyes;
His timely succor doth afford,
    Attentive to his plaints and sighs.

Bestow thy Spirit, gracious Lord!
    Refine my heart, control my will;
Speak to my heart the cheering word
    Say to my passions, " Peace, be still!"

Seal me thine own, and make me pure,
    Infuse thy strength within my breast;
In patient faith may I endure
    Life's labor, while on Christ I rest!

In meekness bear each grief and pain
    Assigned me, while on earth I sigh;
Endure each cross, for richer gain,
    Before the throne of God on high!

GOD'S WAYS.

Jehovah's ways are in the deep,
    His councils none can understand;
His angels guard his saints, and keep
    The chosen ones, whom they attend.

Part of his ways we well can know,
    To man his mercy he reveals;
His judgments can his justice show,
    His brighter glories he conceals.

Our God to know is endless life,
    In Christ revealed, to save the lost;

His garden pangs and dying strife
    Bespeak the price redemption cost.

But when he rends death's iron chains,
    And leaves the mansions of the dead,
Our immortality he gains,
    While all his foes are captive led.

He brings his councils more to light,
    And thus unveils his richest grace;
The face of Christ with luster bright,
    God's highest glory well displays.

We shall immortal robes put on,
    And, like our Lord, his face shall see;
Shall stand entire before the throne
    Adorned with immortality!

THE DAY OF GOD.

The earth, like a shadow, glides on—
    Its pleasures, and honors, and pride;
From peasant to king on the throne,
    Each changes, and naught doth abide.
The heavens themselves shall grow old,
    As raiment, when useless and worn;
Their beauty Jehovah shall fold,
    And orbs from their orbits be torn.

Convulsed with a fear-stirring sound,
    The heavens consume into smoke;
No trace of their glory be found,
    Creation's firm pillars be broke;
The earth and its works shall be burned,
    The ocean be empty and dry;
Their order to chaos returned,
    And all that inhabit them die.

The trumpet shall challenge the dead
  To meet with their Judge on the throne;
The hope of the wicked now fled,
  The devils dismayed and undone;
The book now lies open to tell
  The deeds of earth's numberless host;
The wicked cast down into hell,
  With devils eternally lost!

The righteous caught up in the air,
  To meet with their glorified Lord,
His utmost salvation to share,
  And reap their eternal reward,
Shall gaze on the grace of the Lamb,
  Exult in the smiles of his face;
Shall honor and worship his name,
  In songs of ineffable praise.

THE EIGHT BEATITUDES.

O for that poverty so blest,
  Which Christ in gentle words did show;
For sin to mourn, then from it rest,
  Released from its undying woe!

O for the meekness that he told
  Was heritage more rich and dear
Than shining mines of Ophir's gold—
  More brilliant than the diamond's glare!

O for the hunger and the thirst
  For righteousness and peace divine;
The fullness which their grace confers
  On every lowly, contrite mind!

O for that mercy which obtains,
  The mercy I must gain, or die;

That slays revenge, good-will maintains,
  Infusing Christian charity!

That purity of heart be mine,
  That clears sin's *stains* and *clouds* away;
Revealing God in love divine,
  Of ceaseless and increasing day.

Let bigots rage and persecute—
  My righteousness and peace revile;
Be meek, my heart! my tongue, be mute,
  In lamb-like patience, calm and mild!

Thus did the saints of old endure
  Their cruel rage and malice dire;
The prophets who have gone before
  Did for their holy deeds expire.

Exceeding joys inspire my breast,
  Relying on my risen Lord;
Till with God's people I am blest
  With an exceeding great reward!

ADIEU TO LIFE!

In affliction's fiery trial,
  Though I pass life's failing days,
God I claim in self-denial,
  And his mercy still I'll praise!
Languor all my flesh pervading,
  Warns me that my end is nigh;
Earthly hopes are dimly fading;
  Brighter visions bloom on high.

O for gracious resignation
  To his will, who can not err!
Hope shall be my consolation—
  Joy shall still my bosom cheer!

Claim me not, ye friends who love me!
   Homeward bound I pass before;
Crowns and diadems above me
   Beck me where I'll die no more!

Lay me to my slumbers quiet,
   In my cold and lonely bed;
Till the resurrection fiat
   Wake to life the sleeping dead!
With angelic hosts in glory,
   I will swell redemption's song;
With the blood-washed chant the story,
   While the ages roll along! *

---

* This was the last hymn he wrote.—W P. H.

MISCELLANEOUS POEMS.

REMINISCENCES.

HOW lingers thought upon each distant scene;
    How early visions soften into love!
How loved ones mingle in their wonted mien;
    As erst in life, so now they seem to move.
The colors of the vision yet are bright,
    The sounds I hear seem music's softest lays;
No distance can conceal them from my sight,
    Nor age restrain me from their meed of praise.

My childhood's home seems draped in pleasing guise,
    The rural visions still are dressed as fair
As when in youth those gilded scenes did rise;
    Though sere in age, fond mem'ry lingers there.
There first I heard parental accents sound;
    There filial feeling first began to glow;
Fond memories evoked, come thronging round,
    And re-enact the scenes of "long ago."

I listen to a mother's soothing songs,
    That quieted her weary child to rest;
Or gently hushed me when, for little wrongs,
    I leaned, complaining, on her loving breast.
I roam once more beneath the muscadine,
    Inhale its fragrance with intense delight;
Or 'neath its shade in reverie recline,
    And note the falcon on his airy flight.

The matin songs that, warbled in the grove,
  Brought pensive melancholy o'er my mind—
The plaintive thrush, the moaning turtle-dove,
  With merry notes were touchingly combined.
Prophetical of after life, those songs
  Of joys and griefs that mingle in its scenes;
Its soothing friendships and its cutting wrongs,
  As through dark clouds hope brightly intervenes.

My heart, then sensible to all that passed,
  Still beats responsive to its early joys;
Or mourns in solitude life's sky o'ercast,
  Or plaints or ecstasies my song employs.
Life's early hopes evanishing from sight,
  My early friends thus numbered with the dead,
Admonish me to seek the world of light,
  To which those loved ones have already sped.

EARLY FRIENDS.

From childhood's scenes there comes a cheering voice,
  And bright the visions seen through vistas drear;
Or sights or sounds reveal and speak the joys
  That did my ardent, childish fancy cheer.
I dwell on memories of friendships past,
  And reconstruct past images of love;
Affection's sunlight o'er blithe scenes was cast,
  Along the paths where I did early rove.

The wooing speech maternal soothed my ear,
  And called my truant steps from folly's way;
Intense affection and parental care
  Allured me back when I was wont to stray.
The hymn devout, resounding eve and morn,
  Seems chanting still in melody of praise;
The prayer of faith, ascending to God's throne,
  Still comforts me in life's declining days.

Loved ones, so lovely!—they have gone before,
  And I am wending still life's pilgrim way;
The mortal strife with them for aye is o'er,
  And fast I hasten to life's final day.
Prepared by grace, may I death's summons meet,
  And peacefully resign my fleeting breath!
On Eden's plains those loved ones I shall greet,
  Beyond the strife of life or pain of death!

LIFE'S EARLY MEMORIES.

I sing of memory's early, pleasing dawn,
  Where intellectual rays converge in night.
As golden sunlight streaks the blushing morn,
  So glide young visions on my eager sight.
From out a screen of ebon folds, it seems
  Loved forms, relieved, stand gracefully to view,
All habited in guises so like dreams;
  Yet waking infancy those faces knew.

Central to all, a mother's face appears,
  Adored, and radiant with affection's smiles;
Those smiles shed luster on my childhood years—
  Their reminiscence manhood's toil beguiles.
Her notes are vocal in the breeze that brings
  The accents which affection stirred to lays
O'er cradled innocence, and childish things,
  When, jocund, we were at our artless plays.

The oaken spinning-wheel sends back its sound;
  Monotonous and humming though it be,
Its whirl and spindle yet possess a tongue
  Articulating incidents to me.

Blent with the flax-wheel's bass, the tenor sounds,
   That taught me numbers and the sense of verse;
Emotion through my throbbing bosom bounds—
   What pleased in childhood, still that bosom stirs.

The farm, and orchard clad in green and red,
   Appear to me as then they lay and stood;
The bleating flocks are feeding as they fed
   Along the oozy glade beside the wood.
The cat-bird, in its thorny bowers, still cries
   As sadly as when I its young did steal;
The quail still whistles, and as swiftly flies,
   As when I startled it amid the fields.

Hard by the spring there grew a muscadine,
   That flung sweet odors on the balmy air;
Its tendrils soft the apple-tree did entwine,
   'Neath which I played forgetful of all care.
The cattle lowing at the eve, bespoke
   The nectar-feast of snow-white beverage;
When seated underneath the spreading oak,
   I sipped it from my little basin's edge.

The whippoorwill at nightfall sings its lay,
   With weird and terror-telling cadences,
As touchingly as when, at close of day,
   It used to sing among the chestnut-trees.
The sleepless ghosts, that fancy painted then,
   Seem almost starting to my frighted sight,
'Mid Tory * grave-yards in the shady glen,
   That, legend told me, might be seen at night.

---

* Where certain persons were buried who were reputed to have been Tories in their day.

Full many a scene evolves that stirs my heart—
  Or friendly faces, or the friendly skies;
Each glides along, and acts its pleasing part,
  Before my fascinated, eager eyes.
O! where are they who acted all those parts?
  And where the drama? They are far away—
The smiling ones I knew, with feeling hearts,
  That sported with me in my boyhood days!

The stern realities of life ensued,
  And scattered all our visionary bliss;
These images upon my eyes obtrude,
  But fail to change the dread realities.
Cut from those ties and tender sympathies,
  My heart bleeds freely at the touching sight;
The panorama glides before my eyes,
  And reinvolves them in the screen of night.

Naught but the hope of endless life can stay
  My confidence, in treading such a stage;
'Reft of youth's warm, intensive friendships, aye,
  I test the cold alternatives of age.
Let resignation calm my troubled heart,
  And patience smooth the rugged path I tread,
Till I obtain the ever-during rest
  Remaining for the faithful, holy dead! *

---

* He has reached it now. These touching lines were written after the death of his beloved wife, whose death cast a shadow over his remaining days.—W. P. H.

"MIRZA'S VISION" VERSIFIED.

A Picture of Human Life.

The sacred time forefathers had long set—
The moon was only five days old, as yet ;
This time I kept in ceremonial rite,
And trod the dizzy, venerated height
O'er Bagdad, girt with foe-defying walls,
While loud the minaret to worship calls.
To pass the day in thoughtful mood I went,
While all the scene its mild enchantment lent.
Soft breezes did my dripping temples greet,
Surcharged with aromatic odors sweet,
Which came to stir the contemplative mood,
And all my sympathies of being wooed.
The scenery and the time did thus conspire
To raise within my breast untold desire
To know man's state, so much beset with woes ;
Its vanities, its blasted hopes, its close.
I said : " Vain man is but a shadow, life a dream,
And its realities but phantoms seem.
If life's intent be more, O who can tell?"
With thought so vast my aching heart did swell.
While pensively I mused, I raised my eye
Toward a venerated rock hard by.
The rock was famous as the mystic haunt
Of some celestial genius, whose weird chant
Was wont to soothe and cheer the hearts of men,
As they gave heed, but ne'er was seen ere then.
One habited in shepherd's guise I spied,
Who to his practiced lips then gently plied
A pipe of ever-varying harmonies,
That thrilled my heart with untold ecstasies.

My breast was soothed to tender, tranquil mood,
By wondrous airs that opportunely flowed,
To lift my thoughts that I might fully see
The wisdom of his words who spake to me.
His smile complacent me did kindly greet,
And, graciously, he pointed to a seat.
With veneration due to one so great,
Charmed by his Orphean notes so passionate,
I fell upon the ground, o'erwhelmed and weak,
As o'er strange joys still stranger sorrows break.
"Mirza," he said, and caused me to arise;
"I've heard thy lone and sad soliloquies;
Now follow me"—as kind my hand he took,
And led me to the summit of the rock.
He said: "Now turn thy downcast, tearful eyes,
And note the visionary shapes that rise."
I said: "A valley huge now opes to view;
A tide prodigious sweeps that valley through."
The genius said: "That vale is Misery;
This tide, a portion of eternity,
Set off to man, admeasured by the sun,
As all-impelling time doth onward run."
"What mists are these," I said, "which darkly hide
Both ends of this stupendous, dreary tide?"
Quoth he: "One end imports when time first rose;
The other typifies its final close.
The sea, so darkly bounded at each end—
To it thy thoughts direct, and well attend
To what appears surmounting that dread sea—
Of what vast architecture it may be,"
The genius said, and waited then for me.
"O'er it," I said, "I see a massive bridge."
"'Tis human life, as thou canst safely judge,"
Rejoined my guide; and then continued he:
"Survey it well; its many arches see;

Vast lessons it contains for man below;
Look well for arches all that fabric through."
As leisure served, I found the bridge upstaid
By four-score arches, deeply underlaid.
Still other arches, rent and reeling, stood—
A doubtful basis, on so vast a flood.
The genius said: "That bridge once lay secure
On near a thousand arches, till of yore,
A trying deluge left them but four-score,
To type man's years on earth, or less, or more;
But note attent what happens all that pass
Along this thoroughfare, from first to last."
Through faithless trap-doors, ever and anon,
I saw men plunging, and they soon were gone.
The middle of the bridge seemed less beset
With deadly pit-falls for man's heedless feet;
At either end they thickly multiplied,
To show how pilgrims on their march had died;
Toward the farther end the ranks grew thin—
So many had been caught by trap and gin.
In hobbling march, o'er broken arches, went
Wan forms and weak, with weary travel bent.
Nor tide nor bridge would e'er consent to spare
Earth's travelers, except two cases rare.
Deep melancholy stole upon my mind,
That men in jollity and mirth should find
A sudden, horrid, unexpected end—
Through hidden pit-falls instantly descend,
And struggling cling to anything they could,
Aghast to plunge the dismal, greedy flood!
In thoughtful posture, some with lifted eye
Of speculative frame, fell through to die;
And countless multitudes sought bubbles bright,
That danced before their pleasure-cheated sight,
Till when they thought they had those airy toys,
Their touch, alas! exploded all their joys.

Some armed with cimeters, ran to and fro
To thrust at others; urging them to go
Aside on traps that lay not in their course
Who else had longer 'scaped but for that force!
"Lift now thine eyes from off this dismal scene,"
The genius said, with tender look serene;
"If mystery involve the scene in view,
'T is mine to lend the doubt-dispelling clew."
I said: "What mean these flights of bird I see,
That mount aloft in fierce and bloody glee?
The cormorants and ravens wildly shriek,
And vultures with their gory, dripping beak,
And harpies—all a hateful, bloody brood—
Seem eager for man's flesh as dainty food;
And little winged boys in airy march,
Dart on, or perch them on some center arch
Of that portentous, woe-revealing bridge;
Or chirping bird-like, trip along its edge."
Quoth he: "All these vile things are avarice,
And superstition, fell despairing cares;
Dread passions that infest the life of man,
And make thee doubt but he was formed in vain."
I heaved a heavy sigh, and said: "Alas!
That wretched man is given o'er to pass
Life's thoroughfare with misery so bestead,
And in such grief to join the myriad dead!"
"Look not on man's incipient stage of life,
His mishaps here on earth and mortal strife,
But cast thine eyes toward yon heavy mists,
To which death's tide impels life's votaries;
Or great or small who launch life's untold deeps,
Toward those mists, this tide resistless sweeps—
All generations bears to viewless shades."
The Genius says: "Not one its force evades."
My eyes I quickly turned, as I was bid,
Toward the mists whose sable foldings hid

Close from my sight all beauty and all bliss;
I saw the heavenly contrast—happiness!
And whether thus my guide did aid my sight,
Or waved the mists that veiled those visions bright,
I could not guess; but wide the vale did ope
At its remoter end to yield the scope
Through which at once an ocean spread to view,
Which by a massive rock was sundered through.
Upon the left, all things were hid from sight;
The right lay basking in celestial light.
This sea-born heaven I saw quite studded o'er
With islands fair, and bright the guise they wore;
An archipelago in that celestial sea,
Where joy and gladness reign eternally.
Bright forms I saw in glorious robes arrayed;
Their brows wore garlands, and serene they strayed
Along smooth promenades o'erarched by trees,
Or near the fountain's marge reclined at ease,
On rosy couches quieted to rest,
Where mortal woes can ne'er invade the breast.
Confused, rich harmonies of birds I heard,
Or humming water-falls my bosom cheered;
Angelic harpers played their sweetest lay;
How glad I grew upon the rapt survey!
I longed for eagle's wings to aid my flight,
And waft me to those realms of pure delight.
"O Mirza," finally the Genius said,
" Is not that sea with glory's isles inlaid,
An image grand enough to type the worth
Of bliss, that can repay man's pain on earth?
Is life so fraught with ills, that gives thee chance
To make its ills those richer joys enhance?
Is death too dread, which shall convey thee home
To seas that smile and isles that ever bloom?
Nor erring, think that man was made in vain,
Whose well-wrought effort can such glory gain!"

With untold rapture, still my eager gaze
Was fixed upon those isles and lucid seas.
"Show me," I said, "the secrets 'neath that cloud,
Left of that adamantine rock, whose shroud
Involves in night that portion of the sea—
The things there hid—O tell me what they be!"

   The mystic Genius deigned me no reply;
I turned, but he had vanished from my eye;
Then to my vision turned, and it had flown!
Upon the sacred rock I stood alone!
Instead of tide and bridge and Eden-bowers,
And glory-spangled scenes of blooming flowers,
And humming water-falls, and warbling notes,
And angel-symphonies of singing lutes,
The hollow vale of Bagdad, lo! I spied,
As oxen, sheep, and camels grazed its side.

Smooth Addison, in prose, did first rehearse
The visionary fabric of my verse;
Ye critic-sages, only tell me why
His prose *may* live, my humble verse *must* die?
'T will not impugn your literary fame
To give things equal honors all the same.
Just in your grace, my naughty boast forgive,
And *prose* and *verse* fraternally shall live;
Henceforth *conjoined*, shall grace fair wisdom's page—
For youth a moral, and a song for age.

THE END.

www.ingramcontent.com/pod-product-compliance
Lightning Source LLC
Chambersburg PA
CBHW051231300426
44114CB00011B/696